A PEOPLE'S GUIDE TO
LOS ANGELES

1900   Los Angeles mourns and reveres Grandma Mason.

A PEOPLE'S GUIDE TO
LOS ANGELES

Laura Pulido   Laura Barraclough   Wendy Cheng

University of California Press Berkeley Los Angeles London

University of California Press, one of the most distinguished university presses
in the United States, enriches lives around the world by advancing scholarship in
the humanities, social sciences, and natural sciences. Its activities are supported by
the UC Press Foundation and by philanthropic contributions from individuals
and institutions. For more information, visit www.ucpress.edu.

University of California Press
Berkeley and Los Angeles, California

University of California Press, Ltd.
London, England

© 2012 by The Regents of the University of California
Photos by Wendy Cheng unless credited otherwise.

Library of Congress Cataloging-in-Publication Data
Pulido, Laura.
A people's guide to Los Angeles / Laura Pulido, Laura Barraclough,
Wendy Cheng. — 1st ed.
        p.   cm.
Includes bibliographical references and index.
ISBN 978-0-520-27081-7 (pbk. : alk. paper)
1. Los Angeles (Calif.)—Guidebooks.   2. Los Angeles Region (Calif.)—Guidebooks.
3. Los Angeles (Calif.)—Social conditions.   4. Los Angeles (Calif.)—History.
I. Barraclough, Laura R.   II. Cheng, Wendy, 1977–   III. Title.
F869.L83P85 2012
979.4'94–dc23   2011039098

Manufactured in the United States of America

21   20   19   18   17   16   15   14   13   12
10   9   8   7   6   5   4   3   2   1

The paper used in this publication meets the minimum requirements of ANSI/NISO
Z39.48-1992 (R 2002) (Permanence of Paper).

To the people of Los Angeles: past, present,

and future—especially those in the struggle,

those who teach, and those who learn;

and to Leela, Amani, and Alessandro

The publisher gratefully acknowledges the
generous support of the Lisa See Endowment Fund
in Southern California History and Culture of the
University of California Press Foundation.

Contents

Maps

An Introduction to *A People's Guide to Los Angeles*

In the middle of the day, the sun shines indifferently on the paved lot at 4115 South Central Avenue. The north side of the long, narrow lot at this address faces a two-story strip mall painted yellow. Hand-painted lettering and vinyl banners slung over the railings advertise photo services, seven-dollar haircuts, and *"toda clase de herramientas"* (all kinds of tools). The south side of the lot abuts a faded brick building with *"frutas y verduras* [fruits and vegetables], 99 cents & up" hand-painted on the wall. A row of small, irregular metal squares runs along the top—fasteners of support beams meant to prevent the walls from collapsing in the event of an earthquake. The squares testify to the building's age, since this type of reinforcement was often used for brick buildings built before 1933; this is an old neighborhood, and these buildings have been around for a while. This brick building, currently home to a corner grocery store and a hardware store, once had a twin, which filled the now empty lot. In that lost building, in the late 1960s, the Los Angeles chapter of the Black Panther Party for Self-Defense (BPP) made its headquarters. But on one fateful morning in December 1969, in a predawn raid that turned into a four-hour gun battle, hundreds of Los Angeles police officers fired thousands of rounds into the building, used a battering ram and helicopter, and trashed the inside, causing the roof of the building to cave in. Six people were injured and eleven Panthers were arrested, resulting in the retreat of party members to Oakland and the eventual demise of the Southern California chapter. Today on this stretch of Central Avenue, a man lifts the receiver of the pay phone in front of the market, replaces it, and walks away. Cars pass, stopping briefly in traffic and then moving on, in a constant stream. Three men rest on repurposed office chairs and a worn couch in the empty lot, enjoying an afternoon nap. Someone

Paved lot at 4115 South Central Ave., 2009.

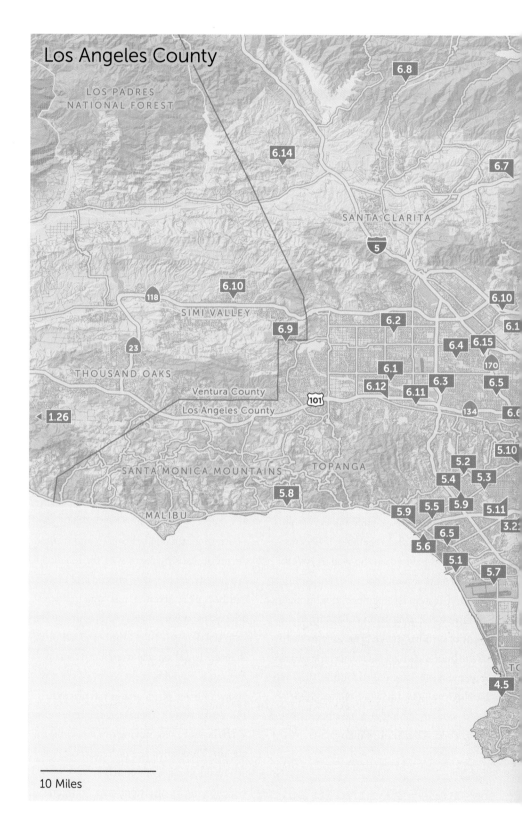

Los Angeles County

LOS PADRES
NATIONAL FOREST

6.8

6.14

6.7

SANTA CLARITA

5

6.10

118

SIMI VALLEY

6.9

6.2

6.10

6.1

23

6.4 6.15

170

THOUSAND OAKS

6.1

6.3

6.5

Ventura County

6.12

6.11

101

134

6.6

Los Angeles County

1.26

5.10

SANTA MONICA MOUNTAINS   TOPANGA

5.2

5.4   5.3

5.8

5.9   5.5   5.9   5.11

MALIBU

3.2

6.5

5.6

4.5

5.1

5.7

TO

10 Miles

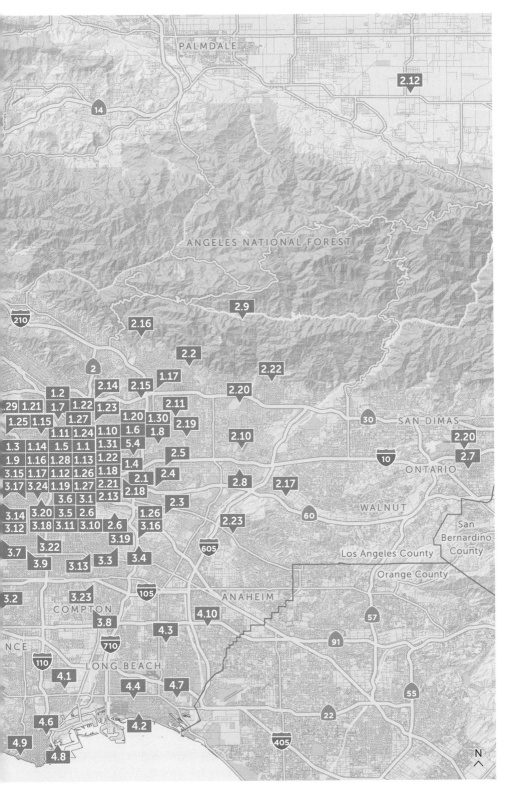

has planted a triangular patch of roses in the raised curb of a parking lot divider. The Panthers, and the building in which they did their work, are long gone.

Less than a mile to the east of the former BPP headquarters, an immense field filled with nothing but weeds and dirt and enclosed by chain-link fence affords an open view of the high-rises of downtown Los Angeles. If you look hard, you might find a few nopal plants—evidence that, not long ago, this was the site of the South Central Farm, the largest urban farm in the nation, and before that, it was the site of a successful community-led struggle to prevent the building of a toxic incinerator. But if you don't look closely or know these histories, this is just another ugly, abandoned industrial lot in South L.A.

In a park five miles farther east, teenagers bounce a basketball back and forth. On this weekday, the swing sets and slides of the modest playground are empty and the dirt baseball field goes unused. There is no trace of the footsteps and chants of the tens of thousands of people who filled this park on a hot day in August 1970 to protest the Vietnam War. The Chicano Moratorium, as it is known, was the largest antiwar action on the part of any ethnic community in the United States. Nor would you know that the tiny clothing store on nearby Whittier Boulevard was once a café where the renowned Mexican American journalist Rubén Salazar was shot and killed by an L.A. sheriff's deputy during his coverage of the event, and that that is why the park—formerly known

as Laguna Park—has been named Ruben Salazar Park, in his honor.

Los Angeles is filled with ghosts—not only of people, but also of places and buildings and the ordinary and extraordinary moments and events that once filled them. There are many such places throughout the region; still others are being created while you read this. This book is a guide to such landscapes, moments, and events. Taking the form of a tourist guidebook, it both celebrates the victories occasionally won through popular struggles and mourns those struggles that have been lost.

A People's Guide to Los Angeles is a deliberate political disruption of the way Los Angeles is commonly known and experienced. A guidebook may seem an unusual or unlikely political intervention, but as representations of both history and geography, guidebooks play a critical role in reinforcing inequality and relations of power. Guidebooks select sites, put them on a map, and interpret them in terms of their historical and contemporary significance. All such representations are inherently political, because they highlight some perspectives while overlooking others. Struggles over who and what counts as "historic" and worthy of a visit involve decisions about who belongs and who doesn't, who is worth remembering and who can be forgotten, who we have been and who we are becoming. Since all historic processes occur somewhere, these questions inherently involve geographic priorities, biases, and exclusions, as some places are celebrated, others are de-emphasized, and still others are literally left off the map. Thus, while not usually thought of as "political," guidebooks contribute to inequality in places like Los Angeles, not only by directing tourist and investment dollars toward some places and not others, but also by socializing visitors and locals alike about who and what is valuable, and—by implication—who and what is not.

Los Angeles, a city that has been built on tourism and self-promotion for more than 150 years, certainly has no shortage of guidebooks.* They range from the conventional, such as *Fodor's Los Angeles* or *Time Out Los Angeles,* to the whimsical, such as *Los Angeles Off the Beaten Path* or the Zagat *Los Angeles Dating and Dumping Guide.* However, these guidebooks convey a severely limited image of Los Angeles as a place of glamour, wealth, and fame or the home of eccentric, creative individuals; such representations clearly ignore the vast majority of the city's population, as well as the social relations that shape their lives. Furthermore, mainstream guidebooks typically describe and interpret their sites through the story of one person—almost always a man, and usually the capitalist who invested in a place, or its architect or designer. In doing so, they reinforce an individualized and masculinist way of thinking about history. Meanwhile, the collectives of people who actually cre-

ated, built, or used the space remain nameless. The Bradbury Building in downtown Los Angeles is an excellent example. Most mainstream guidebooks credit the creative contributions of the architect, George Wyman. We agree that the Bradbury Building is significant, but most accounts of it are incomplete. Who were the workers that constructed the edifice? How did Lewis Bradbury, who commissioned the building, make his fortune? (He owned a mine in Mexico). How has the building been used? How has it fit into a larger pattern of urban development in downtown Los Angeles?

Such conventional interpretations correspond to larger geographic biases and exclusions. Most mainstream guidebooks direct visitors primarily to the Westside, Hollywood, and downtown Los Angeles. Sometimes, portions of the San Fernando Valley and Long Beach are also included. These areas have historically been—and, to some extent, still are—inhabited disproportionately by people who are white, prosperous, famous, or powerful; they are also persistently overrepresented not only in guidebooks but also in other depictions of Los Angeles, such as movies and television shows. Meanwhile, South Los Angeles and East Los Angeles are regularly and systematically excluded.

In South Los Angeles, only the Watts Towers and occasionally the historic Dunbar Hotel are featured; in the Eastside, just a few restaurants, such as the upscale La Serenata de Garibaldi or the renowned El Tepeyac Café, are considered worthy of tourists'

---

*A word on our usage of the term *city:* Although the municipality of Los Angeles is the largest and the dominant city in Los Angeles County, we often use the term *city* simply to refer to the greater metropolitan area, which includes nearly 90 distinct municipalities as well as swaths of unincorporated county land. We make it clear when the term refers to the city proper.

PERSONAL REFLECTION BY GARY PHILLIPS, ACTIVIST AND AUTHOR OF THE IVAN MONK MYSTERY SERIES

There is a Los Angeles of gloss and career angst and virtual whiteness, as depicted in the cable show *Entourage* and books like *The Informers,* that is not your L.A. It is not an L.A. of Korean barbecue taco trucks after *medianoche* in Pico Union, old heads playing dominoes and reminiscing about catching the Chi-Lites at Maverick's Flat back when, or the struggle by organizers and agitators to make this a sustainable city for all its residents, fighting for decent conditions and a say. This is the substrata informing my genre fiction . . . and I wouldn't have it any other way.

(and locals') time and energy. Indeed, in some guidebooks, maps literally stop at the 10 freeway—excluding the vast communities to the south, most of them Black and Latina/o—and at the Los Angeles River, which separates the Greater Eastside and its historic Latina/o and Asian American communities from the rest of the city. These omissions are hardly accidental. They deflect attention away from some of the county's most impoverished, segregated, and polluted neighborhoods, and therefore away from the forces of systematic neglect and oppression that have created such conditions. Such representations also obscure the collective efforts, past and present, of the creative ordinary people who live and work there—people who have raised healthy families and built strong communities amid formidable conditions, and who have led vibrant, in-

novative movements to resist environmental racism, the expansion of the prison-industrial complex, state violence, and residential segregation, among other forces.

What would happen if we refocused our attention on those people and places that are systematically left off the map? This book does exactly that. *A People's Guide to Los Angeles* creates a dramatically different perspective on the region: one that centers on the analysis of power and inequality. It shares the perspectives and histories of those who have been systematically excluded from most representations of the city's history: the working class and the poor, indigenous peoples, people of color, women, immigrants, gays and lesbians, environmental justice activists, political radicals, and other marginalized groups. We question common thinking about which places are desirable and worthy of time, money, and attention. We uncover the labor and hope of subordinated people and places. We show how everyday people are exploited and disenfranchised by capital and the state; how those same people sometimes mobilize to create alternative forms of power; how racism, sexism, class differences, and homophobia lead to struggle and conflict; how dominant ideas are memorialized in landscapes; and how Los Angeles has been a constant site of struggle between nature and people. Through this process we "flip the script" of the typical tourist guidebook, not only in terms of which stories and places we focus on, but also how those stories and places are interpreted.

Recasting the narrative in this way requires a fundamentally different approach to seeing and experiencing physical space. Specifically, it requires an appreciation for vernacular landscapes—landscapes of the ordinary and everyday. *Landscape* refers to what a place looks like, or to its character. To understand what a landscape is, you need only stand outside and look around. Everything you see creates a unique, interesting, and constantly changing landscape. All landscapes reflect the contemporary period, offering information about the practices and everyday life of the people currently using and inhabiting a place. Yet landscapes also provide evidence about past generations, economic and political regimes, and ecologies. History is literally embedded in the landscape. Even if certain histories are excluded from guidebooks and other representations of a place, they cannot be entirely silenced, because there will almost always be some piece of evidence in the landscape itself—an abandoned building, a paved-over lot, a nopal plant—that we can use to challenge dominant historical narratives and recover hidden histories. Landscapes also exist in documents, photographs, and various media such as newspapers, music, and literature, and in individual and collective memories. All of these sources offer clues that we can use to rethink commonsense understandings of history and local geography, and of the unequal relationships of power that sustain them.

Less obvious to the casual observer, but central to our approach in this book, are the structural forces that shape vernacular landscapes. Corporate and governmental decisions that create landscapes are typically obscured or, in some cases, deliberately disguised. This is, in fact, one of landscape's greatest tricks and one of the most important ways in which landscape operates in the service of maintaining an unequal status quo. Because it is not always apparent why a landscape looks the way it does, it becomes easy to assume that it somehow naturally reflects the character, qualities, and moralities of the people who inhabit it. Yet in reality, all landscapes are the result of much larger historical, social, and economic forces that both enable and constrain individual actions and choices. While working on this book, we were continually struck by the mundane nature of landscapes that symbolized the engagement of people with larger structural forces. Take the case of residential discrimination, which has a violent history in Los Angeles County. We found numerous houses throughout the county that had become sites of struggle when people of color tried to buy them or move in, in defiance of legal policies of segregation enforced by the state, such as restrictive covenants. One would never know by looking at these houses or their neighborhoods now.* But this is precisely how places and landscapes are produced—through millions of individ-

---

*These houses, among numerous other sites in this book, are still private residences. While we think it is very important to highlight such places, we also ask readers to use common sense and be respectful when visiting such sites. Current residents may or may not know the history behind their homes. All private residences listed in the book are identified as such.

ual decisions, all made within the constraints of state policies and capitalist imperatives that are occasionally, and sometimes successfully, resisted by people with an alternative vision of how the world should work.

By rereading vernacular landscapes in this book with attention to the interaction between ordinary people and larger social structures, we hope to create a more complex understanding of how power works. We define power as a transformative capacity, or as a person's or group's ability to use whatever resources they may have to create new opportunities, new relationships, and new ideas. In other words, power is our ability to control the conditions of our lives, to impose our will on others, and to create change. Everybody has some power, but, given the inequalities that exist in the world, the resources through which we can exercise our power are not evenly distributed. Some institutions, such as the state and multinational corporations, have far more power than, say, the mom-and-pop store down the street. The impacts of our actions are likewise uneven; some of us have the capacity to affect the lives of many thousands of people, while some of us are more likely to find our lives affected by the actions of others. For example, when the mom-and-pop store closes, local residents who depended on that store for fresh produce or after-school snacks for their kids are affected differently than when a multinational corporation employing tens of thousands of unionized people at living wages decides to shut down or move elsewhere. Both processes are clearly impor-

tant, but in different ways and at different scales; thinking through this unevenness and how it manifests in everyday landscapes is a crucial part of this guide.

We also wish to call attention to how power works through ideology, or belief systems that guide political action, not only at the ballot box but also in the decisions and activities that guide our everyday lives. Most of us can easily recognize how brute force or violence uphold oppressive social relations, but the role of our ideologies—the products of socialization by our family, friends, schools, the media, and other cultural forces—is far less obvious. In the United States, dominant cultural institutions teach us that inequality is the result of individual failures or deviant subcultures, not that it is created by powerful, vested interests such as political elites and multinational corporations. As a result, we learn to accept unequal distributions of power and resources as natural, justified, and even desirable, so that we may rarely stop to think about how these inequalities have been created, much less organize to challenge them. And yet the reach of such ideologies, like the distribution of power, is also uneven. On occasion, under some circumstances, people ask the "big questions" about why their lives are the way they are. They talk with others, share stories, and formulate their own theories about the structural forces shaping their lives. They forge relationships; they build communities; and sometimes, they organize to resist. When they do, ordinary people can and do create significant change, thereby exercising their power in unexpected ways and showing that even the most dominant ideologies are fragile and contested. These contests occur on the ground, in vernacular landscapes, some of which we feature in this book. In documenting these histories and the everyday landscapes in which they occurred, we hope to cultivate new ways of seeing, thinking, and being in the world that challenge dominant ideologies and the inequalities that they seek to justify.

■

A collaborative project more than 15 years in the making, this book grew out of our deep commitments to both scholarship and activism in Los Angeles, and our refusal to separate the two in our work. The initial idea for the guide came from a book project of Laura Pulido's: *Black, Brown, Yellow, and Left: Radical Activism in Los Angeles*. During her research, Pulido uncovered numerous sites where pivotal events had occurred that were not recorded in standard histories of the city. When she shared this information with friends, local teacher Tony Osumi suggested that these sites should be collected in a volume called "The People's Guide to L.A." His idea immediately resonated, and for several years Pulido sought and saved information on sites that recorded class and racial struggles.

Eventually another friend suggested producing a poster. At this point Pulido reached out to a set of collaborators, including coauthors Laura Barraclough and Wendy Cheng, as well as Sharon Sekhon, director of the Studio for Southern California History.

PERSONAL REFLECTION BY TONY OSUMI, ACTIVIST AND TEACHER

A People's Guide reminds us that teaching history needs to move beyond books and classroom walls. It comes out of the beliefs that "people are the makers of history" and "everything is political." It also comes from taking part in political community tours in Los Angeles' Little Tokyo and seeing the power these tours have in educating young people. It intertwines stories of struggle and justice with our daily lives. It allows us to walk down the same sidewalks and breathe the same air as our history-making brothers and sisters. It transforms history from something you learn into something you feel.

The research and writing became a popular, collective process involving many people. Some worked formally on the project, either as paid research assistants or as unpaid volunteers who sought out nearby restaurants, parks, and museums. Others contributed to the project more informally by sharing a story, helping to pin down an exact address, lending a photo, or connecting us with little-known primary sources. In addition, faculty at a wide range of educational institutions in Los Angeles and beyond incorporated *A People's Guide* into their teaching by assigning students to research and write site histories for papers and independent studies.

Our research process was both traditional (grounded in academic sources) and popular (grounded in storytelling, memory, embodied experience, and alternative sources of knowledge). We pored over many scholarly books and articles on Los Angeles, particularly those written from a critical perspective in recent years. Many of these sources, along with readings on landscape and critical cartography, are included in the list of suggested readings in the appendix. But our research also grew out of our relationships with people and organizations working within Los Angeles' progressive and radical activism circles. We participated in many of the campaigns, rallies, protests, workshops, and alternative tours highlighted in this book, and so we had an embodied knowledge of the geography of struggle and resistance in the city upon which to draw. This knowledge was particularly helpful in researching the sites of structures that had been proposed but never materialized, such as the East L.A. prison defeated by the Coalition Against the Prison, or the waste-to-energy incinerator defeated by the Concerned Citizens of South Central Los Angeles. Through our relationships, we also heard stories about places where important events had occurred many years ago, in some cases before our lifetimes. Part of our task, when we heard such stories, was simply to put on our geographer hats and ask: "Where did that happen?" Through this process, we discovered an extensive body of knowledge about L.A.'s progressive and radical past that was not recorded anywhere, existing solely in memory and passed on through stories, myths, rumors, and jokes.

Given this rich history, it was sometimes enormously difficult for us to decide which places and histories to include and exclude. There are hundreds of fascinating stories

to be told, and *A People's Guide* represents only a taste of what is out there. However, over time we developed a few guidelines for our selection process. First, we generally did not include places that had already been designated as historically significant, although we do offer new insights on some very well-known and frequently visited places. Second, we decided not to highlight established institutions such as ethnic museums, monuments, and memorials, because our goal is to focus on lesser-known and vernacular landscapes. Instead, we list these other kinds of places in the "Nearby Sites of Interest" feature that accompanies most of the sites. Third, we prioritized diversity—of geography, historical eras, power dynamics, axes of difference, and the like—giving particular time and attention to those neighborhoods and regions within Los Angeles that have been systematically overlooked by mainstream guidebooks and other cultural representations.

Recovering and retelling the histories of ordinary people and places raised some unique challenges. Foremost, the places associated with people who have limited power are more likely to be destroyed. Indeed, many of the buildings or other structures associated with the struggles that we highlight here, like the Black Panther Party headquarters or the South Central Farm, are gone; they have been erased by urban redevelopment, destroyed by state violence, or simply forgotten because they were embedded in the everyday. Similarly, many of the movements for change we document could be categorized pessimistically as failures. Some activists and organizations were short-lived at best, and viciously repressed, imprisoned, or killed at worst. Nonetheless, because their stories offer important lessons about the exercise of power and resistance, it is crucial to document these stories, to honor them, to learn from them.

We developed a specific approach to visual material that helped surmount some of these difficulties. Coauthor Cheng, a photographer as well as a Los Angeles scholar, had been inspired by cultural landscape studies and the New Topographics school of photography, both of which have sought to recast vernacular landscapes as rich aesthetic, social, and historical documents in their own right. She approached the photographs as being not merely illustrative but a vibrant means of social and intellectual inquiry and an essential part of the storytelling process. Traveling hundreds of miles over Los Angeles' dense and ever-changing landscape, Cheng negotiated the physical and formal challenges of traversing the occasional pedestrian-unfriendly overpass for a good vantage point, looking for addresses that no longer existed or roads that had been moved, and trying to increase the visual interest of architecturally bland strip malls and parking lots that had once been the sites of extraordinary events. She learned firsthand about the operation of power in the landscape and issues of public access through encounters with wary security guards and suspicious property owners: to many, the act of taking a photograph itself was automatically suspect. To others, however, taking

photographs had positive significance, indicating recognition, respect, and the recuperation of stories of struggle. For instance, at Salazar Park in East Los Angeles, a young Chicano man approached and wanted to know why Cheng was taking pictures. She explained the project and told him the park was included as a key site of the Chicano Moratorium. "I thought nobody cared," the man said. Then he introduced himself, shook hands, and offered his help, as he had some stories to share.

In these ways, a visual and embodied engagement with vernacular landscapes can be a fundamentally democratic way to begin critical conversations about the operation of power. All people, regardless of language, levels of literacy, citizenship status, or age, can observe and feel inequalities between communities and the unequal distribution of resources in space. Such observations and experiences can be (and often have been) the starting point for organized resistance to inequality. We hope that, through their considered representations of ordinary places, the images in this book—Cheng's contemporary photographs, as well as carefully selected archival images—will enable viewers to draw intuitive comparisons with their own experiences of space and place and encourage readers to deconstruct all landscapes with a more critical eye.

■

It is crucial to note that *A People's Guide to Los Angeles* is just one contribution to a dynamic reimagining of what Los Angeles has been and will become. In particular, social historians are using archival materials in creative ways, and conducting oral histories with previously overlooked groups of people, to capture the experiences of ordinary people and center them in the constantly evolving story of Los Angeles. Alternative institutions of social and popular history have been established from these efforts. For example, the Studio for Southern California History, created by historian Sharon Sekhon, documents and preserves the region's everyday histories of life and place. The community-based organization Inland Mexican Heritage sponsors public history initiatives that celebrate Mexican culture. Descendants of residents of Hicks Camp, a farmworkers' colony in El Monte, created La Historia Society to document local Mexican American labor and family histories. There are many other such efforts, both institutional and informal. Historic preservation in Los Angeles, traditionally led by the state and by well-financed nonprofit organizations, is also undergoing a dynamic uprising of popular initiatives. For instance, through a project known as The Power of Place (which later became the title of a related book), architectural historian Dolores Hayden led an effort to develop a monument that honors Biddy Mason, a remarkable African American slave who eventually became a free woman in Los Angeles.

Alternative tourism is being similarly reworked. Japanese American activists have created walking tours of Little Tokyo to highlight the community's rich, multiethnic history. The Southern California Library for Social Studies and Research trained high school students from South L.A. to conduct oral histories with family members and community elders to find out about important places in their neighborhoods. Gilda Haas, founder of Strategic Actions for a Just Economy, led a studio class and community outreach program at UCLA on the subject of community-based tourism. This led to the creation of the Tourism Industry Development Council, now known as the Los Angeles Alliance for a New Economy (LAANE), one of the region's foremost economic justice collaboratives.

Finally, a reimagining of Los Angeles is occurring in the realm of cartography and spatial representation. Critical geographers have created new kinds of maps of Los Angeles that capture the structural and institutional dynamics of power, such as the exhibit Just Spaces, hosted by Los Angeles Contemporary Exhibitions in 2007, and the multigenre selections featured in Lize Mogel and Alexis Bhagat's *Atlas of Radical Cartography,* among others.

We wish to honor this extraordinary work while also building on it. Most of these initiatives are, for good reason, defined by a localized geography or a specific social group. By comparison, the central theme that links all the sites in our guide is not a particular racial or ethnic group, nor a particular type of building, activity, or locale, but power, inequality, and resistance. Collectively, the sites we highlight in this guidebook reveal a myriad of power relations that shape Los Angeles County.

We have sought to uncover and share places that might be overlooked as unremarkable, places where people have nevertheless confronted power and, in doing so, have been transformed by those struggles. Our goal is to inspire tourists, residents, and activists to seek out these places in order to reimagine themselves, their histories, their communities, and their ambitions for the world. *A People's Guide to Los Angeles* is meant to be used, to become dog-eared, and to travel with you throughout the city. We hope that you go and visit the places that are profiled here. We believe you will have a different understanding of Los Angeles and how power works in the region just by being there. We encourage you, when you go, to see the landscape as a text—as something that can be read, interpreted, and interrogated to develop a better understanding of how power works. But we are also aware that our guidebook, like any guidebook, is incomplete and partial, and that places that may be important to you may not appear here. For that reason, we encourage you to think of *A People's Guide* as part of an ongoing conversation in which we invite you to participate. We hope that, equipped with this book, you will look at the everyday places and landscapes you pass through in your own life from a new perspective. As we have learned again and again while putting this book together, it is in the apparently common and ordinary places that extraordinary histories have been made—including, perhaps, the everyday landscapes of your own life. So flip the page and join with us in commemorating and learning from the dynamic histories of struggle, community, and imagination in Los Angeles. *¡Adelante!*

1

North Los Angeles

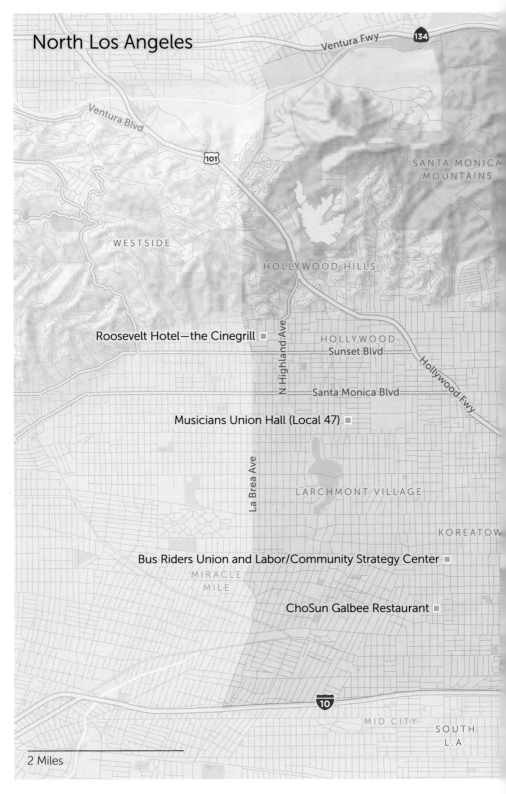

North Los Angeles

Ventura Fwy

134

Ventura Blvd

101

SANTA MONICA
MOUNTAINS

WESTSIDE

HOLLYWOOD HILLS

Roosevelt Hotel—the Cinegrill ▫

N Highland Ave

HOLLYWOOD
Sunset Blvd

Hollywood Fwy

Santa Monica Blvd

Musicians Union Hall (Local 47) ▫

La Brea Ave

LARCHMONT VILLAGE

KOREATOWN

Bus Riders Union and Labor/Community Strategy Center ▫

MIRACLE
MILE

ChoSun Galbee Restaurant ▫

10

MID CITY

SOUTH
L.A.

2 Miles

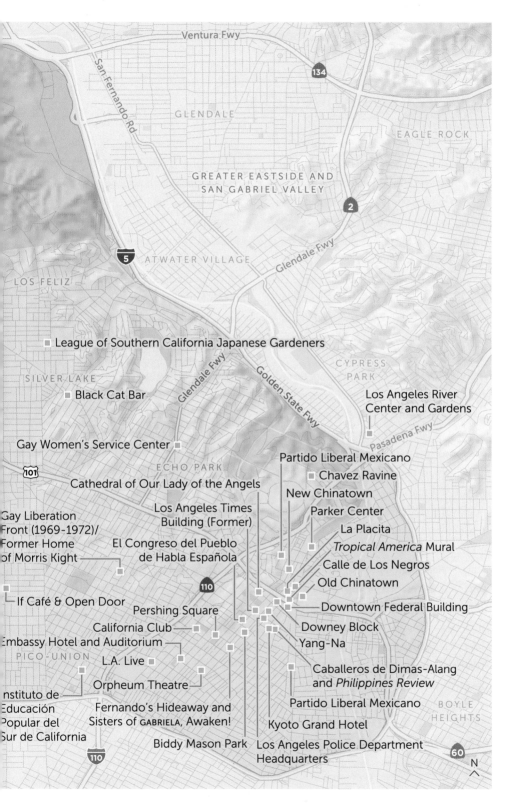

Ventura Fwy

134

GLENDALE

San Fernando Rd

EAGLE ROCK

GREATER EASTSIDE AND
SAN GABRIEL VALLEY

2

Glendale Fwy

5 ATWATER VILLAGE

LOS FELIZ

League of Southern California Japanese Gardeners

Glendale Fwy

Golden State Fwy

CYPRESS
PARK

SILVER LAKE

Black Cat Bar

Los Angeles River
Center and Gardens

Gay Women's Service Center

Pasadena Fwy

101

ECHO PARK

Cathedral of Our Lady of the Angels

Partido Liberal Mexicano

Chavez Ravine

New Chinatown

Gay Liberation
Front (1969-1972)/
Former Home
of Morris Kight

Los Angeles Times
Building (Former)

El Congreso del Pueblo
de Habla Española

Parker Center

La Placita

Tropical America Mural

Calle de Los Negros

110

Old Chinatown

If Café & Open Door

Pershing Square

California Club

Embassy Hotel and Auditorium

PICO-UNION

L.A. Live

Downtown Federal Building

Downey Block

Yang-Na

Caballeros de Dimas-Alang
and *Philippines Review*

Orpheum Theatre

Instituto de
Educación
Popular del
Sur de California

Fernando's Hideaway and
Sisters of GABRIELA, Awaken!

Biddy Mason Park

Partido Liberal Mexicano

BOYLE
HEIGHTS

Kyoto Grand Hotel

Los Angeles Police Department
Headquarters

110

60

N

An Introduction
to North Los Angeles

For hundreds of years the region we will call North L.A. in this book has been the historic core of Los Angeles. When the Tongva, the local indigenous people, dominated the region, one of their largest settlements was Yang-Na (near the current L.A. City Hall). Spanish and Mexican settlers also concentrated nearby, at the plaza. In the U.S. period, the central business district and political infrastructure, too, developed in this area. Starting in the 1900s, however, following the rail, Los Angeles grew in a leapfrog fashion, with multiple urban centers spread across the landscape. Since then, many observers have claimed that L.A. has no "real" downtown. This claim, however, is untrue. This part of the metropolis continues to be crucially important in structuring relationships of power and inequality that affect life not only here but also across the entire Los Angeles metropolitan area and beyond.

The linked processes of urban development, displacement, and resistance have fundamentally shaped life and landscape in North L.A. These dynamics began when Yang-Na was sold to a German investor who evicted the native residents. During the twentieth century, city leaders and capitalists consistently tried to lure people and investors downtown through a range of cultural, political, and economic inducements. Often they used eminent domain and other techniques to eradicate "blighted" areas

(and their inhabitants), thereby making way for development projects. Episodes of displacement include the eviction of Chinese residents from Chinatown in the early 1930s to accommodate Union Station; the forced evacuation of Japanese Americans from Little Tokyo during World War II; the eviction of Mexican residents from Chavez Ravine in the early 1950s to acquire land for public housing that was never constructed, land on which Dodger Stadium was later built; and the complete destruction of Bunker Hill, beginning in the 1950s and continuing in the present (thus constituting the longest redevelopment project in L.A. history), to make way for upscale office buildings as well as a music and performance complex intended, according to city boosters, to turn Los Angeles into a "world class city."

Nowadays, it is in North L.A. that the most concrete efforts to reinvent the central city as an engine of growth, an investment opportunity, and a playground for the rich and upwardly mobile are occurring; all of these processes are part of a neoliberal economic regime that rests on largely unregulated (and therefore often exploitative) private market forces to generate urban growth and provide services. The development projects that have been changing the southern edge of downtown in recent years—for example, the Staples Center, the L.A. Live entertainment complex, and countless loft apartments—continue the linked trends of urban development and displacement into the twenty-first century. Although the area is experiencing higher and higher densities, there is less and less space for the poor and working class, who struggle to make a life amid the visions and decisions of the metropolis's political and social elite. These conflicts are apparent in the area's contemporary landscapes. Here are the governmental buildings and informal social settings where political and economic leaders plan the region's future. The sleek, postmodern skyscrapers where they work cast a shadow on tenement buildings owned by absentee landlords who refuse to make repairs while anxiously awaiting the condemnation of their properties for urban redevelopment. Garment factories–cum–sweatshops, which constitute a major part of L.A.'s manufacturing economy, are clustered in downtown industrial buildings, discreet except for the telltale clatter of sewing machines emanating from small windows. Skid Row and Pershing Square, two (forced) gathering places of the homeless, are also in this area.

Yet the tradition of resistance to displacement and exploitation is as strong and old in this part of the city as the history of urban development. This region's neighborhoods have long been a cultural and political crossroads, where people from different backgrounds have converged, shared, and created new ideas and movements. Some of the region's most vital and groundbreaking progressive social movements were formed in North L.A.'s neighborhoods, often led by immigrants and oriented to the needs and demands of the working class and poor. For example, a revitalized labor movement, led by Justice for Janitors and the former Hotel Employees and Restaurant Employees Union, has demanded workers' rights to unionize and to be paid a living wage; the Bus Riders Union has mobilized for an efficient, clean, and affordable mass transit system; and immigrants, homeless people, and LGBT people have organized against harassment and police brutality. Indeed, the very diversity of North L.A., as well as the leftist traditions that have developed within it, have made this part of the city particularly attractive to all kinds of marginalized people. Notably, in this part of the city there has always been a large cluster of sites important to LGBT people, who have found in the bookstores, bars, and clubs a safe place for the expression of their identities and the formation of queer communities. In these same places, people have often developed politicized gay identities and worked collectively for sexual justice. Through all of these struggles, marginalized people have consistently demanded their "right to the city" while articulating alternative visions of urban life and community that we find inspiring.

As any Angeleno knows, there is no such place actually called "North L.A." Instead, mainstream tour guides and other purveyors of cultural representation, as well as many inhabitants, identify and celebrate the area's distinct neighborhoods associated with past and present immigrant ethnic groups— Koreatown, Thai Town, Little Tokyo, Chinatown, the Greek-Byzantine Corridor,

Olvera Street—often presenting these neighborhoods as worthwhile places to consume food, art, and other cultural artifacts of "exotic" people and distant lands. Absent a structural analysis, such patterns of geographic representation feed into dominant ideologies of immigrant upward mobility, including the "model minority" myth, while pathologizing Black people and the poor. Furthermore, such representations reinforce damaging stereotypes of immigrants (particularly Asians) as "perpetually foreign." Since one of our goals in the *People's Guide* is to encourage reflection on the power of place-names and the ideological "work" they do, we felt it was useful to name this broad area "North L.A.," partly in recognition of the shared structural and ideological processes that have shaped all of these neighborhoods precisely *because* of their immigrant and ethnic origins, and partly as a response to the highly politicized and racialized place-name

"South L.A.," which glosses over and ignores the distinctiveness of individual neighborhoods as well as the diversity of the people who live there.

The other reason we felt the need to name this collection of places in broader terms is the tremendous influence this area has on the larger metropolitan region. This is where the power of the state—local and national—is wielded: L.A. City Hall, L.A. County Hall of Administration, and numerous federal buildings, courthouses, and jails are located in this sector. In addition, many corporations and key cultural and political institutions have their headquarters here. And just as power is not distributed equally among people, the same is true of places. North L.A. exercises a disproportionate influence over the entire region. In sum, it is here where the aspirations of the city's power brokers meet and collide most visibly with its laborers, poor, and homeless.

North Los Angeles Sites

1.1 Biddy Mason Park

333 S. Spring St., Los Angeles 90013

(between W. 3rd St. and W. 4th St.)

DOWNTOWN

Bridget "Biddy" Mason was born a slave in Georgia in 1818. In 1836, she was purchased by Robert and Rebecca Smith, who later became Mormons and moved to Utah. In 1851, the Smiths relocated to San Bernardino, California, to start a new Mormon community. Fortunately for Mason, California had been admitted to the union as a free state in 1850. Technically speaking, this meant that all the Smith slaves were free. However, a few years later, when Mason's owner tried to convince her and the other slaves that moving to Texas—a slave state—would not imperil their freedom, she sought assistance from free African Americans. A lawsuit ensued, and the judge affirmed that Mason was a free person. The ruling was just in time, because the very next year, in 1857, the *Dred Scott* decision would have affirmed her status as property.

PERSONAL REFLECTION BY DOLORES HAYDEN, URBAN HISTORIAN AND AUTHOR OF *THE POWER OF PLACE: URBAN LANDSCAPES AS PUBLIC HISTORY*

Biddy Mason's life and work inspired many Los Angeles residents in the nineteenth century. Researching and writing her story in the 1980s, presenting a public history workshop about her, and organizing the subsequent artists' projects all provided a strong focus for the downtown itinerary of The Power of Place, which I based on the lives of working women, men, and children. Ultimately my 1995 book, *The Power of Place: Urban Landscapes as Public History,* brought Biddy Mason's life to people far from Southern California as part of a commitment to urban history. More than two decades later, the project lives on in many forms and many places.

Mason was a skilled midwife, and as a free woman, she invested all her savings in real estate, beginning with her first house at 331 South Spring Street. Her home eventually became the site of the First African Methodist Episcopal Church, which she helped found, as well as Los Angeles' first child care center. Mason used much of her wealth to assist other African Americans, particularly recent arrivals, and the poor of all races. Mason died in 1891 and is buried in Evergreen Cemetery.

Biddy Mason Park features a mural dedicated to Mason and a

Biddy Mason Park, 2008.

time line tracing key events in her life. The park itself was developed in 1989 as part of a project called The Power of Place, spearheaded by Dolores Hayden, which was an effort to begin documenting and preserving important sites in Los Angeles that were not associated with great white men and their buildings.

NEARBY SITE OF INTEREST

Bradbury Building

304 S. Broadway, Los Angeles 90013

(213) 626-1893

Architecturally significant office building designed by George Wyman and built in 1893. Featured in many films, including *Blade Runner*. Visitors welcome.

FAVORITE NEIGHBORHOOD RESTAURANTS

Homegirl Café

130 W. Bruno St., Los Angeles 90012

(213) 617-0380 (homegirlcafe.org and www.homeboy-industries.org)

A project of Father Greg Boyle's Homeboy Industries, which provides youth with an alternative to gangs, the Homegirl Café is staffed by young women who receive training in the food service industry. Boasting "Latina flavors with a contemporary twist," the café's menu includes roasted pineapple guacamole and carne asada tacos with peanut chipotle sauce. Recipes are made with ingredients grown in Homegirl's own organic garden.

Philippe's the Original

1001 N. Alameda St., Los Angeles 90012

(213) 628-3781 (www.philippes.com)

Established in 1908, Philippe's is an L.A. landmark and the original home of the French-dip sandwich, which remains the house specialty.

1.2 Black Cat Bar

3909 W. Sunset Blvd., Los Angeles 90029

(between Sanborn Ave. and Hyperion Ave.)

SILVER LAKE

Le Barcito (formerly Black Cat Bar), 2008.

In 1967, a police conflict at the Black Cat Bar led to Los Angeles' first known public protest for LGBT rights—two years before New York's better-known Stonewall Riot. A few minutes into New Year's Day 1967, after seeing customers kiss at midnight, undercover LAPD officers began beating patrons of two gay bars on Sunset Boulevard. Raiding first the Black Cat and then New Faces, police severely injured several people and arrested sixteen (for more on police abuse of LGBT folk, see entry 1.28 Pershing Square). Officers charged thirteen people with lewd conduct, two with drunkenness, and one with assault on an officer. Six weeks later, on February 11, approximately 200 people gathered in front of the Black Cat to protest police harassment of queer people. The event helped to mark Silver Lake as a gay neighborhood and establish connections between the emerging gay liberation movement and other radical movements at the time, including the antiwar, Black liberation, and Chicana/o movements. It was coordinated to coincide with similar protests planned in Watts by African American activists, in East Los Angeles and Pacoima by Chicana/o activists, and in Venice and on the Sunset Strip by hippies. Collectively, these protests challenged police abuse and drew links between racial and sexual oppression and the development of radical activism. Unfortunately, the Black Cat's proposed alliances between Black, Chicana/o, and gay liberation implicitly designated "gay" as white. Subsequently, neighborhood activists attempted to counter this assumption, for example by organizing the Sunset Junction street festival and forming Gay and Lesbian Latinos Unidos. This address is currently the site of Le Barcito, a gay bar. *(Courtesy of Emily Hobson)*

NEARBY SITE OF INTEREST

Metropolitan Community Church
4953 Franklin Ave., Los Angeles 90027
(323) 669-3434 (www.mccla.org)
The founding MCC church, which explicitly welcomes LGBT people.

FAVORITE NEIGHBORHOOD RESTAURANTS

Alegria on Sunset
3510 W. Sunset Blvd., Los Angeles 90026
(323) 913-1422 (www.alegriaonsunset.com)
Popular Mexican restaurant in a Silver Lake strip mall. Try the *dobladitas de mole* (corn tortillas folded around melted cheese and smothered in rich mole sauce) or *pollo en mole.*

Café Tropical
2900 W. Sunset Blvd., Los Angeles 90026
(323) 661-8391
Cuban bakery. Customer favorites include fresh-pressed *café con leche* and guava cheese pie.

TO LEARN MORE

Moira Kenney, *Mapping Gay L.A.: The Intersection of Place and Politics* (Temple University Press, 2001).

1.3 Bus Riders Union and Labor/Community Strategy Center

3780 Wilshire Blvd., Suite 1200, Los Angeles 90010 *(at Western Ave.)* (213) 387-2800 (www.thestrategycenter.org)

KOREATOWN

Despite Los Angeles' reputation as an autopia, it also has the largest mass transit system in the United States and therefore has become a prime site for struggles over transit equity. During the 1980s and 1990s, the Metropolitan Transit Authority (MTA) became locked in a fierce battle over how best to meet the city's public transportation needs—should it expand and empower its old, run-down bus fleet, or build a new light rail system? Political and transit leaders clearly favored rail, and their decisions to fund massive, expensive light rail projects that catered to suburbanites ignited protests among working-class bus riders, who saw the issue as a matter of transportation equity. At the time, 88 percent of Los Angeles bus riders were people of color, more than 50 percent had annual family incomes under $12,000, and 57 percent were women. Although buses carried 94 percent of the system's ridership, they received only 30 percent of MTA subsidies. Conversely, MTA rail projects served only about 6 percent of all riders (a disproportionate percentage of whom were white), but received

Damon Azali organizing on the bus, circa 2004.

together Black, white, Latina/o, and Asian (especially Korean) transit users. The BRU recognizes that, despite their ethnic, linguistic, and national differences, bus riders are linked by their dependence on a public transit system that is inadequate, undependable, and expensive.

Pairing up with the NAACP Legal Defense Fund, the BRU charged the MTA with establishing a separate and unequal mass transit system in violation of Title VI of the 1964 Civil Rights Act, which prohibits agencies that receive federal funds from spending those funds in a racially discriminatory way. In 1996, the BRU won a consent decree that obligated the MTA to reduce overcrowding, maintain equitable fares, expand bus service, replace old diesel buses with cleaner ones, and generate a plan to dismantle the city's two-tier system of transit segregation. During the next ten years, implementation of the decree was uneven and the BRU had to fight the MTA at every step. The consent decree was not renewed when it expired in 2006, even though the MTA had not carried out the court's mandates. However, the BRU has continued its organizing work on the buses, leading people in resisting the MTA's persistent proposals to cut bus service and increase fares even while it approves millions of dollars for light rail. The BRU is now the nation's largest grassroots mass transit advocacy group and has been a model for transit organizing work in other cities. The Labor/Community Strategy Center and the BRU are housed in the Wiltern Theatre, a beautiful art deco concert venue.

more than 70 percent of public transit dollars.

The Bus Riders Union (BRU), a project of the Labor/Community Strategy Center, emerged in the early 1990s to challenge these conditions (for more on the origins of the Labor/Community Strategy Center, see entry 6.4 General Motors Van Nuys). The BRU is a good example of what has been called the "new organizing" in Los Angeles. Unlike traditional labor unions that organize workers within a specific workplace or industry, the Bus Riders Union organizes literally on the city's buses, where a broad spectrum of the working class converges daily. The Bus Riders Union embraces an explicitly multicultural, multilingual approach, bringing

PERSONAL REFLECTION BY GRACE SUMMERS, BRU MEMBER

Early in 1997 . . . I read about a hearing that involved some [bus] lines I used. I didn't make it to the meeting, so I called the MTA headquarters. . . . And after three phone calls netted no one who would speak to me, I [called] the Bus Riders Union. . . . I got . . . a hearty greeting from Della Bonner, who told me that I had a right to good public transportation. She gave me a summary of the hearing in question, . . . and [I] felt great goodwill for this Bus Riders Union.

Meetings were in two languages—three if you count the food—and we who spoke only English were properly humbled by the experience of listening through headsets to the simultaneous translations from Spanish.

My job at the time was as a substitute aide in the Burbank Schools. I could take a day off any time I wished. Counting standees on buses sounded constructive. I donated my Tuesdays to standing at the corner of San Fernando Road and Fletcher from 6 to 9 A.M. and 3 to 6 P.M. I knew this was a check on whether the MTA was meeting its agreement for the consent decree. I felt useful.

At the intersection of Western Ave. and Wilshire Blvd., a city bus pulls up behind a Metro stop sign and in front of the Wiltern Theatre (home to the office of the Bus Riders Union), 2009.

NEARBY SITES OF INTEREST

Petersen Automotive Museum
6060 Wilshire Blvd., Los Angeles 90036
(323) 930-2277 (www.petersen.org)

Los Angeles County Museum of Art
5905 Wilshire Blvd., Los Angeles 90036
(323) 857-6000 (www.lacma.org)

Architecture and Design Museum
6032 Wilshire Blvd., Los Angeles 90036
(323) 932-9393 (www.aplusd.org)

La Brea Tar Pits/Page Museum
5801 Wilshire Blvd., Los Angeles 90036
(323) 934-7243 (www.tarpits.org)
Famous fossil collection preserved in tar.

Ambassador Hotel (former)
3400 Wilshire Blvd., Los Angeles 90010
The Ambassador was a famous Los Angeles hotel and the site of Robert F. Kennedy's assassination. The Los Angeles Unified School District acquired the land and razed the hotel in 2006—despite the fierce opposition of preservationists. The Robert F. Kennedy Inspiration Park and Community Schools now occupy the space.

FAVORITE NEIGHBORHOOD RESTAURANTS

Papa Cristo's Taverna

2771 W. Pico Blvd., Los Angeles 90006

(323) 737-2970 (www.papacristos.com)

Family-owned Greek restaurant and market. Try the roasted lamb-and-feta sandwich, or take some fresh-baked spanakopita and baba ghanoush to go. Their baklava is considered to be among the best in the city.

Ma Dang Gook Soo

869 S. Western Ave., Suite 1, Los Angeles 90005

(213) 487-6008

Korean restaurant specializing in noodles. Customer favorites include the chicken noodle soup with hand-cut noodles and mountain vegetable *bibimbap*. The chilled noodles in soybean broth make for a refreshing meal on a hot day.

TO LEARN MORE

Drop in to the Labor/Community Strategy Center.

Check out the film *Bus Rider's Union*, directed by Haskell Wexler (1996).

Eric Mann, *L.A.'s Lethal Air* (Labor/Community Strategy Center, 1991).

1.4 Caballeros de Dimas-Alang and *Philippines Review*

126–128 Astronaut Onizuka St., Los Angeles 90012 *(between E. 1st St. and E. 2nd St.)*

DOWNTOWN/LITTLE TOKYO

This address on Onizuka Street was once home to the offices of the Caballeros de Dimas-Alang, a Pilipino fraternal order, and the organization's newspaper, the *Philippines Review.* The building was a centerpiece of a thriving Pilipina/o immigrant community known as Little Manila during the 1920s and 1930s. The district, which housed restau-

rants, barbershops, tailors, and boarding-houses, was roughly bounded by San Pedro Street on the east, Sixth Street on the south, Figueroa Street on the west, and Sunset Boulevard on the north. These businesses catered to an almost exclusively male population of migratory Pilipino agricultural workers who traversed the Pacific Coast from Seattle to San Diego, as well as a much smaller population of urban Pilipina/o domestic workers and students.

Because the Philippines was a colony of the United States, Pilipina/o migrants were not subject to the immigration restrictions that excluded most other Asian immigrant groups during this period, and they could enter the United States freely. However, like other Asians, they were considered "aliens ineligible for citizenship" and so were unable to own property, apply for naturalized citizenship, or live outside the city's central districts. Although the neighborhood was formed largely through exclusion and restriction, Little Manila nonetheless thrived as a multiracial center of working-class recreation, political information, and social networking.

The Caballeros de Dimas-Alang was among the most prominent of Little Manila's 24 Pilipina/o organizations. The Caballeros was an international organization founded in the Philippines in 1906. One of its chief objectives was to promote Philippine liberation from the United States following the American seizure and colonization of the Philippines in the Spanish-American War. Dimasalang was a pseudonym of Jose Rizal, the Philippine national hero. In 1921,

A parking lot and a bicycle shop occupy the former site of the offices of Caballeros de Dimas-Alang, 2009.

the Caballeros inaugurated its first U.S. branch in San Francisco, and by the mid-1930s it counted twenty-six lodges, including the one in Los Angeles. The Los Angeles branch of the Caballeros published the *Philippines Review* twice monthly. The newspaper featured information about political developments in the Philippines and frequently demonstrated a nationalist position that was intolerant of American colonial policies there, especially after the Tydings-McDuffie Act of 1934 promised Philippine liberation from the United States by 1945.

Virtually all of Little Manila was destroyed by urban renewal and the construction of the 110 freeway in the mid-1950s. This street was originally known as Weller Street; it survived redevelopment but was absorbed by the Weller Court Shopping Center and renamed Onizuka Street in 1986 in honor of the Japanese American astronaut Ellison Onizuka. In 2002, city officials designated a different Pilipina/o neighborhood, near the intersection of Temple and Beverly boulevards west of downtown, as "Historic Filipinotown." In the new neighborhood, a vibrant Pilipina/o labor movement, led by the Pilipino Workers Center, continues to link the conditions of Pilipina/o workers in the United States with those in the Philippines resisting U.S. domination. Simultaneously, however, the older Little Manila of the 1920s and 1930s has been all but forgotten as a historically Pilipina/o space.

FAVORITE NEIGHBORHOOD RESTAURANTS

Daikokuya Ramen

327 E. 1st St., Los Angeles 90012 (213) 626-1680 (www.dkramen.com or www.daikoku-ten.com) Best ramen in L.A., according to many who make up the perpetual queue in front of Daikokuya. Daikokuya makes ramen broth in the Kyushu *tonkotsu* style, with special *kurobuta* black pork bone stock. The shredded *kurobuta* pork bowl is another crowd pleaser.

Señor Fish

422 E. 1st St., Los Angeles 90012

(213) 625-0566 (www.senorfish-la.com)

This popular Mexican restaurant and bar is part of a small local chain. Known for its fish tacos and burritos, it offers lunch specials, happy hour (4–9 P.M.), and happier hour (9 P.M.–midnight). Vegetarian options.

TO LEARN MORE

Search to Involve Pilipino Americans (SIPA) and Temple Gateway Youth and Community Center, 3200 W. Temple St., Los Angeles 90026. A community development organization.

Linda España-Maram, *Creating Masculinity in Los Angeles's Little Manila: Working-Class Filipinos and Popular Culture, 1920s–1950s* (Columbia University Press, 2006).

1.5 California Club

538 S. Flower St., Los Angeles 90071

(between W. 5th St. and W. 6th St.)

(213) 622-1391 (www.californiaclub.org)

DOWNTOWN

The California Club is one of the foremost exclusionary clubs in Southern California. Founded in 1887, the club offers dining, recreation, and meeting facilities to its members. While the club always excluded women, it was originally open to all men but became increasingly discriminatory in the 1920s—echoing the national trend of escalating xenophobia and racism at that time—and eventually excluded all people of color and Jews. In 1987, the Los Angeles City Council made it illegal for such clubs to discriminate. Not only is overt discrimination unethical and illegal, but such exclusionary practices continue to give white men an unfair professional and social advantage, as valuable contacts are made, networks established, and information exchanged in such venues. Amazingly, the California Club opposed the new ordinance, and in fact a segment of the membership waged a campaign to circumvent it, seeking to keep women and African Americans out of the club. Their opposition shows that, although the late 1980s is generally considered to be part of the "post–civil rights era," meaning that the demands of the civil rights and feminist movements had supposedly been achieved, the Reagan presidency in fact inaugurated a rollback of civil rights. After a tense battle, the club eventually decided it would adhere to the new ordinance. Inter-

Entrance to the California Club, 2008.

PERSONAL REFLECTION BY ACTIVIST, PLANNER, AND SCHOLAR GILDA HAAS, ALSO KNOWN AS DR. POP

I was working for Michael Woo when he was on the city council [1985–93]. I was his planning deputy. We had a breakfast date with some important people at the California Club. I was the first to arrive. I scanned the dining room and the maître d' said, "May I accompany you to the ladies' room?" I replied, "No, thank you." He insisted, "I really must accompany you to the ladies' room." I said, "Well, I really don't have to go to the ladies' room." He proceeded to tell me that unaccompanied women (as in without a man) needed to wait in the ladies' room. When Michael came I told him what happened, and we left and had breakfast at the Seventh Street Bistro [no longer open].

Grand Central Market

317 S. Broadway, Los Angeles 90013
(213) 624-2378 (www.grandcentralsquare.com)
Historic market, founded in 1917, with vendors selling produce, delicacies, and specialty items. A popular lunch spot for downtown workers.

1.6 Calle de los Negros

Nearest address: Garnier Building, 425 N. Los Angeles St., Los Angeles 90012 *(at Arcadia St.)*
DOWNTOWN

estingly, when Laura Pulido went to the club in the summer of 2002 to inquire about its history, the people to whom she spoke denied that the club had ever been exclusionary. In fact, when asked about the exclusion of women, one of the workers replied that the practice was not really exclusionary, since women would naturally want to be in their *own* spaces, right?

Calle de los Negros was a street in early Los Angeles' historic downtown, known as El Pueblo de Los Angeles, which formed in the years soon after U.S. conquest. The street was populated by Chinese, Mexican, and indigenous people and was considered a vice district. It is remembered as the site of the Chinatown Massacre, arguably the city's first "race riot." The conflict began on October 24, 1871, when two rival tongs, Nin Yung Company and Hong Chow Company, disagreed over the possession of a young prostitute-slave, Ya Hit, who had run away. A well-respected Anglo, Robert Thompson, intervened in the conflict and was accidentally shot. Soon after, a white saloonkeeper began firing randomly at Chinese homes on Calle de los Negros. As news spread, Anglo and Mexican vigilantes poured into the area and began attacking Chinese residents and their property. Mob leaders included city councilman George Fall and city tax collector Marshal Francis Baker, who told participants to "shoot any Chinese who try to escape." All told, 18 to 22 Chinese people were killed in the violence. More than 500 Angelenos

NEARBY SITE OF INTEREST

Los Angeles Central Library

630 W. 5th St., Los Angeles 90071
(213) 228-7000 (www.lapl.org)
Great free tours. Check hours, which have been reduced due to budget cuts.

Calle de los Negros, date unknown.

participated in the attack. Eventually, 37 rioters were indicted, but fewer than 10 were convicted. The California Supreme Court overturned those convictions a year later.

The Chinatown Massacre resulted from California's powerful anti-Chinese movement of the 1870s and 1880s. Although today Latina/o immigrants bear the brunt of anti-immigrant sentiment, the country's first restrictive immigration laws and anti-immigrant hostilities were actually aimed at Asians, who were despised because most were not Christians and because many people believed they undercut the wages of white workers. The Chinese were subjected to harassment, labor exploitation, and a vast array of exclusionary national and state measures, notably the 1882 Chinese Exclusion Act, which severely

limited their immigration to the United States until 1943, and the similar 1891 California exclusion act. They were also prevented from becoming naturalized citizens or owning property, in this way subjecting them to the constant threat of displacement, harassment, and violence.

Calle de los Negros was razed in 1887. The anti-Chinese movement proliferated for several more decades. The Garnier Building, which is immediately adjacent to where the

The Garnier Building, which houses the Chinese American Museum, sits adjacent to what was formerly Calle de los Negros. Los Angeles City Hall looms in the background, 2009.

Any person who shall knowingly bring into or cause to be brought into this State, by land or otherwise, or who shall aid or abet the same, or aid or abet the landing in this State, from any vessel or otherwise, of any Chinese person not lawfully entitled to enter this State, shall be deemed guilty of a felony, and shall on conviction thereof be fined in a sum of not exceeding one thousand dollars, and imprisoned in the State's Prison for a term not exceeding one year, and, if a Chinese person, shall be sentenced to deportation as in other cases. *(Section 5, Chapter CXL, California Statutes, March 20, 1891)*

street was situated, was a vital part of Los Angeles' earliest Chinatown and now houses the Chinese American Museum.

NEARBY SITES OF INTEREST

Chinese American Museum
425 N. Los Angeles St., Los Angeles 90012
(213) 485-8567 (www.camla.org)

The Chinese Historical Society
411 Bernard St., Los Angeles 90012
(323) 222-0856 (www.chssc.org)

FAVORITE NEIGHBORHOOD RESTAURANT

Phoenix Inn
301 Ord St., Los Angeles 90012 (213) 629-2812
(www.phoenixfoodboutique.com)
Family-owned restaurant established in 1965. Popular dishes include fish and lettuce porridge (with a side order of Chinese donuts for dipping) and steamed chicken.

TO LEARN MORE

Jose Luis Benavides, "'Californios! Whom Do You Support?' *El Clamor Publico's* Contradictory Role in the Racial Formation Process in Early California," *California History* 84, no. 2 (2006): 54–73.

On the history of El Pueblo de los Angeles, see Las Angelitas del Pueblo, www.lasangelitas.org/links.htm#.

For a series of downtown walking tours, see the site developed by Curtis Roseman, http://dornsife.usc.edu/la-walking-tour/.

1.7 Chavez Ravine

Nearest address: San Conrado Mission, 1820 Bouett St., Los Angeles 90012 *(at Amador St.)*

ELYSIAN PARK

Chavez Ravine consisted of three semirural Mexican American communities established in the early 1900s: Palo Verde, La Loma, and Bishop. These neighborhoods were threatened and ultimately destroyed as a result of the Los Angeles Planning Commission's decision, first announced in 1946, to develop new housing in blighted areas to accommodate the county's extraordinary post–World War II population growth. The commission envisioned building 10,000 new housing units throughout the city with federal funds. It promised that rents would be based on a sliding scale, that the new housing would be racially inclusive, and that residents displaced by any land acquisition would have first chance at the new housing. Although beloved by its residents, Chavez Ravine was declared blighted on account of the area's rural land-use and poor infrastructure, as well as its juvenile delinquency and community health problems, and was slated for a

A police vehicle patrols the vast parking lot of Dodger Stadium, 2009.

Bulldozed ruins of former Chavez Ravine home, 1959.

Aurora Vargas is removed from her home, 1959.

new housing project. In July 1950, residents were notified of the project and told that the city would buy their land. In the cold-war climate, however, the idea of public housing was considered "creeping socialism," and conservatives across the country opposed it. For the next decade a legal and political battle ensued regarding the future of Chavez Ravine. Opponents of the housing project red-baited the housing official Frank Wilkinson, ultimately derailing his career.

Many Chavez Ravine residents sold their properties to the city, but others stayed, committed to preserving their homes and community. In May 1959, citing eminent domain, police and bulldozers evicted the remaining residents. Aurora Vargas, a 38-year-old widow and daughter of activists Manuel and Avrana Arechiga, was dragged out of her home by sheriff's deputies, kicking and screaming in front of the media. She was jailed for 30 days. Opponents of the housing development, buoyed by the strength of the Red Scare, ultimately won out and the public housing plans were abandoned. The city later sold the cleared land to Walter O'Malley, who built Dodger Stadium for the relocated Brooklyn Dodgers.

The story of Chavez Ravine has become part of Los Angeles lore and is emblematic of the city's corruption, cold war politics, and the persistent displacement of Mexicans. The story lives on in plays, music, and literature. Former Chavez Ravine residents and their descendants still get together. *(Special thanks to Ron Lopez for his help in researching this entry.)*

NEARBY SITE OF INTEREST

Elysian Park

835 Academy Rd., Los Angeles 90012

(213) 485-5054 (www.laparks.org/dos/parks /facility/elysianpk.htm)

A vast park boasting hilly trails, picnic areas, and stunning views of downtown.

TO LEARN MORE

Chavez Ravine, play by Culture Clash.

Chavez Ravine, album by Ry Cooder (2005, Nonesuch Records).

Ronald Lopez, "The Battle for Chavez Ravine: Mexican Americans and Public Policy in Los Angeles, 1945–1962" (PhD dissertation, UC Berkeley, 1999).

Don Normark, *Chavez Ravine: 1949: A Los Angeles Story* (Chronicle Books, 2003).

Don Parson, *Making a Better World: Public Housing, the Red Scare, and the Direction of Modern Los Angeles* (University of Minnesota Press, 2005).

Gary Phillips, *Bad Night Is Falling* (Penguin, 1998). A novel that explores how the history of Chavez Ravine reverberates in the present.

1.8 Chinatowns

New Chinatown Central Plaza

727 N. Broadway, Los Angeles 90012

(between Ord St. and Alpine St.)

CHINATOWN

Old Chinatown Union Station,

800 N. Alameda St., Los Angeles 90012

(between E. Cesar Chavez Ave. and Arcadia St.)

DOWNTOWN

New Chinatown Central Plaza, 2009.

Before the completion of Union Station in 1939, this area on Alameda Street was Los Angeles' first Chinatown. As early as 1857, Chinese residents of Los Angeles had settled along Calle de los Negros, adjacent to the plaza, but by 1900, as the population grew to 3,000 people, the settlement spread eastward across Alameda Street. Chinese residents of this area worked primarily in laundries and produce markets. However, because Chinese immigrants could not become citizens or own property, they were constantly vulnerable to displacement and relocation.

By the early 1910s, Old Chinatown was beginning to decline, and rumors of impending redevelopment led many landlords to neglect upkeep on their properties. In addition, the remaining opium dens (which often catered to "slumming" non-Chinese tourists), and tong warfare had prompted many outsiders to avoid the area. In 1913, a six-acre portion of Old Chinatown was sold to the Southern Pacific Railroad, and one year later the remainder of Old Chinatown lying east of Alameda was sold to L. F. Hanchett, a San Francisco capitalist who planned to turn the area into an industrial and warehouse district. For the next two decades, plans for the property were stalled, though the clear consensus among civic leaders was that a major railroad terminus should be built on that location. On May 19, 1931, the California Supreme Court approved a decision to condemn the land and construct the new Union Station on the site of Old Chinatown. The Plaza Development Association, a consortium of seventy corporations, was charged with the evacuation of the Chinese residents.

For the next two years, during Union Station's design and planning, civic leaders debated how and where to relocate the Chinese. One proposal was put forth by Christine Sterling, a wealthy socialite who had been instrumental in the development of Olvera Street as a tourist-

oriented "Mexican village." Sterling wanted to create a "China City" at the plaza featuring stalls and booths on narrow, crowded streets, where Chinese people could make money by catering to tourists' exotic expectations. China City opened in 1937 between Spring and Main streets, but was damaged by two fires in the late 1930s and early 1940s and closed down in the early 1950s.

Meanwhile, native-born Chinese American Peter SooHoo, a USC graduate who would eventually be the first Chinese American to join the Los Angeles Department of Water and Power, advocated a relocation plan that would be led, designed, and financed by the Chinese themselves. Acting on a tip from the chief engineer for Union Station, SooHoo approached Herbert Lapham, land agent for the Santa Fe Railroad, who owned a large storage yard on North Broadway. Chinese merchants organized the New Chinatown Association, and

David SooHoo, in the security uniform, and Peter SooHoo, second from left, with an unidentified man at a Chinatown festival, 1940.

at a historic meeting in April 1937 at the old Tuey Far Low restaurant on Alameda and Marchessault streets, Lapham and the New Chinatown Association struck a deal. The association raised more than $100,000, without bank loans or financing, to purchase the land, and then led the design and development process, which was to feature modern and airy buildings, both commercial and residential, and wide streets that conformed to earthquake, fire, and safety regulations. New Chinatown's grand opening took place on June 25, 1938, at the New Chinatown Central Plaza and was attended by L.A. Mayor Frank Gerriam and other civic leaders. Although rooted in histories of displacement and eviction, the New Chinatown is notable as the first modern American Chinatown that was owned and planned from the ground up by Chinese people. Now, Chinatown is being transformed again as Southeast Asian immigrants from Vietnam and Cambodia diversify the area. In addition, markers of gentrification such as loft condominiums and trendy art galleries are replacing old family-run restaurants and souvenir shops.

Union Station itself is notable for its mission-style architecture as well as its role in Southern California transportation infrastructure. While it was pivotal in the early development of Los Angeles, the station largely fell out of use until the region developed a light rail commuter system, beginning in the late twentieth century. It is now, once again, a vital part of Los Angeles' transportation infrastructure. Recent excavations have uncovered a wealth of Chinese artifacts at Union Station—see, for example,

the sculpture at the eastern edge of the station, close to Patsaouras Plaza.

NEARBY SITE OF INTEREST

Los Angeles State Historic Park

1245 N. Spring St., Los Angeles 90012

An old industrial site that has gone through many incarnations, including a "living sculpture" as a cornfield.

FAVORITE NEIGHBORHOOD RESTAURANT

Kim Chuy

727 N. Broadway no. 103, Los Angeles 90012 (213) 687-7215 (www.kimchuy.com)

Specializes in the noodle dishes of the Chiu Chow people of eastern Guangdong province in China. Choose among ten different types of noodles, and try the leek cake.

TO LEARN MORE

Lisa See, *On Gold Mountain: The One-Hundred-Year Odyssey of My Chinese-American Family* (Vintage, 1996).

For more information on both Chinatowns, including oral histories and photos, go to www.chinatownremembered.com.

1.9 ChoSun Galbee Restaurant

3330 W. Olympic Blvd., Los Angeles 90019 *(at S. Manhattan Pl.)* (323) 734-3330 (www.chosungalbee.com)

KOREATOWN

In 1997, ChoSun Galbee, an upscale restaurant and one of Koreatown's largest, became the site of a landmark dispute between immigrant workers and restaurant ownership. ChoSun Galbee fired Myung Jin Park, the head cook, when he refused to sign documents that illegally sought to make him responsible for paying the restaurant's payroll taxes. Such abuses are not uncommon among the thousands of mostly Korean and Latina/o immigrant workers in Koreatown, who typically work 10–14 hours a day for wages as low as $2.50 an hour. For assistance Park turned to the Koreatown Immigrant Workers Alliance (KIWA), which was then known as Korean Immigrant Workers Advocates, an independent worker center that combines worker and community organizing with legal advocacy to end such conditions. KIWA, which developed a strong presence after Los Angeles' 1992 civil unrest with the goal of overcoming ethnic tensions, organized daily community pickets in front of the restaurant, including a 10-day hunger strike, until ChoSun Galbee agreed to pay back wages, comply with basic labor laws, and reinstate Park. Today, according to KIWA, ChoSun Galbee remains one of the few restaurants in Koreatown that adheres to basic labor laws. The Restaurant Workers Association of Koreatown, an outgrowth of the struggle at ChoSun Galbee and campaigns at several other restaurants, continues to educate workers about their employment rights and to monitor standards in the industry.

FAVORITE NEIGHBORHOOD RESTAURANT

Kobawoo House
698 S. Vermont Ave., Los Angeles 90005
(213) 389-7300

This popular eatery specializes in *bossam*: thinly sliced pork wrapped in lettuce leaves, with sliced radishes, pickled cabbage, jalapeños, salty shrimp, and kimchi. The seafood pancake is another favorite.

TO LEARN MORE

Koreatown Immigrant Workers Alliance (KIWA), 3465 W. 8th St., second floor, Los Angeles 90005 (213) 738-9050 (www.kiwa.org).

1.10 Downey Block
312 N. Spring St., Los Angeles 90012
(at N. Main St.)

DOWNTOWN

The northwest corner of Main St. and Temple St., now the site of a federal courthouse, 2010.

After the U.S. takeover of Alta California in 1848, the decline of the indigenous population accelerated, evidenced by a decrease in population; greater political, economic, and social marginalization; and the practice of Indian slavery. During the 1850s and 1860s, L.A.'s indigenous people were routinely incarcerated for loitering, drunkenness, and begging. Then, on most Mondays, a local administrator auctioned off imprisoned Indians for one week of servitude. The ironically named California Act for the Government and Protection of Indians of 1850 allowed any white person to post bail

Drawing of the Downey Block on the northwest corner of Main St. and Temple St., date unknown.

for convicted Indians, whom he could then require to pay off the fine by working for him—a new form of slave labor. According to George Harwood Phillips, in 1850 the Los Angeles Common Council declared, "When the city has no work in which to employ the chain gang, the Recorder shall, by means of notices conspicuously posted, notify the public that such a number of prisoners will be auctioned off to the highest bidder for private service." Most Indians were sold to local ranchers who used them to perform agricultural labor. Indians were sold for anywhere from one to three dollars, one-third of which was to be given to the worker at the end of the week, if he or she had performed satisfactorily. This "wage" was usually paid in the form of liquor, often leading to a repeated cycle of arrest and forced servitude. The rear of the Downey Block served as L.A.'s slave mart and is now a federal courthouse.

TO LEARN MORE

George Harwood Phillips, "Indians in Los Angeles, 1781–1875," in *The American Indian Past and Present,* ed. Roger Nichols (Alfred Knopf, 1986), p. 189.

Robert Heizer, *The Destruction of the California Indians* (Bison Books, 1993).

The Exiles, a film directed by Kent Mackenzie, 1961.

Robert Sundance Family Wellness Center, 1125 W. 6th St., Suite 103, Los Angeles 90017 (213) 202-3970 (www.uaii.org). A community wellness center providing culturally appropriate services to American Indians and Alaska Natives. Named for Robert Sundance, an American Indian from the Standing Rock Reservation in South Dakota, whose "Sundance Court Case" reformed how the criminal justice system addresses alcoholism and public drunkenness.

1.11 El Congreso del Pueblo de Habla Española

233 S. Broadway, Los Angeles 90012
(between W. 2nd St. and W. 3rd St.)

DOWNTOWN

Parking lot at the former site of the offices of El Congreso, 2009.

El Congreso del Pueblo de Habla Española (the Congress of Spanish-speaking peoples) was one of the first national civil-rights organizations for Latinas/os. Established in 1938 by Luisa Moreno (1907–1992), a Guatemalan-born labor organizer with close ties to the Communist Party, El Congreso was part of a larger united front that developed during the 1930s. In organizational documents, El Congreso described itself as "an alliance between the Spanish speaking people and the progressive, all democratic forces among the Anglo-American and minority groups in the United States." Moreno traveled the country recruiting support for El Congreso. The organization was especially strong in Los Angeles. Its main office was located on the property that is now the parking lot at this address. The organization's founding conference was held in Los Angeles in 1938 and was attended by 73 organizations representing 70,000 mostly ethnic Mexican members. El Congreso supported workers' rights, unionization, Latina/o solidarity, immigrants, and the cultivation of Latina/o culture. However, the onset of World War II created tension between the need for national unity and El Congreso's oppositional politics, leading to heavy red-baiting. Ultimately, Moreno was forced to leave the United States and died in Mexico.

Many key Latina/o activists were involved in El Congreso, including Josefina Fierro de Bright, who solicited funds from Hollywood, Eduardo Quevado, and Bert Corona. Corona (1918–2001) is significant because his experience with El Congreso enabled him to serve as a vital bridge between the old Left of the 1930s and the new Left of the 1960s and '70s. Corona came to Los Angeles as a young man and began working as an organizer with the International Longshore

Luisa Moreno at the 1949 California CIO Convention.

and Warehouse Union. Later, Corona, along with Chole Alatorre, cofounded El Centro de Acción Social y Autónomo (CASA), and served as the director of Hermandad Mexicana Nacional.

NEARBY SITE OF INTEREST

Museum of Contemporary Art
250 S. Grand Ave., Los Angeles 90012
(213) 626-6222 (www.moca.org)

TO LEARN MORE

Mario Garcia, "The Popular Front: Josefina Fierro de Bright and the Spanish-Speaking Congress," in *Mexican Americans: Leadership, Ideology, and Identity, 1930–1960* (Yale University Press, 1989), pp. 145–174.

Mario Garcia, *Memories of Chicano History: The Life and Narrative of Bert Corona* (University of California Press, 1995).

1.12 Embassy Hotel and Auditorium

851 S. Grand Ave., Los Angeles 90017
(between W. 8th St. and W. 9th St.)

DOWNTOWN

The Embassy Hotel and Auditorium was built in 1914 as a Beaux Arts–style concert hall and performance venue for the Los Angeles Philharmonic, but it is mostly known as a meeting ground for progressive causes from the 1920s to the 1950s. It was especially important to the vibrant labor movement of the 1930s, including the 1933 dressmaker strike. On September 27, 1933, under the leadership of Rose Pesotta, Los Angeles garment workers gathered here to draw up a list of demands to present to their employers. Working conditions were appalling, and in order to maintain extremely low wages, employers relied on a surplus of labor and high turnover rates. Forty percent of dressmakers earned less than five dollars a week—evidence that employers disregarded California's minimum wage laws requiring $16 for a 48-hour workweek. The employers ignored the workers' demands, and on October 12, the garment workers went on strike.

Initially, the strike included both the cloak makers, who were mostly Anglo and Jewish men, and the dressmakers, who were predominantly Mexican women. But on October 13, the workers gathered at the Embassy and the cloak makers announced that, after just one day, they had settled with the employers and would no longer participate in the strike. Consequently, the garment workers' strike turned into the dressmakers' strike. Approximately 2,000 women from 80 factories went on strike for 26 days. Seventy-five percent of them were ethnic Mexicans and the rest were Italian, Russian, and Jewish immigrants and native-born white women.

Embassy Hotel, 2008.

An injunction was issued against picketing, but given the number of women picketing (more than 1,000 at one point), it was difficult to enforce. Nevertheless, 50 women were arrested, many were fired, and both the Los Angeles Police Department and the Merchants and Manufacturers Association worked to assist employers. On October 30, the workers and employers agreed to arbitration.

The final settlement did not result in major economic benefits for the workers, but the strike was nonetheless extremely significant in terms of regional labor, gender, and racial politics. First, it laid the groundwork for the formation of the International Ladies' Garment Workers' Union in Los Angeles. Second, the strike was one of the first instances when ethnic Mexican workers bargained under American unions rather than through independent unions or worker associations. Third, it provided Mexicanas in Los Angeles with their first taste of what it was like to participate in organized labor. Fourth, it proved to the world that Mexican women could and would organize (which many people had doubted), challenging stereotypes of Mexicanas as docile, nonconfrontational, and easily exploitable workers.

The University of Southern California bought the Embassy in 1987 and used it as a housing and educational annex for 400 students until 1998, at which time the university sold the complex to a New York–based de-

Women at the garment workers' strike headquarters, 1933.

velopment group called Chetrit. Originally, working with another developer, Chetrit planned to refurbish the building to create a performance space that drew on the theater's original architectural features. However, the deal fell through and the Embassy now sits empty in a state of disrepair. Riding the wave of redevelopment that is currently reworking downtown, Chetrit says it still plans on developing a hotel at the site.

FAVORITE NEIGHBORHOOD RESTAURANTS

Original Pantry Café

877 S. Figueroa St., Los Angeles 90017
(213) 972-9279 (www.pantrycafe.com)
The Pantry has been serving up pancakes, om-

elets, country fried steak, and assorted American comfort foods since 1924. An L.A. institution open 24/7.

Más Malo

515 W. 7th St., Los Angeles 90014

(213) 985-4332 (www.masmalorestaurant.com)

A hip Mexican eatery known for its distinctive, house-made chips and featuring such L.A. innovations as vegan *menudo*.

TO LEARN MORE

Clementina Durón, "Mexican Women and Labor Conflict in Los Angeles: The ILGWU Dressmakers' Strike of 1933," *Aztlán* 15, no. 1 (1984): 145–161.

1.13 Fernando's Hideaway and Sisters of GABRIELA, Awaken!

519 S. Spring St., Los Angeles 90013

(between W. 5th St. and W. 6th St.)

(213) 327-0699

DOWNTOWN

Fernando's Hideaway is a print shop, Internet café, and art gallery. It frequently hosts exhibits and events related to political, economic, and social issues, especially those related to immigrants, workers, and Pilipinas/os and Pilipina/o Americans in the diaspora. For example, in 2010 it organized fund-raisers to raise money for travel to Phoenix, Arizona, in protest of Arizona's Senate Bill 1070, which, until its most controversial provisions were blocked by a federal judge, would have allowed police to engage in racial profiling by interrogating suspected unauthorized immigrants on their legal status, among other possible civil rights violations. Fernando's Hideaway has hosted lectures by inter-

Fernando's Hideaway/F Square Printing, 2010.

national human rights leaders; screenings of independent films; book readings and signings; and parties where attendees create posters, banners, and other materials for direct action in support of immigrants' and workers' rights.

One organization that has held several events here is the Sisters of GABRIELA, Awaken! (SiGAw), an organization that strives to build a mass movement among Pilipina women in Los Angeles. SiGAw is a member of GABRIELA-USA, the first overseas chapter of the Philippines-based organization GABRIELA, which is a coalition of 250 organizations and institutions that formed in 1984 to resist the political and economic conditions of the Marcos dictatorship. Members have worked against issues that adversely affect women, such as landlessness, militarization, the foreign debt crisis, International Monetary Fund and World Bank programs, antipeople development projects, the violation of women's health rights, violence against and trafficking in women and children, and prostitution. GABRIELA stands for

General Assembly Binding Women for Reforms, Integrity, Education, Leadership, and Action; the coalition is also named in honor of Gabriela Silang, the first Pilipina to lead a revolt against the Spanish colonization of the Philippines. Like the umbrella organizations to which SiGAw belongs, members of SiGAw connect the struggles of Pilipinas/os in the diaspora, including those in Los Angeles, to conditions in the Philippines. According to its members, the word *SiGAw* holds a deeper meaning beyond the acronym. In the Tagalog language, the word *sigaw* means "shout," and so the acronym is emblematic of the work that SiGAw strives to accomplish in speaking out against injustice.

On May 21, 2010, SiGAw sponsored Diwang Pinay (Spirit of the Pilipina), an annual performance featuring Pilipina and Pilipina American writers, performers, and artists, at Fernando's Hideaway. The event, titled "Pasanin Mo Pasanin Ko: Bridging the Struggle of Pilipinas," highlighted issues of immigration/migration, family, and the hardships and expectations of Pilipinas and Pilipina Americans, and also coincided with and commemorated the hundredth anniversary of International Women's Day.

NEARBY SITE OF INTEREST

The Latino Museum of History, Art, and Culture
514 S. Spring St., Los Angeles 90013
(213) 626-7600 (www.thelatinomuseum.org)

FAVORITE NEIGHBORHOOD RESTAURANTS

Angelique Café
840 S. Spring St., Los Angeles 90014
(213) 623-8698

Charming French restaurant serving hearty breakfasts and lunches. Expect a wait on weekend mornings.

Nickel Diner
524 S. Main St., Los Angeles 90012
(213) 623-8301 (nickeldiner.com)
Comfort food for urbanites. Known for its delectable baked goods.

1.14 Gay Liberation Front (1969–1972)/Former Home of Morris Kight

1822 W. 4th Street, Los Angeles 90057
(between S. Bonnie Brae St. and S. Burlington St.)
WESTLAKE
Private residence

In December 1969, lesbian, gay, bisexual, and transgendered (LGBT) activists in Los Angeles launched a branch of the Gay Liberation Front (GLF), which had recently been founded by New York activists in response to the Stonewall Riots there in late June. At Stonewall, police had stormed a bar catering to LGBT people in Greenwich Village, but patrons had fought back and occupied the streets for three days, demanding an end to police abuse. In the aftermath of these events, New York activists founded the GLF, naming their group explicitly after the National Liberation Fronts in Algeria and North Vietnam. While LGBT activism had been growing and becoming more radical throughout the late 1960s, Stonewall and the GLF helped to fundamentally transform the gay movement and connect it to the antiwar, Black liberation, feminist, and anti-imperialist movements of the time.

In Los Angeles, the GLF operated out of

the Westlake home of Morris Kight, a gay antiwar activist. The group supported the struggles of other marginalized and radical groups (including, briefly, the Black Panthers) and fought homophobia. One of the more famous actions it took was a protest against the "no fags" sign at Barney's Beanery in West Hollywood. As an individual, Kight

Former home of Morris Kight, 2008.

was also instrumental in establishing Christopher Street West, a march and parade commemorating the anniversary of the Stonewall Riots that is now known as L.A. Pride. In 1971, Kight and other GLF leaders also helped to form the Gay Community Services Center, which continues to serve the city today as the Los Angeles Gay and Lesbian Center. Kight was a colorful and controversial figure and was criticized by many as a domineering and eccentric person whose leadership made the Los Angeles GLF more moderate than other chapters. Yet Kight is also celebrated for his role in developing LGBT social services and building alliances with other social justice causes. In the late 1970s, Kight helped win LGBT support for the Coors beer boycott (the family funds right-wing causes), and he also supported organizing by Asian American gay men to address racism in the gay community. He remained active in his later years, fighting against the AIDS epidemic and hate crimes. He died in 2003 at the age of 83. *(Courtesy of Emily Hobson)*

NEARBY SITES OF INTEREST

MacArthur Park
2230 W. 6th St., Los Angeles 90057
(213) 368-0520 (www.laparks.org/dos/parks
/facility/macarthurpk.htm)
A Los Angeles Historic Cultural Monument built in the 1880s, and the only site of legalized street vending in Los Angeles. Frequent site of political protests and marches, including the 2007 May Day march for immigrant rights that resulted in police abuse of journalists and protesters.

UCLA Downtown Labor Center
675 S. Park View St., Los Angeles 90057
(213) 480-4155 (www.labor.ucla.edu/downtown)
Links UCLA and L.A. labor activism through resources, programming, and meeting space.

FAVORITE NEIGHBORHOOD RESTAURANTS

Mama's Hot Tamales Café
2122 W. 7th St., Los Angeles 90057
(213) 487-7474 (www.mamashottamales.com
/index_LosAngeles.html)
Mama's not only makes delicious tamales but also trains local residents in culinary skills, helping workers in the informal economy become formal food service employees and business owners. In addition to their international tamale offerings—about a dozen types that change daily,

from a list of about fifty—Mama's also makes a rich and flavorful Oaxacan mole and a five-star tortilla soup.

Langer's Delicatessen

704 S. Alvarado St., Los Angeles 90057

(213) 483-8050 (www.langersdeli.com)

Al and Jean Langer opened this L.A. institution in 1947. According to regulars, it is home to the best pastrami sandwich in the world: thick, juicy slices of hot pastrami, coleslaw, Swiss cheese, and Russian dressing layered between crispy-crusted slices of rye bread.

Paseo Chapín

2220 W. 7th St., Los Angeles 90057

(213) 385-7420

Guatemalan restaurant. Try the *pepian* Mayan stew.

TO LEARN MORE

ONE National Gay and Lesbian Archives, 909 W. Adams Blvd., Los Angeles 90007 (213) 741-0094 (www.onearchives.org). The ONE Archive is not in the immediate vicinity of the Gay Liberation Front, but it is a must for those seriously interested in studying LGBT history. Houses the world's largest library on LGBT heritage and concerns.

1.15 Gay Women's Service Center

1542 Glendale Blvd., Los Angeles 90026

(at Berkeley Ave.)

ECHO PARK

In 1971, activists in Los Angeles founded the first lesbian social services center in the United States on this site. The Gay Women's Service Center (GWSC) was volunteer-run and it functioned as an all-purpose community center; its programs ranged from consciousness raising groups to health services. Among the center's key founders was

Del Whan, one of the few women active in the Los Angeles Gay Liberation Front. The GWSC sought to establish a women's community that would be independent of male leadership and power, since most gay groups at the time were male-dominated and hierarchically run. Indeed, the Gay Community Services Center faced a women's strike in the 1970s and accepted women's leadership only in the 1980s amid the AIDS epidemic.

The Gay Women's Service Center boasted its name on the front window and helped to make Echo Park a hub of lesbian, feminist, and other social justice activism and community building. Though lesbian and feminist groups also worked on the Westside at that time, Echo Park and adjacent areas became home to several prominent groups, including the Alcoholism Center for Women (the first such program on the West Coast, located on Alvarado Street) and the Woman's Building (a women's arts center on Spring Street in Chinatown). Such sites shared neighborhood space with Latina/o, Filipina/o, and immigrant organizations and residents, making Echo Park a site of intersecting efforts to achieve social justice. *(Courtesy of Emily Hobson)*

NEARBY SITE OF INTEREST

Carey McWilliams's former home

2041 N. Alvarado St., Los Angeles 90039

Private residence

Beloved journalist, lawyer, and activist Carey McWilliams lived here from the 1940s until he moved to New York in the 1970s.

A youthful crowd socializes at the Gay Community Services Center at 1614 Wilshire Blvd. in 1971. Courtesy of the Gay, Lesbian, Bisexual, Transgender Historical Society.

The Gay Women's Service Center was located at what is now a flower shop called Exquisite Flowers, 2008.

FAVORITE NEIGHBORHOOD RESTAURANT

Taix French Country Cuisine

1911 Sunset Blvd., Los Angeles 90026
(213) 484-1265 (www.taixfrench.com)
Another longtime L.A. institution, Taix specializes in French country comfort foods such as coq au vin, *croque monsieur,* ratatouille, and traditional French onion soup.

1.16 If Café and Open Door

If Café   810 S. Vermont Ave., Los Angeles 90005 *(between W. 8th and W. 9th sts.)*
Open Door   831 S. Vermont Ave., Los Angeles 90005 *(between W. 8th and W. 9th sts.)*
KOREATOWN

From the late 1940s through the mid-1960s, this block on Vermont Avenue was home to two working-class, racially mixed lesbian bars: the If Café (also known as the If Club) and the Open Door. "Crowd of butch girls, men in 40s, others from area," read the description for the If Café in 1966 in the *Barfly* gay bar guide; for the Open Door, the same guide noted simply, "Same type crowd as at If Café." The clientele of both bars was Black, white, and Latina, demonstrating that queer life in Los Angeles did not exist only in white and affluent areas but was also embedded in working-class communities of color.

This block of Vermont Avenue was home to two working-class lesbian bars.

Women at these clubs developed a strong, oppositional community, with their own styles and slang; for example, butch Black women termed themselves "hard dressers." Women's experiences at the If Café and Open Door also remind us that homophobic and racist police practices overlapped in postwar Los Angeles. Police frequently raided the bars and arrested patrons, charging women either with "masquerading"—that is, wearing men's clothing—or prostitution. While some lesbians did work as prostitutes, many such charges were false and were used simply to harass and criminalize women who did not meet dominant gender and sexual norms. Black women, who were already more likely to be perceived as "loose" or "deviant" by the dominant culture, faced increased risk of arrest for lesbian behavior. The If Café and the Open Door stayed open for years and produced a vibrant culture that carried over into activism and community life among

lesbians of color in subsequent decades. *(Courtesy of Emily Hobson)*

NEARBY SITE OF INTEREST

Jewel's Catch One

4067 W. Pico Blvd., Los Angeles 90019 (323) 737-1159 (www.jewelscatchone.com) Nearby, though not in the immediate vicinity. Established in 1972, Catch One is the oldest continually running Black-owned gay bar in the United States. The owner has developed a range of projects and initiatives that support the health of local residents.

FAVORITE NEIGHBORHOOD RESTAURANT

Beverly Soon Tofu Restaurant

2717 W. Olympic Blvd., Suite 108, Los Angeles 90006 (213) 380-1113 (www.beverlysoontofu.com) Steaming bowls of Korean tofu soup served with rice and high-quality *banchan* (vegetable side dishes).

1.17 Instituto de Educación Popular del Sur de California (IDEPSCA) and Villa Park

IDEPSCA offices 1565 W. 14th St.,
Los Angeles 90015 *(between S. Union Ave.
and Toberman St.)* (213) 252-2952
(www.idepsca.org)

PICO-UNION

Villa Park 363 E. Villa St., Pasadena
91101 *(between N. Garfield Ave. and N. Los
Robles Ave.)*

IDEPSCA's central office, 2009.

During the 1980s, refugees from Guatemala, El Salvador, Honduras, and Nicaragua came to Los Angeles in large numbers, settling primarily in the Pico-Union, MacArthur Park, and Koreatown neighborhoods. They were fleeing civil wars and political violence that was partly caused by U.S. interventions in the political affairs of Central American governments and carried out by military officers who had been trained at the School of the Americas in Georgia. The building on Fourteenth Street, donated by a local church participating in the sanctuary movement, housed several refugee families. This building is now home to the Institute of Popular Education of Southern California (IDEPSCA).

IDEPSCA is the outgrowth of organizing efforts by students and parents who began meeting in Pasadena's Villa Park in 1984. Initially concerned with educational and

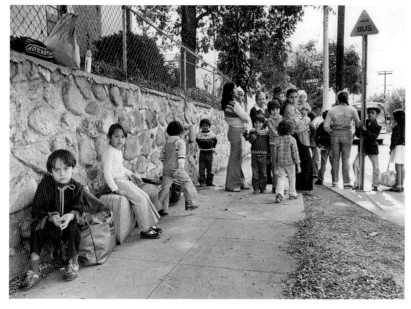

A Salvadoran refugee family waits at a Pasadena bus stop after being released from an INS detention center, 1981.

housing discrimination, activists realized that many community members were illiterate in Spanish, which made their English language acquisition that much harder. As a result, they began offering literacy classes, initially in Pasadena and eventually in other communities throughout Southern California. The classes, in turn, evolved into several organizing projects. Since 1994, IDEPSCA has organized centers for day laborers in several communities throughout Los Angeles. It also runs a variety of programs that address worker health, education, and family literacy and promote economic development, including the highly successful Magic Cleaners, a home-cleaning business that uses eco-friendly practices. In all these programs, IDEPSCA uses popular education methods, influenced by the liberationist philosophy and pedagogy of Paulo Freire, to organize low-income immigrant workers in Los Angeles. IDEPSCA is committed to developing workers' leadership skills and believes in the power of immigrant workers to define and solve problems in their own communities.

FAVORITE NEIGHBORHOOD RESTAURANTS

El Parían
1528 W. Pico Blvd., Los Angeles 90015
(213) 386-7361
Located near IDEPSCA, this restaurant is well known for its *birria,* but we especially like the carne asada and the *carnitas* burrito.

Euro Pane Bakery
950 E. Colorado Blvd., Pasadena 91106
(626) 577-1828
Close to Villa Park, Euro Pane offers freshly baked bread and gourmet sandwiches. Expect a short wait.

Naga Naga Ramen
49 E. Colorado Blvd., Pasadena 91105
(626) 585-8822 (nagaramen.com)
Located in Old Town Pasadena, Naga Naga offers an extensive Japanese menu that is very affordable.

TO LEARN MORE

Nora Hamilton and Norma Chinchilla, *Seeking Community in a Global City: Guatemalans and Salvadorans in Los Angeles* (Temple University Press, 2001).

Hector Tobar, *The Tattooed Soldier* (Penguin, 2000). A novel about a Guatemalan refugee and a death-squad veteran soldier, set in MacArthur Park.

1.18 Kyoto Grand Hotel

120 S. Los Angeles St., Los Angeles 90012
(at E. 2nd St) (213) 629-1200
(www.kyotograndhotel.com)
DOWNTOWN/LITTLE TOKYO

Kyoto Grand, formerly the New Otani Hotel, is a nonunion hotel that exemplifies three distinct power struggles: the gentrification of Little Tokyo, a prolonged unionization fight, and World War II war crimes. Little Tokyo has housed a Japanese and Japanese American population since the turn of the twentieth century, except for the period during World War II when most West Coast Japanese were interned. In the 1970s, the City of Los Angeles' Community Redevelopment Agency was intent on redeveloping the area, as it saw great potential for attracting international investment and making Little Tokyo a hub of the transnational Pacific Rim economy. Consequently, the Kajima Corporation, a major Japanese construction company, proposed a luxury hotel in Little

Boycott sign, directly across from the New Otani Hotel, circa 1996.

Tokyo. Local residents were concerned with maintaining affordable housing so that the nikkei (ethnic Japanese) residents, many of whom were elderly, could continue to live in the area. Asian American activists waged a fierce battle to maintain the community character of Little Tokyo, but the forces of international capital and the state were simply too strong. Kajima won, and built the New Otani Hotel—a move that greatly accelerated the decline of Little Tokyo as a residential community.

In 1993, the Hotel Employees and Restaurant Employees (HERE) Union Local 11 began an organizing drive at the New Otani Hotel. The campaign was challenging because it required the ability to bring together workers who spoke Spanish, Tagalog, Japanese, and English. Led by newly elected Local 11 president Maria Elena

From left to right, Maria Elena Durazo, then president of the Hotel Employees and Restaurant Employees Union, Local 11; Francisca Hinojosa, a New Otani Hotel housekeeper; fired housekeeper Ana Alvarado (in back); and Kathy Masaoka of the Japanese American support committee protest at the New Otani Hotel in Tokyo, Japan, November 16, 1996.

Durazo, demonstrators became a fixture outside the New Otani. HERE wanted the hotel to allow workers to vote on unionization through a "card check" election, as opposed to a secret ballot election. Labor organizers favor card check elections because they allow a union to bargain for workers once 50 percent of employees sign a card authorizing external representation. Many believe that secret ballots aren't really secret, and that employers benefit from such an arrangement. The campaign was brutal: the New Otani hired a union-busting firm and retaliated against workers who supported the union. As an example, three Latina maids were fired despite having worked at the hotel for 16 years. The National Labor Relations Board declared the firings illegal, but its decision was later reversed.

The Los Angeles City Council eventually voted to boycott the hotel because of how it was treating its workers, and because of activists' success in publicizing Kajima's war crimes. Activists had learned that, during World War II, Kajima had profited from slave-labor camps in Manchuria. A global campaign called the Hanaoka Support Committee was created to bring Kajima to justice, and Los Angeles labor and community activists, particularly Asian Americans, were part of it. The New Otani marked a major development in international labor solidarity when, in 1996, Rengo Labor Federation, Japan's largest labor organization, agreed to support the city's boycott and Local 11's campaign. In 1997, John Sweeney, then president of the AFL-CIO, flew to Japan to pressure Kajima and to meet with Japanese labor leaders. Local 11 continued to organize, but it never succeeded in forming a union. In 2007, the Kajima Corporation sold the hotel to 3D Investments, who turned it into the Kyoto Grand.

Although the campaign to organize did not result in a union, there were some positive by-products: it helped renew the Los Angeles labor movement, it built bridges across multiple racial and ethnic lines, and it hinted at the possibilities for international solidarity. The good news is that a handful of Chinese survivors did receive some compensation from Kajima, who admitted to "moral" but not "legal" wrongdoing.

NEARBY SITE OF INTEREST

Japanese American National Museum
369 E. 1st St., Los Angeles 90012
(213) 625-0414 (www.janm.org)

FAVORITE NEIGHBORHOOD RESTAURANTS

San Antonio Winery
737 Lamar St., Los Angeles 90031
(323) 223-1401 (www.sanantoniowinery.com)
One of L.A.'s oldest wineries, in operation since 1917, and the last producing winery in the city. Also the site of a restaurant featuring sandwiches, salads, steaks, and pastas, as well as a wine-tasting room.

Mitsuru Café
117 Japanese Village Plaza Mall, Los Angeles 90012 (213) 613-1028
This hole-in-the-wall in Little Tokyo's Japanese Village Plaza has been serving its famous *imagawayaki* (fluffy moist pastry resembling a pancake, filled with sweet red adzuki bean paste) for more than fifty years, preparing it fresh in the restaurant's front window. Also offers a selection of reasonably priced Japanese *bento*-style lunch specials.

Shojin
333 S. Alameda St., Suite 310, Los Angeles 90013 (213) 617-0305 (www.theshojin.com)
Located on the third floor of the semivacant Little Tokyo Shopping Center, Shojin offers a vegan menu inspired by Buddhist vegetarian

cooking. Popular menu items include the pumpkin croquette, barbecued *seitan,* and *seitan* steak marinated with herb garlic butter.

TO LEARN MORE

Mike Davis, "Kajima's Throne of Blood," *The Nation* (February 12, 1996): 18.

Ralph Frammolino, "The Bolshevik Who Beat Belmont," *Los Angeles Times,* January 7, 2001.

`1.19` L.A. Live

800 W. Olympic Blvd., Los Angeles 90015 *(at Figueroa St.)*

(866) 548-3452 or (213) 763-5483

(www.lalive.com)

DOWNTOWN

L.A. Live is a major sports and entertainment center that first opened in 2007 and continues to expand. It is home to the Lakers, hosts frequent concerts, and includes hotels and condominiums, movie theaters, the Grammy Museum, bowling alleys, and many eateries. The original plan for L.A. Live paid little attention to the new project's social and environmental costs to the local neighborhood. It would have led to significant displacement, a major issue given Los Angeles' perpetual housing crisis, and the remaining residents would have been adversely affected by increased traffic, parking, and crime. But in response to organizing work by the Figueroa Corridor Coalition for Economic Justice (FCCEJ), L.A. Live's owners agreed to an unprecedented set of community benefits in 2001. Strategic Actions for a Just Economy (SAJE) led the effort to create FCCEJ, which was formed to advocate on behalf of and with inner-city residents for an improved quality of life and economic development in the face of severe displacement and gentrification. More than 300 residents and 30 labor, community, and environmental justice organizations joined FCCEJ, which won a historic set of concessions in exchange for its support of the project. These concessions included a preferential-parking district for low-income tenants; guarantees that 20 percent of the new housing units would be reserved for low-income people; $1 million for parks; and a commitment to hiring local residents to fill half of the 5,500 permanent jobs. This community benefits agreement was the first of its kind in the United States and is considered a prototype for resistance to models of downtown development and gentrification that offer little to existing residents, or that threaten to force them out.

FCCEJ's lead organization, SAJE, is also a founding member of a national organization called the Right to the City Alliance. The alliance was created in 2007 "out of . . . an idea of a new kind of urban politics that asserts that everyone, particularly the disenfranchised, not only has a right to the city, but as inhabitants, have [sic] a right to shape it, design it, and operationalize an urban human rights agenda." Five other organizations in Los Angeles are also members of the alliance: the East Los Angeles Community Corporation, Esperanza Community Housing Corporation, Koreatown Immigrant Workers Alliance, South Asian Network, and El Unión de Vecinos.

FAVORITE NEIGHBORHOOD RESTAURANT

NaturaBar

3335 W. 8th St., Los Angeles 90005

(213) 784-0943

Mexican juice bar serving *raspados, licuados,* and ice cream.

TO LEARN MORE

Strategic Actions for a Just Economy, 152 W. 32nd St., Los Angeles 90007 (213) 745-9961 (www.saje.net).

Los Angeles Alliance for a New Economy (LAANE), 464 Lucas Ave., Suite 202, Los Angeles 90017 (213) 977-9400 (www.laane.org).

Right to the City Alliance, www.righttothecity .org.

Neil Smith, *The New Urban Frontier: Gentrification and the Revanchist City* (Routledge, 1996).

A banner at the side entrance to La Placita expresses the church's commitment to immigrant rights, 2008.

1.20 La Placita and Cathedral of Our Lady of the Angels

La Placita 535 N. Main St., Los Angeles 90012 *(at Arcadia St.)* (213) 629-1951 (www.laplacita.org) DOWNTOWN

Cathedral of Our Lady of the Angels

555 W. Temple St., Los Angeles 90012 *(between N. Hill St. and N. Grand St.)* (213) 680-5200 (www.olacathedral.org) DOWNTOWN

Dedicated on December 8, 1822, La Placita is the oldest formal church in Los Angeles, and for many years it was the only Catholic church in the area. It is still a functioning church with a long history of serving Los Angeles' Latina/o population. In the 1980s, La Placita became a safe haven for refugees, specifically Central American immigrants, and a key site associated with the sanctuary movement led by Father Luis Olivares,

a Mexican American priest. Olivares was branded a "communist" by Howard Ezell, then western regional commissioner for the Immigration and Naturalization Service. Many believe that the Catholic leadership was opposed to Olivares's growing popularity and his overt politics, and that they planned to transfer him to a less visible post in Texas. However, Father Olivares was diagnosed with HIV/AIDS and never made the move. He died in 1993. In the early twenty-first century, as anti-immigrant sentiment reached new heights, La Placita, along with a small group of other churches, opened its doors to immigrant refugees once again as part of the New Sanctuary Movement.

La Placita's level of commitment to the poor and vulnerable stands in direct contrast to that of the Cathedral of Our Lady of the Angels. The cathedral was completed in 2002 at a cost of $189.7 million. It was

Cathedral of Our Lady of the Angels, 2008.

intended to replace St. Vibiana's (built in 1885), which had been damaged in the 1994 Northridge earthquake. The cathedral is a postmodern structure designed by Spanish architect Rafael Moneo. Although Cardinal Roger Mahony was a strong defender of immigrants and generally supportive of labor, many criticized him for spending an exorbitant sum to build such a lavish structure when the diocese (the largest in the United States) counts millions of impoverished among its faithful. Mahony's leadership was further criticized when he refused to take responsibility for the sexual abuse scandal among Catholic priests. He not only sought to protect sexual molesters but also resisted sharing their files with the county until he was forced to do so by the courts. These events greatly weakened the church's moral authority in Los Angeles and seriously damaged its coffers. In 2010, upon Mahony's retirement, Jose Gomez became his replacement. Gomez is the first Latino archbishop in the United States.

FAVORITE NEIGHBORHOOD RESTAURANT

Sushi Gen
422 E. 2nd St., Los Angeles 90012
(213) 617-0552 (www.sushigenla.com)
Very popular sushi restaurant known for its fresh sashimi. On the pricier side. Expect a wait.

1.21 League of Southern California Japanese Gardeners
1646 N. Hoover St., Los Angeles 90027
(between Clayton Ave. and Prospect Ave.)
LOS FELIZ
Private residence

A nondescript apartment building stands at the former site of Shoji Nagumo's home, 2008.

Restricted from owning property by California's Alien Land Laws of 1913 and 1920, many Japanese immigrants in Los Angeles, even those with college degrees and skilled trades, turned to gardening. Gardening allowed immigrants to start their own businesses with relatively little capital, offered some autonomy, and paid well compared to the few other occupations open to Japanese workers at the time. During the Depression, gardeners could make between $150 and $200 per month, while those working in the produce market made only about $80 a month and worked much longer hours. By

1934, one-third of the Japanese labor force consisted of gardeners. They performed basic lawn care but also created more elaborate garden designs for wealthy white homeowners in some of the city's most elite neighborhoods.

Japanese American gardeners Chiyokichi Yamanaka, Kenzo Nakawatase, and Tom Nakawatase, Redondo Beach, circa 1950.

Yet during the Great Depression Japanese gardeners increasingly faced hostility from their wealthy employers in places like Beverly Hills, where white women's groups launched a "Back to Manchuria" campaign. Many employers favored the European immigrants and rural whites migrating to Los Angeles amid the height of the nation's economic downturn. In 1933, under the leadership of issei Shoji Nagumo, Japanese gardeners formed three local associations, in Hollywood, West Los Angeles / Sawtelle, and Uptown (bordered by Vermont and Western avenues and Pico Boulevard and San Marino Street). The Hollywood association began as a racially mixed coalition when 62 white Americans and 13 Japanese immigrants met in 1933 to exchange ideas on how to stabilize gardening fees. By the end of the decade, however, all the white members had left gardening to join the more lucrative defense industry, from which Japanese people were largely excluded.

The League of Southern California Japanese Gardeners was established in 1937, with its offices at this address, to respond to persistent anti-Japanese hostility and to manage political and economic issues that could not be handled at the local-association level. By 1940, the league reported 900 members and began to publish a monthly newsletter, *Gadena no Tomo* (literally, "Gardener's Friend"), also known in English as *The Gardener's Monthly.* The newspaper featured political commentaries as well as information about tools and techniques. Less than two years later, after the Japanese attack on Pearl Harbor, the FBI raided Nagumo's home and confiscated the league's membership list, minutes of meetings, and financial records. The league disbanded in 1942, although Japanese internees continued to create gardens and beautify the desert landscapes in which they were detained. After the war, many returning Japanese immigrants and Japanese Americans reestablished their prewar gardening routes. In 1955, Japanese gardeners again became politicized in response to the Maloney Bill, which would have required maintenance gardeners to be licensed by the state, and formed the Southern California Gardeners' Federation. The federation is active to this day and has joined with other ethnic groups, especially Latinas/os, to oppose ordinances such as leaf blower bans and to strengthen the gardening industry.

NEARBY SITE OF INTEREST

Griffith Park

4730 Crystal Springs Dr., Los Angeles 90027 (323) 913-4688 (www.laparks.org/dos/parks /griffithpk)

As the largest urban park in the United States, Griffith Park has just about everything you can think of: an observatory, a zoo, golfing, hiking, swimming, tennis, picnicking, horseback riding, the Autry National Center (theautry.org), the Greek Theatre (greektheatrela.com), and more. There are multiple access points and activities, so it's best to check the web site before visiting.

FAVORITE NEIGHBORHOOD RESTAURANT

Yuca's

2056 Hillhurst Ave., Los Angeles 90027 (323) 662-1214 (www.yucasla.com)

This award-winning taco stand in Los Feliz has been delighting Angelenos since 1976. Be sure to try their signature *cochinita pibil* (pork wrapped in banana leaves and cooked for hours until tender, Yucatán style) in a burrito, taco, or *torta*. The restaurant is not recommended for vegetarians.

TO LEARN MORE

Naomi Hirahara, ed. *Green Makers: Japanese American Gardeners in Southern California* (Southern California Gardeners' Federation, 2000).

1.22 Los Angeles Police Department Headquarters and Parker Center

LAPD Headquarters   100 W. 1st St., Los Angeles 90012 *(at N. Main St.)* (877) ASK-LAPD (www.lapdonline.org) DOWNTOWN

Parker Center   150 N. Los Angeles St., Los Angeles 90012 *(at E. 1st St.)* DOWNTOWN

These two sites have both been the headquarters of the Los Angeles Police Department. Parker Center, which was completed in 1954 and entailed the displacement of much of Little Tokyo, was named after the infamous Chief William Parker in recognition of the tremendous impact he had on the LAPD. Before Parker's arrival in 1950, Los Angeles suffered from pervasive police corruption. Under his leadership, the LAPD became professionalized but was also militaristic and one of the most repressive police forces in the country. According to the *Los Angeles Times,* Parker "raised its sense of mission, created its manual, and weaned it from the corrupting influences of city politics. He also was an arrogant racist who . . . fiercely insisted on the LAPD's independence." Parker's racism was evidenced in his description of Mexican Angelenos as "not far removed from the wild tribes of Mexico," and by his fierce opposition to the civil rights movement. Interestingly, his style often conflicted with that of J. Edgar Hoover, the FBI director who kept a file on Parker—poetic justice given the number of people under LAPD surveillance. According to an FBI agent trailing Parker, "Parker received a question from a Negro in the audience [at an event] and it was obvious that he bristled. After-

People gather outside Parker Center during the 1992 civil unrest following the verdict in the Rodney King beating case.

wards . . . I was told that Parker's ingrained action against Negroes is really the major stumbling block to . . . effective community relations." For example, under Parker, the LAPD introduced Special Weapons and Tactics (SWAT), which was deployed against the Black Panthers (see entry 3.5 Black Panther Party Headquarters).

Such attitudes and practices persisted long after Parker's departure in 1966. For decades the LAPD has been accused of renegade behavior, as seen in its response to the 1965 Watts Riot, the 1990s Rampart Scandal, and its handling of the immigrant-rights May Day protest at MacArthur Park in 2007. In 2000, a judge placed the LAPD under federal oversight in exchange for dropping an investigation into its use of excessive force. Bill Lee of the U.S. Attorney General's office accused the LAPD of "engaging in a pattern . . . of excessive force, false arrests, and unreasonable searches and seizures in violation of the Fourth and Fourteenth Amendments to the Constitution." As of this writing the

consent decree is still in effect, although in 2009 former chief William Bratton insisted that the LAPD was now in compliance, and that it was time to end federal oversight.

In October 2009, the administrative headquarters of the LAPD moved from Parker Center to its current address on West First Street. When the new building was completed, a healthy debate ensued regarding Parker's legacy and what to call the building. Ultimately it was named the LAPD Headquarters in the hope that the police department would move beyond its troubled past.

TO LEARN MORE

For a copy of the consent decree, see the LAPD web site, www.lapdonline.org/assets/pdf /final_consent_decree.pdf.

On the Rampart Scandal, see the *Frontline* episode "LAPD Blues," www.pbs.org/wgbh/pages /frontline/shows/lapd/bare.html.

For an account of the Rodney King beating and aftermath, check out Lou Cannon, *Official Negligence: How Rodney King and the Riots Changed Los Angeles and the LAPD* (Basic Books, 1999).

On the Watts uprising of 1965, read Gerald Horne, *Fire This Time: The Watts Uprising and the 1960s* (University Press of Virginia, 1995). On how the LAPD's aggressiveness affects youth of color, see Edward J. Escobar, *Race, Police, and the Making of a Political Identity: Mexican Americans and the Los Angeles Police Department, 1900–1945* (University of California Press, 1999). Cultural representations of the LAPD are vast, legendary, and largely uncritical. Consider the TV series *Dragnet* and *Adam-12* and the novels of Joseph Wambaugh. More critical appraisals can be seen in Gary Phillips's novel *Bangers,* the television show *The Shield,* and movies like *Training Day.*

1.23 Los Angeles River Center and Gardens

570 W. Ave. 26, Los Angeles 90065 *(between Jeffries Ave. and Huron St.)* (323) 221-8900 (www.lamountains .com/parks.asp?parkid=32)

CYPRESS PARK

The L.A. River is a 51-mile, mostly cemented flood channel that was once a vibrant riparian ecosystem. Though routinely depicted in film and television as an urban wasteland best suited to car chases and assorted crimes, the river has actually played a central role in Los Angeles' history and is a key geographical marker of the contemporary city, as it denotes the beginning of the Eastside. Fed by waters from both the Santa Monica and the San Gabriel mountains, the river, though not navigable in the conventional sense, was the only source of water for centuries. Dozens of Tongva villages were

located along the river, which provided these communities with many of their basic needs. In 1765, the Spanish renamed the river El Rio de Nuestra Señora la Reina de Los Angeles de Porciúncula. Under Spanish rule, Californios developed a series of irrigation ditches called *zanjas* that provided water to the agricultural fields and were a vital part of the social fabric. The original *zanja,* the *zanja madre,* can still be seen along Olvera Street. In addition to filling subsistence water needs, the river also produced a rich wetland environment that supported willows, cottonwoods, oaks, and abundant wildlife.

For much of its history the L.A. River flowed west from its source in the San Fernando Valley and took a sharp turn near

View of the Los Angeles River near Los Feliz, 2008.

Elysian Park to head back out to the Santa Monica Bay. But the river was prone to major floods and frequently changed course, which threatened the permanency of urban development patterns in the growing city. In 1825, after a massive deluge, the river shifted southward, flowing through downtown L.A. and continuing straight to the Pacific Ocean. While the river was always characterized by periodic flood-

Women washing clothes in the *zanja madre*, circa 1900.

ing, this change was especially problematic, because it now ran through densely populated areas. Indeed, in 1861–62, 1884, 1914, and 1933, the river flooded to a devastating degree. By the 1930s the U.S. Army Corps of Engineers was busy damming wild waters throughout the U.S. West in the name of progress. In 1938, Los Angeles joined in these efforts and allowed the Army Corps to begin paving over the Los Angeles River to control its occasional floods. These projects allowed developers to construct sprawling suburbs in the city's floodplains without fear of property damage from floods. As water was diverted for agricultural purposes and flood control, the wetlands ecosystem disappeared.

Today activists and residents are attempting to reclaim this metropolitan ecosystem by making the river a living and breathing part of the city once again. Thanks to organizations like Friends of the Los Angeles River, in May 2007 a 20-year blueprint was adopted to promote wildlife, economic development, tourism, and civic participation. In 2010 the river was declared "navigable," which means it can now be protected by the Clean Water Act. The Los Angeles River Center and Gardens provides an entry into the river and offers exhibits on the past, present, and future of the Los Angeles River.

NEARBY SITE OF INTEREST

Rio de Los Angeles State Park
Approximately 1900 San Fernando Rd., Los Angeles 90065 (www.parks.ca.gov/?page _id=22277)
Built on a former railroad yard, the park boasts a restored wetland.

FAVORITE NEIGHBORHOOD RESTAURANT

Good Girl Dinette
110 N. Ave. 56, Los Angeles 90042
(323) 257-8980 (www.goodgirlfoods.com)
The Good Girl Dinette's Vietnamese American comfort food is vegetarian-friendly. Their spicy fries (jalapeño, garlic, and cilantro) top many

folks' lists of the "Best Fries in L.A." The Viet-namese curry chicken potpie is another crowd pleaser.

TO LEARN MORE

Contact the Friends of the Los Angeles River at www. folar.org.

1.24 Los Angeles Times Building (Former)

Northeast corner of S. Broadway and
W. 1st St., Los Angeles 90012

DOWNTOWN

On October 1, 1910, two brothers, James B. McNamara and John J. McNamara (a member of the Bridge and Structural Iron Workers Union), were arrested in the bomb-ing of the L.A. Times building. The building was a target for labor activists because of its fierce antilabor and right-wing politics under the editorial leadership of Harrison Gray Otis, who was also a leading figure in the Merchants and Manufactur-ing Association, a pro-business orga-nization. The Mc-Namara brothers had also planted dynamite at Otis's house, but it did not detonate. The tragic blast at the Times building, which killed 20 people—including many workers—and destroyed

A vacant lot occupies the site of the former Los Angeles Times building, 2008.

the building, led to a tremendous antilabor backlash and helped solidify Los Angeles as a staunch antiunion town. Organized labor supported the McNamara brothers and helped secure Clarence Darrow to represent them. The evidence, however, was over-whelming, and the brothers pleaded guilty in order to avoid the death penalty. There is a memorial that commemorates the victims at the Hollywood Forever Cemetery (6000 Santa Monica Blvd.).

The Los Angeles Times building after the 1910 bombing.

Musicians Union
Hall (Local 47), 2011.

NEARBY SITE OF INTEREST

Los Angeles Times (current offices)

202 W. 1st St., Los Angeles 90012

(213) 237-5000 or (800) 252-9141

TO LEARN MORE

Robert Gottlieb and Irene Wolt, *Thinking Big: The Story of the* Los Angeles Times, *Its Publishers, and Their Influence on Southern California* (Putnam, 1977).

1.25 Musicians Union Hall (Local 47)

817 Vine St., Los Angeles 90038 *(between Waring Ave. and Willoughby Ave.)*

(323) 462-2161 (www.promusic47.org)

HOLLYWOOD

Local 47 was the first musicians union in the United States that, from segregated origins, became racially integrated (New York's and Detroit's musicians unions were always integrated). Local 47, the white—or, more accurately, non-Black union (it allowed Mexican Americans)—was established in 1897, and

Local 767, the "Negro Local" (which actually allowed anyone to join), was formed in 1918. The two unions functioned as separate and unequal entities, as the vast majority of jobs were directed to Local 47, which also offered better wages and benefits. Seeing the limited opportunities for professional Black musicians, various individuals, including legendary jazz musician Buddy Collette, began to work to integrate the two unions. Discussions began in the 1950s and required several years of hard work and negotiation. One of the major issues at stake was the financial implication of transferring death benefits from Local 767 to 47, as the benefits were unequal. Eventually, however, after exploring various strategies and in recognition of the membership's general desire to eliminate segregation, both locals voted for amalgamation. On April 1, 1953, all Los Angeles union musicians became part of Local 47.

While some consider the union's amalgamation to be the first major civil rights

The Jimmy Cleveland Octet rehearses at the Musicians Union Hall on July 31, 1980, with Jimmy Cleveland (trombone), Jackie Kelso (tenor sax), Lanny Morgan (alto sax), Fostina Dixon (baritone sax), Bob Ojeda (trumpet), Janet Thurlow Cleveland (vocals), Jim Hughart (bass), Ray Knehnetsky (piano), and Tim Pope (drums).

victory of the World War II era in Los Angeles, and while it ultimately led to greater opportunity and access for Black musicians, integration did not come without its costs. The amalgamation coincided with other forces, such as police harassment of mixed-race music venues, that ultimately led to the decline of the Central Avenue music scene and the "community musician" vibe from South L.A. As musicians began moving west toward jobs and the union hall, they were less available to stage impromptu performances, foster community learning, and mentor young people. African American musicians did manage to bring some of the community musician ethos into Local 47, as evidenced by such initiatives as the Black and Brown Brotherhood Band in the early 1970s. Local 47 remains active to this day and negotiates with employers to establish fair wages and working conditions for more than 8,000 members.

NEARBY SITES OF INTEREST

Barnsdall Art Park
4800 Hollywood Blvd., Los Angeles 90027
(323) 660-4254 (www.barnsdallartpark.com)
A community park offering a gallery, theater, art classes, and programs. Also home to Frank Lloyd Wright's Hollyhock House.

CBS Television City
7800 Beverly Blvd., Los Angeles 90036
(323) 575-2458 (www.seeing-stars.com/tapings /cbstapings.shtml)
Interested in watching the taping of a television show?

FAVORITE NEIGHBORHOOD RESTAURANTS

Pink's Hot Dogs
709 N. La Brea Ave., Los Angeles 90038
(323) 931-4223 (www.pinkshollywood.com)
An L.A. landmark and site of frequent star sightings.

The Original Farmers Market
6333 W. 3rd St., Los Angeles 90036
(323) 933-9211 (www.farmersmarketla.com)
A historic landmark offering a bounty of fresh produce, prepared foods, and specialty items, since 1934. Du-Par's pancakes are first rate.

1.26 Orpheum Theatre, Sleepy Lagoon Murder, and Ventura School for Girls

Orpheum Theatre   842 S. Broadway, Los Angeles 90014 *(between W. 8th St. and W. 9th St.)* (877) 677-4386 (laorpheum.com)
DOWNTOWN

Former site of José Díaz's home   5500 E. Slauson Ave., Los Angeles 90040 *(between I-710 and S. Eastern Ave.)* COMMERCE

Ventura School for Girls   801 Seneca St., Ventura 93001 *(nearest cross street: Nocumi St.)*

Pachucas in a lineup, 1942.

In the 1940s, two events occurred that have since become emblematic of white Angelenos' racism toward Mexicans in the World War II period: the Sleepy Lagoon murder trial and the Zoot Suit Riots. Sleepy Lagoon was a reservoir used as a swimming hole by Mexican Americans, who, because of discrimination, were allowed only limited access to public pools. On August 2, 1942, José Díaz was found dead at the reservoir. Within 48 hours, racist hysteria ensued, resulting in police picking up 600 Mexican youth and arresting 22 of them. The LAPD was especially vigilant in prosecuting the youth, as it wanted to send a message that the "pachuco problem" was under control. *Pachuco* was a term used to refer to Mexican American youth who developed their own distinctive culture, embodied partly in the zoot suit, as they were neither fully Mexican nor "American."

In a corrupt trial (the largest mass trial in California history up to that point), 17

Orpheum Theatre, 2008.

youth were wrongfully convicted and sentenced to life in prison at San Quentin. In 1944, however, the ruling was overturned, as a result of the work of Arab American attorney George Shibley (with the assistance of Alice McGrath) and the Sleepy Lagoon Defense Committee (which included such individuals as Rita Hayworth and Josefina Fierro de Bright, as well as the Communist Party). The youth were released from San Quentin after spending nine months there, during which time they were harassed and brutalized by guards. Díaz's death remains officially unresolved. Díaz's home was actually located between 5500 and 5560 East Slauson, where currently there is a loading dock. Although the exact location of the reservoir can no longer be determined, we know that it was in the area bounded by the 710 freeway, Bandini Boulevard, Eastern Avenue, and Slauson Avenue on what was then Williams Ranch. Now an industrial area, at the time of Díaz's death it was agricultural land, and most residents worked in packing plants or as farmworkers.

Ten young Mexican American women were also investigated separately for their suspected role in Díaz's murder. Although they were never found guilty, most were sentenced to the Ventura School for Girls, a California correctional facility notorious for its draconian disciplinary measures. Girls with long histories of delinquency, sexual promiscuity, and unsatisfactory stays at other institutions were often sent to the Ventura School for stricter reform. The Mexican American women at the Ventura School and California's other reform institutions were prohibited from speaking Spanish, wearing "gang" clothing, and gathering in groups together as coethnics. These prohibitive practices reflected wartime fears of racial nationalism and political radicalism, as well as anxieties about shifting gender roles. According to Elizabeth Escobedo, in 1944 Nan Allan, the superintendent of the Ventura School, told an investigative committee that the women sent to the school after the Sleepy Lagoon trial "were a particularly dif-ficult group to handle because they were so nationally conscious." One of the young women, Eva Flores, explained the situation somewhat differently, telling her caseworker that she found "it easier to identify with Mexican girls and felt that some of the American girls did not like her." After an average stay of 16 months, the young women were released, but even after their parole, they remained wards of the California Youth Authority until they were 21 years old.

Many consider the Sleepy Lagoon murder and trial to be a precursor to the subsequent Zoot Suit Riots. The riots were so called because many Mexican American youth (and other youth of color) donned zoot suits—long, draped suits seen as marks of defiance—at the time. During a two-week period in May and June 1943, thousands of servicemen and spectators participated in violent attacks against Mexican Americans in Chinatown, Boyle Heights, and other parts of Los Angeles. U.S. sailors stationed in L.A. were offended by Mexican American youth dressed in zoot suits. Not only was such clothing considered to be unpatriotic, but also the presence of pachucos in downtown and other locales signaled their refusal to abide by segregation patterns. Violence erupted as military personnel began beating individual pachucos and eventually assaulting Mexicans in general. White civilians soon joined with sailors, and barrio youth fought back. At one point servicemen entered the Orpheum Theatre and dragged Mexicans from their seats, stripped them, and beat them. In his study of the riots, Luis Alvarez quotes Vicente Morales as saying,

"About eight soldiers got me outside the theatre and they started beating me up. It happened so fast, I passed out. I woke up with a cracked rib, a broken nose, black and blue all over. I was really beat." Morales—not the soldiers—was arrested for disturbing the peace. The Los Angeles City Council responded to the violence by ordering that the victims be arrested, outlawing zoot suits, and instituting curfews. The perpetrators were never brought to justice.

NEARBY SITE OF INTEREST

Broadway Theatre and Commercial District
300–849 S. Broadway, Los Angeles 90014
The Orpheum is part of this historic district that features 12 movie palaces built between 1910 and 1930. Currently, the district is a leading Latina/o shopping center in Southern California.

FAVORITE NEIGHBORHOOD RESTAURANT

Clifton's Cafeteria
648 S. Broadway, Los Angeles 90014
(213) 627-1673 (www.cliftonscafeteria.com)
An old-fashioned cafeteria that fed thousands for free during the Great Depression. Unless you're really into 1940s-style cafeteria fare, don't visit this Los Angeles landmark for its food, but rather its interesting ambience and rich history.

TO LEARN MORE

Luis Alvarez, *The Power of the Zoot: Youth Culture and Resistance during World War II* (University of California Press, 2008).

Elizabeth Escobedo, "The Pachuca Panic: Sexual and Cultural Battlegrounds in World War II Los Angeles," *Western Historical Quarterly* 38, no. 2 (2007): 133–156.

Eduardo Obregón Pagán, *Murder at the Sleepy*

Lagoon: Zoot Suits, Race, and Riot in Wartime L.A. (University of North Carolina Press, 2003).

Catherine S. Ramirez, *The Woman in the Zoot Suit: Gender, Nationalism, and the Cultural Politics of Memory* (Duke University Press, 2009).

Luis Valdez, *Zoot Suit and Other Plays* (Arte Público Press, 1992). The play *Zoot Suit* tells the story of the Sleepy Lagoon murder trial and the Zoot Suit Riots. It was made into a film in 1981.

For more on the riots and pachucas/os more generally, including a PBS documentary, go to www.pbs.org/wgbh/amex/zoot/.

1.27 Partido Liberal Mexicano

809 Yale St., Los Angeles 90012
(at Alpine St.) CHINATOWN
519½ E. 4th St., Los Angeles 90013 *(at Towne Ave.)* DOWNTOWN

Partido Liberal Mexicano propaganda button. Image printed in *Regeneración*, December 2, 1911.

Ricardo and Enrique Flores Magón were brothers and anarchists who played an instrumental role in the Mexican Revolution. Born in Oaxaca in 1874, Ricardo dedicated his life to overthrowing dictator Porfirio Díaz and replacing Díaz's regime with an anarchist politics based on worker control and collective ownership. Although Mexico has always suffered from severe economic and political inequalities, things came to a head with Díaz. Under his leadership the national estate was largely sold off to foreigners, with scant consideration for the millions of displaced and impoverished Mexicans.

In response, revolutionaries throughout Mexico fought for a radically democratic reconstruction of the country (embodied in the slogan "Tierra y Libertad," meaning "Land and Liberty"). Among their efforts was the formation of the Partido Liberal Mexicano (PLM). Ricardo Magón established the newspaper *Regeneración* in 1900, with the assistance of his brother, Enrique, and was promptly imprisoned. Upon his release, the two brothers then sought refuge in Texas, but were persecuted by both Mexican and U.S. officials and forced to flee from city to city. In 1910, the Díaz dictatorship was overthrown and the Magón brothers settled in Los Angeles. They continued producing *Regeneración* at the Fourth Street address, but eventually the PLM headquarters moved to Yale Street, where it also operated La Casa del Obrero Internacional (the International Workers House), which offered lodging and cultural activities. According to historian Emma Pérez, the house was divided into 13 small apartments and also housed La Escuela Racionalista. The Magón brothers were imprisoned under the Espionage Act in 1918 and sent to Leavenworth Penitentiary in Kansas. Ricardo died in his cell in 1922. Although the Mexican Revolution was the first major revolution of the twentieth century, its significance—and in particular its transnational dimensions—is often underappreciated.

> Farewell, O comrades, I
> scorn life as a slave!
>
> I begged no tyrant for my
> life, though sweet it was;

> Though chained, I go uncon-
> quered to my grave,
>
> Dying for my own birth-
> right—and the world's.
> *(Ricardo Flores Magón)*

NEARBY SITES OF INTEREST

Studio for Southern California History

977 N. Hill St., Los Angeles 90012

(213) 229-8890 (www.socalstudio.org)

Near Yale Street, this is a museum and media lab specializing in social history.

Azusa Revival Commemorative Plaque

200 S. San Pedro St., Los Angeles 90012

Near the PML office on Fourth Street, the Azusa Revival, a multiyear event that played a key role in the development of U.S. Pentecostalism, was centered on 312 Azusa Street. The event is marked by a commemorative plaque around the corner at 200 S. San Pedro.

FAVORITE NEIGHBORHOOD RESTAURANT

Hop Li Seafood Restaurant

526 Alpine St., Los Angeles 90012

(213) 680-3939 (www.hoplirestaurant.com)

Customers' favorites include shrimp with honey-glazed walnuts and squid with spicy salt.

TO LEARN MORE

Ward S. Albro, *Always a Rebel: Ricardo Flores Magón and the Mexican Revolution* (Texas Christian University Press, 1992).

Chaz Bufe and Mitchell Cowen Verter, eds., *Dreams of Freedom: A Ricardo Flores Magón Reader* (AK Press, 2005).

On the Magonist assault on Tijuana, see Richard Griswold del Castillo, "The Discredited Revolution: The Magonista Capture of Tijuana in 1911," *Journal of San Diego History* 26, no. 4 (Fall 1980), www.sandiegohistory.org/journal/80fall/revolution.htm.

For the Mexican government's Magón archive, see www.archivomagon.net.

For *Regeneración* articles in English, see http://dwardmac.pitzer.edu/Anarchist_Archives/bright/magon/home.html.

1.28 Pershing Square

532 S. Olive St., Los Angeles 90013 *(between W. 5th St. and W. 6th St.)* (213) 847-4970 (www.laparks.org/pershingsquare/)

DOWNTOWN

Constructed in 1866 as La Plaza Abaja, Pershing Square is the largest park in downtown Los Angeles. At the turn of the twentieth century, it became an important site for leftist political activism because of its central location and proximity to North L.A.'s working-class, ethnically mixed neighborhoods. The Socialist Party, the Industrial Workers of the World (IWW), and the Communist Party gave frequent speeches here to mobilize people who were excluded from traditional political structures because of their race, gender, age, or citizenship status. However, progressive and radical groups faced a climate of intensive repression from law enforcement and the Los Angeles City Council. In 1901, the city council passed an ordinance requiring street speakers to obtain police permits for the right to speak in public parks. In 1903, the ordinance was extended to cover all public streets. In response, the Socialist Party and the nascent IWW

initiated a Free Speech League that purposefully violated the ordinance and flooded the city's courts and jails. In August 1908, they struck a compromise with the city council that abolished the permit requirement in exchange for a "no-speech zone" covering downtown's white-collar districts, a deal that put Pershing Square off-limits. As a result of the deal, and of the growing popularity of automobiles (which decreased pedestrian traffic), the square was largely abandoned as a center of political activity.

Pershing Square, 2008.

People milling about Pershing Square, circa 1956.

Nonetheless, because of its relatively open political atmosphere, Pershing Square became well known as a cruising ground for gay men from diverse racial and class backgrounds. A site for sex and friendship, Pershing Square was an easy walk to gay bars downtown and in Bunker Hill; up until the mid-1960s, the downtown core held Los Angeles' most significant concentration of gay male life. Many gay men describe this crossroads as important to the development of their political consciousness. Harry Hay remembers meeting both other gay men and leftist radicals at Pershing Square during the Depression. Hay became a Communist Party member and later helped found two of the first gay rights organizations in the country: the little-known Bachelors for Wallace (1948) and the better-known Mattachine Society (1950), both of which were based in Los Angeles. Archivist Jim Kepner, who was critical in the development of the ONE National Gay and Lesbian Archives (www.onearchives.org), described Pershing Square as continually policed by the LAPD, yet also continually dynamic and vibrant.

Police sweeps and cleanups became harsher in 1959 and 1964, however, and a moral panic over "degeneracy" helped pave the way for the square's redesign. In 1964, Pershing Square's trees, grass, and bushes were removed; it was paved with concrete, and a parking garage was constructed underneath. Urban growth, decentralization, the dominance of automobiles, and the rise of alternative forms of media such as radio and television also eroded the park's political importance. During a redesign process in 1989–90, tight restrictions forbade the inclusion of trees, grass, or other "hiding places," and the public restrooms were removed because they were perceived as a nuisance to maintain (new ones have since been constructed). Pershing Square is now a gathering place for homeless men and women from the nearby Skid Row community, who face near-constant police harassment, as do activist groups such as Food Not Bombs, which seek to raise the visibility of homelessness and poverty in Los Angeles.

NEARBY SITES OF INTEREST

Millennium Biltmore Hotel Los Angeles

506 S. Grand Ave., Los Angeles 90071
(213) 624-1011 (www.millenniumhotels.com
/millenniumlosangeles)
A Los Angeles Historic Cultural Monument built in 1923 and noted for its beautiful Italian Renaissance architecture. Also the site of a Chicana/o activists' protest against Ronald Reagan in 1969 that resulted in the trial of the Biltmore Six.

Walt Disney Concert Hall

111 S. Grand Ave., Los Angeles 90012
(323) 850-2000 (www.laphil.com)
Designed by architect Frank Gehry and famous for its striking stainless steel exterior, the hall is home to the Los Angeles Philharmonic.

TO LEARN MORE

Lillian Faderman and Stuart Timmons, *Gay L.A.: A History of Sexual Outlaws, Power Politics, and Lipstick Lesbians* (Basic Books, 2006).
Mark Wild, "Preaching to Mixed Crowds: Ethnoracial Coalitions and the Political Culture of Street Speaking, 1900–1929," in *Street Meeting: Multiethnic Neighborhoods in Early Twentieth-Century Los Angeles* (University of California Press, 2005).

1.29 Roosevelt Hotel— the Cinegrill

7000 Hollywood Blvd., Los Angeles 90028
(at N. Orange Dr.) (323) 466-7000
(www.thompsonhotels.com/hotels/la
/hollywood-roosevelt)

HOLLYWOOD

Before the mid-1970s, Los Angeles sustained an ethnic Vietnamese community of fewer than 20,000 people. The first wave of 130,000 Southeast Asian refugees, in the care of the U.S. military and various churches, arrived in 1975, following the war in Vietnam. Although the U.S. government had every intention of dispersing them throughout the country, Southern California's warm weather, wealth of public colleges, and abundance of generous refugee sponsors made it a hub of Vietnamese resettlement. Saigon's Cantonese-speaking population, which had access to resources in North America and Asia outside the reach of other Vietnamese, had the easiest time opening restaurants and markets that could appeal to the existing Chinese American population and the emerging Vietnamese one. In 1976, one could shop at Man Wah Company, just off College Street in Chinatown, for bootlegged Vietnamese music cassettes, Chinese herbal medicine, Vietnamese periodicals and books, fish sauce from Thailand, pickled scallions from Japan, and instant noodles from Taiwan. Vietnamese food could also be found at one of a half dozen or so restaurants operating on or near Hollywood Boulevard (near the 101 freeway) in the neighborhood known today as Thai Town.

One of the community's beloved hotspots during this time was the Cinegrill at the Roosevelt Hotel, a once swanky destination that rich and middle-class whites had, by the mid-1970s, deserted for L.A.'s Westside. Beginning in the summer of 1975 and lasting another couple of years, this nightclub hosted Vietnamese music night for the first wave of refugees. Weekends at the Cinegrill were made possible when a refugee busboy was promoted to play piano there and convinced the owner that Vietnamese nights would bring in paying customers to

"Nomads welcome," reads the Cinegrill sign at the Roosevelt Hotel, 2010.

what had become, according to one regular, "a dying place." The band members were refugees fresh out of Camp Pendleton who lucked out in finding a hotel owner whose mission had become the sponsorship of dozens of refugee families. The Roosevelt Hotel was also the place where a young refugee first performed "Farewell, Saigon," a song he had composed in his Inglewood apartment. This song, the first Vietnamese refugee song ever produced, left its usually festive audience in tears, and word of this fantastic piece spread quickly to the rest of the diaspora. The Voice of America and BBC Radio eventually recorded a studio version of this song and broadcast it to Vietnam the following year. Southern California's Vietnamese refugee community has since become centered on the Little Saigon neighborhood of Orange County. *(Courtesy of Phuong Nguyen)*

NEARBY SITES OF INTEREST

Hollywood Farmers' Market
1600 Ivar Ave., Los Angeles 90028
(323) 463-3171
One of the largest farmers' markets in the Southland. Open Sundays 8 A.M.–1 P.M.

Amoeba Records
6400 Sunset Blvd., Los Angeles 90028
(323) 245-6400 (www.amoeba.com)
One of L.A.'s leading independent record stores; regularly features free live music.

FAVORITE NEIGHBORHOOD RESTAURANTS

Ord Noodles
5401 Hollywood Blvd., Los Angeles 90027
(323) 463-1339

Popular Thai Town noodle shop. Try their specialty, *hoy ka* noodles, and the crispy pork.

The Veggie Grill
8000 W. Sunset Blvd., Los Angeles 90046
(323) 822-7575 (www.veggiegrill.com)
Try the Santa Fe Crispy Chickin', the V-Burger, and carne asada. Other crowd pleasers include the Sweetheart (sweet potato) Fries and carrot cake. Very reasonably priced.

1.30 *Tropical America* Mural
644½ Main St., Los Angeles 90012 *(near W. Cesar Chavez Ave.)*, south wall, exterior of the second floor of Olvera Street's Italian Hall
DOWNTOWN

América Tropical Oprimida y Destrozada por Los Imperialismos (*Tropical America* for short) was painted by David Alfaro Siqueiros, one of the great Mexican muralists, and is considered to be the first outdoor public painting in Los Angeles and perhaps the country. L.A.'s civic elites commissioned Siqueiros to paint the mural for the exterior of a Bavarian beer garden, owned by a Nazi, as part of the Olvera Street development project, which was completed in 1932 as an economic development strategy and tourist attraction. City elites wanted Siqueiros to depict a colorful (and apolitical) scene of Mexican peasant life that would appeal to tourists. Instead, Siqueiros, who painted the mural while in exile in Los Angeles, featured a crucified Mexican laborer under the boot of U.S. capitalist interests. In his journal, Siqueiros wrote that his intent was to produce a "great uncovered mural painting in the free air, facing the sun, facing the rain, for the masses." *Tropical America* is a clear

Portion of the Siqueiros mural *Tropical America*.

condemnation of U.S. imperialism and celebrates the resistance of Mexico's indigenous population. Los Angeles' ruling elite found the mural so offensive that, within a week of its unveiling, it was whitewashed; the whitewash has since been removed. Although the mural cannot be fully restored because of its deterioration, there is currently an effort under way to install a viewing stand and interpretation center so that the public can appreciate both the mural and the power of art as sociopolitical critique.

NEARBY SITE OF INTEREST

El Pueblo Historical Monument (Olvera Street)
125 Paseo de la Plaza, Los Angeles 90012 (near entrance to Olvera Street: 845 N. Alameda St.)
Olvera Street is often considered the birthplace of Los Angeles and is both a major tourist destination and a popular shopping district for locals. Its highly romanticized portrayal of early Mexican Los Angeles was the brainchild of the wealthy Anglo-American socialite Christine Sterling, who helped found a development corporation in the early 1930s to design and promote the site as a "quaint Mexican village."

FAVORITE NEIGHBORHOOD RESTAURANT

Cielito Lindo
23 Olvera St., Unit E, Los Angeles 90012
(213) 687-4391 (www.cielitolindo.org)

Cielito Lindo has been serving its signature taquitos and guacamole sauce on Olvera Street since the early 1930s.

1.31 Yang-Na

200 N. Spring St., Los Angeles 90012 (City Hall) *(between W. Temple St. and W. 1st St.)*
DOWNTOWN

Yang-Na, located in the heart of Los Angeles' contemporary civic center, was one of numerous indigenous Tongva villages in Southern California and a favorite trading area for native people from throughout the region. We believe it is located at approximately this address, which is now the L.A. City Hall. Before Spanish colonization, there were approximately 50 politically connected but autonomous villages in the Greater L.A. region. Each village housed between 50 and 100 people. The Tongva people are of the Uto-Aztecan language family. Because their territory encompassed great ecological diversity, they were skilled hunters, gatherers, and fishers. After Spanish conquest, they were called the Gabrieleños because of their association with Mission San Gabriel.

Spanish penetration devastated the lifestyle of the Tongva and nearly destroyed their population. The pueblo of Los Angeles was founded on or near the site of Yang-Na

In 2009, the flags of the United States, the state of California, and the City of Los Angeles fly in front of the Los Angeles City Hall, which was built approximately on the former site of a Tongva village.

Photograph of a drawing depicting a Yang-Na village. Artist and date unknown.

in 1781, and the Tongva people were coerced from their villages into the missions at San Gabriel and San Fernando. Death by disease and abuse at the missions was widespread; six thousand Tongva people died at Mission San Gabriel alone. During the Mexican period (1824–48), the missions were secularized and many Tongva/Gabrieleños moved to the growing city of Los Angeles to work, where they formed a cheap and subordinated labor force that was essential to the city's growth. In 1828, a German immigrant purchased the land upon which Yang-Na stood and, with the help of Mexican officials, evicted the entire community that had

been living there for perhaps two to three thousand years. Then, in 1847, the Mexican elite of Los Angeles passed a proclamation forbidding Gabrieleños to enter the city limits without proof of employment. Conditions only worsened under American rule. For example, laws routinely convicted Indians for "vagrancy" or public drunkenness (see entry 1.10 Downey Block); and indigenous, as well as Mexican, land claims were widely disregarded. Most Gabrieleños survived by keeping their indigenous identity a secret. They instead identified as Mexican, learned to speak Spanish, and converted to Catholicism. The Gabrieleños were largely neglected during federal treaty procedures throughout the nineteenth and twentieth centuries and, partly for this reason, do not have dedicated reservation land (but see entry 2.9 Haramokngna American Indian Cultural Center).

TO LEARN MORE

Albert L. Hurtado, *Indian Survival on the California Frontier* (Yale University Press, 1988).

The Greater East-side and San Gabriel Valley

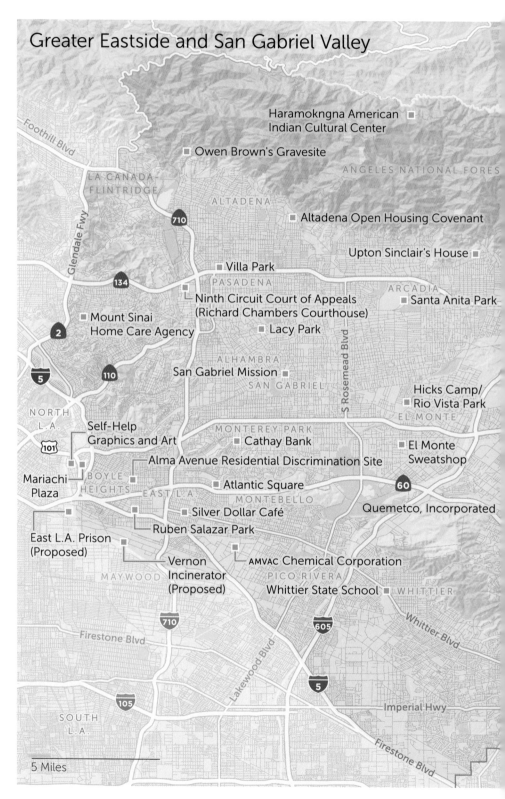

Greater Eastside and San Gabriel Valley

Foothill Blvd

Haramokngna American
Indian Cultural Center ■

Owen Brown's Gravesite ■

ANGELES NATIONAL FORES

LA CAÑADA-
FLINTRIDGE

ALTADENA

Altadena Open Housing Covenant ■

710

Glendale Fwy

Upton Sinclair's House ■ ■

■ Villa Park

134

PASADENA

ARCADIA

Ninth Circuit Court of Appeals
(Richard Chambers Courthouse)

■ Santa Anita Park

2

■ Mount Sinai
Home Care Agency

■ Lacy Park

5   110

ALHAMBRA

San Gabriel Mission ■

SAN GABRIEL

S Rosemead Blvd

Hicks Camp/
■ Rio Vista Park

EL MONTE

NORTH
L.A.

■ Self-Help
Graphics and Art

MONTEREY PARK

■ Cathay Bank

■ El Monte
Sweatshop

101

Alma Avenue Residential Discrimination Site

BOYLE
HEIGHTS

60

Mariachi
Plaza

EAST LA

■ Atlantic Square

MONTEBELLO

Quemetco, Incorporated

■ Silver Dollar Café

Ruben Salazar Park

East L.A. Prison
(Proposed)

Vernon
Incinerator
(Proposed)

MAYWOOD

AMVAC Chemical Corporation

PICO RIVERA

Whittier State School ■   WHITTIER

710

Firestone Blvd

Lakewood Blvd

605

Whittier Blvd

5

105

Imperial Hwy

SOUTH
L.A.

Firestone Blvd

5 Miles

74

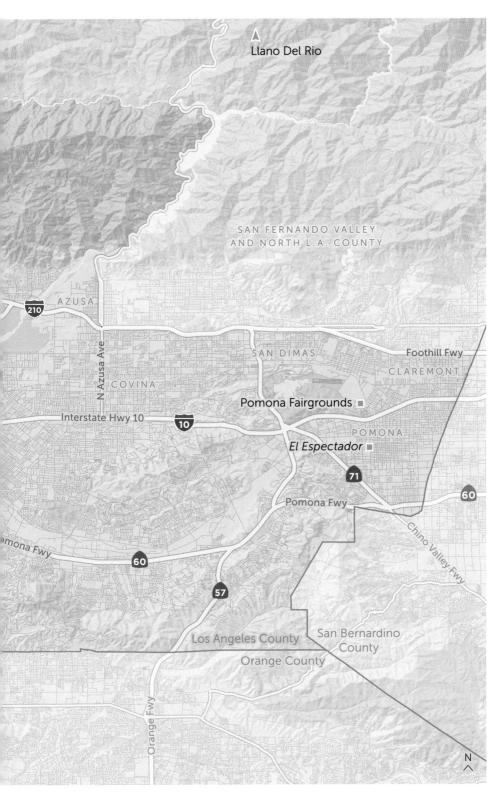

Llano Del Rio

SAN FERNANDO VALLEY
AND NORTH L.A. COUNTY

AZUSA

SAN DIMAS

Foothill Fwy

CLAREMONT

N-Azusa Ave

COVINA

Pomona Fairgrounds ■

Interstate Hwy 10

POMONA

El Espectador ■

Pomona Fwy

mona Fwy

Chino Valley Fwy

Los Angeles County

San Bernardino
County

Orange County

Orange Fwy

N

An Introduction to the Greater Eastside and San Gabriel Valley

Smog. Freeways. The San Gabriel Mountains looming to the north. Signs in Spanish, English, and Chinese. Endless miles of incredibly varied housing interspersed with industrial clusters and large expanses of retail. World-renowned Chinese food. Welcome to the Greater Eastside and San Gabriel Valley (which we'll typically refer to simply as the "Eastside" throughout the rest of this book). The Eastside was the first part of Los Angeles settled by nonnatives. It is divided from the rest of the county by the L.A. River, which was the region's primary water supply for centuries. When the "Spaniards" (who were really a diverse group of indigenous Mexicans, Afro-Mexicans, and Europeans) began exploring the region, the first place they settled was the San Gabriel Mission (1771). There, they introduced many of the agricultural products for which California is now famous, such as wine, and began their forays into what is now downtown Los Angeles.

Three dynamically interrelated processes—labor, immigration, and land use conflicts—have shaped the Eastside's development and are reflected in the sites we have chosen. Because of its proximity to downtown, the L.A. River, and the railroad, the Eastside has historically housed much of the region's industry. Beginning at the turn of the twentieth century, the brick factories and warehouses that provided the raw materials for Los Angeles' growth were located here. Now, the Eastside coordinates much of L.A.'s contemporary manufacturing economy—especially furniture, electronics, and apparel. The concentration of industry has made the area an attractive destination for laborers, who literally built and continue to sustain the area. These conditions have led to the development of a strong working-class consciousness that is reflected in both historic and contemporary movements for unionization and socialism and against labor exploitation, prison expansion, and environmental racism, among other forces.

Many of the Eastside's workers have been immigrants who were restricted from living elsewhere in the city. By the early 1900s the Eastside had become heavily populated by Mexicans, who were pushed out of downtown by the city's elite Anglo boosters. Starting in the 1920s, they were joined by Russian, Jewish, Armenian, and Japanese immigrants, as well as African American migrants from the U.S. South and Midwest. After World War II, with a decline in residential segregation and the expansion of the suburbs, many (especially the children of immigrants) moved farther east, to the suburbs of the San Gabriel Valley—places like Alhambra, San Gabriel, Pasadena, Pico Rivera, Whittier, and Azusa. Some others (especially Jewish Americans) moved to the San Fernando Valley and the Westside. These outward migrations left the older neighborhoods of the Eastside to become almost entirely Mexican and Latina/o spaces, an association that is reflected in popular films such as *Born in East L.A.* However, since the 1980s, waves of newcomers, especially from Asia and Latin America, have continued to come to the San Gabriel Valley and have settled in such places as Monterey Park, El Monte, Hacienda Heights, Walnut, and San Marino. Today, the Greater Eastside is home to a mix of Latina/o, Asian, and white residents. The region's neighborhoods and landscapes reflect its ethnic diversity and the varied trajectories of upward mobility among generations of immigrant groups.

Since the Eastside is simultaneously a hub of industrial activity and a vibrant residential space, innumerable land use conflicts have inevitably ensued. When Mexicans were initially pushed east of downtown, industry and other dangerous land uses were not far behind. This pattern is a result of both industry's need for relatively large parcels of land and a desire to locate hazardous land uses away from population clusters . . . or at least populations that "matter." Working-class Latinas/os have largely borne the brunt of L.A.'s industrial machine. Not only do they live in close proximity to industry and breathe highly polluted air, but they also have been systematically displaced by the maze of freeways that connects the region and allows suburbanites access to downtown. Residents have repeatedly had to battle unwanted land-use projects—such as prisons, the manufacture of toxic chemicals, and incinerators—that serve the entire Los Angeles region but disproportionately affect Eastside communities. Their activism has been an important element of progressive and leftist politics in Los Angeles.

Throughout the Eastside one can find traces of these complex and interlocking histories. This is a region that features greatly contrasting landscapes: urban, suburban, industrial, agricultural, and even wilderness landscapes. It is crossed by major waterways, including the Los Angeles River, the San Gabriel River, and the Rio Hondo, as well as by national and local freeways (5, 10, 60, 710, 210, 605). It also features some of the region's most important recreational areas and some of the steepest mountains in the continental United States. Perhaps most important for the purposes of *A People's Guide,* it is home to a diversity of people who have sometimes been complicit in their own and others' oppression, but who have also struggled to create community and a more socially just world amid these forces. The end result is a fascinating landscape.

Greater Eastside and San Gabriel Valley Sites

2.1 Alma Avenue— Residential Discrimination Site

240 N. Alma Ave., Los Angeles 90063
(between E. Cesar Chavez Ave. and Michigan Ave.) **EAST LOS ANGELES**

Private residence

House at 240 N. Alma Ave., 2008.

In 1923, white residents of the community of Belvedere united when Mr. Shimizu, a Japanese immigrant, bought a house from a white homeowner in the name of his nisei children. Since California's Alien Land Laws prohibited "aliens ineligible for citizenship" (a term that included most nonwhite immigrants) from owning property (which also made it illegal for whites to sell to a Japanese person), many Asian immigrants purchased property in the names of their American-born children. The neighbors protested the Shimizus' purchase and posted a sign that read: "Look Here! Come one, come all! Big meeting 7 o'clock February 24, 1923 Corner of Alma and Brooklyn Avenue To keep the Japs out! Everybody help. The Committee." A white mob, including members of the Asiatic Exclusion League of Southern California, met the Shimizu family and informed them that they were not welcome. When the Shimizus did not leave, the activists set the house on fire and threatened to kill Mr. Shimizu. Within a year the Shimizus had moved back to their previous neighborhood of Evergreen, near Boyle Heights.

Japanese Americans have had a long presence in California, which began when they first arrived as agricultural workers in the late 1800s (see also entry 2.10 Hicks Camp/ Rio Vista Park). Until approximately 1970, Japanese Americans were the third-largest nonwhite group in Los Angeles County (after Mexican Americans and African Americans). Because of legal residential segregation and the hostility of white people like those who protested the Shimizus' move, the only neighborhoods open to Japanese Americans were, for many years, either Little Tokyo, the Crenshaw neighborhood of South L.A., the Harbor area, or Boyle Heights in East L.A. Over time, especially after World War II, Japanese Americans expanded farther south and east, but only through great struggle (see entry 3.17 Kashu Realty and Thirty-sixth Street Residential Discrimination Site).

NEARBY SITES OF INTEREST

El Mercado
3425 E. 1st St., Los Angeles 90063
(elmercadodelosangeles.com)

An indoor Mexican market packed with restaurants, shops, foodstuffs, and a bakery and which also features outdoor food stalls. Try the *nieves* (shaved ice) or *champurrado* with hot churros. An Eastside institution.

Evergreen Cemetery

204 N. Evergreen Ave., Los Angeles 90063
(323) 268-6714

One of Los Angeles' oldest cemeteries (est. 1877), and one of the few places in L.A. County where people of color (including such notable figures as Biddy Mason) were allowed to be buried before World War II. Be sure to check out the Evergreen Cemetery Jogging Path, which is a national model for promoting exercise in low-income neighborhoods.

Breed Street Shul

247 N. Breed St., Los Angeles 90033
(www.breedstreetshul.org)

Once the largest synagogue in the western United States. Currently closed and in disrepair, but plans are afoot for restoration of its two buildings, built in 1915 and 1923.

FAVORITE NEIGHBORHOOD RESTAURANT

Cemitas Poblanas Elvirita no. 1

3010 E. 1st St., Los Angeles 90063
(323) 881-0428

Specializing in the Puebla-style Mexican sandwich.

2.2 Altadena Open Housing Covenant

2393 Glen Canyon Rd., Altadena 91001
(between Grand Oaks Ave. and Roosevelt Ave.)
Private residence

Altadena is an unincorporated community north of Pasadena, and one of Los Angeles' oldest suburbs. Many members of Pasadena's historic African American population relocated north to Altadena beginning in the 1950s, when they were displaced first by redevelopment and, over the next few decades, the construction of the 134 and 210 freeways. While Black in-migration and subsequent school desegregation rulings prompted significant white flight from Pasadena and Altadena to neighboring Arcadia, San Marino, Sierra Madre, and La Cañada Flintridge, many of the remaining white and Black residents were committed to integration. In 1959, the Altadena-Pasadena Human Relations Committee and the Pasadena Area Fair Housing Committee created the Open Housing Covenant, in which individual residents signed an agreement stating that "any family should be free to choose its place of residence." Because few other places in the San Gabriel Valley welcomed people of color at that time, many African Americans

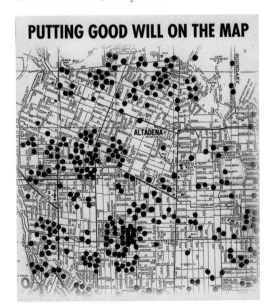

Map by the Altadena-Pasadena Human Relations Committee showing the distribution of residents who signed the Open Housing Covenant, circa 1959.

moved to Altadena in the 1960s and 1970s, and now many Latinas/os are doing so. The particular address listed above, which was the home of a resident who signed this agreement, is noteworthy because it is located east of Lake Avenue, which has historically been a racial and economic dividing line. In general, white people and more expensive real estate could—and still can—be found east of Lake, whereas a more racially and economically mixed population lived west of Lake. As can be seen from the map, most of the signatories were located west of Lake, indicating that fewer whites in exclusively white areas signed; the signatory at this address, therefore, was an exception. Although both Altadena and Pasadena still exhibit internal segregation, on the whole they remain far more racially diverse than surrounding cities, and this diversity is widely celebrated among residents.

NEARBY SITES OF INTEREST

Jackie Robinson Park and Community Center
1020 N. Fair Oaks Ave., Pasadena 91103
(626) 744-7300 (http://cityofpasadena.net
/HumanServices/Jackie_Robinson_Center/)
Jackie Robinson, the famed baseball player who integrated major league baseball in 1947, lived at 45 Glorieta, adjacent to the park. The house itself no longer exists.

Former home of Octavia Butler
108 W. Tremont St., Pasadena 91103
Private residence
Butler (1947–2006), an African American science-fiction writer and recipient of a MacArthur Genius Grant, lived here in 1976.

Cobb Estate
3496 N. Lake Ave., Altadena 91001 (northwest corner of Lake and Alta Loma)
A picturesque hiking area (the 2.7-mile uphill trail is an excellent workout). Includes the remains of the Mount Lowe railroad, a scenic rail line that operated from 1893 until 1936, and which is on the National Register of Historic Places.

School of Self-Reliance
(626) 791-3217 (www.ChristopherNyerges.com)
Want to learn how to survive in the wilds of the San Gabriel Mountains? This school offers regular survivalist classes.

FAVORITE NEIGHBORHOOD RESTAURANT

Bulgarini Gelato
749 E. Altadena Dr., Altadena 91001
(626) 791-6174 (www.bulgarinigelato.com)

2.3 AMVAC Chemical Corporation

2110 Davie Ave., Commerce 90040 (between Corvette St. and Fleet St.) (323) 888-1724 (www.amvac-chemical.com)

AMVAC Chemical Corporation, 2008.

AMVAC is a Newport Beach–based pesticide corporation with a production facility at this address. Among its products are pesticides that either have been banned by the

Environmental Protection Agency (EPA) or are in the process of being banned. To date, AMVAC has bought the rights to ten such pesticides, most of which are organophosphates (a class of pesticides that are acutely toxic). AMVAC's pesticides are sold in California, the United States, and internationally. Critics charge that not only has AMVAC sought to prevent the EPA from banning certain pesticides, but also that the sale and distribution of such products has resulted in numerous poisoning incidents and environmental damage across the globe.

In 2007, AMVAC settled a lawsuit (without admitting to any wrongdoing) brought by 30 workers on a Dole banana plantation in Nicaragua, who charged that DBCP (dibromochloropropane) manufactured by AMVAC and used on the bananas resulted in the workers' sterility. DBCP is known to cause sterility in humans. A Los Angeles jury awarded six workers $3.2 million in damages, and a subsequent judgment ordered Dole to pay $2.5 million as punishment for knowingly sending Nicaraguan workers into contaminated fields without warning. Dole's lawyers then argued that the "new Dole," which apparently refers to a new, socially responsible company, should not have to pay for the conduct of the "old Dole." In 2009, however, the case was reopened with evidence that some of the banana workers' testimony was coerced. In 2010, Judge Victoria Chaney threw out the initial multi-million-dollar award and dismissed all other claims because of tampering. According to the judge, as quoted in the *Los Angeles Times*, "It is understandable that the [Nicaraguan]

populace is angry and feels impotent. The problem is [that] the focus of their rage is . . . one target: Dole's use of DBCP." Well, who would you be angry at? The Nicaraguan workers did not merely *feel* impotent; they *were* literally impotent. While pollution has never recognized political boundaries, the sale of pesticides too toxic to sell in the United States to industrializing countries with limited regulatory capacity represents a new low.

NEARBY SITE OF INTEREST

Citadel Outlets
100 Citadel Dr., Los Angeles 90040
(323) 725-1450 (www.citadeloutlets.com)
The art deco building was built in 1929 to house the Samson Tire and Rubber Company factory, and later a Uniroyal tire plant, which closed in 1978. This testament to deindustrialization is now an outlet mall.

TO LEARN MORE

Pesticide Action Network (PAN) (www.panna.org), dedicated to advancing alternatives to pesticides in the United States and globally.
Angus Wright, *The Death of Ramón González: The Modern Agricultural Dilemma* (University of Texas Press, 2005).

2.4 Atlantic Square

2230 S. Atlantic Blvd., Monterey Park 91754
(at W. Riggin St. and W. Floral Dr.)
In the late 1980s, the redevelopment of the Atlantic Square Shopping Center was the occasion of struggle among established white and Latina/o residents, and more recent Chinese immigrants, in Monterey Park. Atlantic Square was originally built in the

1950s, and by the late 1980s its deteriorating condition prompted businesses to vacate in favor of newer malls. Faced with decreasing tax revenues, city officials made redevelopment of Atlantic Square a high priority. Yet the shopping center's redevelopment coincided with a period of strong anti-immigrant sentiment, as seen in "slow-growth" and "English-only" initiatives, which in Monterey Park were aimed at the Chinese. The rapid expansion of businesses owned by immigrant Chinese had produced conflicts over what types of businesses, signage, and architectural styles should exist in the community. According to sociologist Leland Saito, these conditions led to the reassertion of white dominance through control of the landscape. Established residents and city officials lobbied publicly for "mainstream" chain stores and a "Mediterranean" architectural style. Residents first suggested a Mexican theme to reflect the early history of the community, but over time that idea was "whitened," to become Spanish and, finally, vaguely "Mediterranean." The Mediterranean style is widely accepted because it is assumed to be European (although, in reality, the Mediterranean Sea is encircled

in part by North Africa and the Middle East as well) and therefore more American than Mexican- or Asian-influenced styles. In addition to debates over architectural style, there were disagreements over whether business signs should be written in Chinese and whether other visual markers of Chinese culture should be permitted. The entire redevelopment process proceeded with little participation or input from ethnic Chinese immigrant residents and business owners.

The redeveloped shopping center, featuring an assortment of national chain stores in the much-desired Mediterranean style, opened in the early 1990s. Today, Atlantic Square Shopping Center serves residents of East Los Angeles as well as the West San

Atlantic Square, 2009.

PERSONAL REFLECTION BY LELAND SAITO, SOCIOLOGIST AND AUTHOR OF *RACE AND POLITICS: ASIAN AMERICANS, LATINOS, AND WHITES IN A LOS ANGELES SUBURB*

What happened in Atlantic Square is, I believe, happening in other cities around the country as city officials work to redevelop their urban business districts into downtown "Main Streets" to compete with suburban malls. Even in communities in which immigrant entrepreneurs are generating new economic vitality in once moribund areas, city officials eagerly target and subsidize franchises of national chains and "mainstream" businesses, which disproportionately are owned and frequented by nonimmigrants, rather than tapping into and supporting the new immigrant entrepreneurs and their clientele.

Gabriel Valley. It retains its "Mediterranean" look, with beige facades, arched entryways, and red faux-adobe roof tiling. Posted conspicuously in front of the Ralphs grocery store, which serves as one of the center's anchor businesses, is a large American flag. Generic Mediterranean style has become emblematic of the late-twentieth- and early-twenty-first-century California landscape. But as demonstrated at Atlantic Square, even at an everyday site as seemingly innocuous as a shopping center, choice of form is not merely a neutral aesthetic decision but can have tremendous material and political significance for issues such as immigration, demographic change, and national identity.

FAVORITE NEIGHBORHOOD RESTAURANTS

Happy Family
500 N. Atlantic Blvd., Monterey Park 91754
(626) 282-8986
Popular vegetarian Chinese restaurant. A few of the many favorites: minced "squab" in lettuce leaf, deep-fried sesame "chicken," spicy eggplant, and sweet and sour "spareribs."

Mandarin Noodle House
701 W. Garvey Ave., Monterey Park 91754
(626) 570-9795
This small, family-run establishment is known for its scallion pancakes and beef noodle soup. The noodles are homemade.

TO LEARN MORE

Timothy Fong, *The First Suburban Chinatown: The Remaking of Monterey Park, California* (Temple University Press, 1994).
Leland Saito, *Race and Politics: Asian Americans, Latinos, and Whites in a Los Angeles Suburb* (University of Illinois Press, 1998).

2.5 Cathay Bank

250 S. Atlantic Blvd., Monterey Park 91754 *(between W. Garvey Ave. and W. Newmark Ave.)* (626) 281-8808 (www.cathaybank.com)

Cathay Bank's first branch location, in Monterey Park, 2009.

This branch of Cathay Bank was the first branch location of a Chinese American bank in the United States. In 1962, the original Cathay Bank was established in Los Angeles' Chinatown near downtown. As the first Chinese American bank in Los Angeles, the institution provided important services to the bank's predominantly ethnic Chinese clientele. For example, it hired Chinese-speaking employees, introduced American-style banking services that took into account cultural and immigrant contexts, and made loans to applicants who were likely to be denied by mainstream institutions.

The opening of the bank's first branch, in Monterey Park in 1979, paralleled the influx of ethnic Chinese immigrants in the west San Gabriel Valley. The majority of these immigrants had come from Taiwan and Hong Kong, fleeing political uncertainty and pursuing economic opportunity. By 1990, Monterey Park had become the first majority-Asian American city on the U.S.

mainland and garnered a host of nicknames, including "the first suburban Chinatown" and "Little Taipei." A growing number of Chinese American banks, including Cathay Bank, played key roles in facilitating ethnic Chinese entrepreneurship and home loans in the San Gabriel Valley. In doing so, they transformed the San Gabriel Valley's commercial and residential spaces into what geographer Wei Li has described as an "ethnoburb."

Today, Cathay Bank, East-West Bank (headquartered in Pasadena), and United Commercial Bank in San Francisco are the three largest minority-owned financial institutions in the United States, and East-West Bank is the second-largest bank headquartered in Los Angeles. A stretch of Valley Boulevard northeast of this site, between Garfield Boulevard and Del Mar Avenue, has been dubbed the "Chinese Wall Street" because of its high concentration of Chinese American banks, as well as East Asian and nonethnic banks, indicating the high demand for financial services and the considerable financial resources of the area. In response to discriminatory lending practices by mainstream financial institutions, minority-owned financial institutions have provided a significant community resource. The history of Cathay Bank exemplifies what the geographer Yu Zhou has termed the "two faces" of the ethnic Chinese economy in North America: on the one hand, it links individuals and institutions in the United States to the dynamic economies of East and Southeast Asia; but on the other hand, this economy's very existence stems from the marginalization of "nonwhite" racial groups in the United States.

NEARBY SITE OF INTEREST

San Gabriel Square

140 W. Valley Blvd., San Gabriel 91776 (www.sangabrielsquare.com)

Shops and restaurants catering to an ethnic Chinese clientele, anchored by the Asian-American-owned supermarket chain Ranch 99.

FAVORITE NEIGHBORHOOD RESTAURANTS

Savoy Kitchen

138 E. Valley Blvd., Alhambra 91801 (626) 308-9535

There is almost always a wait at this tiny, family-run eatery, which is famous for its Hainan chicken.

Wahib's Middle East Restaurant

910 E. Main St., Alhambra 91801 (626) 281-1006 (http://wahibmiddleeast.com)

Try the vegetarian supreme or the kabobs.

Fosselman's Ice Cream

1824 W. Main St., Alhambra 91801 (626) 282-6533 (www.fosselmans.com)

An Alhambra institution for more than 80 years.

TO LEARN MORE

Wei Li, *Ethnoburb: The New Ethnic Community in Urban America* (University of Hawaii Press, 2009).

Denise Hamilton, *The Jasmine Trade: A Novel of Suspense Introducing Eve Diamond* (Scribner, 2001). Mystery novel set in the San Gabriel Valley featuring Asian American "parachute kids" as central characters.

Yu Zhou, "How Do Places Matter? A Comparative Study of Chinese Ethnic Economies in Los Angeles and New York City," *Urban Geography* 19 (2000): 531–553.

2.6 East Los Angeles Prison (Proposed) and Vernon Incinerator (Proposed)

Proposed East L.A. prison Nearest address is 1600 S. Santa Fe Ave., Los Angeles 90021 *(cross street: E. Olympic Blvd.; the prison would have occupied the entire block)* VERNON

Proposed Vernon incinerator 3961 Bandini Blvd., Vernon 90058 *(between S. Downey Rd. and S. Indiana St.)* VERNON

In the late 1980s, the California Department of Corrections (CDC) sought to build a reception center (i.e., a prison) in East Los Angeles in order to house California's expanding prison population. A group of local residents formed the Coalition Against the Prison to fight the CDC, because they felt that the city's poor and minority communities were already burdened with more than their share of dangerous and undesirable land uses. This initiative eventually gave birth to the Mothers of East L.A. (MELA), which waged a David-and-Goliath-type struggle against the CDC. They challenged the CDC's environmental impact report (EIR)—a planning document that outlines the anticipated positive and negative consequences of a proposed development—which in this case was grossly inadequate and underestimated the negative impacts on local communities. The organization also confronted cultural insensitivity, such as the CDC's refusal to provide appropriate translation, and a host of racist assumptions, including the comment made by one public official that the Mexican American women should be thankful the prison would be located nearby, because their children were the ones most likely to be incarcerated. MELA, which was joined in its suit by the City of L.A., won a major victory when Governor George Deukmejian decided he would no longer consider this site as a possibility. This particular struggle was one of many that marked the start of California's unprecedented prison expansion project. Over the past several decades California has built the largest prison system on the globe. Critics have argued that prisons are California's

Proposed site of the East L.A. prison, 2008.

Graphic developed by Ignacio Gomez for the Coalition Against the Prison, circa 1988.

(and increasingly the United States') ineffective response to complex social and economic problems, such as poverty and a lack of employment opportunity, that demand real solutions.

MELA was soon called upon to mobilize again when the California Thermal Treatment Service sought to construct a hazardous waste incinerator in the city of Vernon. This plan was partly a response to Southern California's massive trash problem. City officials in Vernon welcomed the incinerator, despite the fact that it was expected to burn many thousands of tons of hazardous waste annually and would add to the region's acute air pollution. Amazingly, the local regulatory agencies did not require an EIR for the incinerator project. Both the failure to require a full EIR and the plan to site such a facility adjacent to the Latina/o Eastside were seen as blatant acts of environmental racism. MELA, in conjunction with the Natural Resources Defense Council, successfully blocked the project.

These two struggles—resistance to the prison and to the incinerator—and the effort by women in South Central Los Angeles to block another incinerator, the LANCER project, were key events in the development of the environmental justice movement in Los Angeles (see entry 3.1 Alameda Boulevard: The "White Wall," South Central Incinerator, and South Central Farm).

TO LEARN MORE

Mary Pardo, *Mexican American Women Activists: Identity and Resistance in Two Los Angeles Communities* (Temple University Press, 1998).

2.7 El Espectador

915 W. 4th St., Pomona 91768 *(between S. Huntington St. and S. White Ave.)*
Private residence

Ignacio López published *El Espectador* from his home in Pomona (pictured here in 2010) for part of its history, from about 1935 to 1944.

El Espectador (the Spectator) was a Spanish-language newspaper published by Ignacio L. López from approximately 1933 to 1961. Born in Guadalajara, Mexico, in 1908, López was raised in the United States and graduated from Pomona College in 1931. His paper, which was published from his home, was distinct from other Spanish-language publications in that it focused on the local Mexicana/o population, rather than on Mexico. The weekly served the eastern San Gabriel Valley and the area now called the Inland Empire (the inland metropolitan region anchored by the cities of Ontario, San Bernardino, and Riverside).

Aside from its long run and emphasis on Mexicans in the United States, the newspaper was significant because López used it as a tool for social change and racial equality. At that time, the eastern edge of Los Angeles County was primarily an agricultural region, and Mexicans there lived in a Jim

Ignacio López, date unknown.

cans. Finally, *El Espectador* was a strident critic of police abuse. When the newspaper ceased publication, López worked for mainstream political candidates and was eventually appointed as the Spanish-speaking coordinator for the Department of Housing and Urban Development under the Nixon administration.

It is difficult to overstate the role of ethnic media like *El Espectador* in supporting ethnic and immigrant communities. In Latina/o Los Angeles, this history begins with *El Clamor Público,* the first Spanish-language newspaper established in California after U.S. conquest; it was founded in 1855 by a 19-year-old printer named Francisco Ramirez. This history also includes *La Opinión,* founded in 1926, which is the largest Spanish-language newspaper in the United States, and radio personalities such as Eddie "Piolín" Sotelo, who played a pivotal role in convening Los Angeles' largest protest—more than 500,000 persons supporting immigrant rights—in May 2006.

Crow world. López played a key role in challenging segregation and discrimination. Not only did he publicize such injustices in his newspaper, but he also played an active role in dismantling Jim Crow by organizing community boycotts, confronting discriminatory politicians and business owners, and mobilizing Mexican Americans to reject their second-class status. For example, López led a boycott that resulted in the desegregation of the Upland Theatre, and he, along with others, filed a lawsuit against the City of San Bernardino because it allowed Mexican Americans and African Americans to use the public pool only on Fridays—a suit that led to the desegregation of all local public pools. *El Espectador* also supported parents in South Fontana when the school district there lagged in desegregating its schools, and López joined a challenge to the City of Chino when it refused to apply for federal housing funds after it became known that the housing would benefit primarily Mexi-

NEARBY SITE OF INTEREST

Latino Art Museum

281 S. Thomas St., Suite 105, Pomona 91766
(909) 484-2618 (www.lamoa.net)
Small gallery specializing in fine art by Latin American artists living in the United States.

FAVORITE NEIGHBORHOOD RESTAURANT

El Merendero Bakery

301 S. Garey Ave., Pomona 91766
(909) 620-1411
Mexican *panadería* and restaurant with an extensive menu.

TO LEARN MORE

Mario T. García, "Mexican American Muckraker: Ignacio L. López and *El Espectador*," in *Mexican Americans: Leadership, Ideology, and Identity, 1930–1960* (Yale University Press, 1989), pp. 84–112.

Matt Garcia, *A World of Its Own: Race, Labor, and Citrus in the Making of Greater Los Angeles, 1900–1970* (University of North Carolina Press, 2001).

Matthew D. Matsaganis, Vikki S. Katz, and Sandra Ball-Rokeach, *Understanding Ethnic Media: Producers, Consumers, and Societies* (Sage Publications, 2011).

Apartment complex at 2614 N. Santa Anita Ave., El Monte, 2009.

2.8 El Monte Sweatshop

2614 N. Santa Anita Ave., El Monte 91733
(between Owens Wy. and Elliott Ave.)

Private residences

In August 1995, federal investigators raided this apartment complex on suspicion that it housed garment workers who were being held as slaves. They found 72 undocumented Thai workers, mostly women, who had been held captive for up to four years. Recruited from Bangkok by Chinese Thai nationals who promised them well-paying jobs in the United States and weekends and evenings off, they were instead locked in this seven-unit complex with boarded-up windows, surrounded by razor wire. They were forced to work 18 hours a day assembling garments for such clothing lines as B.U.M., High Sierra, Cheetah, and Anchor Blue. They earned less than one dollar per day. Armed guards watched them, and they were forced to buy food and necessities from a "store" run by their captors. All of their phone calls were monitored, and their letters censored.

Eventually, a worker named Win Chuai Ngan found a Thai-language newspaper in the trash. He cut out and hid an advertisement for a Thai temple and the mailing address label for the apartment. One night, carrying the clipping and the mailing label, he jumped the razor wire fence, ran to a taxi

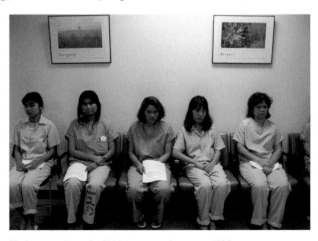

Thai women from the El Monte sweatshop case, 1995.

stand, and asked to be taken to the temple. He told his story to the people at the temple, and the raid soon followed. Eight persons who operated the complex were arrested. Because the workers were unauthorized, they were subject to deportation by the Immigration and Naturalization Service. A groundswell of protest erupted, with demands that the workers be released and granted amnesty. Sweatshop Watch eventually raised bail for all of the workers. After their release, Sweatshop Watch secured legal jobs for them and arranged for housing and medical care.

While much of the media and U.S. public were appalled that slavery could happen in the contemporary United States, this story is far too common both in Los Angeles and globally. In fact, the El Monte complex was just one of several similar local operations, many of which "employed" not only Asian immigrants but also Latinas/os. The fact is that sweatshops are a regular feature of the contemporary manufacturing economy. To maximize profits, clothing retailers routinely subcontract sewing and assembly jobs to smaller companies that agree to meet impossible cost and time demands. Subcontractors pass this pressure on to their workers in the form of illegally low wages and long hours, as well as appalling and inhumane conditions. Between 1995 and 2009, Los Angeles' garment industry workforce shrunk from 112,000 to 79,400 workers. Although garment production is still Los Angeles County's largest manufacturing industry, subcontractors are moving production to less industrialized countries, where similar work conditions often prevail.

Historically, the retailers who initiate this chain of exploitation have not been held liable, but the El Monte case changed this practice. Thai and Latina/o workers, represented by the Asian Pacific American Legal Center, sued retailers, including Mervyn's, charging that retailers are actually joint employers of garment workers and, as such, are bound by federal and state laws. The workers sought $7 million in back wages, but they also wanted to expose the garment industry's horrific practices and conditions. Ultimately, they won $4 million in a landmark settlement that made the larger point of holding corporate giants responsible for the labor exploitation they create through subcontracting. Most of the Thai immigrants stayed in the United States, and in 2008 several became United States citizens. In 2010, a play about their struggle, *Fabric,* premiered locally, and the case has been featured in an exhibit on sweatshops at the Smithsonian National Museum of American History.

NEARBY SITE OF INTEREST

El Monte Legion Stadium
11151 Valley Blvd., El Monte 91734
(http://elmontelegionstadium.com)
Now a post office, this was formerly the site of the El Monte Legion Stadium, one of the Southland's most popular dance spots and a major site of multiracial mixing in the 1950s.

FAVORITE NEIGHBORHOOD RESTAURANT

Valenzuela's
11721 Valley Blvd., El Monte 91732
(626) 579-5384
Known for their *carne asada en su jugo* and *machaca* dishes.

TO LEARN MORE

Coalition to Abolish Slavery and Trafficking—Los Angeles, (888) 539-2373 (www.castla.org).

Edna Bonacich and Richard P. Appelbaum, *Behind the Label: Inequality in the Los Angeles Apparel Industry* (University of California Press, 2000).

Jane L. Collins, *Threads: Gender, Labor, and Power in the Global Apparel Industry* (University of Chicago Press, 2003).

Peter Leibhold and Harry Rubenstein, *Between a Rock and a Hard Place: A History of American Sweatshops, 1820–Present* (UCLA Asian American Studies Center, 1999).

Almudena Carracedo and Robert Bahar, directors, *Made in LA* (Semilla Verde Productions, 2007). An award-winning documentary film about three Latina garment workers in Los Angeles and their struggle to win basic labor protections.

Haramokngna American Indian Cultural Center, 2008.

2.9 Haramokngna American Indian Cultural Center

Angeles Crest Hwy. and Mount Wilson Red Box Rd., La Cañada Flintridge 91101 (626) 449-8975 (call or check www .haramokngna.org/visit-haramokngna for current directions).

Haramokngna is the Tongva word for "the place where people gather," and it is the name of this cultural and educational center that focuses on the local indigenous population. The site, which opened in 1999, used to be a seasonal trading place for the Tongva. Before the Spanish conquest, most native groups in Southern California were hunter-gatherers and used the many diverse environments of the region, including the ocean, shoreline, grasslands, and mountains, to full advantage. Many of their trails and landmarks, such as Tongva Peak in Glendale and Tongva Trail in the Angeles National Forest, still exist. Nowadays, although Los Angeles has the largest urban indigenous population in the United States, and the Gabrieleño/Tongva tribe is one of the county's largest (numbering around 1,500 people), they have no tribal lands and are not federally recognized. This lack of recognition has led to a distinct native landscape in L.A., in which there are no reservations—the spaces most Americans associate with native people—and few places where indigenous people visibly concentrate. As a result, places such as Haramokngna and sacred sites take on special significance. Besides serving as a site for local American Indians to preserve and produce their culture, Haramokngna offers an indigenous perspective on native history, culture, and contemporary issues for the benefit of the larger community. The cultural center is currently open on Saturdays.

NEARBY SITES OF INTEREST

Descanso Gardens
1418 Descanso Dr., La Cañada Flintridge 91011
(818) 949-4200 (www.descansogardens.org)

Hahamongna Watershed Park
Oak Grove Dr. and Foothill Blvd.,
La Cañada Flintridge 91011 (626) 744-7275
(www.lamountains.com/parks.asp?parkid=643)

FAVORITE NEIGHBORHOOD RESTAURANT

Black Cow Café
2219 Honolulu Ave., Montrose 91011
(818) 957-5282 (www.whatscookninc.com
/black_cow1.htm)
This popular eatery has been around for decades.
A pleasant spot for lunch or dinner.

2.10 Hicks Camp/Rio Vista Park
4275 Ranger Ave., El Monte 91732 *(nearest cross street: Dilo St.)* (626) 580-2200

A gate at Rio Vista Park is decorated with an artful
rendition of Hicks Camp, 2008.

This site, a former agricultural workers'
camp, is closely associated with the launch
of the 1933 Los Angeles County Strike (also
known as the El Monte Berry Strike), which
was the largest in the history of California
agriculture up to that date. The strike highlighted the complex dynamic among ethnic
Mexicans, Pilipinos, Japanese, and Anglos
that was typical of the agribusiness industry
in the first half of the twentieth century.
Anglo landowners typically leased land to
Japanese farmers, who could not own land
under California's Alien Land Laws. The
Japanese, in turn, employed Mexican and, to
a lesser extent, Pilipino and other Japanese
workers. Workers lived in local colonias or
on land rented from the farmers. They built
homes of discarded materials that usually
lacked plumbing and heating. Families typically made less than $100 per month.

During the Great Depression, conditions got even worse. The Japanese Growers
Association cut wages from 25 cents to 9
cents per hour. The Cannery and Agricultural Workers Industrial Union (CAWIU),
an independent union with communist
ties, began organizing workers in 1933. In
May, the CAWIU petitioned the Japanese
Growers Association for a wage increase.
Receiving no reply, the organizers called a
general meeting at Hicks Camp for June 1.
Six hundred workers unanimously declared
an immediate work stoppage. A committee
of Mexican, Pilipino, and Japanese workers
coordinated the strike.

Civic leaders and growers immediately
sought to quash the rebellion. The Los
Angeles Police Department's "Red Squad"
assigned undercover agents to infiltrate the
group and convince strikers to follow their
more conservative national consuls instead
of the CAWIU. The Mexican government
directed its consular officials to assume leadership positions on the strike committee.
The new leadership, in turn, expelled the

CAWIU. While the CAWIU continued to distribute leaflets and chase scabs out, they were regularly harassed by the Mexican consul and the LAPD.

Eventually, the Los Angeles Chamber of Commerce pressured the growers to settle. The growers offered 25 cents per hour. The strikers refused it, believing that the existing labor shortage (partly caused by the repatriation of Mexicans in 1931 and 1932) worked in their favor. After a series of secret meetings, the growers and the Mexican consuls (without involvement of the workers) agreed on $1.50 for a nine-hour day, or twenty cents per hour when work was not steady. While this settlement did restore a slightly higher wage, more importantly the strike gave rise to a new union: the Confederación de Uniones Campesinas y Obreras Mexicanas, which represented berry workers and politicized the region's agricultural workers. Five thousand workers eventually joined the rebellion. As they moved to other crops throughout the state, they used strikes to create a militant agricultural labor movement that endured throughout the 1930s.

Hicks Camp, as well as eight other local workers' camps, remains a source of community pride. For many years an annual reunion was held to unite former residents. Out of these reunions grew La Historia Society and El Museo de los Barrios, which seek to document and preserve the area's rich history. In 2008, Hicks Camp became Rio Vista Park, which functions as a living historical, cultural, and educational monument to the workers' camps.

NEARBY SITES OF INTEREST

La Historia Society
3240 Tyler Ave., El Monte 91731 (626) 279-1954
Museum devoted to the history of El Monte, especially from the Mexican American perspective.

Santa Fe Trail Historical Park
3675 Santa Anita Ave., El Monte 91731
Small park commemorating El Monte as the end of the Santa Fe Trail.

TO LEARN MORE

Ronald Lopez, "The El Monte Berry Strike of 1933," *Aztlán* 1 (1970).

Salvador Plascencia, *The People of Paper* (Harcourt, 2006). A magical-realist story set in El Monte.

2.11 Lacy Park

1485 Virginia Rd., San Marino 91108
(at Euston Rd.) (www.ci.san-marino.ca.us/lacy.htm)

Lacy Park is the only public park in the extremely wealthy, politically conservative city of San Marino, where the median income is more than triple that of Los Angeles County as a whole. San Marino was incorporated in 1913, when it was believed that neighboring cities would annex (and therefore gain property tax revenues from and possibly try to develop) the extensive landholdings belonging to the city's "fathers": railroad tycoon Henry Huntington; George Patton, who was the city's first mayor and the father of the World War II general George Patton; and other wealthy ranchers. Incorporation as an independent city enabled these wealthy property owners to preserve and maintain their landholdings under their own control. Huntington's estate supervisor designed the community, and since then San Marino has prided itself on being what the local newspaper calls "the finest, exclusively residential community in the West." San Marino is widely known for its exclusionary city ordinances, which range from the seemingly trivial, such as one prohibiting property owners from placing trash cans in view of the street, to the more significant, such as a ban on apartment buildings and a limit of one family per home. Beginning in the 1980s, the historically old-money, white community changed substantially with a large influx of affluent ethnic Chinese immigrants. Currently, Asians constitute nearly half the residents. However, the community's collective antipathy to change, and its deep investment in property values (with a median home sales price of $1.4 million in 2007) and exclusivity, has changed very little. For example, in 1993 residents resisted a state mandate to provide 13 units of affordable housing.

Two parkgoers approach the fee booth at Lacy Park, 2007.

San Marino's tight control of community boundaries has been perhaps most blatant in Lacy Park. From 1978 to 1988, the park was closed on weekends; city officials claimed the closures were a result of funding problems in the wake of Proposition 13, which slashed public revenues statewide. However, the closures also followed residents' complaints about "criminal elements" and crowding by "outsiders." In 1988, the park reopened on the weekends but instituted a $3-per-person fee for non–San Marino residents (it is now $4). This policy made Lacy Park the first park in California to charge nonresidents for usage. Park officials also instituted a $50 permit fee for any group gathering of more than 15 people (the fee is currently $65). In 1993, following Lacy Park's precedent, homeowner activists in neighboring Arcadia instituted a reservation system and a differentiated fee scale for residents and nonresidents at its Wilderness Park in order to discourage "casual picnicking." Other affluent San Gabriel Valley cities, such as Claremont and La Verne, have since followed suit. Together, these practices demonstrate the continuing power of elite homeowners, especially in independently incorporated areas, to use civic ordinances to maintain their wealth and to control public space for their own benefit.

These exclusionary policies are particularly insidious because of the vast disparities in access to recreational areas that exist in Los Angeles. Los Angeles has long been recognized as one of the most "park-poor" cities in the country. The National Recreation and Parks Association recommends that cities create 6.25 to 10.5 acres of parkland per 1,000 persons, but the City of Los Angeles offers only 4 acres per 1,000 persons. This scarcity is compounded by an equity problem. White-dominant neighborhoods have far greater access to parks and recreational spaces than Black- and Latina/o-dominant neighborhoods. White-dominant neighborhoods in L.A. enjoy 17.4 acres per 1,000 residents, while Latina/o areas have 1.6 acres per 1,000 persons, and Black communities average just 0.8 acres per 1,000 persons. These disparities are associated with unequal health outcomes, including higher rates of diabetes and asthma in communities of color.

In 1996, in response to the general paucity of parkland, voters in Los Angeles passed Proposition K, which generates $25 million annually for 30 years for parks. While a portion of this money is directly allocated, some is available through a competitive grant process. Not surprisingly, an analysis by Wolch, Wilson, and Fehrenbach based on the first two years of the competitive process indicated that applications from white neighborhoods enjoyed the highest success rates, followed by those from African American communities; applications from Latina/o-dominated areas had the lowest success rate. Mayor Antonio Villaraigosa determined that the number-one goal of the Los Angeles Department of Parks and Recreation would be to address these disparities by "providing equal access." In the meantime, residents of Black- and Latina/o-majority neighborhoods often travel to parks and recreational spaces in other cities—yet the policies of Lacy Park (and others like it) seek to block their efforts.

NEARBY SITES OF INTEREST

Huntington Library and Gardens

1151 Oxford Rd., San Marino 91108
(626) 405-2100 (www.huntington.org)

The newest addition to the 270-acre grounds of the Huntington is the Chinese garden, Liu Fang Yuan—Garden of Flowing Fragrance—which opened in 2008. The development of a Chinese garden here might seem bittersweet to some, given that the fortune of railroad magnate Henry Huntington was built partly on the backs of Chinese workers (see entry 6.7 Lang Station).

The Old Mill

1120 Old Mill Rd., San Marino 91108
(626) 449-5458 (www.old-mill.org)

Built in 1816, the Old Mill is the oldest commercial building in Southern California. Self-guided and docent-led tours are offered.

FAVORITE NEIGHBORHOOD RESTAURANTS

Freshwater Pavilion Tea Shop

Huntington Gardens, 1151 Oxford Rd.,
San Marino 91108 (626) 405-2100

Chinese tea and refreshments are available at the tea shop during the garden's public hours.

Heirloom Bakery and Café

807 Merida Ave., South Pasadena 91030
(626) 441-0042

Superb cupcakes and cakes, plus delicious breakfasts and sandwiches.

TO LEARN MORE

Jennifer Wolch, John P. Wilson, and Jed Fehrenbach, *Parks and Park Funding in Los Angeles: An Equity Mapping Analysis* (Sustainable Cities Program, University of Southern California, 2002), available at www.usc.edu/dept/geography/ESPE/documents/publications_parks.pdf.

2.12 Llano del Rio

16773–16849 Pearblossom
Hwy. (State Hwy. 138), Llano
93544 *(approximately ⅓ mile
east of 165th St.; the stone en-
tryway ruins are visible off the
north side of the road; GPS
Coordinates: 34.5071983337,
-117.8290557861; Center for
Land Use Interpretation location map: http://ludb.clui.org
/ex/i/CA3087/)*

Stone ruins of the Llano del Rio colony, 2008.

Llano del Rio was a utopian socialist colony that existed on this site from 1914 to 1917. It is a good example of the complexity and contradictions of the U.S. Left in the first part of the twentieth century. During the 1910s, the Socialist Party enjoyed a period of widespread popularity in Los Angeles and other U.S. cities. The party was less radical than other groups active in Los Angeles at that time, but believed that control of the ballot box and the universal organization of workers would lead to the gradual transformation of capitalism. Llano's primary founder was Job Harriman, a socialist lawyer, labor activist, and politician who moved to L.A. in 1886 and quickly became involved in local leftist politics. Harriman ran for mayor of Los Angeles on the Socialist Party ticket twice, in 1911 (getting 35 percent of the vote) and 1913. His defeats in the political arena led him to embrace an economic, rather than strictly political, base for spreading socialism. He believed that socialism needed a concrete example of successful cooperative life to show working people that it was

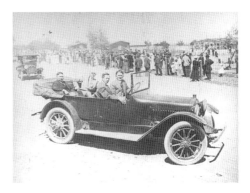

Job Harriman (in front passenger seat), friends, and colonists at Llano del Rio's first-anniversary celebration, 1915.

possible to abandon their current means of livelihood.

The Llano del Rio cooperative embraced socialist principles of joint ownership, political parity, and Karl Marx's idea of "from each according to his ability, to each according to his needs." But the colony often had trouble putting its leftist principles into practice. The co-op was set up as a stock-issuing corporation controlled by its owner-members, with each member required to buy shares of ownership for $2,000 each, which put membership out of reach for most poor and working-class people. In addition, while the colony received applications from diverse racial and ethnic groups, it rejected applications from nonwhites, not because of race prejudice, organizers said, but because they claimed it was not wise to mix the races in these new communities. These practices effectively limited membership at Llano to the white middle class (although African American cooperative towns were also being established elsewhere during this time period and faced their own challenges). The colony at Llano included feminist plans for communal kitchens and underground laundry conveyors to reduce women's labor. Not all of these plans were implemented, but some were, including a Montessori kindergarten that contributed to moving housekeeping and child rearing into the paid, public domain. The colony built an impressive array of industries, including farming, livestock, and construction, and came close to self-sufficiency. Llano was very popular, attracting as many as 500 colonists at any given time; according to estimates, more than 2,000 people total lived at the colony over its three years of existence. The colony could not keep up with demand, and most colonists lived in wood-frame tents.

Despite its popularity, Llano del Rio faced a variety of problems that ultimately led to its demise. Foremost was the desert environment, which made it difficult to sustain crops and secure enough water (made worse by resistance from neighboring ranchers). The colony also suffered from labor shortages caused by the World War I draft, as well as growing anxiety about socialism after the Russian Revolution. In late 1917, the colony closed. About 200 remaining members moved to Louisiana, where they established another colony and prospered until 1937. The site here in Los Angeles was declared a California Historical Landmark in 1982, though its marker was immediately stolen and has not been replaced.

NEARBY SITES OF INTEREST

Mescal Wildlife Sanctuary
223rd St. E. and Hwy. 138 (between 238th St. E. and 243rd St. E.), Llano 93544 (661) 944-2743
One hundred acres of wilderness—no facilities, no established trails.

Theodore Payne Wildlife Sanctuary
235th St. E. (between Ave. U and Ave. V, 1 mile north of Palmdale Road), Llano 93544 (661) 944-2743
This 320-acre sanctuary includes many Joshua trees. Southern California deserts feature stunning floral displays after the winter rains. However, this sanctuary and the Mescal Wildlife Sanctuary may be difficult to access. Call the park office during business hours for assistance.

California Institute of the Arts
24700 McBean Pkwy., Valencia 91355 (661) 255-1050 (http://calarts.edu)
Created in the early 1960s by Walt Disney, CalArts was the first degree-granting higher educational institution for the visual and performing arts, and is now a renowned leader in arts education and training.

2.13 Mariachi Plaza

E. 1st St. and N. Boyle Ave., Los Angeles
90033

BOYLE HEIGHTS

Mariachi Plaza is a street corner where mariachi musicians congregate while waiting to pick up jobs. Mariachi is a musical form that originated in Jalisco, Mexico, and is performed by groups of men (and increasingly women) wearing traditional *charro* outfits and playing violins, horns, and accordions. Mariachis can be found strolling in restaurants and are standard sights at Mexican and Mexican American celebrations such as weddings, baptisms, and *quinceñeras*. L.A. and Guadalajara are arguably the leading cities for mariachi music in the world.

Consumers of mariachi music have long known that they can hire musicians at Mariachi Plaza, making this site one of the older "shape-ups" in Los Angeles. A shape-up is a site where workers in the informal economy congregate while awaiting work. Los Angeles' informal economy has flourished over the past several decades because of both an increase in immigration, which has led to a greater supply of workers, and employers' desire to save money by paying workers under the table and using other practices that lead to the casualization of labor. The growth of the informal sector is part of the region's increasingly polarized economy, which is characterized by both high-wage and low-wage employment. Though mariachi musicians are not usually associated with the day laborers who provoke ire and angst among some segments of the population, they too are caught in the more vulnerable end of this polarized economy as it manifests in Los Angeles.

NEARBY SITES OF INTEREST

La Casa del Mariachi

1836 E. 1st St., Los Angeles 90033
(323) 262-5243 (www.casadelmariachi.com)
Have you ever wondered where mariachis get those cool suits? La Casa offers a full selection of Mexican finery for him and her.

Candelas Guitars

2724 Cesar Chavez Ave., Los Angeles 90033
(323) 261-2011 (www.candelas.com)
Classical, acoustic, flamenco, mariachi, and *bajo sexto* guitars handcrafted since 1948.

Lincoln Heights Jail

401–449 N. Avenue 19, Los Angeles 90031
(http://ludb.clui.org/ex/i/CA3347)
Architecturally interesting jail (art deco and

Mariachi musicians available for hire congregate at Mariachi Plaza, 2007.

Bauhaus modern) that housed many radicals over the years. Closed in 1965. The Bilingual Foundation of the Arts is located within the repurposed building at 421 N. Avenue 19.

FAVORITE NEIGHBORHOOD RESTAURANTS

Al and Bea's Mexican Food
2025 E. 1st St., Los Angeles 90033
(323) 267-8810
Boyle Heights burrito shack loved by locals and visitors alike and recommended by L.A. food guru Jonathan Gold. Excellent bean-and-cheese burrito.

Primera Taza Coffee House
1850½ E. 1st St., Los Angeles 90033
(323) 780-3923 (primerataza.com)
Unpretentious coffee shop offering espresso, pastries, sandwiches, and free wi-fi. Free parking in back.

2.14 Mount Sinai Home Care Agency
4515 Eagle Rock Blvd., Los Angeles 90041
(between N. Ave. 45 and Corliss St.)
EAGLE ROCK

In 2008, two Pilipina/o immigrant home health care workers filed suit against Mount Sinai Home Care Agency, a Pilipina/o-owned business, after the agency failed to pay them for work they had performed. Georgia Danan, a retired teacher who immigrated to the United States from the Philippines in 2005 to join her daughter, worked for Mount Sinai from November 2006 to August 2007. Although Danan is herself elderly, as a recent immigrant she could not take advantage of state-provided benefits for seniors, such as Social Security, so she began to work with Mount Sinai as a home health

care provider. However, the agency did not pay her for 15 of the days she worked as a full-time worker, nor did it pay her minimum wage or overtime. The second worker, Balbert Quintas, a trained and degreed dentist who immigrated to the United States in 1994 after being sponsored by his father, was not able to practice dentistry in the United States because of differences in licensing requirements and examinations, and so turned to work in the home health care industry. Mount Sinai did not pay Quintas for several of the days he worked in July 2006. According to Quintas, "We are a part of the workforce of skilled caregivers that have made Mount Sinai a very profitable business for its owners, and we deserve to be treated with dignity and respect."

These two cases are emblematic of the working conditions that affect workers in the home health care industry, many of whom are Pilipina/o immigrants, since immigration reform in the 1960s. The 1965 Immigration Act overhauled the existing U.S. immigration policy to eliminate racist national origins quotas, including severe restrictions on the number of Asian immigrants, instead prioritizing family reunification and the recruitment of skilled and professional workers to fill labor shortages in growing fields. The United States' labor shortages in the health care and computer industries have been attractive pathways for Pilipina/os, especially those trained in the health sciences, to escape economic hardship in the Philippines and seek a higher quality of life. Yet upon arrival in the United States, they often face barriers to practicing their professions. Some professionals, such as Quintas, who are unsuccessful in getting licenses, accept lower-status and low-paying jobs in the health field, as nursing assistants, orderlies, or clerks, or in the long-term care services field, providing nursing home care, home care, live-in child care, or elder care. Consequently, they experience significant downward mobility and risk the rampant exploitation that is characteristic of much of this industry. These practices grow more widespread and troubling as, in the absence of a comprehensive public health care system, more and more elderly Americans depend on private home health care services for their medical care.

Both Danan and Quintas approached the Pilipino Workers Center (PWC) for help with their cases. Formed in 1997, the PWC provides services and resources that help meet the immediate needs of Pilipina/o workers and their families while also organizing for long-term change. One of the PWC's major initiatives is the Caregivers Organizing for Unity, Respect, and Genuine Empowerment (COURAGE) campaign. The PWC helped Danan and Quintas to file suits with the Department of Labor Standards Enforcement (DLSE). In 2007–8, the DLSE ordered Mount Sinai to pay Quintas more than $3,000, and Danan more than $22,000, in unpaid wages and penalties. However, Mount Sinai ignored the order, as well as offers of mediation, refusing to pay the two workers what they were due. In response, Danan and Quintas, with support from the PWC and a wide network of immigrant rights organizations in L.A., filed a joint civil

suit against the agency in 2008. The court awarded the two workers $104,000. As of 2008, the COURAGE campaign had won more than $100,000 in back wages for Pilipina/o caregivers, apart from the amount owed to Danan and Quintas. Nonetheless, the struggle for the protection of immigrant worker rights continues.

Mount Sinai Home Care is no longer located at this address. However, its office was once located inside this large commercial complex, the Philippine Village Community Center, which hosts community events for the large Pilipina/o community that has settled in Eagle Rock since the 1970s. Several businesses providing goods and services oriented toward Pilipina/os, especially Pilipina/o health care workers, are located inside, including travel agencies, and medical supply stores and other health-care businesses. *(Quote is from a press release dated August 7, 2008, posted on the Facebook page titled "COURAGE Campaign for Georgia and Bobby.")*

NEARBY SITES OF INTEREST

Pilipino Workers Center
153 Glendale Blvd., 2nd floor, Los Angeles 90026 (213) 250-4353 (www.pwcsc.org)

Urban and Environmental Policy Institute, Occidental College
Community office at 2106 Colorado Blvd., Los Angeles 90041 (departments.oxy.edu/uepi) A community-oriented research and advocacy institute that has produced many important studies related to labor organizing, immigrant rights, and economic and environmental justice issues in Los Angeles. It also hosts occasional lectures and events.

Southwest Museum, Arroyo Campus

234 Museum Dr., Los Angeles 90065

The Southwest Museum of the American Indian is now part of the Autry National Center. It is currently closed for renovation but expected to reopen in 2013.

FAVORITE NEIGHBORHOOD RESTAURANTS

Café Princesa

4257 York Blvd., Los Angeles 90041

(323) 474-6860 (www.casaprincesa.com)

Pilipina/o-owned coffee shop and café that frequently hosts live music, often featuring Pilipina/o bands. Spoken-word nights on Thursdays from 7 to 10 P.M.

Blue Hen

1743 Colorado Blvd., Los Angeles 90041

(323) 982-9900 (www.eatatbluehen.com)

Vietnamese comfort food made with organic and locally sourced produce whenever possible. Customer favorites include hand-cut turmeric fries and organic chicken *pho*.

The Oinkster

2005 Colorado Blvd., Los Angeles 90041

(323) 255-6465 (www.theoinkster.com)

Pastrami and burger joint with a gourmet flair. Try the Belgian fries with garlic aioli and *ube* (purple yam) shake. Also serves beer.

Auntie Em's Kitchen

4616 Eagle Rock Blvd., Los Angeles 90041

(323) 255-0800 (www.auntieemskitchen.com)

Named after Dorothy's aunt in the *Wizard of Oz*. Auntie Em's changes its menu seasonally but is known for comfort foods: mac and cheese, meatloaf sandwich, grilled skirt steak, and great salads. Then there's the diet-busting bakery, including irresistible red velvet cupcakes.

TO LEARN MORE

Caregiver, a film directed by Chito Roño (Star Cinema, 2008).

2.15 Ninth Circuit Court of Appeals (Richard Chambers Courthouse)

125 S. Grand Ave., Pasadena 91105

(between Del Rosa Dr. and Maylin St.)

(626) 229-7250

The Ninth Circuit Court of Appeals presides over a lush residential neighborhood in Pasadena, 2011.

The Los Angeles 8, better known as the L.A. 8, was a group of immigrants who were persecuted by the government for 20 years in one of the longest-running immigration battles in recent history. In January 1987, eight immigrants (seven Palestinian men and one Kenyan woman) were arrested because of their association with and political support for the Popular Front for the Liberation of Palestine (PFLP), a constituent organization of the Palestinian Liberation Organization (PLO). Essentially, the U.S. government did not like their politics, but because the immigrants had done nothing illegal, authorities pursued other means to harass and eliminate them. It is important to realize that the L.A. 8's political activity, which they never attempted to hide, consisted of fund-raising and public speeches, which would be perfectly legal if carried out by U.S. citizens. However, because they were immigrants they were denied their First Amendment rights.

Initially, the PFLP and the PLO were classified as terrorist organizations under the provisions of the McCarran-Walter Act of 1952, which made affiliation with a group that "advocated the doctrines of world communism" a deportable offense. Consequently, the members of the L.A. 8 were targeted for deportation solely based on their political opinions. Over the years, they were tried *six* different times by the federal government, but were never found guilty of any crime. These different cases produced mixed legal results. In 1988, the federal district judge hearing the PFLP's case ruled that the McCarran-Walter Act was unconstitutional because it denied immigrants their First Amendment rights. Yet the harassment and repeated suits against the L.A. 8 proceeded anyway. On January 30, 2007, Judge Bruce Einhorn dismissed the final two defendants of the L.A. 8 because the government did not have any evidence of wrongdoing but simply did not like their political beliefs. Einhorn also acknowledged their 20 years of suffering and called the proceedings "an embarrassment to the rule of law." The prosecution of the L.A. 8 is instructive because it combines a witch hunt with a larger attack on individual democratic rights using "antiterrorism" as a guise. In fact, some have argued that the government's tactics in the PFLP case were forerunners to the 2001 U.S. Patriot Act.

One of the L.A. 8's many hearings was held in the Richard H. Chambers courthouse, which is actually the historic Vista Del Arroyo Hotel. The hotel was built in 1903 and catered to wealthy easterners. It was refurbished in 1985. Self-guided tours are available, and group tours can be arranged.

NEARBY SITES OF INTEREST

Chihuahuita Memorial, Pasadena Community College's Community Education Center
3035 E. Foothill Blvd., Pasadena 91107
Adjacent to the former site of the Chihuahuita School (est. 1916), a segregated school that served Mexican Americans.

Norton Simon Museum
411 W. Colorado Blvd., Pasadena 91105
(626) 449-6840 (www.nortonsimon.org)

Gamble House
4 Westmoreland Pl., Pasadena 91103
(626) 793-3334 (www.gamblehouse.org)
Arts-and-crafts-style house built in 1908 for the owners of the Procter and Gamble Company, who used it as a retirement home.

Rose Bowl
1001 Rose Bowl Dr., Pasadena 91103
(626) 577-3101 (www.rosebowlstadium.com)
Features the Kidspace Children's Museum, an aquatic center, a golf course, a massive flea market the second Sunday of every month, running/walking tracks, and more. Many walkers and joggers use the three-mile loop around the Bowl's exterior.

Armory Center for the Arts
145 N. Raymond Ave., Pasadena 91103
(626) 792-5101 (www.armoryarts.org)

Pacific Asia Museum
46 N. Los Robles Ave., Pasadena 91101
(626) 449-2742 (www.pacificasiamuseum.org)

Little Round Top, the bluff on which Owen Brown's gravesite is located, 2010. In the foreground, blackened trees are visible, a result of the 2009 Station Fire, in which more than 160,000 acres of the Angeles National Forest burned.

Pasadena Museum of History

470 W. Walnut St., Pasadena 91103
(626) 577-1660 (www.pasadenahistory.org)
The museum houses a collection of interviews that historian Robin D. G. Kelley conducted with Black residents of Pasadena, among other offerings.

FAVORITE NEIGHBORHOOD RESTAURANTS

Daisy Mint

1218 E. Colorado Blvd., Pasadena 91106
(626) 792-2999 (www.daisymint.com)
Offers a creative and flavorful selection of pan-Asian dishes.

Green Street Restaurant

146 S. Shoppers Ln., Pasadena 91101
(626) 577-7170 (www.greenstreetrestaurant.com)
Known for its signature Dianne Salad. A little more expensive than most of our recommendations.

Hey That's Amore

27 E. Holly St., Pasadena 91103 (626) 844-8716
Italian American sandwich shop.

TO LEARN MORE

Committee 4 Justice, www.committee4justice
.com / index.php.

2.16 Owen Brown's Gravesite

Nearest address: 4630 Rising Hill Rd., Altadena 91001 *(nearest cross street: Canyon Crest Rd.)*

Directions: Drive to the end of Rising Hill Rd. and continue up the private road for approximately 0.2 miles. Park on the left, across from the first house. Walk back the way you came (about 65 paces from the edge of the parking area), and you will see a small trail on your right. After a few minutes you will see the hill, Little Round Top. Go off the trail and climb to the top.

In 1859, abolitionist John Brown led an attack on the federal armory at Harper's Ferry, Virginia. Although Brown was convicted and hanged and most of his comrades were captured, a handful escaped. John's son Owen fled north, via the underground railroad, where he waited out the Civil War. In 1884, he, along with his sister Ruth and brother Jason, settled in Altadena, where they became local celebrities. Ruth married and became a teacher at Garfield School, while the brothers homesteaded in the foothills of Altadena and named a local peak

Jason and Owen Brown by their cabin on Brown's trail, date unknown.

after their father (Brown Mountain). Owen Brown was buried in 1889 near his cabin, and his gravesite has been the site of countless visits and memorials. Owen Brown's gravesite is located on a hill called Little Round Top in the Meadows area. The grave is on private land but is accessible to the public. It is uncertain if Brown is buried in the hole on the southern edge of the knoll, or near the tree on the northern edge. The gravestone mysteriously disappeared in 2002.

NEARBY SITE OF INTEREST

Christmas Tree Lane
Santa Rosa Ave., between Woodbury Ave. and Altadena Dr., Altadena 91101
(www.christmastreelane.net)
Christmas Tree Lane is the oldest large-scale Christmas lighting spectacle in the United States. On display from mid-December through early January.

FAVORITE NEIGHBORHOOD RESTAURANT

Amy's Patio Café
900 E. Altadena Dr., Altadena 91001
(626) 798-4737

Lovely café with tasty breakfast and lunch menu. Hours may be limited—call in advance.

TO LEARN MORE

Michele Zack, *Altadena: Between Wilderness and City* (Altadena Historical Society, 2004).

2.17 Quemetco, Incorporated

720 S. 7th Ave., City of Industry 91745 *(at Salt Lake Ave.)* (626) 330-2294

Quemetco is one of the greatest toxic polluters in L.A. County. According to the Community Right-to-Know Act that was passed in 1996, businesses emitting toxins over a certain threshold are required to report their

Entrance to Quemetco, 2008.

emissions to the Environmental Protection Agency (EPA), which makes them public. The Community Right-to-Know law is an important accomplishment of the environmental justice movement, because it gives local communities the information they need to more effectively challenge polluters. According to the EPA's Toxic Release Inventory, toxins may be released into any media, including the air, soil, water, landfills, or underground injection. A toxin is defined as a chemical that is a known mutagen (causes mutations), teratogen (causes birth defects or disturbs fetal development), or carcinogen (causes cancer).

In 2005, Quemetco, which does secondary smelting and chemical manufacturing, ranked as the greatest toxic polluter in Los Angeles County. That year, Quemetco reported 2.1 million pounds of toxic emissions. The number two and three spots were occupied by ExxonMobil (located in Torrance) and Chevron U.S.A. (located in El Segundo), respectively. As recently as 2002, ExxonMobil and Chevron occupied the first and second spots, respectively, but managed to cut their emissions significantly, so that each now emits just over 1 million pounds annually.

Air toxins in the county have an interesting geography. Although the Eastside, where Quemetco is located, has a much larger number of polluting firms than the Harbor/South Bay, these firms tend to be relatively small. The air pollution on the Eastside is a function of the concentration of many small polluters here and prevailing winds. In contrast, the Harbor/South Bay, where ExxonMobil and Chevron are located, is home

to a smaller number of much larger firms. Historically, the county's top polluters have hailed from the petrochemical industry, and the Harbor/South Bay, with its concentration of refineries, produces the greatest toxic emissions in the L.A. region.

TO LEARN MORE

For more on the Community Right-to-Know law and to identify local polluters, see www.epa.gov/epahome/r2k.htm.

Manuel Pastor Jr., James L. Sadd, and Rachel Morello-Frosch, "Environmental Inequity in Metropolitan Los Angeles," in *The Quest for Environmental Justice: Human Rights and the Politics of Pollution,* ed. Robert Bullard (Sierra Club Books, 2005).

Laura Pulido, "Rethinking Environmental Racism: White Privilege and Urban Development in Southern California," *Annals of the Association of American Geographers* 90 (2000): 12–40.

2.18 Ruben Salazar Park and Silver Dollar Café

Salazar Park   3864 Whittier Blvd., Los Angeles 90023 *(between S. Alma Ave. and S. Ditman Ave.)* (323) 260-2330 (parks.lacounty.gov/Parkinfo.asp?URL=cms1_033236.asp&Title=Salazar) EAST LOS ANGELES

Silver Dollar Café   4945 Whittier Blvd., Los Angeles 90022 *(between S. Ferris Ave. and S. La Verne Ave.)* EAST LOS ANGELES

During the late 1960s and early 1970s, East L.A. emerged as a major center of Chicana/o activism. Inspired by the civil rights movement, concerned about the Vietnam War, and frustrated with racism and poor community conditions, Mexican American youth began agitating for social

Two youths hold a banner during the Chicano Moratorium march, August 29, 1970.

change. Two linked events, in particular, formed a turning point for *el movimiento* (the movement), as it was called: the Chicano Moratorium and the assassination of Rubén Salazar.

On August 29, 1970, approximately 30,000 protesters marched six miles from Belvedere to Laguna Park. They were protesting the fact that Chicanos were disproportionately drafted and killed in the Vietnam War but also oppressed at home. As the crowd reached the park, more than 500 police attacked the marchers, resulting in the arrest of over 200 persons, hundreds of injuries, and three deaths. The Chicano Moratorium was the largest antiwar action on the part of any ethnic community in the United States. Many marchers were deeply politicized by the event and realized they needed to create a strong and united movement to defend their rights.

Closely linked to the Chicano Moratorium is the assassination of Rubén Salazar. Born in Ciudad Juárez, Mexico, in March 1928, Salazar was a journalist who became an important voice for social change. He worked for the *L.A. Times* and the Spanish-language television station KMEX. Over time Salazar became increasingly critical of the war and social injustice, and emerged as a key commentator on the Chicana/o

Interior of the Silver Dollar Café, where Rubén Salazar was shot during the Chicano Moratorium, in 1970; this photo was taken through the mail slot two days after the event.

movement. After covering the Chicano Moratorium on August 29, Salazar went to the Silver Dollar Café, where he was shot by L.A. County sheriff's deputy Tom Wilson. The projectile came from outside the café and hit Salazar in the head. A coroner's panel ruled that the killing was a homicide, but Wilson was never brought to trial. Before his death, Salazar was being investigated by both the LAPD and the FBI, who opposed his increasingly critical news coverage. In August 2010, Sheriff Lee Baca refused to release the records related to Salazar's shooting. In February 2011 the Sheriff's Office of Independent Review released a report saying that Salazar's death was not a conspiracy but the result of poor decisions. Eyewitnesses remain unconvinced. Laguna Park's name was changed to Ruben Salazar Park in his honor.

PERSONAL REFLECTION BY MARGARITA RAMIREZ, DEPUTY DIRECTOR OF GRANT MAKING, LIBERTY HILL FOUNDATION

When we got to the park, we were sitting there, listening to a number of speakers, [such as] Dolores Huerta, and then all of a sudden, we heard people screaming. It looked like a school of fish, I remember, when the tear gas hit, because people were running one way, and then they went the other because of the tear gas seemingly from nowhere. . . . And pretty soon we found ourselves screaming and running and trying to get out of there. . . . That was my first sort of "hit" of any social movement or political activism.

NEARBY SITE OF INTEREST

Estrada Court Murals
3200–3355 E. Olympic Blvd., Los Angeles
(www.lamurals.org/MuralFiles/ELA
/EstradaCourts.html)
Vast collection of murals in a public housing complex.

FAVORITE NEIGHBORHOOD RESTAURANT

Tacos Baja Ensenada
5385 Whittier Blvd., Los Angeles 90022
(323) 887-1980
Specialties include fish and shrimp tacos, Ensenada style. And you can't beat the price, particularly the Wednesday specials.

TO LEARN MORE

Ruben Salazar, *Border Correspondent: Selected Writings, 1955–1970*, ed. Mario T. García (University of California Press, 1995).

Lorena Oropeza, *¡Raza Si!, ¡Guerra No!: Chicano Protest and Patriotism during the Viet Nam War Era* (University of California Press, 2005).

2.19 San Gabriel Mission

428 S. Mission Dr., San Gabriel 91776
(at S. Ramona St.) (626) 457-3035
(sangabrielmission.org)

The San Gabriel Mission was built in 1771 under the Spanish crown. It was the first mission in the Los Angeles area and the fourth in California. The mission was originally located near Whittier Narrows, but after flooding there it was moved to its current location in 1775. The California mission system has been highly romanticized as an idyllic period in which Spanish padres cared for and converted the indigenous population to Catholicism, Spanish culture, and produc-

San Gabriel Mission, 2007.

tive labor habits. Such mythology, however, obscures the conquest, dispossession, widespread death, and forced labor that occurred at the missions. Tony Pinto, a Kumeyaay from San Diego, tells the story this way: "I am now 73 years old. My grandfather and grandmother told me what happened at the missions. . . . The Indians were slaves. They did all the work, and after a day's work, the priests locked them up. . . . They fed them actually as little as possible. They beat them and killed them if they were sick or couldn't work." Under the Franciscans, Indians were forced to work the 1.5 million acres of land that constituted the San Gabriel Mission. It was one of the most productive missions, and the site of widespread death: an estimated 6,000 indigenous people died at San Gabriel Mission.

In 1775, mission Indians formed alliances with residents of eight local villages, includ-

ing Sibapet, Juvit, and Jajamovit, to attack the mission and its priests. The uprising was led by Nicolas José, a mission Indian, and Toypurina, a nonbaptized woman from Juvit. Unfortunately, the plot was discovered and 21 Indians were arrested. Most were whipped and released. Governor Pedro Fages described the lashes as "the most serious scolding for their ingratitude, making ugly their perverseness, and showing them the . . . powerlessness of their practices against we who are Catholic." Nicolas José was banished from San Gabriel and sentenced to six years of hard labor with irons, and Toypurina was banished to the Monterey mission, where she lived out her days. The San Gabriel Mission is still a functioning church, as well as a major tourist spot and frequent field-trip destination for fourth-grade students. *(All quotes are from Steven Hackel, "Sources of Rebellion: Indian Testimony and the Mission San Gabriel Uprising of 1785,"* Ethnohistory *50 (2003): 643–669.)*

NEARBY SITES OF INTEREST

Grapevine Arbor

324 S. Mission Dr., San Gabriel 91776
Planted in 1861, this historic site is now a popular place for weddings.

San Gabriel Playhouse

320 S. Mission Dr., San Gabriel 91776
(626) 308-2865 (www.missionplayhouse.org)
Built by California poet laureate John Steven McGroarty for performances of *The Mission Play.*

La Laguna de San Gabriel, Vincent Lugo Park (a.k.a. "Monster Park")

1305 Prospect Ave., San Gabriel 91776

Kids love climbing on Benjamin Dominguez's massive sculptures of sea creatures.

FAVORITE NEIGHBORHOOD RESTAURANTS

Golden Deli Vietnamese Restaurant

815 W. Las Tunas Dr., San Gabriel 91776

(626) 308-0803 (www.goldendelirestaurant.com)

Always bustling, Golden Deli is one of the best *pho* places in town. The crispy spring rolls and chicken curry with vermicelli also come highly recommended.

Pizza Place California

303 S. Mission Dr., San Gabriel 91776

(626) 570-9622

Has a wide and interesting pizza selection. Also features pan-Asian and other comfort foods. The warm bread starter is hard to resist.

Newport Tan Cang Seafood Restaurant

518 W. Las Tunas Dr., San Gabriel 91776

(626) 289-5998 (www.newportseafood.com)

Another favorite food destination in the San Gabriel Valley. The specialty is lobster, but the kung pao chicken and French-style beef are also popular.

TO LEARN MORE

The Huntington Library has a computerized repository that documents the lives of more than 100,000 California Indians who lived at the missions in the eighteenth and nineteenth centuries; see www.huntington.org /huntingtonlibrary.aspx?id=576.

Douglas Monroy, *Thrown among Strangers: The Making of Mexican Culture in Frontier California* (University of California Press, 1990).

Luis J. Rodriguez, *Always Running: La Vida Loca, Gang Days in L.A.* (Curbstone Press, 1993). This important memoir is set in San Gabriel.

2.20 Santa Anita Park and Pomona Fairgrounds

Santa Anita Park   285 W. Huntington Dr., Arcadia 91007 *(at Civic Center Pl.)*

(626) 574-RACE (www.santaanita.com)

Pomona Fairgrounds   1101 W. McKinley Ave., Pomona 91768 *(at Paige Dr.)*

(909) 623-3111 (www.fairplex.com/fp/)

The racetrack at Santa Anita Park is one of the most historic horse-racing sites in the United States, and the scene of some of the greatest victories by Seabiscuit—the "people's champion"—during the Great Depression. Less well known is that Santa Anita served as a temporary detention center for many of the Japanese Americans who were interned during World War II. On February 19, 1942, President Franklin D. Roosevelt signed Executive Order 9066, which authorized the mass incarceration of Japanese Americans living on the West Coast. Beginning on March 30, almost 100,000 Japanese Americans in Cali-

View overlooking the horse stables at Santa Anita Park, 2007.

Japanese American internees arrive at Santa Anita, 1942.

fornia were sent to temporary detention or assembly centers, such as Santa Anita Park and the Pomona Fairgrounds. Because of the haste with which they had to evacuate, Japanese Americans were forced to sell their homes, businesses, and possessions for a pittance and to leave most of their remaining belongings behind. Internees were held at temporary detention centers until the more permanent concentration camps, such as Manzanar and Tule Lake, were completed. The internment of Japanese Americans is recognized as one of the gravest violations of civil rights in U.S. history. In the 1980s, Japanese Americans mobilized for reparations, and in 1988 President Ronald Reagan offered a formal apology, acknowledged that the internment had been a result of "racial hysteria," and provided monetary compensation.

NEARBY SITE OF INTEREST

Los Angeles County Arboretum

301 N. Baldwin Ave., Arcadia 91007

(626) 821-3222 (www.arboretum.org)

FAVORITE NEIGHBORHOOD RESTAURANT

Din Tai Fung

1088 and 1108 S. Baldwin Ave., Arcadia 91007

(626) 574-7068 and (626) 446-8588

(www.dintaifungusa.com)

This family-owned chain specializes in handmade *xiao long bao* (Shanghai soup dumplings). The original Din Tai Fung, in Taipei, was ranked as one of the world's top 10 restaurants by the *New York Times*. Try their popular juicy pork and juicy pork/crab dumplings. Expect a wait.

TO LEARN MORE

Nikkei for Civil Rights and Redress, www.ncrr-la .org/index.php.

2.21 Self-Help Graphics and Art

1300 E. 1st St., Los Angeles 90033
(at S. Anderson St.) (323) 881-6444
(www.selfhelpgraphics.com)

BOYLE HEIGHTS

Self-Help Graphics, 2011.

Self-Help Graphics is a community-based arts center serving the Chicana/o and Latina/o communities in East Los Angeles. The center specializes in printmaking and was instrumental in popularizing the celebration of Dia de los Muertos (Day of the Dead) in the United States. Founded in the early 1970s by local artists who were interested in producing art that reflected the reality of their community, Self-Help Graphics was both an outcome of the Chicano Movement and an active contributor to it. It was critical to the development of key Chicana/o artists such as Gronk, Barbara Carrasco, and Frank Romero. Originally based in a garage, Self-Help moved to the location at 3802 Cesar Chavez Avenue in 1978 under the leadership of Sister Karen Boccalero. Boccalero belonged to the Order of the Sisters of Saint Francis and was, according to Frank Romero in a *Los Angeles Times* article, "the heart and soul of the place." Af-

ter her death in 1997, Self-Help faced financial troubles and entered a period of great turmoil. In 2005, the arts center closed its doors for three months. The Sisters of Saint Francis transferred the deed for the building to the Los Angeles Archdiocese, which then sold it on their behalf in 2008. There was great concern that Self-Help would lose its home because of this transaction (and tremendous outrage at the diocese). Although the collapse of the real estate market in 2009 allowed the organization to afford the rent for another two years, in 2011 Self-Help Graphics moved to its current location on First Street, a former sea-urchin-processing plant across from the light-rail tracks. A new board of directors has recently been installed that, it is hoped, will enable Self-Help to survive another forty years. Self-Help regularly offers innovative exhibits, classes, and workshops. The stunning mosaic-tiled exterior of the former Self-Help building on Cesar Chavez Avenue is also worth a visit, although the impressive statue of the Virgen de Guadalupe that graced the parking lot behind the old building has been moved to the interior of the new location.

NEARBY SITES OF INTEREST

Corazón del Pueblo

2003 E. 1st St., Los Angeles 90033
Community-based performance space and cultural center.

Libros Schmibros

2000 E. 1st St., Los Angeles
90033 (323) 302-9408
(http://librosschmibros
.wordpress.com)

Libros Schmibros, whose title
acknowledges Boyle Heights'
Jewish and Latina/o heritages,
was opened by David Kipen in
the wake of budgetary cuts to local libraries that resulted in reduced hours and services. It is a
used bookstore that lends books
for free to local community
residents. Limited hours—check
before visiting.

The former home of Upton Sinclair, 2008.

FAVORITE NEIGHBORHOOD
RESTAURANTS

La Serenata de Garibaldi

1842 E. 1st St., Los Angeles 90033
(323) 265-2887 (www.laserenataonline.com)

A Boyle Heights institution offering upscale
Mexican cuisine and specializing in seafood. On
the pricier side.

Antojitos Carmen

2510 E. Cesar Chavez Ave., Los Angeles 90033
(323) 264-1451

Mexico City–style street food from a beloved
street vendor turned restaurateur. Try the *huara-
ches con huitlacoche* (fried masa topped with corn
fungus), pan-fried quesadillas, and house-made
habanero salsa.

2.22 Upton Sinclair's House

464 N. Myrtle Ave., Monrovia 91016
(at E. Scenic Dr.)

Private residence

Upton Sinclair was a journalist, writer, socialist, political activist, and the author of
such critical books as *Oil!* and *The Jungle*.

Sinclair was born in Baltimore and moved
to Pasadena around 1915. Although nationally known for his writing, locally he led
antipoverty campaigns and participated in
the struggles to protect the freedoms of
speech and assembly. In 1923, in order to
support a rally called by the striking Industrial Workers of the World, he read the U.S.
Constitution to a crowd of 3,000 people at
Liberty Hill in San Pedro. Four lines into the
First Amendment, Sinclair was arrested by
the LAPD and charged with criminal syndicalism, which made it a crime to belong
to any organization that advocated—or was
perceived by those in power to be advocating—violent changes to the existing political
system (see entry 4.6 Port of Los Angeles
and Liberty Hill). After his release, he went
on to create the Southern California chapter
of the American Civil Liberties Union. His
actions inspired the founding in 1976 of the
Liberty Hill Foundation, which supports

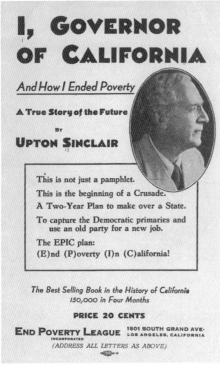

I, GOVERNOR OF CALIFORNIA

And How I Ended Poverty

A True Story of the Future

BY

UPTON SINCLAIR

This is not just a pamphlet.
This is the beginning of a Crusade.
A Two-Year Plan to make over a State.
To capture the Democratic primaries and
use an old party for a new job.
The EPIC plan:
(E)nd (P)overty (I)n (C)alifornia!

The Best Selling Book in the History of California
150,000 in Four Months

PRICE 20 CENTS

END POVERTY LEAGUE 1501 SOUTH GRAND AVE.
INCORPORATED LOS ANGELES, CALIFORNIA
(ADDRESS ALL LETTERS AS ABOVE)

Pamphlet promoting Sinclair's plan, End Poverty In
California.

progressive community activism in Los Angeles County.

Sinclair ran for public office numerous times, often on the Socialist Party ticket, and always lost. However, in 1934, during the Great Depression, he ran for governor of California on the Democratic ticket and mounted his famous End Poverty In California (EPIC) campaign. The heart of EPIC was the redistribution of wealth. A key part of the platform was to create state-owned factories and field cooperatives to put people back to work. The cooperatives would focus on production for use rather than for profit. EPIC also advocated repeal of the state sales tax, the creation of a system of graduated

income and inheritance taxes, an increased tax on public utilities, and pensions for the elderly and disabled. Sinclair was enormously popular among the working class during his run for governor but was attacked by Republicans and mainstream Democrats, who portrayed him as a communist. Even Democratic president Franklin Delano Roosevelt withheld his support. Sinclair won 45 percent of the vote, and Republican Frank Merriam won the election by a slim margin. Although Sinclair lost, 26 EPIC candidates were elected to the California State Assembly, and the EPIC platform inspired 75 agricultural cooperatives. Though many political analysts insist that Americans are inherently opposed to socialist ideas, the EPIC campaign suggests that such policies can and do engender significant support when capitalism is thought to have failed. Many EPIC ideas were eventually incorporated into New Deal legislation, exemplified by the creation of Social Security in 1935.

Sinclair lived in several Southern California communities, including Belmont Shores and Pasadena, and here in Monrovia from 1942 to 1966. His house is a national historic monument.

NEARBY SITES OF INTEREST

Monrovia Historical Museum

742 E. Lemon Ave., Monrovia 91016
(626) 357-9537 (www.monroviahistorical
museum.com)
Built on the former site of a racially segregated swimming pool. Limited hours; call before visiting.

Old Town Monrovia on Myrtle Avenue

A charming commercial district that comes alive every Friday evening from March through December for a street fair and farmers' market. The Monrovia Public Library is a good place to get oriented: 321 S. Myrtle Ave., Monrovia 91016.

TO LEARN MORE

Lauren Coodley, ed. *The Land of Orange Groves and Jails: Upton Sinclair's California* (Heyday Books, 2004).

2.23 Whittier State School

11850 E. Whittier Blvd., Whittier 90601

(at Sorenson Ave.)

In the early twentieth century, the eugenics movement was extremely popular on the international stage, and leaders in California played a pivotal role in its development. Eugenicists advocated the selective breeding of the U.S. population in order to ensure the fitness of the white race. They also applied emerging ideas from biology and medicine to supposedly solve social problems. In particular, they believed that genetic intel-

ligence was immutable, meaning that it was not affected by social factors such as poverty, literacy rates, or cultural knowledge. Eugenicists pioneered the application of IQ tests to large segments of the human population. They used their data—which, with few exceptions, they claimed, "proved" the genetic superiority of whites—to advocate immigration restrictions, segregated schools, and the forced sterilization of African Americans, Mexicans, Puerto Ricans, American Indians, developmentally disabled persons, and others. These policies were intended to prevent "irresponsible breeding" among the "inferior races" and to minimize their social and genetic mixing with whites.

Eugenicists did much of their work here at the Whittier State School, a facility for male juvenile offenders under age 16. The Whittier State School was operated by the state's Department of Institutions, which also operated the Ventura School for Girls (see entry 1.26 Orpheum Theatre, Sleepy Lagoon Murder, and Ventura School for

The grounds of Whittier State School, later the Fred C. Nelles Youth Correctional Facility, pictured here in 2009, are now used for television and motion picture filming.

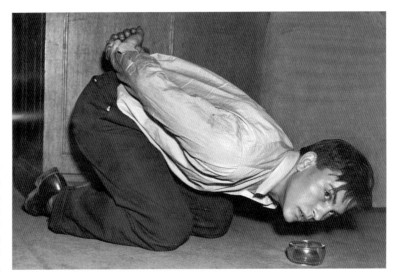

Layton Clark, after his release from Whittier State School, shows how he was forced to eat off the floor during his detention, 1940.

Girls). In 1916, the Department of Institutions created the California Bureau of Juvenile Research (CBJR), which was, according to historian Alexandra Stern, the first unit in the country devoted exclusively to research into the "causes and consequences of delinquency and mental deficiency." CBJR staff members conducted intelligence tests and other psychometric research on inmates at the Department of Institutions' facilities, most of whom, in Southern California, were impoverished Mexican, Black, and American Indian youth. Given IQ tests, they were uniformly found to be "feebleminded" or "dull" compared to their white counterparts. Those so deemed were frequently institutionalized in higher-security facilities throughout the state, where they were often sterilized, which was a mandatory precondition for their release. Inmates were also tracked into "appropriate" rehabilitative programs—for boys, vocational training in menial and agricultural work; for girls, lessons in housekeeping, cooking, and sewing; and for immigrants, Americanization programs. In 1941, the CBJR was disbanded and replaced by the California Youth Authority—a major contributor to California's massive prison expansion—which has since been the subject of extensive protest by the Youth Justice Coalition (see entry 3.7 Chuco's Justice Center and FREE L.A. High School).

The Whittier State School was renamed the Fred C. Nelles Youth Correctional Facility, in honor of its former superintendent who served during the height of the eugenicist movement. The school closed in 2004, although in 2006 Governor Arnold Schwarzenegger proposed that the site be used for a new men's prison. Currently, the facility is used for television and motion picture filming.

NEARBY SITES OF INTEREST

Pio Pico House

6003 Pioneer Blvd., Whittier 90606

(526) 695-1217 (www.piopico.org)

Former home of the last Mexican governor of California.

Whittier Museum

6755 Newlin Ave., Whittier 90601 (562) 945-3871 (www.whittiermuseum.org)

Documents and exhibits the history of Whittier, primarily in the nineteenth century. Open Saturdays and Sundays only. Free.

Pico Rivera Sports Arena

11003 Rooks Rd., Pico Rivera 90601

(562) 695-0747

Features big-name musical acts from Mexico, as well as *charreadas* (Mexican rodeos), almost every Sunday during the summer months.

TO LEARN MORE

Alexandra Stern, *Eugenic Nation: Faults and Frontiers of Better Breeding in Modern America* (University of California Press, 2005).

3

South Los Angeles

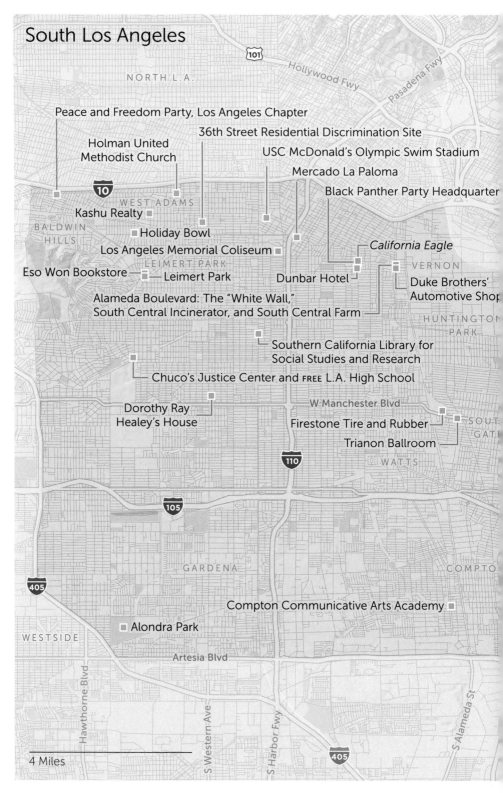

South Los Angeles

NORTH L.A.

Hollywood Fwy

Pasadena Fwy

Peace and Freedom Party, Los Angeles Chapter

36th Street Residential Discrimination Site

Holman United
Methodist Church

USC McDonald's Olympic Swim Stadium

Mercado La Paloma

Black Panther Party Headquarter

WEST ADAMS

Kashu Realty

BALDWIN
HILLS

Holiday Bowl

California Eagle

Los Angeles Memorial Coliseum

LEIMERT PARK

VERNON

Eso Won Bookstore

Leimert Park

Dunbar Hotel

Duke Brothers'
Automotive Shop

Alameda Boulevard: The "White Wall,"
South Central Incinerator, and South Central Farm

HUNTINGTON
PARK

Southern California Library for
Social Studies and Research

Chuco's Justice Center and FREE L.A. High School

Dorothy Ray
Healey's House

W Manchester Blvd

Firestone Tire and Rubber

SOUT
GAT

Trianon Ballroom

WATTS

GARDENA

COMPTO

Compton Communicative Arts Academy

Alondra Park

WESTSIDE

Hawthorne Blvd

S Western Ave

S Harbor Fwy

Artesia Blvd

S Alameda St

4 Miles

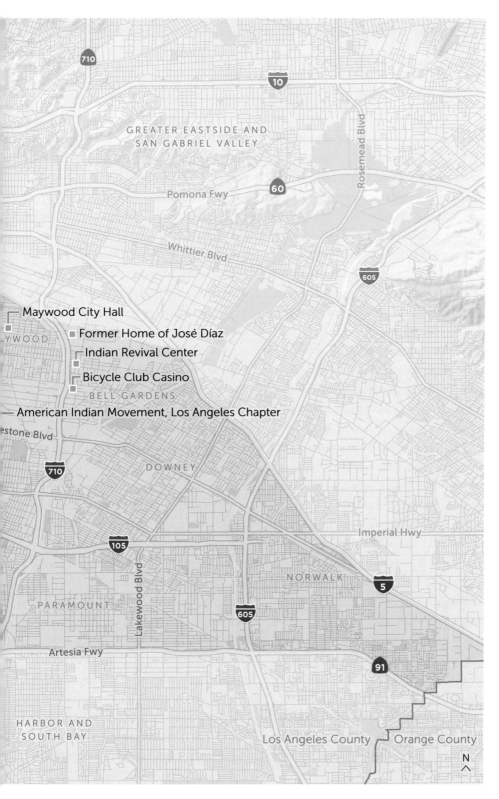

GREATER EASTSIDE AND
SAN GABRIEL VALLEY

Rosemead Blvd

710

10

60

Pomona Fwy

Whittier Blvd

605

Maywood City Hall

Former Home of José Díaz

Indian Revival Center

Bicycle Club Casino

YWOOD

BELL GARDENS

American Indian Movement, Los Angeles Chapter

estone Blvd

710

DOWNEY

105

Lakewood Blvd

PARAMOUNT

Imperial Hwy

NORWALK

5

605

Artesia Fwy

91

HARBOR AND
SOUTH BAY

Los Angeles County   Orange County

N

An Introduction to South Los Angeles

Along with Hollywood and Beverly Hills, South Los Angeles—which was known until 2003 as "South Central L.A.," a name that still sticks in the minds of many people—is one of the most famous communities in Southern California. The region's notoriety derives not from its reputation as a place of wealth and glamour but from the countless films, television shows, news programs, and songs that depict South L.A. as a Black space haunted by poverty, gangs, crime, and bad schools. While there is no denying that these factors exist in South L.A., our task in this guide is to situate these social patterns within dynamics of power and structural inequality. We contend that South Los Angeles cannot be understood outside of four powerful and intertwined dynamics: residential segregation, police repression, economic restructuring, and collective resistance.

Beginning in the late 1800s, wealthy people built beautiful Victorian and Craftsman-style homes in the neighborhoods just north of the University of Southern California, such as West Adams. For these people, South L.A. was an exclusive suburb of downtown Los Angeles, where most of them owned or managed the city's formative industries, including agriculture, oil, and construction. But South Los Angeles was not intensely developed until the 1920s and 1930s, when real estate developers and community-builders constructed massive tracts

of small, affordable, single-family homes in close proximity to the thousands of factories and assembly plants that flourished all through the southern flatlands, particularly along the Alameda Corridor. These communities attracted working-class whites, often from the U.S. South, who became first-time homeowners. South Los Angeles changed dramatically during World War II, however, when large numbers of African Americans arrived, again mostly from the U.S. South. Black Angelenos were instrumental in creating a thriving cultural scene along Central Avenue, which attracted diverse audiences and participants from throughout the region. Yet local Black people faced major legal and social barriers in finding housing. Although residential segregation existed in many parts of the county, it was most intense in South L.A., where African Americans faced violence and intimidation by white homeowners, many of whom were influenced by Jim Crow ideologies. Thanks in part to the work of antiracist real estate agents such as Kazuo Inouye (see entry 3.17 Kashu Realty and Thirty-sixth Street Residential Discrimination Site), as well as multiracial homeowner organizations among Black and Japanese Americans, the area became home to a growing number of people of color. By 1970, antidiscrimination laws began to take effect and middle-class African Americans moved to more affluent communities to the west, such as Baldwin

Hills, and to the north, such as the Mid City area, although they still faced (and continue to face) barriers to integration in many parts of the city.

Residential segregation and white violence in South L.A. were facilitated by unabashed police violence. Consequently, no account of South L.A. would be complete without acknowledging the powerful role of police brutality, and resistance to it, in shaping life in this part of the city. In August 1965, Watts exploded in response to a confrontation that ensued when a white police officer pulled over a Black motorist. The confrontation escalated, the driver's mother got involved, and observers openly challenged the police. The rest is history. The most important thing to understand is that this incident was simply the straw that broke the camel's back in terms of community/police tensions. For decades, the African American population in South L.A. had experienced intense police repression. From 1950 to 1966, Chief William Parker, who was highly antagonistic toward African Americans, led the Los Angeles Police Department (see entry 1.22 Los Angeles Police Department Headquarters and Parker Center). Parker saw the civil rights movement as a communist plot and was determined to stomp out any attempts at social change. In fact, it was the repressive nature of the police that led to such formations as the Black Panther Party for Self-Defense in 1968 and, in later years, the Coalition Against Police Abuse. The Watts riot itself was the largest instance of urban unrest in U.S. history up to that time, and it

led to the almost complete out-migration of whites and abandonment of the area by corporate retail outlets, who feared damage to their properties and property values.

A mere decade later, the factories along the Alameda Corridor began to relocate or close down as part of the process of deindustrialization that has affected most U.S. cities. Those factories that stayed often restructured, substituting low-wage, non-unionized work with few benefits for the well-paid, unionized, benefited jobs of a previous era. The end result was the loss of stable employment, leaving an overwhelmingly African American population with few economic opportunities. This area had not known prosperity for decades, and consequently it was hardly surprising that South L.A. again went up in flames in 1992, once again precipitated by an incident of police brutality (see entry 6.10 Simi Valley Courthouse and Site of Rodney King Beating). This time, however, African Americans were joined by their Latina/o neighbors, who had since moved into the area in large numbers. As a result of expanded immigration since the 1970s, particularly from Latin America and Asia, and the relative affordability of this part of Los Angeles, South L.A.'s population is now 50 percent Latina/o. However, rarely do we see Latinas/os in popular depictions of South Los Angeles. Nor, for that matter, do we see the hundreds of thousands of hardworking people—of all races—who are trying to make ends meet, raise their children, and forge community. Instead, we consistently see racist and sexist images of young African American men engaged in antisocial behavior. To many outsiders and in much of the popular media, the 1992 uprising merely confirmed the popular stereotype, so often depicted in the media, of South Los Angeles as a criminal, chaotic space.

Nowadays, South L.A.'s main thoroughfares are filled with storefront churches, check-cashing stores, pawnshops, nail salons, beauty parlors, fried chicken or fish stands, and Latina/o corner markets. These vernacular landscapes attest to the mixed origins of the region's inhabitants: the Southern roots of Black residents who first came to Los Angeles during the 1940s, and the Latin American and Asian origins of more recent immigrants. These commercial landscapes also provide evidence of the efforts by small-scale entrepreneurs to offer necessary goods and services to local residents amid the void left by corporate capital since the 1960s. The area's extensive residential landscapes consist mostly of modest homes and apartments, which testify to its long-standing importance to Los Angeles' working-class populations of all racial groups.

Perhaps the most important theme of life in South L.A. is the long history of radical politics and community activism that has evolved in response to structural conditions of inequality. Such resistance has taken many forms: the popular uprisings of 1965 and 1992; visionary community organizations like the Black Panther Party and American Indian Movement; churches such as Holman United Methodist and the Indian Revival Center; the alternative press, such as the *California Eagle;* and direct action, like that taken by the farmers and supporters of the South Central Farm. Through these venues and many more, residents of South L.A. have consistently found ways to challenge the conditions that shape their lives and to work toward the more just world they envision. As a result, South L.A. must be appreciated as a place occupied and shaped by many generations of people—including the current generation—who are not afraid to fight for their dreams for the future.

In 2003, the Los Angeles City Council renamed this area "South Los Angeles" in an effort to break with the negative connotations of "South Central." In this guide, we too use the label "South Los Angeles," not because it is the official, state-sanctioned term, but because our boundaries include communities (such as Artesia, Bell Gardens, and South Gate) that are not typically included in popular understandings of South Central, but which still fall in this general territory. In grouping these diverse communities together, we aim to reflect on how South L.A.'s diversity—as well as the area's long history of structural discrimination and resistance—is obscured by sensationalistic media depictions and popular understandings of South Central.

South Los Angeles Sites

Alameda Boulevard: The "White Wall," South Central Incinerator, and South Central Farm

4100 Long Beach Ave., Los Angeles 90058
(between E. 41st St. and E. Vernon Ave.)

VERNON

Before World War II, South L.A.'s working-class neighborhoods were racially segregated by an invisible barrier known as the "White Wall" along Alameda Boulevard. African Americans lived to the west of Alameda, whites to the east. During the Watts uprising in 1965, Alameda emerged as a racial dividing line. Police officers were stationed along Alameda, and the mayor of Huntington Park, Larry Walsh, even got the Southern Pacific Railroad company to line the tracks along Alameda with railroad cars to prevent the spread of agitation and property destruction into white neighborhoods. Many whites fled South Los Angeles immediately after the Watts uprising, citing Black violence and fears of school integration, and taking advantage of racially exclusive housing in the suburbs. As a result, nonwhites, particularly Latinas/os, were able to buy properties on the east side of Alameda for the first time.

As Los Angeles' economic and ethnic geography has changed since the 1960s, Alameda Boulevard has retained its importance as a crucial industrial corridor. Freight rail lines along the corridor connect the port at Long Beach with the vast industrial districts in southeast L.A. that produce, assemble, and distribute manufactured goods to global consumers. As a result, the neighborhoods lining the Alameda Corridor house both the manufacturing facilities of local and global firms who have been enticed by various government incentives to locate here and hundreds of thousands of working-class, mostly nonwhite families struggling to eke out a living. Not surprisingly, South Los Angeles neighborhoods are highly polluted, and the area's children have higher-than-average blood lead levels and suffer disproportionately from asthma.

Such conditions have generated innovative community activism to resist further industrial and hazardous development. Two environmental justice struggles, both of which occurred at this address, were pivotal. First, in the mid-1980s, the City of Los Angeles planned to build waste-to-energy incinerators throughout the city in order to address the growing trash problem. Not surprisingly, the first incinerator (known as the LANCER project) was targeted for South Central Los Angeles, at this intersection. Research has shown that such facilities are consistently more likely to be located in low-income neighborhoods and communities of color, because it is assumed that residents will not protest. But in this case, that assumption was wrong. A group of largely African American women mobilized as the Concerned Citizens of South Central Los Angeles and successfully challenged the accuracy of the environmental impact report, defeating the project. The group went on to

The former site of South Central Farm and the proposed incinerator (the LANCER project), now a vacant lot, 2007.

play a key role in the region's environmental justice movement, built community housing, and was a major force in the development of a citywide recycling program.

After the 1992 Los Angeles uprising, which exposed the lack of sufficient access to fresh food as a major problem in South L.A., the same plot of land was turned into a community garden. The South Central Farm, as it became known, was a 14-acre farm divided into 350 plots that were allocated to low-income families, primarily Latina/o immigrants, who used them as "survival gardens" to provide food and medicine. The farm eventually became the largest urban garden in the United States. However, the ownership of the land itself was contested because of a series of legal entanglements between the city, a wealthy private property owner, and community organizations. After a prolonged struggle on the

part of community activists and their advocates (including 61 legal claims) and a weak effort by the city to save the farm, the city authorized the eviction of the farmers. Despite widespread media coverage, celebrity involvement, and public outrage, the farm was bulldozed in June 2006. One group of farmers established a farm on a small plot farther south under power lines at 111th and Avalon streets, while others began farming on a donated plot of land near Bakersfield. Both groups are currently selling their produce at farmers' markets in Los Angeles. Ralph Horowitz, the contested owner, has stated that he plans to use the land for a megawarehouse, but his plans were recently defeated by a broad coalition of community protesters, a scathing report by the Air Quality Management District, and a *Los Angeles Times* exposé linking Horowitz's warehouse plans with the clothing retailer Forever 21, which is notorious for encouraging sweatshop conditions. The plot of land remains vacant and its future is uncertain, although

Farmer at the South Central Farm in May 2006, before its destruction.

the farmers continue their legal challenges to reclaim the land. Meanwhile, the South Central Farm has set up a community center across the street from the bulldozed farm (at the southeast corner of East Forty-first St. and Long Beach Ave.), and an oral history project has been initiated to collect the stories of those involved.

Golfers at Alondra Park, 2009.

FAVORITE NEIGHBORHOOD RESTAURANT

Taqueria La Carreta
1471 E. Vernon Ave., Los Angeles 90011
(323) 232-7133
Popular neighborhood Mexican restaurant that is open late. Regulars swear by the quesadillas, homemade tortillas, and salsa bar with free beans.

TO LEARN MORE

South Central Farmers, www.southcentral farmers.com.

The Garden, a film directed by Scott Hamilton Kennedy (Black Valley Films, 2008).

On the LANCER project, see Louis Blumberg, Robert Gottlieb, and Jim Hightower, *War on Waste: Can America Win Its Battle with Garbage?* (Island Press, 1989).

Communities for a Better Environment, 5610 Pacific Blvd., Huntington Park 90255 (323) 826-9771 (http://cbecal.org). This organization offers a "Toxic Tour" that shows the effects of pollution on marginalized communities.

3.2 Alondra Park

3850 W. Manhattan Beach Blvd., Lawndale 90260 *(between Prairie Ave. and S. Doty Ave.)*

Wilbur Gordon, an African American doctor turned real estate developer, sought to create a housing development for the Black middle class on this site in 1925. At that time, because of restrictive covenants, harassment, and violence, the vast majority of L.A.'s Black residents—even those who were middle class or wealthy—were confined to a congested area in the city's central districts. To cater to their interests, Gordon planned to create an economically exclusive community, called Gordon Manor, similar in status to the restrictive white neighborhoods of Wilshire and Hollywood. However, almost immediately after Gordon purchased the property and announced his intentions, a coalition of powerful white real estate developers decided that the site would be the perfect place for a regional park serving the South Bay. In reality, they simply did not want a Black-occupied housing development—even an elite neighborhood of wealthy homeowners—in the vicinity of the racially exclusive white residential neighborhoods where they did their business. In April 1926, they pushed a resolution through the Los Angeles County Board of Supervisors to claim Gordon's land through eminent domain. Simultaneously, a group of white residents submitted a petition to claim 100 acres of adjacent agricultural land farmed by Japanese tenant farmers, who were restricted from owning land by California's Alien Land Laws. Using bond money authorized by the recently passed Mattoon Act, the L.A. County Board of Supervisors paid cash to compensate Gordon and the bank that had leased the land to the Japanese tenant farmers. The farmers' leases were terminated and they received nothing. The *California Eagle* criticized the board of supervisors for catering to "the Ku Klux Klan and Southern Crackers." As evidence that the land acquisitions were not part of a larger park initiative, surrounding residents and municipalities then balked at tax assessments to pay for the park's development. Consequently, the land was not developed into a regional park until after World War II. Currently, Alondra Park consists of 84 acres with numerous recreational facilities, including a lake for fishing and a public golf course. It also functions as habitat for migratory wetland birds and features a native plant garden.

NEARBY SITES OF INTEREST

Frontier Logistics Services
19200 Western Ave., Los Angeles 90501
A violent clash between striking and nonstriking workers took place here on July 31, 1965, when this site was occupied by Harvey Aluminum.

Dow Chemical Company Plant
305 Crenshaw Blvd., Torrance 90503
In the 1960s, Dow Chemical produced napalm at this plant. Students for a Democratic Society protested it, and the Torrance Police Department attacked them.

FAVORITE NEIGHBORHOOD RESTAURANTS

Spoon House Bakery and Restaurant
1601 W. Redondo Beach Blvd., Gardena 90247
(310) 538-0376
Popular hole-in-the-wall specializing in Japanese-style pasta dishes.

Al-Noor
15112 Inglewood Ave., Lawndale 90260
(310) 675-4700 (www.alnoor-restaurant.net)
Unassuming but popular Pakistani restaurant known for its excellent chicken *tikka masala*.

3.3 American Indian Movement, Los Angeles Chapter
4304 Clara St., no. 1, Cudahy 90201
(between Otis Ave. and Atlantic Ave.)
Private residence

Apartments at 4304 Clara St., Cudahy, former headquarters of the Los Angeles chapter of AIM, 2009.

In 1968, George Mitchell, Dennis Banks, and Clyde Bellecourt gathered 200 Native American community members in Minneapolis to discuss ways to combat decades of exploitative and weak federal Indian policy, as well as discrimination and police abuse. The meeting gave rise to the American Indian

Movement (AIM). Chapters soon proliferated across the country, including several in Los Angeles, one of which operated at this address. At that time, AIM was more militant than other American Indian initiatives. Although many indigenous people distinguish their struggles from those of other people of color in the United States, AIM's members believed they had much in common with contemporary organizations such as the Black

AIM leader Russell Means running away from federal marshals—who had a warrant for his arrest after his involvement at Wounded Knee—at the Los Angeles Indian Center, 1973.

Panther Party, the Brown Berets, and the Young Lords. Besides challenging police abuse and federal Indian policy, AIM was also adamant about fighting for the survival of Indian nations, land, and sovereignty.

In addition to AIM, there were many other organizations and activists working on behalf of indigenous people, including the National Council on Indian Opportunity. The National Council convened a forum in 1968 that resulted in increased funding for Los Angeles colleges and universities to recruit Native American students through such initiatives as the High Potential Program (HPP) and Equal Opportunity Program (EOP). At UCLA, the Native American student population numbered 70 in 1969 (up from seven students in previous years), and new courses such as Liberation of the American Indian, American Indian Community Development and Interaction, and American Indian Studies in Literature were offered.

L.A.'s American Indians were actively and centrally involved in many of AIM's national campaigns and strategies. On November 20, 1969, 89 Native Americans landed on Alcatraz Island, reclaimed it as Indian property under a little-known government statute that allowed indigenous occupation of abandoned federal lands, and proposed using it as a cultural center. Thirty-five of the protesters were new UCLA students recruited through the HPP and EOP. Participation in the occupation led to a closer relationship between the Native American population in Los Angeles and the national AIM movement. In 1973, AIM members allied themselves with leaders on the Pine Ridge Reservation in South Dakota to occupy Wounded Knee in protest of the 1890 massacre of Sioux peoples by the U.S. Army. Over the course of the 71-day occupation and an armed standoff between AIM and U.S. Marshals that resulted in the death of two protesters, United People for Wounded Knee (UPWK) came together in Los Angeles to raise financial support. AIM press secretary Mark Banks, the older brother of AIM cofounder Dennis Banks, generated publicity and raised funds in Southern California. After the standoff, UPWK continued building local support for the national AIM movement by raising money for members who had been indicted and were on trial for their involvement. Charges were dropped in 1974. Later that year, Los Angeles supporters of AIM formed the Skyhorse-Mohawk Defense-Offense Committee to garner financial support for Paul Skyhorse and Richard Mohawk, who were accused of murdering a cab driver in Ventura County. Over the next four years, the committee organized rallies, fund-raisers, and demonstrations in support of the incarcerated Skyhorse and Mohawk. Charges were dropped and the men were released in 1978.

Unlike similar organizations of the 1960s and 1970s, AIM still exists and continues to fight for the rights of native peoples across the world. In 1993 there was an ideological break, and one faction, the AIM-Grand Governing Council (GGC), won rights to the organizational name. There are still autonomous chapters throughout the United States that continue to function outside of the GGC, however.

FAVORITE NEIGHBORHOOD RESTAURANT

Famous Hamburger
4143 Florence Ave., Bell 90201 (323) 562-0744
Popular gathering spot for young Muslims from the surrounding community. Full menu of halal and kosher meats, as well as Mexican food and pizza.

TO LEARN MORE

Paul Chaat Smith and Robert Warrior, *Like a Hurricane: The Indian Movement from Alcatraz to Wounded Knee* (New Press, 1996).

Author, activist, and theologian Vine Deloria Jr. published the first of his many notable books, *Custer Died for Your Sins: An Indian Manifesto* (Macmillan, 1969), in the year of AIM's founding. This and any of Deloria Jr.'s other 20-plus books are worthwhile reads.

Nicolas Rosenthal, "Re-imagining Indian Country: American Indians and the Los Angeles Metropolitan Area" (PhD dissertation, UCLA, 2005).

3.4 Bicycle Club Casino

7301 Eastern Ave., Bell Gardens 90201
(between Florence Ave. and Live Oak St.)
(562) 806-4646 (www.thebike.com)

The Bicycle Club Casino was built in 1984 and was initially the largest poker club in the world (it is now the second largest). The casino is significant because it represents the outcome of a series of public finance and economic processes that have plagued low-income cities in Los Angeles County, particularly in the southeast, since the passage of Proposition 13. Approved in 1978 by California voters, Proposition 13 was ostensibly about protecting seniors on fixed incomes from escalating property taxes by freezing the tax rate until a property was sold, at which point a reassessment could take place. However, less understood by the public is the fact that the proposition also created huge tax breaks for commercial real estate. Because of their ability to avoid actual sales and property transfers (which would trigger

Entrance to the Bicycle Club Casino, 2010.

lion in city revenues. Key to its success was Pai-Gow, a Chinese game with a large following. However, gambling as a source of municipal financing in California suffers from at least two problems—aside from corruption, which led the U.S. government to temporarily assume ownership of the casino. First, gambling is most successful when there is limited competition. In southeast Los Angeles, however, there are at least five or six cities with card houses. In fact, each time a new casino has opened, the other cities have lost players and revenues. Second, in California, municipal gaming is not the same as Vegas-style gambling, because players are not betting against the house. The house simply hosts the games by providing the venue and amenities. In contrast, gambling on nearby Indian reservations is the real thing, and local poker clubs have been losing players to reservation gambling. For these reasons, gaming is not a viable regional economic development strategy. The Bicycle Casino is an example of an economy of last resort, and further evidence that simply shifting money around is not a long-term economic solution.

a reassessment) through the formation of shell companies, corporations' real estate tax bills have, since the proposition went into effect, been absurdly low and much lower than those of homeowners. The decline in corporate real estate tax revenues has greatly contributed to the economic crisis facing California municipalities. Cities and counties have sought to compensate by imposing user-fees, reducing services, levying special taxes, increasing sales taxes, and attracting other tax-generating enterprises. The southeast part of L.A. County was especially hard hit because it had also suffered from deindustrialization. Much of the region's old industrial infrastructure was located in this working-class area. In addition, these communities, which were rapidly becoming majority Latina/o, were not able to attract large retailers that could provide an alternative revenue stream via sales taxes. The solution? Gambling.

In 1981, Bell Gardens passed an ordinance allowing gaming, which, it was promised, would be a solution to budget woes. George Hardie developed the Bicycle Club Casino, which, in its first five years, generated $8 mil-

NEARBY SITES OF INTEREST

Plaza Mexico

3100 E. Imperial Hwy., Lynwood 90262
(310) 631-6789 and (310) 631-4989
(www.plazamexico.com)
Mexican shopping and dining complex built by Iranian developers that has become an important

site for Mexican immigrant community formation and activism.

Ted Watkins Memorial Park
1335 E. 103rd St., Los Angeles 90002
(323) 357-3032

Site of the historic Bloods and Crips gang truce and frequent unity events attended by rival gangs.

3.5 Black Panther Party Headquarters

4115 S. Central Ave., Los Angeles 90011
(between E. 41st St. and E. 41st Pl.)

HISTORIC SOUTH CENTRAL

The Black Panther Party for Self-Defense (BPP) was the leading revolutionary nationalist organization in the United States in the late 1960s and early 1970s. The organization was founded in Oakland, California, in 1966, and the Southern California chapter was established in 1968 under the leadership of Alprentice "Bunchy" Carter. The BPP defended the Black community against the police, created "survival programs" that focused on meeting people's basic needs, and built bridges with other organizations across the globe that were fighting poverty and oppression. In 1969, the director of the FBI, J. Edgar Hoover, proclaimed that the BPP "represents the greatest threat to the internal security of the country."

In December of 1969, the Los Angeles Police Department launched a predawn raid on the headquarters of the Southern California chapter of the BPP, which was located at this address. Committed to obliterating the Panthers, the LAPD initiated the attack in search of illegal weapons and two Panthers wanted on assault charges. The four-hour gun battle, in which the department deployed the newly created Special Weapons and Tactics (SWAT) team, involved hundreds of officers attacking the building. The LAPD fired thousands of rounds into the building, used a battering ram and helicopter, and subsequently trashed the inside of the building. The roof of the building caved in. The attack resulted in the injury of three Panthers and three patrolmen and the arrest of eleven Panthers. Soon after the attack, the BPP leadership called for retrenchment and

The former site of the Black Panther Party headquarters, photographed in 2007, is now a parking lot flanked by a Mexican market and small businesses.

Black Panther Party members in their South L.A. office in December 1969, just before it was raided and destroyed by hundreds of LAPD officers.

BPP headquarters after the raid, December 9, 1969.

the relocation of party members to Oakland, contributing to the eventual demise of the Southern California chapter.

TO LEARN MORE

41st & Central: The Untold Story of the L.A. Black Panthers, a film directed by Gregory Everett (Ultra Wave Vision, 2009).

The FBI's War on Black America, a film directed by Deb Ellis and Denis Mueller (CreateSpace, 2009).

Charles Jones, ed., *The Black Panther Party (Reconsidered)* (Black Classic Press, 1998).

3.6 *California Eagle*

4071–4075 S. Central Ave., Los Angeles 90011 *(at E. 41st St.)*

HISTORIC SOUTH CENTRAL

The *California Eagle,* published from 1879 to 1964 in this building, was the longest-running Black-owned newspaper on the West Coast. In the early twentieth century, Los Angeles was considered a relative haven for African Americans, because the city offered possibilities for Black home ownership and entrepreneurship, a rich cultural life (especially centered on jazz), and three Black-owned newspapers. The *California Eagle* (originally *The Owl*) was founded in 1879 by John Neimore, an escaped slave from Missouri. In 1910, Charlotta Bass began selling subscriptions to *The Owl,* and in 1921 she purchased the newspaper from Neimore and changed its name to the *California Eagle.* She edited the paper with her husband, Joseph, until his death in 1934, after which Charlotta ran it alone.

Under Bass's leadership, the paper became

The building that housed the offices of the *California Eagle* is now occupied by an appliance store and a furniture store, 2007.

California Eagle publisher and editor Charlotta Bass (center) with her staff, date unknown.

a leading voice for social change in L.A. and was known for defending the rights of people of color and workers. The *Eagle* typically covered issues that were either ignored or negatively portrayed by the white press, and prodded its readers to challenge racial discrimination in all spheres. At times, the *Eagle* even challenged Black elites and the Black middle class, such as the leaders of the NAACP, when they were overly accommodationist. Nor did the paper limit its

coverage to African Americans. It covered incidents of police brutality, such as the Sleepy Lagoon trial, and endorsed Mexican American Edward Roybal as the L.A. City Council representative for the Ninth District (which included Boyle Heights, Chinatown, Little Tokyo, and Central Avenue).

Charlotta Bass retired in 1951, partly to run for vice president on the Progressive Party ticket. She was the first African American woman to be nominated for national office. Upon her retirement, she sold the *Eagle* to Loren Miller, a civil liberties lawyer who had effectively defended African Americans. In 1964, Miller was appointed judge of the California Superior Court and sold the paper to fourteen local investors. In less than a year, however, the paper closed as a result of mismanagement.

TO LEARN MORE

Watts Labor Community Action Committee, 10950 S. Central Ave., Los Angeles 90059

(323) 563-5639 (www.wlcac.org). A community-based organization committed to improving life in the Watts area.

Regina Freer, "L.A. Race Woman: Charlotta Bass and the Complexities of Black Political Development in Los Angeles," *American Quarterly* 56, no. 3 (2004): 607–632.

3.7 Chuco's Justice Center and FREE L.A. High School

1137 E. Redondo Blvd., Inglewood 90302
(at West Blvd.)

Chuco's Justice Center, 2009.

Chuco's Justice Center is a radical art space and gathering place where the movement to end California's prison-industrial complex is taking shape and rapidly growing. For years, the California State Legislature and governor have slashed funding for public education while expanding budgetary outlays for prisons and youth detention centers (see entry 2.6 East Los Angeles Prison [Proposed] and Vernon Incinerator [Proposed]). California now has more prisons and detention facilities than public universities, and it spends four times as much to keep a young person locked up in a prison cell for a year as it does to educate a youth in the public school system. Meanwhile, California has the highest

youth dropout rate, youth unemployment rate, and youth incarceration rate of all 50 states. This system is having a particularly devastating effect on Black and Latina/o youth, who are enormously *over*represented in California Youth Authority (CYA) facilities and enormously *under*represented among high school graduates and in higher education.

The Youth Justice Coalition (YJC), which has its offices here at Chuco's, is helping build a movement to challenge these patterns. The YJC is a grassroots organization that challenges the massive expansion of prisons, especially youth detention centers, in California. The coalition is made up of youth between the ages of 8 and 24 who have been incarcerated in one of the CYA's facilities or who have parents or siblings who have been locked up. They protest the increasingly prisonlike conditions of public schools in Los Angeles, and they work to challenge systemic racial, economic, and gender inequality in the prison industrial complex. The YJC's campaigns include its efforts to end life-without-parole for minors, fight gang injunctions and the building of gang databases, repeal graffiti injunctions, and remove questions about past criminal history on job applications. In addition to its extensive work on the outside, the YJC also organizes within youth prisons, where members coordinate leadership development, legal and political education, and court support. The organization has built bridges with county probation and police departments and extensive coalitions with other progressive organizations in Los Angeles. It has also effectively stopped the practice of transferring youth from juvenile facilities to county jails, and has helped to improve living conditions within the CYA. The YJC's ultimate goal is to shut down the California Youth Authority completely.

In September 2007, the Youth Justice Coalition and John Muir Charter School started FREE L.A. High School to support young people with experience in the prison system so they could earn their high school diplomas. The school serves as one of L.A.'s few community-based alternatives to detention and incarceration for young people. It uses a unique and innovative curriculum that integrates core academic skills in math, science, English, and social studies with "street education" (community organizing) and education about "troublemakers" (that is, the study of social movement history, philosophy, and leadership). The school is envisioned as a base on which personal and community power can be built and sustained to create a more just world. The school celebrated its first graduation in 2009.

Chuco's Justice Center is named for Jesse "Chuco" Becerra, a talented and beloved YJC organizer who was gunned down outside a party in 2005, at the age of 24. Becerra had been working on building a truce between gangs in three rival neighborhoods. Chuco's also houses the offices of the Los Angeles chapter of Critical Resistance, a national prison abolition organization; the October 22 Coalition Against Police Brutality; and TEEAMWORKS, a gang intervention program led by former and inactive gang members, among others. Artistic and community events are held here frequently.

NEARBY SITE OF INTEREST

Kenneth Hahn State Recreation Area

4100 S. La Cienega Blvd., Los Angeles 90008 (323) 298-3660 (www.parks.ca.gov/?page _id=612)

A large park with five miles of trails, a fishing lake, lotus pond, and community center.

FAVORITE NEIGHBORHOOD RESTAURANTS

Serving Spoon

1403 Centinela Ave., Inglewood 90302 (310) 412-3927 (theservingspoon.net)

Regulars recommend anything on the breakfast menu, as well as the fried catfish. Expect a wait on weekends.

Inglewood Rose Donut Shop

917 N. La Brea Ave., Inglewood (310) 672-9471

Be sure to try the buttermilk donuts.

TO LEARN MORE

Ruth Wilson Gilmore, *Golden Gulag: Prisons, Surplus, Crisis, and Opposition in Globalizing California* (University of California Press, 2007).

3.8 Compton Communicative Arts Academy

The Happening House: 102 E. Indigo St., Compton 90220 *(at S. Willowbrook Ave.)*

The Compton Communicative Arts Academy was one expression of a vibrant community arts movement that developed in Los Angeles and other U.S. cities during the late 1960s. In L.A., this movement included Self-Help Graphics and the mural program that became SPARC, among other groups (see entries 2.21 Self-Help Graphics and Art, and 6.5 *The Great Wall* and Social and Public Art Resource Center). The community arts movement opposed the elite and Eurocentric biases of the city's dominant artistic institutions and the nearly wholesale exclusion of artists of color from exhibits, galleries, and museums. Participants believed that all people need and deserve expressive outlets, that art can be a powerful force for positive social change, and that the arts are vital to the building of strong communities.

In 1968, the Compton Willowbrook Community Action Council, a War on Poverty agency, invited local artist Judson Powell to create an arts program in Compton at an old two-story house donated by the Salvation

Children's art class at the Compton Communicative Arts Academy, 1970s.

Army. The academy sponsored a wide variety of programs, including a jazz band that performed original music at local concerts and in other venues (including local prisons), as well as workshops in dance, theater, the visual arts, and children's arts and crafts. By 1973, the academy had expanded, occupying five locations throughout Compton, including the original donated house, which was called the "Happening House"; the Arena; a playhouse used for theater and music; a cinema workshop on Alondra Boulevard; and a sculptural workshop on Rosecrans Boulevard. Many renowned artists participated in the academy as both teachers and students, including John Outterbridge, a painter and sculptor who later went on to direct the Watts Towers Art Center. The academy was widely considered to be a vibrant and inspirational environment, especially for African American artists and other artists of color, for many of whom it was a formative life experience. After struggling with funding for years, however, the Happening House here on Indigo Street was torn down. This address is now the site of a commercial strip mall.

TO LEARN MORE

Daniel Widener, *Black Arts West: Culture and Struggle in Postwar Los Angeles* (Duke University Press, 2010).

3.9 Dorothy Ray Healey's House

1733 W. 84th St., Los Angeles 90047
(at S. Western Ave. and S. Harvard Blvd.)
MANCHESTER SQUARE
Private residence

This was one of Dorothy Ray Healey's homes in Los Angeles in which she lived as

Former home of Dorothy Ray Healey, 2009.

an adult. Healey was a lifelong leftist who was active not only in Los Angeles but also nationally. Born in 1914 to parents who were Hungarian Jewish immigrants, Healey moved with her family to Los Angeles when she was a child. She got her first taste of class exploitation and labor organizing while working at a peach-processing plant. She joined the Young Communist League at the ripe old age of 14, and the Communist Party at age 18. Healey brought a deep commitment to labor organizing and antiracism to the Southern California branch of the party. For example, she became actively involved in the defense of the Mexican youth tried for the Sleepy Lagoon murder (see entry 1.26 Orpheum Theatre, Sleepy Lagoon Murder, and Ventura School for Girls), was active in the Congress of Industrial Organizations, and in 1933 played a key role in leading the multiethnic strike of Mexican and Japanese berry pickers in El Monte (see entry 2.10 Hicks

Camp / Rio Vista Park). Healey became the chairwoman of the Southern California branch of the Communist Party in the mid-1940s and helped to make it one of the leading chapters in the country by building bridges between unions, civil rights movements, and progressive electoral coalitions.

Like other leftists, Healey was subjected to repeated harassment and prosecution because of her political views. During the Red Scare of the 1950s, she was one of the original Smith Act defendants, who were arrested, jailed, and tried for "attempting to overthrow the government," until the Supreme Court declared the law unconstitutional. In the 1960s, she was fined under the McCarran Internal Security Act of 1950, which required the registration of communist organizations and authorized the investigation of people engaged in "subversive activities." Both the Smith and McCarran Acts sought to limit the work of labor and

Dorothy Ray Healey debates state senator Jack Tenney (hands in pockets) during a Los Angeles City Council hearing on a proposed communist registration ordinance, August 1956.

social justice activists. Although Healey's work was instrumental in building the American Communist Party, in the 1950s she disavowed the U.S.S.R. after learning of Stalin's horrific regime of terror and ultimately left the Communist Party itself. Instead, she forged ties with the social movements of the 1960s and 1970s, serving as a bridge between the old Left and new Left and working for a more humane world not based on capitalism. Healey died in 2006 in Maryland, where she had moved to be closer to her son.

FAVORITE NEIGHBORHOOD RESTAURANT

M'Dear's Desserts, Bakery, and Bistro

7717 S. Western Ave., Los Angeles 90047
(323) 759-2020 or (323) 759-2222
A small, unassuming neighborhood place. Regulars recommend the soul food burrito, chicken and waffles plate, and homemade lemonade.

TO LEARN MORE

Dorothy Ray Healey and Maurice Isserman, *California Red: A Life in the American Communist Party* (University of Illinois Press, 1993).

Dorothy Healey Collection at University Library, Special Collections, California State Long Beach University, 1250 Bellflower Blvd., Long Beach 90840 (562) 985-4087 (www.csulb.edu /library/guide/serv/speccol.html).

Community Coalition, 8101 S. Vermont Ave., Los Angeles 90044 (323) 750-9087 (www .cocosouthla.org). An economic and social justice organization that has a great track record in bringing together African American and Latina/o residents of South L.A. around a wide range of political, social, and health-related issues.

3.10 Duke Brothers' Automotive Shop

4154 Long Beach Ave., Los Angeles 90011
(at E. 41st Pl.)

CENTRAL-ALAMEDA

This site is home to the original Duke brothers' automotive shop, founded by the Ruelas brothers—Julio, Oscar, Fernando, and Ernie—who became legendary for their role in the custom car circuit of lowriding. The Ruelas brothers emigrated with their mother from Tijuana to Los Angeles in the 1950s. The brothers were introduced to auto mechanics at a young age while living with their Uncle Tinker—who originally owned the automotive shop and hoped to keep them off the street—and they quickly learned to build and modify cars. The brothers, along with others from the neighborhood, organized the Duke's Car Club in 1962. It is the largest and longest-surviving known lowrider car club. The club has several chapters and now includes third-generation members.

Lowriding involves the practice of lowering and customizing one's car with painstaking care and then cruising to show it off. It is now popular around the globe, including in Japan, but lowriding first emerged after World War II in Mexican American working-class communities throughout the U.S. Southwest as car ownership became more widespread. Lowriding has played an especially important role within Chicana/o culture. In particular, it created a way to express a distinctly Mexican American identity at a time when Mexicans were stigmatized and subject to daily discrimination. Lowriding allowed for a positive articulation of

Lineup of restored classic cars in front of the Duke brothers' shop, 1977.

Chicana/o identity—albeit one not shared by the larger society. Indeed, for decades the police often equated lowriders with gang members, and many cities felt that cruising was a public nuisance and banned it. But lowriders persisted in their passion. Lowriding culture has always been much more than an expression of one's personal identity; it is also about family and community—thus, the car clubs. Yet lowriding is largely a male-centered activity. Within lowriding culture, women are often seen as "accessories," exemplified by their physical presence as passengers in the cars; as painted representations on the vehicles; and in the lowrider car club magazines, where they are usually scantily clad. However, there is a growing number of women learning how to repair and stylize their own cars, and family (especially mothers, wives, and sisters) is highly respected in the lowrider scene.

Throughout its history, the Duke's Car Club has taken its responsibility to the community seriously. The Dukes played a central role in forming the West Coast Association of Low Riders in 1978, with the express purpose of uniting car clubs to serve the Chicana/o community. Members assisted Cesar Chavez and the UFW back in the day, have raised money for holiday toys for children, and have taken the "Duke's Bus" to local prisons to put on lowrider shows for the inmates. The club has also been a vehicle for unifying people despite their turf, affiliation, or race. Given its location in a historically Black community that has attracted large numbers of Latinas/os in recent years, the Duke's Car Club has been especially important in building bridges between African Americans and Mexican Americans. These two groups, although often seen in conflict, could—and still can—sometimes be found working under the same car at the Duke automotive shop. Fernando Ruelas, longtime president of the car club, died in 2010.

TO LEARN MORE

Duke's Car Club, www.dukescarclub.com.
Denise Michelle Sandoval, "Bajito y Suavecito/ Low and Slow: Cruising through Lowrider Culture" (PhD dissertation, Claremont Graduate University, May 2003).

3.11 Dunbar Hotel

4225 S. Central Ave., Los Angeles 90011
(at E. 42nd Pl.)

HISTORIC SOUTH CENTRAL

Dunbar Hotel, 2007.

The Dunbar Hotel, formerly known as the Hotel Somerville, was originally named for the Los Angeles dentist and African American civil rights activist John Somerville, who was instrumental in founding the Los Angeles branch of the National Association for the Advancement of Colored People (NAACP). Somerville launched a successful campaign to bring the organization to Los Angeles for its 1928 convention. It was the first time that the NAACP had decided to hold its annual conference on the West Coast—and so the event promised to link Los Angeles and the West with the civil rights movement based on the East Coast. To lure the NAACP to Los Angeles, Somerville had promised to build a high-quality convention hotel, which he did. As quoted in Douglas Flamming's book, *Bound for Freedom,* Somerville recalled that it became "the finest hotel in America catering to colored people."

The hotel's location at Forty-second and Central avenues was far south of the existing hub of Black activity then centered on Twelfth and Central. But shortly after the convention, businesses and residences were constructed around the Somerville, prompting the *California Eagle* to call the area the "Brown Broadway." John Somerville went bankrupt during the Great Depression and was forced to sell the hotel. Lucius Lomax eventually purchased the hotel and renamed it the Dunbar in honor of poet Paul Laurence Dunbar. The Dunbar Hotel continued to occupy a central place in Black Los Angeles, especially the city's jazz scene, by hosting such performers as Duke Ellington, Count Basie, and Bill "Bojangles" Robinson. In addition, poets and intellectuals like Langston Hughes and W. E. B. DuBois gathered here. With racial integration, however, the Dunbar began to decline in the late 1950s. A development corporation was established in 1988 to restore the building, which was converted to low-income housing, primarily for seniors. The hotel is a protected historical site and houses the Museum In Black. As of this writing, the city may take over the hotel because of nonpayment of taxes, and its future is uncertain.

**NEARBY SITES AND
RELATED EVENTS OF INTEREST**

Watts Towers Arts Center
1761–1765 E. 107th St., Los Angeles 90002
(213) 847-4646 (www.wattstowers.us)
Home of the Watts Towers, an L.A. landmark constructed by Italian immigrant Simon Rodia entirely of found materials such as broken glass, tile, and sea shells. Also at the same location: the Watts Towers Day of the Drum Festival, which

highlights international percussion every year in late September.

Central Avenue Jazz Festival
Central Ave., between Martin Luther King Jr. Blvd. and Vernon Ave. (www.centralavejazz.org)
A free jazz festival held annually every summer.

Chester Himes's home (former)
4433 Crocker St., Los Angeles 90011
Private residence
The acclaimed African American novelist Chester Himes lived here during the 1940s.

Dolphin's of Hollywood Record Store
1061 E. Vernon St., Los Angeles 90111
John Dolphin, a Black recording pioneer, established a record store at this address in the late 1940s to "bring Hollywood to the Negros," since Black people could not own property or operate a business in Hollywood at that time.

3.12 Eso Won Bookstore and Leimert Park
4331 Degnan Blvd., Los Angeles 90008
(between W. 43rd St. and W. 43rd Pl.)
(323) 290-1048 (www.esowonbookstore.com)
LEIMERT PARK

Eso Won—which, in the Amharic language of Ethiopia, means "water over rocks"—is one of a dwindling number of independent bookstores in Southern California. It specializes in books by and about African Americans. The store is known for its popular book signings and author events, including visits to the store by Muhammad Ali, Johnnie Cochran, Patti LaBelle, Berry Gordy, and not one, but two, U.S. presidents: Bill Clinton and Barack Obama (twice). Unlike so many of its counterparts (Aquarian Bookstore in Central Los Angeles, Grass Roots in South Los Angeles, and the Black and Latino Multicultural Bookcenter in Altadena), Eso Won has managed to survive despite tough economic times, the vagaries of Los Angeles development politics, and the fickle tastes of the book-buying public.

The store was founded by James Fugate and Tom Hamilton, who began selling 100 titles out of milk crates in Fugate's car. In the late 1980s, they sold books at the African Marketplace and Cultural Faire and at other local events, dubbing their efforts "Books On Wheels." In 1989, they moved into their first brick-and-mortar store: three small upstairs rooms on Slauson Avenue. They moved an-

Eso Won Bookstore, 2009.

Demonstration and rally by the Los Angeles Free South Africa Movement in Leimert Park, 1989.

other three times before finally landing, in 2006, at this address in Leimert Park, which is the heart of Los Angeles' vibrant African American arts scene and home to multiple performance spaces, cultural centers, galleries, and political meeting places. Reflecting Leimert Park's identity as an artistic and political place, the outside of Eso Won features a mural reflecting Black internationalist and community themes.

Fugate and Hamilton had briefly hoped, in 1996, to move into a storefront with more floor space at a newly remodeled mall in the relatively affluent African American neighborhood of Ladera Heights, until it was sold to a group of investors that included Earvin "Magic" Johnson—the All-Star former Laker—who offered leases to large chain stores instead of locally owned businesses. In a *Los Angeles Times* article, Hamilton characterized Eso Won's experience with the developers by saying, "That means to have somebody else come in, set up their businesses, have black people go and support those businesses and then run the money out of the

community." Eso Won has managed to keep its doors open continuously since 1989, but faces multiple challenges, including not only a troubled economy and competition with online and discount booksellers (problems that all independent bookstores are facing) but also the threat of redevelopment and gentrification of Leimert Park.

NEARBY SITES OF INTEREST

World Stage Performance Gallery
4344 Degnan Blvd., Los Angeles 90008
(323) 293-2451 (www.theworldstage.org)

Lucy Florence Cultural Center
3351 W. 43rd St., Los Angeles 90008
(323) 293-1356 (lucyflorencecc.square space.com)
A coffeehouse and cultural center.

FAVORITE NEIGHBORHOOD RESTAURANTS

M&M Soul Food
3552 W. Martin Luther King Jr. Blvd., Los Angeles 90008 (323) 299-1302
Southern food. Regulars recommend the oxtails, fried chicken, cornbread muffins, and mac 'n' cheese.

Phillips Barbecue

4307 Leimert Blvd., Los Angeles 90008

(323) 292-7613

Kansas City–style barbecue. Try the ribs and baked beans. Very limited seating; ordering take-out is recommended.

Earlez Grille

3630 Crenshaw Blvd., Los Angeles 90008

(323) 299-2867 (earlezgrille.net)

A rare find: a barbecue place offering excellent vegetarian options, including delicious meat-free versions of chili, hot links, tamales, and hot dogs.

3.13 Firestone Tire and Rubber

2323–2525 Firestone Blvd., South Gate 90280 (between S. Alameda St. and Santa Fe Ave.)

Beginning in the 1920s, Los Angeles—especially the southeastern part of the county—was a magnet for manufacturing. Developers lured industry by selling land for cheap just outside city boundaries, enabling manufacturers to buy city services without paying city taxes. Moreover, because Los Angeles was an "open shop," firms did not have to pay union wages. Attracted by these incentives, numerous firms relocated to Los Angeles, including Bell Foundry, A. R. Maas Chemical Company, General Motors, Pittsburgh Steel, and Firestone Tire and Rubber. Many of these new factories were branch plants of firms headquartered on the East Coast.

Firestone Tire and Rubber built a factory on a 40-acre lot at this site, which had been a bean field. In 1928, the first tire rolled off the assembly line. Eventually the plant employed 2,500 people. Starting in the 1930s, as part of a larger wave of worker activism, Firestone became unionized, and after World War II its workers, represented by United Rubber Workers Local 100, were able to negotiate solid wage and benefit packages.

By 1964, South Gate was home to more than 600 plants and employed more than 37,000 workers, with thousands more employed in the surrounding areas. Although the communities along the industrial corridor became strong union supporters in the 1940s and 1950s, their approach epitomized "business unionism," in which workers were primarily concerned with compensation instead of demanding democracy at the workplace, promoting a working-class culture, or challenging capitalism. They also remained politically conservative—and white. Despite strong support for integration from the union leadership, workers of color were able to access these jobs only through struggle. Nor were they able to live in surrounding residential communities until both the jobs and white people left in the late 1960s and the 1970s.

Beginning in the mid-1960s, two major events dramatically changed South Gate and its environs. First, in 1965, there was the Watts civil unrest, which triggered a massive exodus of whites from all of South Los Angeles. As whites left the area, they were replaced by Latina/o immigrants, leading to some tensions but also to new avenues of community and labor organizing among African Americans and Latinas/os. Second, and perhaps more profound, was deindustrialization. Beginning in the late 1970s, the branch plants and many other manufacturers left the region in search of lower production costs. Firestone, for example, closed

A multiracial group of Firestone workers on strike in front of the plant's main gate, April 1967.

Students taking LAUSD adult education classes exit from what was formerly the main entrance of the Firestone plant, 2010.

its doors in 1983. The consequences were disastrous for Los Angeles generally, and the Southeast industrial corridor in particular. By the mid-1980s, South Gate alone had lost 12,500 jobs, which had particular consequences for workers of color. According to L.A. scholar Mike Davis in a 1991 issue of *Heritage*, "While white workers for the most part were able to retire or follow their jobs to the suburban periphery, nonwhites were stranded in an economy that was suddenly minus 40,000 high-wage manufacturing and trucking jobs."

Yet the industrial base of the Alameda Corridor was not totally abandoned or destroyed; rather, it was transformed. The Firestone plant eventually reopened as an industrial park that houses, among other businesses, a nonunion furniture factory employing primarily immigrants. The site is also now home to an adult school that offers courses for high school diploma completion, English proficiency, and vocational training. These dynamics—epitomized right here on the site of Firestone's former plant—are emblematic of the changing nature of Los Angeles' manufacturing economy. As historian Becky Nicolaides has noted, "Paying minimum wage (and sometimes less), these operations turned the clock backward about 100 years in terms of wages, work conditions, and the prevalence of the open-shop."

FAVORITE NEIGHBORHOOD RESTAURANT

La Barca Jal
3501 Firestone Blvd., South Gate 90280
(323) 564-5141
Traditional Mexican family-style restaurant.

TO LEARN MORE

Becky Nicolaides, *My Blue Heaven: Life and Politics in the Working-Class Suburbs of Los Angeles, 1920–1965* (University of Chicago Press, 2002).

3.14 Holiday Bowl

3730 Crenshaw Blvd., Los Angeles 90018
(between Rodeo Rd. and Coliseum St.)

CRENSHAW

The former Holiday Bowl, now converted to a Starbucks and a Walgreens drugstore, 2006.

The Holiday Bowl was a bowling alley founded by five Japanese Americans in 1958. Building the Bowl was part of the process of rebuilding the nikkei community after internment during World War II. Owners sold shares throughout the community in order to finance its construction. Given the Bowl's location on Crenshaw, it was an important site in the desegregation of Los Angeles, as it served a Black, Japanese American, and white clientele. Reflecting the multiethnic and working-class nature of its customer base, the

Bowl's coffee shop featured grits, *udon,* chow mein, and hamburgers and was open round-the-clock to serve workers on the swing and graveyard shifts. As a result of poor management, the Bowl was closed in May 2000 and targeted for demolition. However, supporters of the Bowl mobilized and persuaded the Los Angeles Cultural Heritage Commission to designate the coffee shop as a historical-cultural monument on account of its 1950s-style Googie architecture and its importance in creating an integrated Los Angeles. Although most of the building was destroyed, the facade of the coffee shop was preserved and now encloses a Starbucks, while on the site of the former bowling alley now stands a new structure that houses a Walgreens drugstore.

FAVORITE NEIGHBORHOOD RESTAURANT

The Cobbler Lady

3854 Crenshaw Blvd., Los Angeles 90008
Regulars recommend the peach cobbler and red velvet cupcakes, as well as soups (try the navy bean) and sandwiches.

Champion women's bowling team at the Holiday Bowl, November 1962.

TO LEARN MORE

Nina Revoyr, *Southland* (Akashic Books, 2008).

Top of Their Game, a film directed by John Esaki (Japanese American National Museum, 2000).

Sharon Sekhon, "Why the Holiday Bowl Matters," Holiday Bowl History Project, www .holidaybowlcrenshaw.com/community.htm.

3.15 Holman United Methodist Church

3320 W. Adams Blvd., Los Angeles 90018
(between 3rd Ave. and 4th Ave.)

(323) 731-7285 (www.holmanumc.com)

JEFFERSON PARK

In 1945, seven people met in Ulysses Griggs's home to develop a plan to meet the needs of Los Angeles' rapidly growing Black population. The result was Holman United Methodist Church, a key Black institution that is closely associated with social justice causes. Originally known as Morgan Chapel, Holman UMC had many homes—including a dance hall at Jefferson and Normandie, a Japanese church during the Japanese American internment, and a Jewish synagogue—before it finally purchased the Pepperdine mansion here on West Adams Boulevard (so named because the building was once owned by the founder of Pepperdine University). The church has had many pastors, but we include it in the *People's Guide* mainly because of the Reverend James M. Lawson Jr., who came to Holman UMC in 1974 and made peace and justice central to his ministry.

Lawson, the son of a Methodist preacher, was a major figure in the civil rights movement and a practitioner of nonviolence. While he was a student, Lawson was a member of the Congress of Racial Equality and helped to stage sit-ins and protests. During the U.S. war in Vietnam, when Lawson received his draft letter he registered as a conscientious objector and spent 13 months in prison. Upon his release, he went to Nagpur, India, as a missionary and studied Satyagraha (Sanskrit for "force of truth/ love"), or what is known in the United States as nonviolent resistance. He returned to the United States and began conducting workshops in the U.S. South for the Southern Christian Leadership Conference. Lawson was at the forefront of such events as the 1964 Civil Rights Act, 1965 Voting Rights Act, Poor People's Campaign, and Black Sanitation Workers' strikes—all before he joined the ministry. Martin Luther

Rev. James Lawson Jr. of Holman United Methodist Church (second from left) with civil rights leaders and elected officials at a memorial march in honor of Martin Luther King Jr., January 1978.

King Jr. once described Lawson as the "leading nonviolence theorist in the world."

Rev. Lawson was the pastor of Holman UMC for 25 years, until he retired in 1999. The mission of the church is "to make disciples for Jesus Christ by bringing to the people of Los Angeles, and particularly the historic West Adams community, hope-filled, Christ-inspired responses to urban needs." As of this writing, the Reverend Dr. Henry L. Masters Sr. is the senior pastor of Holman UMC. Lawson remains an active figure in many social justice causes in Los Angeles.

FAVORITE NEIGHBORHOOD RESTAURANTS

Natraliart

3426 W. Washington Blvd., Los Angeles 90018
(323) 732-8865

Jamaican restaurant known for its oxtails, jerk chicken, and fried plantains. Closed on Sundays and Mondays.

Tacos Chabelita

2001 S. Western Ave., Los Angeles 90018
(323) 734-0211

Locals favor the carne asada burritos and chicken tacos.

TO LEARN MORE

For more on the architectural history of the area, see the West Adams Heritage Association, www.westadamsheritage.org. West Adams is one of the many older districts in L.A. struggling with both historic preservation and gentrification.

William Andrews Clark Memorial Library, 2520 Cimarron St., Los Angeles 90018 (323) 735-7605 (www.humnet.ucla.edu/humnet/ClarkLib/). A little-known treasure of rare books, specializing in English literature and history.

3.16 Indian Revival Center

5602 E. Gage Ave., Bell Gardens 90201
(at Specht Ave.)

This church was built in 1956 by American Indians who moved to L.A. through the relocation programs organized by the federal government from the 1940s to the 1970s. After World War II, the U.S. federal government became increasingly concerned about the cost of maintaining treaty obligations with American Indian nations. In addition, many politicians representing districts in the U.S. West, which became increasingly numerous and powerful in the postwar era, saw Indian lands as impediments to regional economic development. Influenced by the anticommunist ideologies of the McCarthy era, such political and economic elites disdained the communal land ownership system of the reservations. Since Indians did not have the capacity or inclination to develop these lands, they reasoned, the lands should be opened up for development to those who *could* and *would* develop them. Despite these underlying political and economic motivations, in public discourse the Bureau of Indian Affairs (BIA) merely cited the need for Indians to "assimilate." It argued that life on the reservations prevented them from doing so and, in fact, "inhibited" their economic progress. So, in the official BIA rhetoric, relocation was actually a favor to Indians. In the late 1940s, the federal government initiated the Urban Indian Relocation Program and set up field offices in major cities to encourage and facilitate American Indian relocation. The BIA originally provided transportation, job placement, and subsistence funds until the first paycheck; vocational training was added in 1956.

Los Angeles was one of the original relocation cities, and by the late 1960s it had the largest American Indian urban population in the United States. In just six years, between 1960 and 1966, the Indian population of Los Angeles more than doubled, from 12,405 persons to more than 25,000, and Los Angeles' Indian population accounted for more than one-third of the number of American Indians in California. Two residential concentrations emerged: (1) the area bordered by Western Avenue, Beverly Boulevard, Figueroa Street, and Pico Boulevard, which was the original federal location for relocated Indian families; and (2) the city's southeastern suburbs, especially Cudahy, Bell, Bell Gardens, and Huntington Park. Many American Indians also settled outside these two clusters, throughout Los Angeles' other suburbs. The majority of L.A.'s Indian population during this period migrated from Oklahoma, Arizona, New Mexico, the Dakotas, and Montana. Most Indian persons identified with the following tribes: Navajo (the largest group, at 14 percent), Sioux (12 percent), Cherokee (6 percent), Creek (6 percent), Pueblo (5 percent), Choctaw (4 percent), and Seminole, Cheyenne, Chippewa, and Apache (each constituting approximately 3 percent).

While maintaining their tribal identifications (particularly among the larger groups), American Indians in Los Angeles also forged a pantribal identity as Indians, which was further facilitated by the larger Angeleno population's inability or unwillingness to make distinctions among American Indians on the basis of linguistic, ethnic, and cultural differences. Social institutions such as athletic leagues, clubs, cultural centers, and churches were vital to the construction of a pan-Indian identity. Although most American Indians did not attend church regularly, religious institutions were nonetheless important community pillars that eased the transition to urban life. A 1966 survey conducted by anthropologist John Price found that nine fundamentalist Protestant churches and one Latter Day Saints church in L.A. had predominantly Indian memberships. One of these was the Indian Revival Center, an Assembly of God church, which had the largest and most active Indian congregation in Los Angeles during the 1960s and 1970s. By the mid-1960s, 250 persons, many of whom were Navajo, regularly attended services here. The church conducted Sunday school classes in the Navajo language and had a choir that sang Christian hymns in Navajo. In 1968, Price wrote: "Of all the large Indian social groups in Los Angeles, this is one of the least assimilated." In fact, the very name *Indian Revival Center* might be interpreted in at least two ways: as a space for religious revival, but also as a place for the revival and perpetuation of Indianness. In this respect, the church—along with the many other Indian social and cultural institutions in Los Angeles—functioned as a place of adaptation to the new urban context while also meeting community needs and allowing for cultural resistance.

The church is still active today and continues to sponsor many events and programs, including not only regular religious services but also health and wellness programs, presentations by visiting Native speakers from across the country, and political forums for candidates to elected office, among others. The church celebrated its fiftieth anniversary in 2006. Los Angeles remains the largest urban Indian population in the country, with more than 200,000 Indian-identified people.

NEARBY SITE OF INTEREST

Henry Gage Mansion

7000 E. Gage Ave., Bell Gardens 90201
Considered the oldest house in L.A. County.

TO LEARN MORE

John Price, "The Migration and Adaptation of American Indians to Los Angeles County," *Human Organization* 27, no. 2 (1968): 168–175.

Donald Lee Fixico, *The Urban Indian Experience in America* (University of New Mexico Press, 2000).

Susan Lobo and Kurt Peters, eds., *American Indians and the Urban Experience* (AltaMira Press, 2001).

Indian Country Diaries: A Seat at the Drum, a television documentary produced by Native American Public Telecommunications, 2006, www.pbs.org/indiancountry.

3.17 Kashu Realty and Thirty-sixth Street Residential Discrimination Site

Kashu Realty 3112 W. Jefferson Blvd., Los Angeles 90018 *(between Edgehill Dr. and 11th Ave.)* JEFFERSON PARK

Residential Discrimination Site 1772 W. 36th St., Los Angeles 90018 *(between S. St. Andrews Pl. and W. Western Ave.)*

EXPOSITION PARK

Private residence

Before World War II, many neighborhoods in South L.A., particularly those close to downtown and west of Alameda Boulevard, were gripped by racially restrictive covenants. To make matters worse, few lenders would approve mortgages for minorities to purchase homes in white neighborhoods. Consequently, the few neighborhoods where people of color could live suffered from severe overcrowding. West Jefferson was one of these neighborhoods. West Jefferson had been integrated after World War I by wealthy, professional Black people and then middle-class African Americans and Asian Americans, who worked with enterprising real estate agents to "bust" all-white blocks despite the restrictive covenants. "Blockbusters" played on white homeowners' fear of integration and took advantage of the pent-up demand for housing by people of color to generate quick sales and large profits for real estate agents. Those white homeowners who remained became incensed at efforts to integrate their neighborhoods and used both legal and extralegal means to resist.

An example of white resistance to integration can be seen in the story of a house on Thirty-sixth Street formerly at this address, which has since been replaced by a large stucco apartment building. In 1925, the Crestmore Improvement Association, a homeowners association in West Jefferson, placed a twenty-five-year renewal on race restrictions that were about to expire—even though many people of color had already moved in. Black, Japanese, and other non-

A white mob gathers to protest the sale of this home in South L.A. to a Black family, 1949.

white residents were then sued for violating the restrictive covenants, and many were evicted. In July 1933, two hundred white property owners (including several local judges) organized a campaign to drive out all "Mongolians" and "Negroes" still living around the Thirty-sixth Street Elementary School. Margaret Walker, spokesperson for the campaign, stated, "We shall have all Caucasians by themselves in residential districts and we should certainly restrict property against the Japanese. I don't see why we can't save our part of town for our people." Mrs. Tsurue Kuranaga, who rented no. 1772, across the street from the school, had been targeted by the campaign. Kuranaga was charged with violation of racially restrictive covenants and forcibly removed by court order in November 1933. Through the end of the 1940s, other Japanese Americans and African Americans experienced similar evictions in other parts of the city.

After World War II, however, residential integration gained traction as federal and state courts began to strike down restrictive covenants and other forms of *de jure* segregation, and as veterans of color, in particular, pointed to their patriotic service and demanded their civil rights. Black real estate agents, calling themselves "realtists," formed the National Association of Real Estate Brokers in 1947, with the goal of securing minority access to equal housing opportunities. Kashu Realty, owned by nisei Kazuo Inouye, also played an instrumental role in the desegregation of many white neighborhoods in South Los Angeles. Inouye, the son of Japanese immigrants, was born in Los Angeles in 1922 and grew up in ethnically mixed Boyle Heights. Like many Japanese Americans, Inouye had worked on farms and in produce markets before being incarcerated at Manzanar during World War II. To regain his freedom, he accepted a job topping sugar beets in Montana and then tried unsuccessfully to secure work with Ford Motors in

Although the real estate agency has since changed hands, the Kashu Realty sign still hangs at 3112 W. Jefferson Blvd., 2009.

Detroit. Despite having served in the highly decorated all-Japanese 442nd Regiment, Inouye repeatedly encountered employment discrimination and racial hostility. In 1947, he returned to Los Angeles to take over his brother-in-law's realty business. Propelled by his personal experiences with discrimination, Inouye made it his business to open up all-white neighborhoods to people of color. He worked with Japanese Americans and African Americans to purchase homes, often from Jewish homeowners or others who were sympathetic to racial integration. One of his first clients was a Mexican American woman, legally classified as "white," who had long endured the hostility of her neighbors and made Inouye promise to sell her home to a person of color. When he found a Japanese American buyer, a rival white real estate agent broke all the windows in the home. Inouye confronted him directly, calling himself a "kamikaze" and threatening to shoot the white real estate agent if he set foot on the property again. Through such tactics, Inouye sold a record number of homes in the Crenshaw district during the 1950s and 1960s. He advertised regularly in the Black press and facilitated the area's demographic shift from an all-white to a multiethnic African American, Japanese, and Latina/o place. Kashu Realty opened branch offices on Wilshire Boulevard and in Los Feliz and Monterey Park, where his firm performed similar feats. While these branches closed early on, the Crenshaw office remained open into the twenty-first century.

NEARBY SITES OF INTEREST

Black Power mural, *To Protect and Serve: A Moment in African American History*
3406 11th Ave., Los Angeles 90018

Noni Olabisi's stunning forty-foot mural, painted on the side of a barbershop.

Former offices of the Coalition Against Police Abuse

2824 S. Western Ave., Los Angeles 90018

Founded by activist Michael Zinzun, CAPA challenged police violence and helped broker L.A.'s historic gang truce in 1992.

FAVORITE NEIGHBORHOOD RESTAURANTS

Harold and Belle's Creole Restaurant

2920 W. Jefferson Blvd., Los Angeles 90018 (323) 735-9023 (haroldandbellesrestaurant.com)

Not cheap, but an L.A. landmark serving decadent soul food, including an excellent crawfish étouffée.

CJ's Café

5501 W. Pico Blvd., Los Angeles 90019 (323) 936-3216 (http://cjscafe.net)

An interesting and tasty mix of Mexican and soul foods.

TO LEARN MORE

Scott Kurashige, *The Shifting Grounds of Race: Black and Japanese Americans in the Making of Multiethnic Los Angeles* (Princeton University Press, 2008).

The Japanese American National Museum has an extensive oral history collection that includes an interview with Inouye. Search "Inouye" at www.inthefirstperson.com.

3.18 Los Angeles Memorial Coliseum

3939 S. Figueroa St., Los Angeles 90037 *(at W. Martin Luther King Jr. Blvd.)* (213) 747-7111 (www.lacoliseumlive.com/joomla/)

EXPOSITION PARK

For most Angelenos, the Los Angeles Memorial Coliseum is a landmark most closely

The entrance to the Los Angeles Memorial Coliseum, 2009.

associated with major sports events. Originally commissioned in 1921 as a memorial to World War I veterans, the stadium has hosted two Olympiads, two Super Bowls, and one World Series. Once home to the Rams, the Dodgers, and the Raiders, the coliseum is now home to the USC Trojan Football Team. But the coliseum has also hosted many political activities, including a much-celebrated appearance in 1990 by Nelson Mandela, who spoke to a packed crowd of more than 75,000 people to build support for the African National Congress's fight against apartheid. Also worth highlighting is the August 1972 Wattstax concert, a vibrant celebration of Black self-expression and self-respect that sought to positively empower the community to rebuild after the devastation of the 1965 uprising. Wattstax brought together more than 100,000 people and was the second-largest gathering of African Americans in U.S. history, after Dr. Martin Luther King's March on Washington. The event featured an array of African American talent such as the Staple Singers, the Bar-Kays, Albert King, Isaac Hayes, and the Dramatics. Later, the event became known as "the Black Woodstock." The event was filmed and, along with footage featuring everyday Black life in Los Angeles, was turned into a Golden Globe–nominated picture that was screened at the Cannes Film Festival and locally. However, the film never enjoyed wide theatrical release because mainstream Hollywood deemed its material too controversial. Wattstax is fondly remembered by many in the South L.A. neighborhood and has been commemorated by a collection of images and memorabilia curated by the Stax Museum of American Soul Music in Memphis, Tennessee. In fall 2007, the exhibit was on display at the California African American Museum, which is located near the coliseum in Exposition Park.

The Bar-Kays perform in the Wattstax concert at the L.A. Coliseum, 1972.

NEARBY SITE OF INTEREST

Exposition Park
700 Exposition Park Dr., Los Angeles 90037
(213) 744-7458 (www.expositionpark.org)
Features the California African American Museum (www.caamuseum.org), Rose Garden, Natural History Museum (www.nhm.org), California Science Center (www.californiascience center.org), and IMAX Theatre.

FAVORITE NEIGHBORHOOD RESTAURANT

La Taquiza
3009 S. Figueroa St., Los Angeles 90007
(213) 741-9795 (lataquizausc.com)
Vast Mexican menu, including their specialty, the *mulita*. Also try the refreshing *aguas frescas*.

TO LEARN MORE

Wattstax, a film directed by Mel Stuart (Warner Brothers, 2004).

3.19 Maywood City Hall

4319 E. Slauson Ave., Maywood 90270
(at Flora Ave.) (323) 562-5700
(www.cityofmaywood.com)
Maywood is a small residential suburb in southeastern Los Angeles that is known for its pro-immigrant politics. Once a primarily white city, the community is now 96 percent Latina/o and has declared itself a sanctuary city. Sanctuary cities are places in which local residents have decided not to enforce federal immigration laws that they consider to be unjust. Yet this approach is not a "natural" result of the city's heavily Latina/o population, but rather of a concerted political struggle, for Maywood was not always this way. In the 1990s, while al-

ready a Latina/o-majority city, but one with a white-majority city council, Maywood had instituted a series of traffic checkpoints. Ostensibly intended to identify drunk drivers, the checkpoints, in reality, were attacks on immigrants. In 1993, California had passed a law (SB 976) requiring applicants to present proof of legal U.S. residency when requesting a driver's license. As a result, unauthorized immigrants could no longer legally drive in the state. Those who were stopped at checkpoints without a license had their cars impounded, which were then held at least 30 days at $30 per day. In 2002, 1,800 cars were impounded, while only seven drunk drivers were cited, illustrating that the policy was intended to harass immigrants rather than reduce drunk driving and create safer streets.

In response to this "tax on immigrants," community members mobilized. Organizations including One Los Angeles–Industrial Areas Foundation, Comité Pro Uno, and Saint Rose of Lima Church got the city to agree to substantial policy modifications and then, joined by other organizations, gained public oversight of the police department and challenged numerous other anti-immigrant policies. Eventually, activists elected several immigrant-rights activists to the city council, changing its composition and leading Maywood to become an explicitly pro-immigrant city and ultimately a sanctuary city.

Interestingly, Maywood's pro-immigrant rights groups have faced their most intense opposition from *outside* the city. In 2006, anti-immigrant activists from Orange County, including members of Save Our State (the proud sponsors of California's Proposition 187, which denied social, educational, and health services to undocumented immigrants) and the Minutemen, came to Maywood City Hall to protest its immigrant-friendly policies and politics. Their action came on the heels of several extremely hostile legislative proposals that had been introduced in Congress, where they were being debated, especially the Sensenbrenner-King Immigration Restriction Bill (HR 4437). HR 4437's key objective was the criminalization of unauthorized immigrants and those who sought to assist them. The anti-immigrant activists' intent was to "punish" Maywood by disrupting traffic and making the city pay for extra police time (it cost the city $20,000 to $30,000 to police this action). Pro-immigrant activists from across the region responded by staging a counterdemonstration in defense of Maywood and immigrant rights. Afterward, on a white pride web site, one person commented, "I hate to say this, but I think these mestizos are going to eventually make the black civil rights riots look like a cake walk, just in their sheer numbers alone." *(Quote is from Storm-front.org, a web site promoting "White Pride World Wide": www.stormfront.org/forum/showthread.php?t=321772.)*

NEARBY SITE OF INTEREST

Maywood Riverfront Park
5000 E. Slauson Ave., Maywood 90270
(323) 562-5020
A greening project in a heavily industrial area.

TO LEARN MORE

Genevieve Carpio, Clara Irazábal, and Laura Pulido, "The Right to the Suburb: Rethinking Lefebvre and Immigrant Activism," *Journal of Urban Affairs* 33, no. 2 (2011): 185–208.

3.20 Mercado La Paloma

3655 S. Grand Ave., Los Angeles 90007 *(at W. 37th St.)* (213) 748-1963 (www.mercado lapaloma.com)

HISTORIC SOUTH CENTRAL

The Mercado La Paloma is a comprehensive community development project, market, and gathering place that opened its doors in 2000. A project of Esperanza Community Housing Corporation, the Mercado is an effort to address the area's limited avenues for economic development and its widespread poverty (South Los Angeles suffers from a 30 percent poverty rate—twice the average of Los Angeles County). The Mercado functions as an incubator for small businesses by providing subsidized rent, business training, financial consulting, and a jointly operated delivery service for restaurants. These services have enabled many immigrant

Mercado La Paloma, 2008.

entrepreneurs from local neighborhoods to successfully launch their own businesses, including arts and crafts stores, alterations, and shoe repair, in addition to restaurants. The idea is for profits to stay local so they can be reinvested in the community. The Mercado also houses a health education and information center staffed by Esperanza's health promoters, as well as the offices of numerous nonprofit organizations on its second floor. It offers community workshops and classes, such as English as a second language, computer literacy, and yoga. The building itself is a former warehouse that was refurbished, and it provides a much-needed community space in South L.A. Be sure to drop by and check out the great food and beautiful arts and crafts!

TO LEARN MORE

Esperanza Community Housing Corporation, 2337 S. Figueroa St., Los Angeles 90007 (213) 748-7285 (www.esperanzacommunity housing.org).

Strategic Actions for a Just Economy (SAJE), 152 W. 32nd St., Los Angeles 90007 (213) 745-9961 (www.saje.net). A community-based organization focused on building power among, and economic justice for, South L.A. residents.

3.21 Peace and Freedom Party, Los Angeles Chapter

2617 Hauser Blvd., Los Angeles 90016 *(between W. Adams Blvd. and Westhaven St.)* (www.peaceandfreedom.org)

WEST ADAMS

The Peace and Freedom Party (PFP) is a political party committed to socialism, democracy, environmentalism, feminism, and racial equality. It was founded on June 23, 1967, in California and was born out of the Black liberation and anti–Vietnam War movements. The first registration initiative took place at a demonstration against Lyndon Johnson in Century City. The party achieved ballot status in 14 states, including California, where it was placed on the ballot in January 1968. The PFP is composed primarily of middle-class whites and students and initially provided a vehicle through which whites could support the struggles of people of color. For example, several Black Panthers ran for office on the PFP ticket, and the Panther Party was often considered the PFP's representative in many Black communities. The party also experimented with a bicameral organizational structure that allowed for greater political autonomy for people of color. The question of how whites can best work with people of color and support antiracist organizing is a challenging one, and the PFP is one innovative solution. Over time the Party's platform has changed from its original emphases on war resistance and Black liberation to focus more on ecology and feminist issues, although always within a socialist context.

Headquarters of the Peace and Freedom Party Los Angeles, 2009.

secured few endorsements. The California party, including the Los Angeles chapter, is an exception—it still has a presence in the county. Between 1967 and 2008, the PFP nominated 10 presidential and California gubernatorial candidates. Locally, the party has enjoyed some electoral success with representatives on city councils, school boards, and special district boards throughout the state. This address on Hauser Boulevard is one of many offices that the PFP has used over the years.

Unfortunately, most PFP chapters in other states dissolved after 1968 as a result of election law changes and because they

Peace and Freedom Party rally at MacArthur Park, 1967.

NEARBY SITES OF INTEREST

Center for Land Use Interpretation

9331 Venice Blvd., Culver City 90232

(310) 839-5722 (www.clui.org)

A small museum and research center offering exhibits and educational resources about human-environment interactions and landscape form.

Museum of Jurassic Technology

9341 Venice Blvd., Culver City 90232

(310) 836-6131 (www.mjt.org)

FAVORITE NEIGHBORHOOD RESTAURANTS

Café Brasil

10831 Venice Blvd., Los Angeles 90034

(310) 837-8957 (www.cafe-brasil.com)

Culver City gem offering great lunch specials with Brazilian-style meats, *feijoada,* beans, rice, and plantains. Features a lovely outdoor patio.

Sky's Gourmet Tacos

5408 W. Pico Blvd., Los Angeles 90019

(323) 932-6253 (www.skysgourmettacos.com)

Sky's has been dishing up "Mexican food with a splash of soul" since 1992. Their shrimp taco is a perennial favorite, and they have recently introduced a vegetarian and vegan menu. Also try the sorrel lemonade.

Tender Greens

9523 Culver Blvd., Culver City 90232

(310) 842-8300 (www.tendergreensfood.com)

Organic soups, salads, and sandwiches.

TO LEARN MORE

James Elden and David Schweitzer, "New Third Party Radicalism," *Western Political Quarterly* 24, no. 4 (1971): 761–74.

3.22 Southern California Library for Social Studies and Research

6120 S. Vermont Ave., Los Angeles 90044

(between W. 61st St. and W. 62nd St.)

(323) 759-6063 (www.socallib.org)

VERMONT-SLAUSON

Truly a "people's library," the Southern California Library for Social Studies and Research moved to this address in 1969. Its roots, however, go back to 1929, when Emil Freed began collecting books, pamphlets, flyers, posters, buttons, and other ephemera from Los Angeles' social struggles. He focused on grassroots working-class groups such as the unemployed councils of the Depression era (grassroots organizations that protested mass unemployment and inadequate relief programs), the Communist Party, the Congress of Industrial Organizations, and various workers' schools. Beginning in 1952, the political landscape was transformed by McCarthyism, which suppressed not only communism but also all dissenting voices. As a result, the Los Angeles Workers' School (along with many other like-minded institutions) closed and its library collections languished. In 1962, Freed, along with several friends, began cleaning and organizing the materials, and he added them to his own collection. As other activists learned of Freed's project, they donated their materials. Freed's collection of leftist materials soon outgrew his home, and he began using friends' garages and other storage spaces throughout the city. In 1969, Freed bought this building, which had been a furniture and home appliance store before

Southern California Library for Social Studies and Research, 2008.

the Watts uprising. He negotiated a price of $35,000 for the property and began by securing $10,000 in loans and donations from friends. When Freed was unable to secure a formal bank loan for the remainder, however, a white Southern migrant—who had come to one of Freed's previous shops/storage locations in search of taped lectures by Angela Davis—donated $25,000.

The library is a vital resource for the study of Los Angeles' radical past. Among the many notable materials are the papers of the Los Angeles chapters of the Committee for the Protection of the Foreign Born, Asociación de Vendedores Ambulantes, and a full run of the *California Eagle* newspaper. In addition, the Library continues to collect materials associated with Los Angeles' contemporary social and political struggles. It hosts special events, speakers, public forums, and exhibits dedicated to unraveling power relations in Los Angeles and supporting local activists. Be sure to check out the library's renowned twice-annual sale of progressive, leftist, and rare books.

NEARBY SITE OF INTEREST

Los Angeles Black Worker Center

6569 South Vermont Ave., Los Angeles 90043
(323) 752-7287 (http://labor.ucla.edu)
A special project of UCLA's Labor Center, the Black Worker Center focuses on enhancing the employment and economic opportunities of African American workers. Located in the Paul Robeson Center.

FAVORITE NEIGHBORHOOD RESTAURANT

Barbecue King

5309 S. Vermont Ave., Los Angeles 90037
(323) 750-1064 (texasbbqking.com)
Texas-style barbecue. Try the spareribs, tri-tip, beans, potato salad, and collard greens.

3.23 Trianon Ballroom

2800 Firestone Blvd., South Gate 90280 (between Santa Fe Ave. and Long Beach Blvd.)

During the Great Depression, thousands of people were forced to flee the Dust Bowl region because of extensive drought, soil erosion, and the collapse of the agricultural economy. Three hundred and fifty thousand "Okies," as they were called, migrated to California in hopes of securing work as agricultural laborers; ninety-six thousand of them settled in Los Angeles, especially its southeastern industrial suburbs, including South Gate, Bell Gardens, and Lynwood. As John Steinbeck poignantly depicted in his classic novel *The Grapes of Wrath,* the Dust Bowlers—poor and working-class whites—experienced tremendous discrimination, rejection, and impoverished working conditions in California's fields, where they joined Mexican, African American, and Asian American laborers. They were considered such a threat that, in 1936, the Los Angeles Police Department actually sent officers to the California-Arizona state line to try to block them. According to Thomas McManus, a leader of the anti-Okie movement, "No greater invasion by the destitute has ever been recorded in the history of mankind." As a result of the widespread hostility toward them, Okies were the target of eugenics campaigns, and in 1937 California made it a crime (punishable by up to six months in prison) to assist in the transport of indigent migrants. Historian Peter La Chapelle has argued that Okies were one of the few white groups who experienced racial downward mobility: while they were initially considered white, upon their arrival in California they were so despised that they became nonwhite. However, with the onset of World War II, they migrated from rural areas in California to Los Angeles, where they found employment in the booming defense economy and were eventually able to claim whiteness and middle-class status once again.

Though the Dust Bowlers are best known for helping to build Southern California's manufacturing economy, their cultural contributions are often overlooked. Specifically, they brought with them their musical traditions, which made Los Angeles into the capital of the genre that would eventually become known as country-western music. For example, Woody Guthrie had an immensely popular radio show on KFVD, on

The former site of the Trianon Ballroom, now a vacant lot, 2010.

which he sang hillbilly songs with a sharp political edge. Defense workers organized square dances, and western swing was born in the dance halls of Southern California. The Trianon Ballroom was one such place. Located near GM South Gate, Douglas Aircraft, and the Firestone Tire and Rubber plant, the Trianon catered to industrial workers, especially women, who made up the bulk of the workforce during World War II. A 1942 survey found that dancing was the favorite leisure activity of young women in the Los Angeles area. Places like the Trianon even offered women free nylons—a precious commodity during the war.

After the war, with the return of the male population, Dust Bowlers flocked to suburbia, where they tried to blend in and shed those much-maligned Okie roots. They embraced a far more conservative ideology that privileged their whiteness over their working-class status. The Trianon closed down after that and, as of this writing, is an empty lot. *(Quotes are from Peter La Chapelle, Proud to Be an Okie.)*

NEARBY SITE OF INTEREST

South Gate Civic Center Museum
8680 California Ave., South Gate 90280
(323) 357-5838 (www.sogate.org/index.cfm
/fuseaction/detail/navid/105/cid/484/)
Open Wednesdays from 10 A.M. to 4 P.M. only.

TO LEARN MORE

Peter La Chapelle, *Proud to be an Okie: Cultural Politics, Country Music, and Migration to Southern California* (University of California Press, 2007).

3.24   USC McDonald's Olympic Swim Stadium

University of Southern California Campus, Los Angeles 90007 *(nearest intersection: W. 34th St. and McClintock Ave.)* (www .usctrojans.com/facilities/usc-swim-stadium .html)

UNIVERSITY PARK

USC McDonald's Olympic Swim Stadium was built in 1983 with a $3-million donation from the McDonald's Corporation and was used for competitive swimming and diving events during the 1984 Olympics. It was one of the first athletic facilities in Olympic history to be built entirely with private funds. However, a widely publicized agreement required that the pool be available for use by members of both the university and the community after the Olympics. McDonald's Corporation's CEO, Paul Schrag, in a *Los Angeles Times* article, explained the company's desire to be a serious partner in the Los Angeles Olympics: "The fact that McDonald's Olympic Swim Stadium will be made available to community residents makes our commitment doubly worthwhile." This was confirmed by then mayor Tom Bradley and the Los Angeles Olympic Organizing Committee. As the committee noted, "The facility proved fully satisfactory for Olympic use and will be well used by area residents and USC students for years to come."

Unfortunately, when USC completed construction of its fitness center (the Lyon Center) in 1988, it physically blocked public access to the pool. Community member Suleiman Edmondson, who regularly used the pool after running with his group, the

USC McDonald's Olympic Swim Stadium, 2009.

Trojan Master Track Program (no relation to USC), reported that he found the gate locked and access denied. In order to access the pool, a person was now required to possess a student or faculty ID and to enter through the Lyon Center. Edmondson, who was alarmed by these changes, insisted that a subsidiary agreement obligated USC to open the pool to summer use by local youth. James Dennis, then vice president of student affairs, responded that he didn't know of any subsidiary agreement. When asked about the initial agreement signed by USC and the McDonald's Corporation, both parties claimed not to have copies. In addition, USC insisted that the pool was never intended for "recreational use," as it conforms to the requirements of the International Swimming Federation for competitive use, and argued that the pool does not comply with the California Health and Safety Code and is unsuitable for recreation. While recreational and competitive swim pools are indeed different,

questions remain: Why were these issues not clarified earlier? Why did representatives claim that community members would be able to use the pool indefinitely? Why did USC not protest the media blitz, from which its community-relations image benefited greatly, when McDonald's donated the money and broke ground? Why was access suddenly denied? These questions remain unanswered.

Currently, the pool is not available for general recreational use, but it is available to organizations such as Universal Diving, the Youth Diving Club, and a water polo team. On an individual basis, people older than 15 who do not have a university ID may apply for access to the pool, but they must do so in writing, pass a swimming test, and state that they understand the pool is not for recreation but for competition and training. *(Quotes from the Los Angeles Olympic Organizing Committee, "Official Report of the Games of the XXIIIrd Olympiad Los Angeles, 1984")*

NEARBY SITE OF INTEREST

"Blacklist" Monument and Garden

Harris Hall Sculpture Park, USC Campus (behind
Fisher Art Gallery abutting Exposition Blvd.)
A moving monument honoring those artists who
were blacklisted in the McCarthy era.

FAVORITE NEIGHBORHOOD RESTAURANT

La Barca

2414 S. Vermont Ave., Los Angeles 90007
(323) 735-6567
Excellent Mexican food, affordably priced. Attracts a real cross section of South Los Angeles
residents.

4

The Harbor and South Bay

Harbor and South Bay

W Imperial Hwy
105

WESTSIDE

Vista del Mar

Artesia Blvd
405
Artesia Fwy

REDONDO
BEACH

Hawthorne Blvd

TORRANCE

Western Ave

CARSON

110

Miramar Park ▪
1

Baypoint Avenue Residential Discrimination Site ▪

LOMITA

WILMINGTON

RANCHO PALOS VERDES

Former Japanese Community
Port of Los Angeles Liberty Hill Plaza
Port of Los Angeles Administrative Building ▪
Bethlehem Steel Shipyard ▪
SAN PEDRO
Terminal Island Federal Correction Institution
White Point Preserve and Education Center ▪

ICE Prison
(closed)

4 Miles

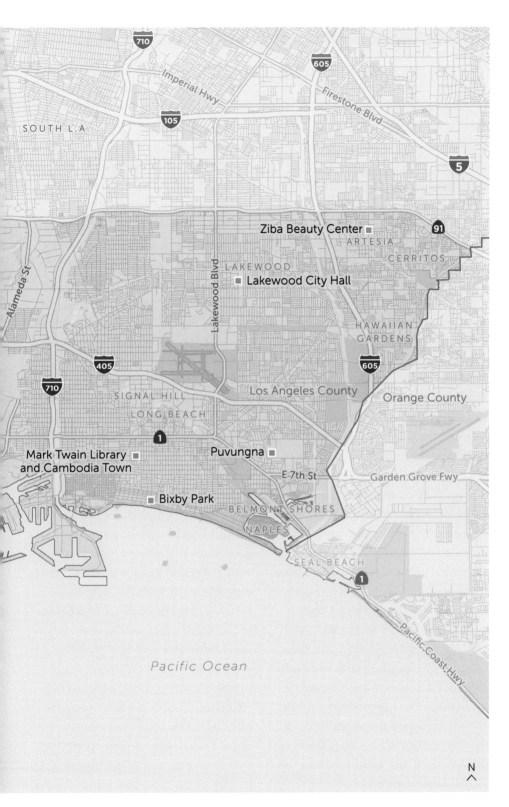

Ziba Beauty Center

ARTESIA

CERRITOS

LAKEWOOD

Lakewood City Hall

HAWAIIAN
GARDENS

SOUTH L.A.

Imperial Hwy

SIGNAL HILL

LONG BEACH

Los Angeles County

Orange County

Mark Twain Library
and Cambodia Town

Puvungna

E 7th St

Garden Grove Fwy

Bixby Park

BELMONT SHORES

NAPLES

SEAL BEACH

Pacific Ocean

Alameda St

Lakewood Blvd

Pacific Coast Hwy

N

An Introduction to the Harbor and South Bay

Although most people think of Olvera Street and the San Gabriel Mission as the birthplace of Los Angeles, the first point of European contact was actually near San Pedro. In 1542, the Portuguese sailor Juan Rodríguez Cabrillo found his way to San Pedro and dubbed it the Bay of Smokes because of the fire the locals used when hunting. The Spaniards subsequently ignored the bay for the next several centuries, during which time they established a solid foothold in the interior. California Indians had lived on the coast for centuries, and beginning in the 1830s they were joined by ethnic Mexicans. Both groups worked on ranches owned by wealthier Mexicans and Americans. Starting in the late nineteenth century, other immigrant groups, including Croatians, Slavs, Italians, and Japanese, settled in the region.

The Harbor and South Bay area has long seemed separate and removed from L.A., because of the large number of immigrant and ethnically defined peoples (who tended to stick to their own), the centrality of the maritime economy, and the geographic distance from central Los Angeles. Laura Pulido's mother, who moved to San Pedro from East L.A. as a young bride in the early 1960s, used to remark that she felt like she was moving to the edge of the world. Not all of the region was so isolated, however. Important exceptions were Long Beach, Redondo Beach, and perhaps to a lesser extent, Terminal Island. As early as 1890, these places developed into resort areas visited and inhabited by Angelenos from elsewhere in the region.

Despite its relative isolation and distinctiveness from central Los Angeles, however, the Harbor and South Bay region has long been fundamental to the entire Southern California economy. Beginning in the late nineteenth century, the coastal communities of Long Beach, Wilmington, San Pedro, and Redondo Beach developed in conjunction with early maritime industries, including fishing, canning, warehousing, sailing, cargo handling, shipbuilding, salt mining, and oil extraction. While downtown L.A. was bustling in 1900, these harbor communities were small but growing and vital to the overall development of the region. The Harbor and South Bay has been especially important because of its local infrastructure that serves all of Southern California. Redondo Beach was the region's first harbor, although it was soon eclipsed by San Pedro. Actually, Santa Monica and San Pedro vied to be the home of Los Angeles' port, and San Pedro ultimately won. This incident led to the strange shape of the city of Los Angeles: a narrow stretch of land, commonly known as the "shoestring," was deliberately annexed to connect the port to the rest of the city. The city of Long Beach, too, built a port, which is adjacent to the port of Los Angeles, and the two are called the "twin ports."

Like all of Los Angeles and Southern California, the harbor and South Bay were fundamentally transformed by World War II. Shipbuilding exploded along the harbor, as did aviation and aerospace in north Long Beach and throughout the South Bay, creating an arc of industrial plants along the coast up to the Los Angeles airport. In many ways, defense contracts constituted a massive subsidy to Southern California, and to the South Bay in particular, by the federal government. The ports are of even greater economic importance. Currently, 40 percent of U.S. imports arrive via the twin ports. These goods are then sent by train and truck to every corner of the country, with many in-between steps also handled in Southern California. Over the last couple of decades, warehousing has increasingly moved from the coast to the Inland Empire (the counties to the east of Los Angeles) in the search for cheaper land and nonunion workers. This kind of economic activity, and the growth of Asian economies—from which Los Angeles, as a gateway to the Pacific Rim, benefits enormously—has made the twin ports the busiest port complex in the United States and one of the most profitable in the world.

These economic forces have contributed to the development of a strong working-class culture in the Harbor and South Bay region. The expansion of the defense industry provided thousands of well-paying jobs for both blue-collar workers, such as assembly line workers, and the highly skilled engineers and technical workers who designed the bombs and jets that maintained U.S. military strength during the cold war. Industrial growth was accompanied by the construction of hundreds of thousands of homes for workers and their families. Many of the new neighborhoods consisted of modest, affordable homes targeted at blue-collar workers, but others were elite. Of particular note is the Palos Verdes Peninsula. Before World War II, the peninsula had been home to Japanese American farmers, but then it was transformed into an exclusive hilltop community housing legions of engineers and scientists employed in the South Bay's defense economy. This new round of residential real estate development not only led to new geographic and demographic patterns but also further stimulated the port economically. For example, all the lumber for those new houses arrived via ship and had to be unloaded by someone; dockworkers, in turn, took advantage of their centrality to the regional economy and the fixed location of the ports to organize and enhance their position. Such conditions account for the power of the International Longshore and Warehouse Union, which not only has achieved exceptionally good wages, benefits, and a powerful voice in establishing good working conditions but also routinely uses its clout (e.g., via work stoppages) to assist other workers and make political statements.

A downside to this economic powerhouse, however, is rampant pollution. The polluters here are not the small "mom-and-pop" polluting industries of the Eastside, such as metal-platers, or even of the restructured Alameda Corridor. To the contrary, this is big industry—transnational firms such as ExxonMobil, Texaco, and Northrop are here. These industries, and the infrastructure that supports them, pour massive amounts of pollution into the air, soil, and water. The ports themselves generate more than 20 percent of Southern California's diesel particulate matter. Making matters worse, there are few environmental regulations targeting ships' air emissions. Yet because of prevailing winds, the area as a whole does not appear to be as polluted as, say, unincorporated East L.A. Don't be fooled, however: petrochemical and defense production is a dirty business that is affecting the health and well-being of humans, plants, and animals.

Nowadays, the Harbor and South Bay region consists of a diverse collection of communities. The South Bay, which includes such municipalities as Manhattan Beach, Redondo Beach, and Hermosa Beach, is a solidly middle-class area that is largely white and Asian. Given the desire of so many people to live near the ocean, these communities have some of the region's most expensive real estate per square foot. As a result, many beach communities are characterized by cramped little houses and yards, as well as by a relaxed, leisurely ambience. In contrast, both San Pedro and Long Beach

are much more economically and racially diverse. In 2006, Long Beach, the second-largest city in Los Angeles County, became the most ethnically diverse city in the United States. To many, Long Beach feels like a microcosm of Los Angeles but is, some might argue, more livable. It has its upscale coastal neighborhoods, such as Belmont Shores and Naples, as well as its ghettos and barrios. To the north of Long Beach lie the cities of Gardena, Lawndale, and Compton, which morph into South Los Angeles along their northern edges. These three cities are socially integrated with the historic Black communities there. To the east of Long Beach is the community of Seal Beach and then Orange County, which for many reasons is considered culturally, politically, and demographically distinct.

Today, the Harbor and South Bay region is fully integrated with all of Southern California and the global economy. Yet the influences that have historically shaped the region continue to create a sense of distinctiveness. A visit to the Harbor and South Bay today reveals the wealth, power, and influence of global industry, the hope of working-class people and immigrants from around the world, and the degree to which the physical environment still shapes our lives.

Harbor and South Bay Sites

4.1 Baypoint Avenue Residential Discrimination Site

1571 Baypoint Ave., Wilmington 90744
(between E. Q St. and E. Proctor St.)

Private residence

House at 1571 Baypoint Ave., Wilmington, 2009.

In 1962, James and Doris McLennan, an African American couple, sought to purchase a home at this address in the Sun-Ray Estates, which was then a new housing development. Since James was a veteran, they attempted, like thousands of other veterans, to use his Veterans Administration benefits to facilitate the purchase of this home. However, when they inquired about the property, they were told the tract had no vacancies. The couple subsequently learned that half of the properties were unsold, and they attempted once again to initiate a purchase. The salesman refused and threatened to call the police.

The McLennans returned a third time with representatives from the American Civil Liberties Union and the Centinela Bay Human Relations Council, at which time the salesman accepted a deposit. However, four months later the developer, Banning Gardens, claimed that the VA had not accepted the McLennans' loan application and that the house had been sold to someone else. To find out if the property had actually been sold, a test couple attempted to purchase the same property. They made a deposit and walked away with the key. After a 35-day "dwell-in," numerous arrests, and a legal order addressed to Banning Gardens, the developer finally allowed the McLennans to open escrow on the property—a year and a half after their first bid.

Acts of residential discrimination such as this occurred with regularity throughout

Robert Martell, in an American Nazi uniform, engages in counter-picketing against members of the Congress of Racial Equality, who were opposing the California Real Estate Association's efforts to rescind the Rumford Fair Housing Act, 1963.

Southern California during the slow, painful process of integration. Desegregation depended on the persistence of people like the McLennans, as well as on legislative efforts. In 1963, state representative W. Byron Rumford, working with African American legislators, successfully introduced California State Assembly Bill 1240 (the Rumford Act), which prohibited discrimination based on race or creed in the sale or rental of real estate property in California. A year later, the California Real Estate Association, capitalizing on white homeowners' widespread opposition to integration, successfully petitioned California voters to pass Proposition 14, which nullified the Rumford Act. Ultimately, the California Supreme Court held that Proposition 14 was unconstitutional. The Rumford Act remains a landmark piece of legislation for civil rights in California, and it predated the national Fair Housing Act of 1968 by several years. *(Daniel Martinez HoSang conducted all the research for this entry.)*

NEARBY SITE OF INTEREST

Banning Park and Banning Residence Museum
401 E. M St., Wilmington 90744 (310) 548-7777 (banningmuseum.org)
A museum dedicated to Phineas Banning, the man who financed the dredging of the harbor.

TO LEARN MORE

Daniel Martinez HoSang, *Racial Propositions: Ballot Initiatives and the Making of Postwar California* (University of California Press, 2010).

4.2 Bixby Park

130 Cherry Ave., Long Beach 90802
(between E. Broadway and E. Ocean Blvd.)
(562) 570-1601 (www.longbeach.gov/park /parks_and_open_spaces/parks/bixby_park.asp)

In 1926, a Ku Klux Klan (KKK) march here at Bixby Park drew thousands of Klansmen and -women from throughout the Los Angeles region. The march testified to the growing power and popularity of the KKK in the 1920s, both nationally and locally in Southern California, as well as to the degree to which white supremacy was embedded in the lives of many working-class and middle-class white migrants to metropolitan areas like Los Angeles. For Long Beach's ordinary white residents, most of whom were recent emigrants from the Midwest, the Ku Klux Klan functioned as much as a social organization as a racist hate group because it helped them to meet new people and to sustain relationships with others who had moved to L.A. from the same town or county. In fact, Long Beach was dubbed "Iowa by the Sea" during the 1920s because of its large population of Midwest émigrés. Yet these migrants were also deeply invested in the maintenance of racial hierarchies and their white privilege in their new home. Long Beach, like many Southland cities, remained segregated through the 1960s and witnessed several intense struggles over desegregation (see entry 4.1 Baypoint Avenue Residential Discrimination Site). The Klan was one of the most powerful organizations in Long Beach, allegedly claiming prominent members of the city's police and fire departments.

Ironically, by some measures Long Beach

Bixby Park, 2009.

is now the most racially and ethnically diverse city in the country. Contemporary Bixby Park's frequent concerts, community classes, and other public events are a vibrant cultural mélange. And local historical memory tends to paint over Long Beach's exclusionary past: a large mural at the park's community center depicts Long Beach's history as an idyllic home to large numbers of Midwestern whites. Some of the scenes were painted to look like old snapshots of community picnics, including a reception for former Iowa residents; another scene features the Long Beach Municipal Band playing in 1926. The racist activity these residents engaged in, including the 1926 KKK rally, is not featured on the mural. If a mural were to be painted depicting park use today, it would include children of various ethnicities receiving free lunches and participating in summer activities, student-athletes from nationally recognized Long Beach Polytechnic High School practicing on the grassy hill just south of Ocean Boulevard, and homeless

people hard hit by the South Bay's deindustrialization seeking shelter in the band shell.

NEARBY SITES OF INTEREST

Museum of Latin American Art
628 Alamitos Ave., Long Beach 90802
(562) 437-1689 (www.molaa.com)

Long Beach Heritage Museum
653 Grand Ave., Long Beach 90814
(562) 433-4156 (http://.longbeachheritage
museum.org)

FAVORITE NEIGHBORHOOD RESTAURANTS

Café Ambrosia
1923 E. Broadway, Long Beach 90802
(562) 432-1098 (www.cafeambrosialong
beach.com)
Greek-inspired menu for breakfast, lunch, and dinner, with a focus on healthy cooking.

Café Piccolo
3222 Broadway, Long Beach 90803
(562) 438-1316 (www.cafepiccolo.com)
Italian food in an intimate setting. Dinner is a bit pricey.

Que Sera Sera

1923 E. 7th St., Long Beach 90802

(562) 599-6170

Historic lesbian bar where musician Melissa Etheridge got her start. Now a variety of acts play to a mixed crowd most nights.

4.3 Lakewood City Hall

5050 Clark Ave., Lakewood 90712

(between Hardwick St. and Del Amo Blvd.)

(562) 866-9771

The city of Lakewood has played a key role in the development of contemporary suburbia because of two innovations—one technical, one legal—that took shape here. First, Lakewood is noted for the use of pioneering assembly-line techniques in the construction of housing. In 1949, developers Louis Boyer, Mark Taper, and Ben Weingart began building tract-style housing faster, cheaper, and at a higher density than had previously been done: builders broke ground for more than 500 homes per week. Whereas previous subdivisions yielded five houses per acre, Lakewood boasted eight homes per acre. The increase in residential density (and therefore in the number of consumers) was very attractive to retailers. Consequently, plans for Lakewood included the Lakewood Shopping Center, which became the largest retail center in the United States upon its completion.

Lakewood's second, and per-

haps more significant, contribution to suburban history was a new form of municipal incorporation called the "Lakewood Plan." After World War II, new communities seemed to develop overnight in Los Angeles County (partly on account of new assembly techniques, partly because of federal home loan guarantees and VA benefits). While many of these new communities wanted to become independent cities, few could afford it. Only those with wealthy residents, such as San Marino, or those with an industrial base, such as Vernon, could provide the necessary tax base that the establishment of municipal services required. Instead, most communities were located on unincorporated county

Aerial view of Lakewood Shopping Center under construction, 1952.

land and therefore perennially vulnerable to annexation by larger cities, such as Los Angeles, Long Beach, and Pasadena, which were perceived as being corrupt and wasteful and as catering to the interests of racial minorities. In 1954, Los Angeles County allowed Lakewood to become an independent city and to contract services with the county at the same rate paid by county residents. This innovation, known as the Lakewood Plan, created a flood of incorporations by small communities. While there were various motives for incorporation, many voters and city leaders sought to exclude certain groups and activities by using tools such as zoning. As Los Angeles scholar Mike Davis has argued, "Residents of minimal cities could zone out service-demanding low-income and renting populations, eliminate (through service contracting) homegrown union or bureaucratic pressures for service expansion . . . or fiscal redistribution." As a consequence, dozens of cities were, as William Fulton describes them, "created on the cheap." The incorporation movement was further supported by the Bradley-Burns Act (1956), which allowed cities to collect a one-cent sales tax for their own use. This meant that everyone who shopped in Lakewood, for example, paid a tax that the city could use however it wished. Most cities chose to use this extra income to subsidize property taxes, which as a result were artificially low.

While the Lakewood Plan and its implementation had tremendous implications for class and racial segregation, equally important were the implications of extensive municipal incorporation for regional policy.

The Los Angeles area became a collection of dozens of cities, each controlling its own land use plans, and planners were unable to engage in meaningful regional planning for decades. This political geography has had horrendous consequences for issues such as air quality and transportation that inherently cross municipal boundaries.

TO LEARN MORE

Mike Davis, *City of Quartz: Excavating the Future in Los Angeles* (Vintage Books, 1990).

William Fulton, *The Reluctant Metropolis: The Politics of Urban Growth in Los Angeles* (Johns Hopkins University Press, 2001).

D. J. Waldie, *Holy Land: A Suburban Memoir* (W. W. Norton, 1996).

4.4 Mark Twain Library and Cambodia Town

1401 E. Anaheim St., Long Beach 90813 *(at Gundry Ave.)* (562) 570-1046 (www.lbpl.org/location/mark_twain /default.asp)

This public library holds the largest popular (nonacademic) collection of Khmer-language materials in the United States, numbering more than 3,000 volumes. The collection includes an extensive selection of children's books and folklore, as well as materials on subjects ranging from computers and cooking to history, poetry, and philosophy. The library also hosts a free Khmer-language class each Saturday. These resources serve Long Beach's large Cambodian American community, which is estimated to number around 50,000 people and constitutes the largest concentration outside of Cambodia.

Library patrons approach the entrance of Mark Twain Library, 2010.

The first Cambodians came to Long Beach in the 1950s and 1960s to attend California State University (CSU), Long Beach, as part of an exchange program between the United States and Cambodia. This initial migration created an established Cambodian community in Long Beach that subsequently attracted refugees fleeing the genocidal Khmer Rouge regime in the 1970s.

The revitalization of literature, music, and the arts holds special significance to Cambodians, since traditional arts

Long Beach residents march on Anaheim St. in the 1993 International Festival and Unity Walk, coorganized by the Cambodian Business Association and the City of Long Beach.

and culture were particular targets of the Khmer Rouge. Nearby galleries specialize in both ancient and contemporary Khmer and Khmer American art, and community organizations teach traditional Cambodian dance. CSU Long Beach hosts the Nou Hach Literary Project, which publishes fiction and essays by Cambodian writers in journal form. In recent years a number of Cambo-

dian American hip-hop artists, such as Prach Ly and Tiny Toones, have emerged in Long Beach, telling the contemporary history of Cambodian immigrants through music and dance while creating diasporic connections through their popularity in both Cambodia and the United States.

The library sits at the center of a twenty-block stretch of Anaheim Street (bounded by Junipero and Atlantic avenues) that was officially designated Cambodia Town in 2007. The several-years-long effort to name the area was spearheaded by the organization Cambodia Town, Inc., the leadership of which includes business owners like Richer San, founder of Golden Coast Bank, the first Cambodian American bank. Although about 70 percent of the restaurants and shops in the district are Cambodian owned, some locals (including a number of Cambodian Americans) opposed the designation, feeling that it might increase gang activity or exclude non-Cambodian businesses. However, community-based efforts in Cambodia Town both celebrate Cambodian culture and identity and emphasize unity among the increasingly diverse population that has made Long Beach its home in the past few decades. An annual Cambodian New Year parade runs along Anaheim Street in April, with themes such as "Cambodia Town for Diversity," "Cambodia Town for Prosperity" and, as in the photo featured here, "Unity Walk."

NEARBY SITES OF INTEREST

2nd City Council Arts and Performance Space
435 Alamitos Ave., Long Beach 90802
(562) 901-0997 (www.2ndcitycouncil.org)
A contemporary Khmer and Khmer American art gallery and performance space.

Holy Redeemer Vietnamese Church
2458 Atlantic Ave., Long Beach 90806
(562) 424-2041
A Catholic church that was crucial to the resettlement of the first wave of Vietnamese refugees in Southern California.

FAVORITE NEIGHBORHOOD RESTAURANTS

Lily Bakery and Food Express
1171 E. Anaheim St., Long Beach 90813
(562) 218-7818
Very affordable *banh mi* (sandwiches) are their specialty.

Siem Reap Restaurant
1810 E. Anaheim St., Long Beach 90813
(562) 591-7414
Popular Cambodian restaurant.

La Lune Restaurant
1458 Atlantic Ave., Long Beach 90813
(562) 599-5457
Cambodian restaurant featuring live music and karaoke on the weekends.

TO LEARN MORE

Susan Needham and Karen Quintiliani, *Cambodians in Long Beach* (Arcadia Publishing, 2008).

United Cambodian Community of Long Beach, 2201 E. Anaheim St., Suite 200, Long Beach 90804 (562) 433-2490.

Khmer Girls in Action, 1355 Redondo Ave., Suite 9, Long Beach 90804 (562) 986-9415 (www.kgalb.org). A community organization that seeks to enable young Southeast Asian women to advocate for the immediate needs of their communities and for social, political, and economic justice.

Applied Social Research Institute of Cambodia, CSU Long Beach, Dr. Leakhena Nou, executive director (562) 985-7439 (www.asricjustice.org). The institute collects survivors' stories from the Cambodian genocide.

Nou Hach Literary Project, CSU Long Beach, www.nouhachjournal.net.

4.5 Miramar Park

201 Paseo de la Playa, Torrance 90505

(between Calle Miramar and Paseo de la Concha)

The El Segundo blue butterfly, which is found nowhere in the world except the southeastern shores of the Santa Monica Bay, has been endangered for many years. Originally, the butterfly flourished along El Segundo's extensive sand dune system, but the development of the Los Angeles Airport, the Hyperion Sewage plant, the Chevron Oil Refinery, and waterfront homes decimated the dune system. To make matters worse, the dunes were planted with ice plant to prevent the sand from blowing away; the ice plant subsequently edged out the native plant population, which was essential habitat for the butterfly. Consequently, the El Segundo blue was listed as an endangered species in 1976. By 1988, the butterfly's habitat had been reduced to only three places. In 2004, a group of conservationists began tearing out the ice plant in Torrance and Redondo Beach and replacing it with native plants such as buckwheat and deer weed. Amazingly, by the summer of 2007 the butterfly had made a comeback. It is now

thought that tens of thousands exist—still a relatively small population, but a remarkable achievement—and you can see them at this site.

Three hundred and nine species (130 animal, 179 plant) are currently listed as threatened or endangered in California, which is the largest number of any state in the continental United States. The single most important reason for species endangerment is habitat loss, which, in the case of Southern California, is a result of urban and suburban development. When a species is identified as threatened or endangered, a recovery plan is developed; however, the vast majority of actually threatened and endangered

Native California plants bloom along the Esplanade between Torrance and Redondo beaches, 2008.

species are never listed because of intense political pressure, primarily from developers and large landowners. Even with recovery plans, however, relatively few species make a comeback.

Given this context, the El Segundo blue butterfly's resurgence is an especially important success story that was made possible by the vision and commitment of two organizations: the Urban Wildlands Group and the Los Angeles Conservation Corps' Science, Education and Adventure Lab. When you visit, be sure to take a walk along the Esplanade, which features informational signs about native wildlife.

FAVORITE NEIGHBORHOOD RESTAURANTS

Happy Veggie

709 N. Pacific Coast Hwy., Redondo Beach 90277 (310) 379-5035 (happyveggie.com) The vegetarian *pho,* spring rolls, and "chicken" curry are among the favorites.

Addi's Tandoor

800 Torrance Blvd., Suite 101, Redondo Beach 90277 (310) 540-1616 (www. addistandoor.com) This popular Indian restaurant boasts generous servings. Reservations recommended.

King's Hawaiian Bakery and Restaurant

2808 W. Sepulveda Blvd., Torrance 90505 (310) 530-0050 (www.kingshawaiianrestaurants .com) Traditional Hawaiian plate lunch.

Ichimiann Bamboo Garden

1618 Cravens Ave., Torrance 90510 (310) 328-1323 (www.ichimiann.com) Reasonably priced *soba* and *udon.* Buckwheat noodles handmade in their kitchens daily. Try their popular shrimp tempura bowl with hot *soba* or *udon.*

TO LEARN MORE

Visit the web site of the Urban Wildlands Group, www.urbanwildlands.org.

4.6 Port of Los Angeles and Liberty Hill

Port of Los Angeles Administrative Building 425 S. Palos Verdes St., San Pedro 90731 *(at W. 5th St.)* (310) 732-7678 (www .portoflosangeles.org)

Port of Los Angeles Liberty Hill Plaza 100 W. 5th St., San Pedro 90731 *(at Harbor Blvd.)*

From the first moment of U.S. conquest, the San Pedro Bay has been continually subject to major alterations, especially dredging, in order to meet the needs of a rapidly indus-

Liberty Hill Plaza, 2009. A California Historical Landmark plaque adjacent to the parking lot commemorates the 1923 Industrial Workers of the World strike.

trializing capitalist economy. Today, the Port of Los Angeles is the largest container port in the United States. It covers 7,500 acres and features 270 berths and 25 major cargo terminals. In 2008, the port handled 170 million metric tons of cargo worth approximately $244 billion. Currently, the U.S. Army Corps of Engineers is engaged in a $253-million program to deepen the port's channels from 45 feet to 53 feet in order to accommodate the increasing size of cargo ships that ply the Pacific Ocean. This investment will allow Los Angeles to accept even more global trade, much of it generated through free trade agreements with Mexico, Central America, and South America.

There are several reasons why the twin ports of Los Angeles and Long Beach are so massive. First, they are the points of entry to a vast consumer market. Ninety-five percent of all U.S. imports arrive via ships bringing consumer goods to local and national consumers; Southern California alone is home to more than 13 million people, who buy a lot of stuff. Second, Los Angeles is the leading manufacturing county in the United States, and while many of its products are domestically consumed, many are also exported. And third, the Pacific Coast is the easiest point of access for key Asian trading partners, such as China and Japan. Consequently, the port is absolutely crucial to the flow of goods coming into and out of the region and the country as a whole.

Although all ports are becoming increasingly mechanized, people built them and continue to operate them. The twin ports at Los Angeles and Long Beach supply more than 1 million jobs in California, and the waterfront is populated by a diversity of workers. One of the most important groups is the longshoreworkers (they are no longer called *longshoremen,* in recognition of the fact that women are now, following a hard-fought battle, represented among their ranks). Longshoring, which involves the loading and unloading of cargo ships, is an ancient profession that was long marked by intense teamwork and camaraderie, but also by dangerous working conditions, unpredictable and intermittent work schedules, and low wages. To address these conditions and secure better wages for their families, longshore workers across the United States organized and eventually developed, under the leadership of Harry Bridges (an alleged communist), into the powerful International Longshore and Warehouse Union (ILWU).

Unionization was a brutal fight, and Liberty Hill marks a key battle in the war to extend and protect the freedoms of speech and assembly upon which collective action relies. During the late 1910s and early 1920s, the Marine Transport Workers Industrial Union 510, an affiliate of the Industrial Workers of the World (IWW), or "Wobblies," was attempting to organize the workers. The IWW was a radical labor organization that believed in worker solidarity regardless of race and employed forceful organizing tactics, including direct action and civil disobedience. Their work was particularly difficult in Los Angeles' notorious open-shop climate. San Pedro shippers and police were fiercely opposed to the unionization of sailors and longshoremen, and they used

PICKET DUTY MAY 15, 1934

THE BIRTH OF THE ILWU IN LOS ANGELES HARBOR . . . . . .

STOCKADE AND SHIP USED AS LIVING QUARTERS AND BARRACKS FOR GUARDS AND FINKS

FINKS UNLOADING GRACE LINE SHIP.

BERTH 145

THE LONGSHOREMEN, OUTNUMBERED BY THE POLICE, GUARDS AND FINKS, FOUGHT FOR THEIR JOBS AND THE RIGHT TO ORGANIZE.

DRAWING BASED ON EYE WITNESS REPORTS. PODUE LOCAL 63

Drawing of strikers trying to evict scab workers on May 15, 1934, Berth 145, Wilmington. The year 1934 saw violence along the entire West Coast, which eventually resulted in the birth of the ILWU. Because the Wilmington confrontation took place at night, no photos were taken. This partly explains why the San Francisco struggle is better known. Illustration by Nick Podue (n.d.) based on eyewitness accounts. Many thanks to Art Almeida for bringing this image to our attention and helping interpret it.

a wide variety of tactics to prevent workers from organizing and gaining more power. For example, local authorities outlawed all street meetings in San Pedro, the American Legion formed a "military branch" in 1919 to help "drive the reds out," efforts were made to blacklist activist workers, and California passed the dreaded Criminal Syndicalism Act (which outlawed a whole host of organizing activities) in 1919. Los Angeles chief of police Louis Oaks declared that "any attempt by IWW members or sympathizers to start street meetings or demonstrations

of any sort [would] be dealt with immediately."

It was in this context that novelist and political activist Upton Sinclair sought to support the workers (see entry 2.22 Upton Sinclair's House). On May 15, 1923, the Wobblies at San Pedro and San Francisco harbors went on strike to demand higher wages, better working conditions, and the repeal of the Criminal Syndicalism Act. Since the IWW was banned from holding street meetings on public land in San Pedro, Minnie Davis, a local resident, offered the use of her property on Liberty Hill, and Sinclair and others convened there. Protesting California's unconstitutional restrictions on freedom of speech and assembly, they read foundational U.S. texts such as the Bill of Rights to a crowd of 3,000 people. Sinclair and IWW leaders were promptly arrested by the LAPD and charged with criminal syndicalism. From the Wobblies' perspective, the arrests were a victory. In fact, they were hoping to get arrested, and refused to testify on their own behalf. Their goal was to flood the jails with workers arrested merely for exercising their First Amendment rights, in this way creating overcrowding, which would attract media attention while at the same time mocking the state's efforts to limit free speech. Sinclair and most of the IWW leaders were released after four days, but some were subsequently sentenced to prison at San Quentin on charges of violating the Criminal Syndicalism Act, which was not repealed until 1968.

Ultimately, the strike fizzled and the charges against Sinclair were dropped. However, the Liberty Hill incident signaled the rebirth of the Los Angeles labor movement, led to the formation of the Southern California chapter of the American Civil Liberties Union, and laid the foundation for the subsequent organizing successes of the International Longshoremen's Association (ILA). The ILA was the predecessor of the ILWU on the West Coast. One of the ILWU's most important gains, in addition to good wages, benefits, and safer working conditions, was worker control of the hiring hall, which was previously controlled by the employers.

PERSONAL REFLECTION BY LOUIS PULIDO, RETIRED ILWU MEMBER

The things that stand out in my mind about my 51-year career in the ILWU are many. I reflect on the financial benefits of having such a high-paying job, the tremendous health benefits, and the generous pension benefits and medical coverage after I retired. I reflect on the fact that I was afforded the opportunity to advance from the lowest rung of the ladder, a basic longshoreman, working in the hold of the ship, to the highest rung, becoming a forklift operator, a gantry crane driver, a hatch boss, and finally a ship boss. I cannot emphasize enough the profound effect my membership in the ILWU has had on my life!

Liberty Hill is now registered as California Historic Landmark no. 1021. The name was adopted by the Liberty Hill Foundation, an organization inspired by Sinclair's act, which provides funding and support for social-change organizations throughout the county. *(All quotes are from Martin Zanger, "Politics of Confrontation: Upton Sinclair and the Launching of the ACLU in Southern California," Pacific Historical Review 38, no. 4 [1969]: 383–406.)*

NEARBY SITES OF INTEREST

Harry Bridges Institute for International Education and Organization
350 W. 5th St., Suite 209, San Pedro 90731 (310) 831-2397 (www.harrybridges.com)

Los Angeles Maritime Museum
Berth 84, 6th St. and Harbor Blvd., San Pedro 90731 (310) 548-7618 (www.lamaritime museum.org)

Former site of Yuri Kochiyama's childhood home
879 W. 11th St., San Pedro 90731
Private residence
Kochiyama is a Japanese American human-rights activist who works across racial lines.

FAVORITE NEIGHBORHOOD RESTAURANTS

San Pedro Fish Market and Restaurant
Ports O' Call Marketplace, Berth 78,
1190 Nagoya Way, San Pedro 90731
(310) 832-4251 (www.sanpedrofishmarket.com)
Always packed. Try one of their famous shrimp trays with a large slab of garlic bread. Affordable.

Ante's
729 S. Ante Perkov Way, San Pedro 90731
(310) 832-5375 (www.antesrestaurant.com)
A San Pedro fixture since 1945, specializing in Croatian food. On the pricey side.

TO LEARN MORE

Harvey Schwartz, *Solidarity Stories: An Oral History of the ILWU* (University of Washington Press, 2009).
For more on the ILWU, visit its web site, www.ilwu.org.
On local free-speech struggles, see Judy Branfman's documentary, *The Land of Orange Groves and Jails,* or the edited volume of the same name by Lauren Coodley.

4.7 Puvungna

1250 Bellflower Blvd., Long Beach 90840
Directions: From E. State University Dr., enter campus on Earl Warren Dr. and park in the first lot on the left. Walk north from the parking lot.
Puvungna was a Tongva Indian village and burial ground located on land now occupied by California State University, Long Beach. It is a spiritual center for the Tongva, for not only was it the birthplace of Chungichnish, their god and lawgiver, but it was also Chungichnish's place of instruction. In 1972, campus workers uncovered the burial ground, which was then listed on the National Register of Historic Places along with two adjacent sites. Twenty years later, however, university officials developed plans for a strip mall to be built on the site. Local Indians, aided by students and community members, organized, held prayer vigils, and peaceably occupied the area. University officials ordered the Indians to leave. Over the next decade, a battle was waged in the courts in which the ACLU joined forces with the Tongva. During the campaign, the CSULB Board of Trustees refused to commit to the preservation of the site, calling into

Ceremonial objects at Puvungna, 2007.

question the ancestry and beliefs of well-known Indian leaders and denying the site's sanctity, despite a sign previously placed there by the university itself reading: "Gabrielino [sic] Indians once inhabited this site, Puvungna, birthplace of Chungichnish, lawgiver and god." In 1998, CSULB's president, Robert Maxon, abandoned the development plans, and in 2006 a new university president, F. King Alexander, was appointed who has said that he would continue to protect the site. As of this writing, the Tongva continue to have access to and carry out ceremonies on the site, but they are also ever wary of development pressures.

NEARBY SITES OF INTEREST

Earl Burns Miller Japanese Garden

On the California State University, Long Beach, campus, 1250 Bellflower Blvd., Long Beach 90840 (562) 985-8420 (www.csulb.edu /~jgarden/)

Bolsa Chica Wetlands

3842 Warner Ave., Huntington Beach 92649 (714) 846-1114 (http://bolsachica.org) A bit of a drive from Puvungna (6½ miles), but well worth a visit.

Belmont Shore

E. 2nd St., Long Beach 90803 (between Pacific Coast Highway and Livingston Drive) Relaxing beach community with charming shops, eateries, and coffee shops.

Long Beach Aquarium of the Pacific

100 Aquarium Wy., Long Beach 90802 (562) 590-3100 (www.aquariumofpacific.org) A great place for the whole family. Lots of hands-on activities for kids.

Urban Ocean Boat Cruise

(562) 590-3100, ext. 0 (www.aquariumofpacific .org/education/programdetails/urban_ocean _cruise/)

This 2½-hour excursion focuses on the environmental impact of the port on the ocean. Reservations are required and can be made through the Aquarium of the Pacific.

FAVORITE NEIGHBORHOOD RESTAURANTS

George's Greek Café

135 Pine Ave., Long Beach 90802 (562) 437-1184 (www.georgesgreekcafe.com) Popular family-owned and -operated restaurant. Try their signature lamb chops and Greek salads.

Open Sesame Mediterranean Grill

5215 E. 2nd St., Long Beach 90803 (562) 621-1698 (www.opensesamegrill.com) Lebanese cuisine. Almost always a wait, but well worth it. Fried potatoes with garlic sauce are a favorite appetizer. The hummus is also excellent.

4.8 Terminal Island

Immigration and Customs Enforcement prison (now closed) 2001 S. Seaside Ave., San Pedro 90731 *(nearest cross street: Wharf St.)*

Terminal Island Federal Correction Institution 1299 S. Seaside Ave., San Pedro 90731 *(nearest cross street: Wharf St.)*

Former Japanese community Tuna St. *(between Terminal Wy. and Fish Harbor)*

Bethlehem Steel Shipyard Berth 240, approximately 220 S. Seaside Ave. *(just north of the federal prison, near Wharf St.)*

Terminal Island is a largely human-made landmass and a central part of the harbor area's geography, landscape, and history. Known previously as Isla Raza Buena Gente,

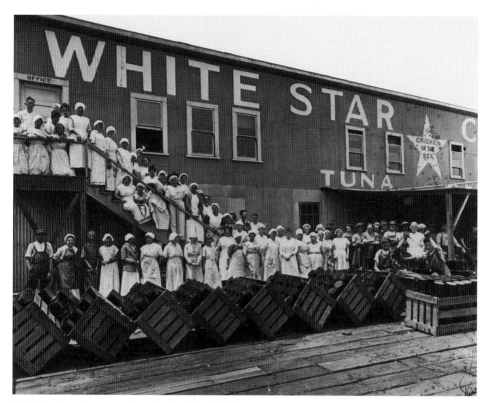

White Star Tuna Cannery workers, Terminal Island, 1945.

and then as Rattlesnake Island, it was re-named Terminal Island in 1891 because it was expected to become the terminus for a rail system linking the nation's interior via the Los Angeles and Salt Lake Railroad (this plan fell through). Originally, this strip of sediment in the estuary of the Los Angeles River attracted many elites, who built homes on the island's Brighton Beach. However, its resort character did not last, as city leaders realized the island's potential for industrial and infrastructure development.

The cities of Long Beach, San Pedro, and Los Angeles fought for ownership of Terminal Island—all with grand visions of constructing a port there. The City of L.A.

Road sign on Terminal Island, 2009.

prevailed, annexing Terminal Island (as well as Wilmington and San Pedro) in 1909 and creating the city's notable "shoestring," a narrow swath of the Alameda Corridor that connects central Los Angeles to the harbor. Almost immediately thereafter, designs for infrastructure development began. Since the region lacked a natural deep harbor, the Santa Monica Bay had been initially targeted for the creation of an artificial one. However, local entrepreneur Phineas Banning, who is often

Cannery St., with cargo cranes in the background, 2009.

called the "Father of the Harbor," successfully lobbied Congress for money to dredge the channel from the ocean to Wilmington, the town he had established, where he also owned a transport and shipping company that would profit directly from the dredging. The first dredging occurred in 1916 and allowed ships to dock along what is now the port's main channel. The island grew in size as dredge spoils were used for landfill, and it changed from a resort to an industrial area, as fisheries, canneries, and even a Ford auto plant sprouted next to shipping and transport businesses.

Needless to say, the elites abandoned their mansions and Terminal Island was quickly transformed into a multiethnic, working-class place. Most of the workers were Japanese, Pilipina/o, and Mexican. During the Great Depression, they were joined by whites. The Japanese, in particular, established a toehold in the area's fishing industry.

In fact, before World War II, Terminal Island was home to one of the largest Japanese American settlements in Southern California. Japanese Americans called the community East San Pedro or "Fish Harbor." As many as 3,000 people lived there and created an array of ethnic businesses and social institutions. Within just 48 hours of the Japanese attack on Pearl Harbor, however, the Japanese community at Terminal Island was forcibly disbanded because of its proximity to the island's vast concentration of national defense and economic activities. The majority of nikkei ultimately went to Manzanar Internment Camp in the Owens Valley, and none resettled on Terminal Island. However, in 1974, survivors and their children formed the Terminal Islanders Club, and in July 2002 a memorial was dedicated to the Japanese American community that had once lived there.

Evacuated of "enemy aliens," Terminal

Island became a hub of national defense activity during and after WWII. Japanese American homes were razed, and the settlement was converted into a naval training center called Roosevelt Base. The seaplane ramp at Reeves Field became the primary operating base for seaplanes assigned to the Pacific Fleet. Terminal Island was also the site of many other wartime activities, especially ship and airplane production. The military aircraft produced at nearby plants such as Lockheed, Douglas, and Vulty were shipped to Terminal Island, where they were equipped and flight tested. More than 90,000 workers were employed in the shipbuilding industry by such companies as Bethlehem Steel, which had a shipyard on the island.

Terminal Island is also part of the prison-industrial complex. Although the island is only 4.4 square miles, it houses two federal prisons: the Federal Correctional Institution–Terminal Island, which is a low-security prison for men; and an immigration detention center. In 1938, the San Pedro Processing Facility was established to process incoming immigrants. During the 1980s, in keeping with the larger trend of criminalization that began in that decade, it became an immigration detention center, where immigrants awaiting resolution of their cases were held. Horrific conditions and inmate neglect were frequently reported, and between 2004 and 2007 more than 70 people died while awaiting sentencing or deportation.

One of the most widely publicized cases was that of Victoria Arellano, an undocumented Mexican immigrant who was HIV-positive and transgendered. Arellano died in July 2007 because Immigration and Customs Enforcement (ICE) officials refused to administer her HIV medications. In the face of such blatant disregard by the state, her fellow inmates cared for her and even went on strike to demand that she be taken to a hospital, but they were ignored until it was too late. After her death and associated media attention, ICE abruptly closed the prison and transferred 400 prisoners to Texas and other states, without even telling the attorneys of many of the prisoners. Although the facility lost its accreditation from the American Correctional Association in August 2007, officials said the closure was unrelated to Arellano's death and the result only of "maintenance needs," which would take approximately one month to complete. As of this writing, the facility has not reopened.

NEARBY SITES OF INTEREST

Drum Barracks Civil War Museum
1052 Banning Blvd., Wilmington 90744
(310) 548-7509

San Pedro Bay Historical Archives
638 S. Beacon St., Room 626, San Pedro 90731
(310) 548-3208
Be sure to check hours in advance.

FAVORITE NEIGHBORHOOD RESTAURANTS

Los Tres Cochinitos
803 W. Pacific Coast Hwy., Wilmington 90744
(310) 549-0921
Inexpensive and tasty Mexican food. Also serves burgers.

Isaac's Café
632 N. Fries Ave., Wilmington 90744
(310) 830-4933

This family-owned and -operated restaurant is known for its carne asada burritos.

TO LEARN MORE

The Lost Village of Terminal Island, video available from www.terminalisland.org.

Detailed map of Nikkei Terminal Island, available from Japantown Atlas, japantownatlas.com /map-terminal.html.

The Japanese American National Museum's collection of oral histories conducted with former residents of Terminal Island can be accessed at http://content.cdlib.org /view?docId=kt367n993t.

4.9 White Point Preserve and Education Center

1600 W. Paseo del Mar, San Pedro 90731
(between Western Ave. and Weymouth Ave.)
(310) 541-7613 (www.pvplc.org)

From the late 1940s to the early 1970s, millions of pounds of dichlorodiphenyltrichloroethane (commonly known as DDT) and polychlorinated biphenyls (PCBs) were discharged into the ocean off the coast of Southern California. Most of the DDT originated from the Montrose Chemical Corporation's manufacturing plant in Torrance and was discharged into the Los Angeles County Sanitation District's wastewater collection system, which emptied at White Point, in a submarine area known as the Palos Verdes Shelf. Montrose also dumped DDT-contaminated waste into the ocean near Santa Catalina Island. According to the U.S. Geological Survey, in the early 1990s an estimated 100 tons of DDT was found over a 17-square-mile area 200 feet below the ocean surface. The area is now a Superfund site. The highest concentrations of DDT and PCBs were discovered near the mouth of the

White Point Preserve and Education Center, 2008.

White Point wastewater outfall, although the pollutants extend from the Palos Verdes Shelf into Santa Monica Bay.

DDT was banned in 1972, thanks to the efforts of the United Farm Workers and the Environmental Defense Fund, because it is a carcinogen with great longevity. Not surprisingly, 30 years after DDT was banned it continues to affect Southern California wildlife. Local eagles have yet to recover their reproductive ability, because DDT enters the food chain and causes weakened eggshells. Likewise, it continues to accumulate in women's breast milk. It was not until 1990 that the U.S. government and the State of California filed a lawsuit against Montrose Chemical Corporation under the federal Superfund law. Montrose agreed to a consent decree on March 15, 2001, to settle the lawsuit. The Montrose Settlements Restoration Program focuses on "capping" the sediment, but there is doubt outside the EPA whether this solution will actually work.

White Point has a long history in the area as a popular beach, a military site (it contained gun placements in World War II and later a Nike Missile facility), and most recently, a nature preserve. But don't let the beautiful coastline fool you. In 2011, health authorities warned that certain fish species caught between Santa Monica and Seal Beach—white croaker, barracuda, topsmelt, black croaker, and barred sand bass—were toxic and should not be eaten.

NEARBY SITES OF INTEREST

Cabrillo Beach and Marine Aquarium
3720 Stephen M. White Dr., San Pedro 90731 (310) 548-7562 (www.cabrillomarineaquarium .org)

Point Fermin Lighthouse
807 W. Paseo Del Mar, San Pedro 90731 (310) 241-0684 (www.pointferminlighthouse.org)

Wayfarers Chapel
5755 Palos Verdes Dr. South, Rancho Palos Verdes 90275 (310) 377-1650 (www.wayfarers chapel.org)
A beautiful chapel and gardens.

TO LEARN MORE

For more on the Palos Verdes Shelf Superfund site, visit the Environmental Protection Agency's web site: yosemite.epa.gov/r9/sfund /r9sfdocw.nsf/vwsoalphabetic?openview.

For more on the clean-up efforts, go to the Montrose Settlements Restoration Program web site, www.darrp.noaa.gov/southwest /montrose/msrphome.html.

4.10 Ziba Beauty Center

17832 Pioneer Blvd., Artesia 90701 *(between 178th St. and Ashworth St.)* (562) 402-5131 (www.zibabeauty.com)

Ziba Beauty Center is the site of an ongoing labor struggle involving primarily South Asian immigrant women. Ziba operates 13 salons throughout Southern California and is headquartered in Artesia. It specializes in "Eastern beauty," by offering such services as threading (a form of hair removal) and *mehndi* (temporary henna tattoos). Ziba has "styled" such celebrities as Salma Hayek, Paula Abdul, Gwen Stefani, and Madonna. The company lists "trust" and "empower-

Ziba Beauty Center, 2010.

ment" among its core values, but numerous workers have alleged unfair working conditions. There are two sets of complaints. First, Ziba previously required employees to sign a noncompetition agreement stating that they would treat henna application and threading as proprietary secrets (despite the fact that both are centuries-old cultural practices). Second, workers charged that Ziba did not provide sufficient overtime pay and breaks. Some of the workers testified that they were paid a flat rate of $50 for a workday lasting 8 to 11 hours.

In January 2008, five workers were fired for refusing to sign the noncompetition agreement. Working in conjunction with the South Asian Network (SAN), the workers staged a public protest in front of Ziba's headquarters and eventually filed a class-action lawsuit based on the other alleged violations. Ziba has since rescinded the noncompetition agreement. In March 2010, the Los Angeles Superior Court ruled

that all workers who had been employed at Ziba since 2004 could be part of the lawsuit. Lawyers anticipate that they will represent anywhere from 150 to 200 workers. An attorney for Ziba's CEO in an article in the *Los Angeles Times* declared, "There is absolutely no merit in the lawsuit against Ziba."

Ziba is just one business among many in the Artesia area that centers on South Asians and their culture. California has long had South Asian residents, such as Punjabi farmworkers in the early twentieth century, but most of the state's South Asian immigrants are relatively recent, having arrived after the overhaul of U.S. immigration policy in 1965. Starting in the 1980s, Artesia began to emerge as a "Little India." In 1990, SAN was formed to defend the political, labor, and human rights of South Asians, but the organization has also targeted domestic violence in the South Asian community and has sought to build solidarity with other immigrant communities and communities of color.

Currently, SAN is organizing both Latina/o and South Asian workers along Pioneer Boulevard and attempting to establish the Los Angeles Taxi Workers Alliance.

NEARBY SITES OF INTEREST

South Asian Network

18173 Pioneer Blvd., Suite I, 2nd floor, Artesia 90701 (562) 403-0488 (www.southasian network.org)

Cerritos Center for the Performing Arts

12700 Center Court Dr., Cerritos 90703 (562) 916-8501 (www.cerritoscenter.com)

TO LEARN MORE

For more on Ziba's labor practices, see http://zibabeauty.blogspot.com.

For more on South Asians in Southern California, see South Asian Network, www.southasian network.org, and Satrang, an organization supporting queer South Asians, www.satrang.org.

Prema Kurien, "Constructing 'Indianness' in Southern California: The Role of Hindu and Muslim Indian Immigrants," in *Asian and Latino Immigrants in a Restructuring Economy: The Metamorphosis of Southern California,* ed. M. López-Garza and D. Díaz (Stanford University Press, 2001), pp. 289–312.

The West-side

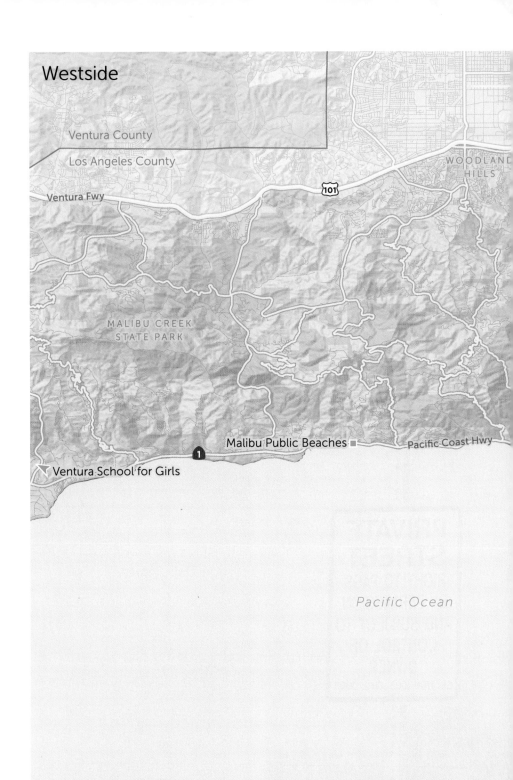

Westside

Ventura County

Los Angeles County

Ventura Fwy

101

WOODLAND HILLS

MALIBU CREEK STATE PARK

Malibu Public Beaches ■

Pacific Coast Hwy

1

Ventura School for Girls

Pacific Ocean

4 Miles

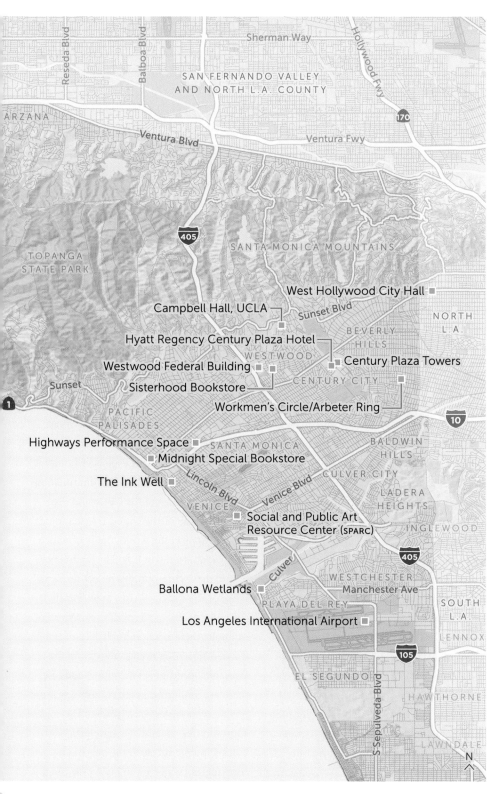

West Hollywood City Hall

Campbell Hall, UCLA

Sunset Blvd

Hyatt Regency Century Plaza Hotel

Century Plaza Towers

Westwood Federal Building

Sisterhood Bookstore

Workmen's Circle/Arbeter Ring

Highways Performance Space

Midnight Special Bookstore

The Ink Well

Social and Public Art
Resource Center (SPARC)

Ballona Wetlands

Manchester Ave

Los Angeles International Airport

An Introduction to the Westside

Breathtakingly beautiful beaches, sunny skies, and young, tanned bodies glistening on the sand. These are the iconic images of Los Angeles broadcast to the world everyday by films, television shows, and other media. They represent the mythic "California Dream" of fantastic year-round weather and the leisurely good life. Southern California's boosters have promoted the California Dream for more than a century, attracting migrants with expectations of fame, fortune, good health, and recreation in the California sunshine. As a result, such images, along with everyday celebrity encounters, are what many people associate with and expect from Los Angeles. And, in fact, such landscapes do exist, but in a limited set of places—especially the Westside—where many of the county's wealthiest and most prestigious residential communities, as well as its glorious beaches, are located. Yet popular representations of the landscapes associated with the California Dream err on three counts. First, they obscure the Westside's significant *internal* diversity, including its historic Black and Latina/o neighborhoods, working-class communities, and pockets of poverty. Second, by suggesting that all of L.A. is like the Westside, they obscure the larger reality of life in L.A. for the vast majority of the city's residents. Finally, such imagery elides the fact that the processes creating the California Dream have too often rested on rampant exploitation and overdevelopment of the natural environment, as well as on the exclusion of social "undesirables."

The majority of Los Angeles' wealthiest residential communities are located on the Westside. While Malibu, Pacific Palisades, and Santa Monica line much of Los Angeles' 27 miles of coastline, Brentwood, Beverly Hills, and Bel-Air are located slightly more inland. These communities are known by name to tourists and consumers of popular media throughout the country and the world, through, for example, television shows such as *Beverly Hills, 90210* and media coverage of the O. J. Simpson case. These neighborhoods also have some of the United States' most expensive homes, which are owned or leased by multimillion-aires, celebrities, and the CEOs and managers of some of the largest transnational corporations in the world, many of which are headquartered in L.A. The landscapes within these communities reflect residents' sense of their social status, as well as their desire for privacy and social exclusivity. For example, there is a noticeable lack of public transportation, or even sidewalks, in the Westside's prestigious neighborhoods, but there are numerous gated communities and private security forces. Several of the coastal communities, meanwhile, have effectively blocked public access to the beaches by constructing wall-to-wall luxury housing, illegally blocking access points, and posting false "no parking" signs. It is not that poor and working-class people do not inhabit these spaces—there is a veritable army of housecleaners, cooks, gardeners, and nannies, most of them Latina/o, who either live in these homes or travel to them daily for low-wage domestic work—but the social boundaries between them and their wealthy employers are structured into the landscape itself and felt by "outsiders" of all stripes.

Meanwhile, in the Westside's flatlands, far away from its hillside communities, is a far more diverse range of neighborhoods. Some of L.A.'s oldest African American communities—such as the concentration near the Santa Monica Civic Auditorium that was displaced by freeway and infrastructure construction, or the Oak Park neighborhood of Venice, which still exists—are located in the Westside. In Venice, Mar Vista, and parts of Santa Monica, large populations of renters and workers enjoy highly walkable communities with a generally well-run public transportation system and affordable housing—thanks to some of the most tenant-friendly rent control laws in the country. Collectively, these neighborhoods also constitute a veritable cradle for the arts, intellectualism, and a progressive counterculture. As students, artists, and intellectuals have met in these spaces, progressive ideas have flourished, leading to movements for rent control, gay rights, sanctuary for the homeless, and environmental protection, as well as multiracial political alliances. Many of the Westside's landscapes reflect its progressive, creative

vibe: cozy cafes peopled with students and writers; independent bookstores selling rare texts; and theaters and performance spaces featuring avant-garde artists who push the boundaries of creative expression. The Westside is also home to a sizeable Jewish community. Many Jewish Angelenos moved here from the Eastside or from occupied Europe during the 1940s and 1950s, especially as residential restrictions against Jews (though not necessarily other groups) in Los Angeles began to ease up in the aftermath of World War II. The Westside's Jewish community was instrumental in the election of Tom Bradley, Los Angeles' first African American mayor, in 1973, as part of a "rainbow coalition." Given this eclectic array of landscapes, the Westside is simultaneously a wealthy, exclusive, and socially progressive place, where a high value is placed on the social and environmental quality of life, and where the question of who shall have access to that lifestyle, and on what terms, is struggled over daily.

Pursuit of the California Dream has come with a hefty price tag: rampant environmental degradation. As millions of people have sought access to the Westside's beautiful landscapes, hyperdevelopment has endangered numerous plant and animal species—some of which are found nowhere else in the world—leading many to the brink of extinction and, ironically, threatening to destroy the same factors that have attracted so many people in the first place. In response, many environmental groups have emerged in the Westside that focus on restoration of the area's unique coastal habitat. There is an increasing number of preserves and natural areas scattered throughout the region. An equally vibrant movement focuses on opening up the Westside's beaches to public use by Angelenos from throughout the metropolitan region. In sum, the Westside is a more diverse, complex, and interesting place than popular media images would suggest.

We have chosen to label this part of the city "the Westside" because that is what most locals call the area. The cognitive map associated with the Westside is well established, reflecting the sense among both Westside residents and those who inhabit other parts of the city that the Westside is a "place apart"—a spatially and culturally distinctive part of Los Angeles.

Westside Sites

5.1 Ballona Wetlands

Entrance to saltwater marsh and dunes, 303 Culver Blvd., Los Angeles 90293 *(at Pershing Dr.; enter the marsh from the far corner of the parking lot for Gordon's Market)* PLAYA DEL REY

Entrance to freshwater dunes, northwest corner of W. Jefferson Blvd. and Lincoln Blvd., Los Angeles 90094 PLAYA VISTA

Wetlands are the land where the ocean's salt water and the land's freshwater meet. The result is an incredibly rich environment that provides critical habitat to many plant and animal species. Migratory birds in particular rely on wetlands as resting places in their annual migrations. In the Americas, the Pacific Flyway, a major migration path

that traverses from the Mexican border to Ventura County, passes through Southern California. In addition, wetlands have a filtering function that helps to protect ocean waters. Because they exist on the highly desirable coastline, however, wetlands have been systematically destroyed by human development. While wetlands once thrived along the coast, 95 percent have now been destroyed. In Los Angeles County, only two wetlands survive: Ballona and Los Cerritos.

Ballona was originally 2,000 acres and provided nesting and feeding grounds for 185 bird species. It was also home to many indigenous villages. The destruction of the area began in the 1930s and 1940s with oil

Residential and commercial development looms over the Ballona Wetlands, 2007.

development and subsequent projects by the U.S. Army Corps of Engineers. In the 1950s and 1960s the vast majority of the wetland area was destroyed by residential and commercial development projects, including Marina del Rey. In response, activists began rallying around the wetlands in 1978 with the establishment of Friends of Ballona Wetlands. Since then, the Friends and other environmentalists, such as SCOPE (Strategic Concepts in Organizing and Policy Education) have fought off megaprojects. One particularly legendary struggle centered on the Playa Vista Development, which was supposed to include Steven Spielberg's Dreamworks as the star tenant; Spielberg ultimately stayed in Glendale, but organizers who worked to make Playa Vista a more socially and environmentally responsible project helped to create Workplace Hollywood, which secures job and business opportunities in the entertainment industry for members of L.A.'s disadvantaged communities. Finally, in 2003, Governor Gray Davis acquired 547 acres to begin restoration. More recently, docents have begun offering tours of a portion of the wetlands.

FAVORITE NEIGHBORHOOD RESTAURANTS

Uncle Darrow's
2560 S. Lincoln Blvd., Marina del Rey 90291 (310) 306-4862 (www.uncledarrows.com) Cajun and Creole food.

Aunt Kizzy's Back Porch
523 Washington Blvd., Marina del Rey 90292 (310) 578-1005 (www.auntkizzys.com) Southern food. Though a little on the pricey side,

the servings are large. Regulars love the fried chicken, mac and cheese, and sweet potato pie.

TO LEARN MORE

Friends of Ballona Wetlands, 211 Culver Blvd., Suite K, Playa del Rey 90293 (310) 306-5994 (www.ballonafriends.org).

Heal the Bay, 1444 9th St., Santa Monica 90401 (310) 451-1500 (www.healthebay.org). An environmental group working to protect the Santa Monica Bay and local waters.

5.2 Campbell Hall, UCLA

405 N. Hilgard Ave., Los Angeles 90024
(between Wyton Dr. and Warner Ave.)
WESTWOOD

Campbell Hall, 2009.

Local universities played an important role in the political mobilization of communities of color during the 1960s and 1970s. Students demanded greater access to higher education and the establishment of ethnic studies programs, which, in turn, fostered greater connections between students and broader communities of color. One result of these efforts was UCLA's High Potential Program, which sought to bring historically underrepresented students to campus.

Black Panthers of Southern California held a press conference in January 1969 to speak out against police brutality. Seated from left to right: Michael Pennewell, Shermont Banks, and Raymond Hewitt.

Through High Potential, the Black Power movement developed a campus presence. At that time, there were two rival organizations in Los Angeles vying for the hearts and minds of young African Americans: US, a cultural nationalist organization that emphasized the importance of cultivating a distinctive African American culture linked to Africa; and the Black Panther Party, which was more revolutionary nationalist and linked the struggle of Black people to the need to end capitalism. Relations between the two organizations became hostile because of their competing ideologies and because both groups wanted to lead the Black Power movement. In January 1969, there was a shoot-out in Campbell Hall that resulted in the deaths of two Panthers: Alprentice "Bunchy" Carter and John Huggins. One former activist, quoted in Laura Pulido's *Black, Brown, Yellow, and Left*, described Carter in the following way: "Bunchy was a natural leader, he had been the leader of the renegade Slausons, he had been to prison, he was well-educated, he was a poet. He knew history. He could fight. He didn't have any fear. He could dance, he could drink, and he could lead." It was subsequently learned that the FBI had played a critical role in fostering tension and conflict between the two groups, as it had done within the larger Black Power movement throughout the country.

More recently, UCLA again became the site of state violence, this time involving campus police. On November 14, 2006, campus police asked Mostafa Tabatabainejed, a UCLA student, to present identification as part of a random check at Powell Library. He refused to do so in order to protest what he saw as a case of racial profiling in the post-9/11 era. Tabatabainejed, who was double-majoring in philosophy and North African Studies, was hit three to five times by a Taser gun; some of the Taser shots were administered after he had been handcuffed for not leaving the library after refusing to show his ID. Each shot delivered 50,000 volts of electricity. Widespread outrage ensued on the UCLA campus. Students demanded that Taser guns no longer be used on campus and that an independent investigation of the incident be conducted. Eventually, a new Taser policy was adopted, and Tabatabaine-jed won the federal civil lawsuit that he filed against the university.

NEARBY SITES OF INTEREST

Fowler Museum, UCLA
North Campus, UCLA, Los Angeles 90095
(310) 825-4361 (www.fowler.ucla.edu)

Charles E. Young Research Library, Department of Special Collections, UCLA
405 Hilgard Ave., Los Angeles 90095
(310) 825-4988 (www.library.ucla.edu
/specialcollections/researchlibrary/index.cfm)
If you like *A People's Guide*, check out the "Extremist Collection" at UCLA Special Collections.

Skirball Cultural Center
2701 N. Sepulveda Blvd., Los Angeles 90049
(310) 440-4500 (www.skirball.org)

Getty Museum
1200 Getty Center Dr., Los Angeles 90049
(310) 440-7300 (www.getty.edu)

FAVORITE NEIGHBORHOOD RESTAURANT

Diddy Riese Cookies
926 Broxton Ave., Los Angeles 90024
(310) 208-0448 (www.diddyriese.com)
Inexpensive cookies and ice cream cookie sandwiches. A longtime UCLA neighborhood institution.

TO LEARN MORE

Philip Foner, ed., *The Black Panthers Speak* (Da Capo Press, 1995).

5.3 Century City

Century Plaza Towers   2029 and 2049 Century Park East, Los Angeles 90067 (at W. Olympic Blvd.) CENTURY CITY

Hyatt Regency Century Plaza Hotel
2025 Avenue of the Stars, Los Angeles 90067 (between Constellation Blvd. and W. Olympic Blvd.) (310) 228-1234 (centuryplaza.hyatt .com/hyatt/hotels/index.jsp) CENTURY CITY

Century Plaza Towers, 2008.

Many protests are held in Century City because it is symbolic of both political and economic power. Presidents, world leaders, and captains of capitalism often stay at the Century Plaza Hotel, and some have offices in the Century Plaza Towers. Century City had its origins in the 1920s film industry, when the land that currently houses the hotel was a back lot of Fox Films (later 20th Century Fox). With the advent of television, however, the studios sold part of their holdings. The Aluminum Company of America (Alcoa) built the Century Towers Apartments, the Century Plaza Hotel, and the Century Plaza

Police hold back antiwar protesters in Century City, June 1967, just before President Lyndon Johnson's speech at the Century Plaza Hotel.

Towers (also known as the "Twin Towers"); the latter were designed by architect Minoru Yamasaki, who also designed the World Trade Center in New York. Past tenants in these complexes have included ABC Entertainment, Northrop Grumman, and former president Ronald Reagan. Corporations currently housed in the Century Park Towers include the facility service contractors American Business Maintenance; Morgan Stanley and Nuveen Investments; international real estate developers CB Richard Ellis and Westfield; and FOX Entertainment.

Two important public protests that occurred at Century Plaza Towers and the Century Plaza Hotel resulted in police abuse. In June 1967, 10,000 to 15,000 people gathered to protest President Lyndon Johnson's policies in the Vietnam War. They were met with batons, clubs, and tear gas. A similar incident took place on June 15, 1990, when approximately 500 members and sup-

porters of Justice for Janitors (JfJ), representing primarily immigrant janitors who were subcontracted to clean the buildings, and the Service Employees International Union (SEIU) staged a peaceful protest in their effort to seek union recognition. JfJ has been a leader in rebuilding the labor movement in Los Angeles by emphasizing organizing and labor/community relations. JfJ also was a leader at this historical moment, in trying to hold property owners—not just the contracted company—liable for the wages and working conditions of subcontracted employees (see entry 2.8 El Monte Sweatshop to read about a similar struggle). The LAPD responded violently to the demonstration, resulting in many injuries, arrests, and one miscarriage. JfJ organizers worried that the violence would prompt workers to drop their bid for unionization, but such was not the case. Instead, workers were angered and mobilized by the way they had been treated.

Indeed, so was the larger public, whose pressure helped motivate the owners to settle with the workers. And in 1993, the City of Los Angeles agreed to pay $2.35 million in damages as a result of the police abuse. JfJ commemorates the protest annually.

The Century Plaza Hotel is considered an iconic architectural landmark. In 2009, when its existence was threatened by redevelopment plans, it was named one of the 11 most endangered historic places in the United States by the National Trust for Historic Preservation. In August 2010 its owner proposed a remodel that would preserve the building's architectural integrity.

FAVORITE NEIGHBORHOOD RESTAURANT

S&W Country Diner
9748 W. Washington Blvd., Culver City 90232
(310) 204-5136
Cozy neighborhood diner. Breakfast served till 3 p.m. Nearly four miles from Century City, but worth the drive.

TO LEARN MORE

Bread and Roses, a film directed by Ken Loach (Parallax Pictures, 2000).
Roger Waldinger, Chris Erickson, Ruth Milkman, Daniel J. B. Mitchell, Abel Valenzuela, Kent Wong, and Maurice Zeitlin, "Helots No More: A Case Study of the Justice for Janitors Campaign in Los Angeles" (Working Paper no. 15, Los Angeles: UCLA School of Public Policy and Social Research, Lewis Center for Regional Policy Studies, April 1996, www.lewis.ucla.edu /publications/workingpapers/15A.pdf).

5.4 Federal Buildings

Westwood 11000 Wilshire Blvd., Los Angeles 90024 *(between S. Sepulveda Blvd. and Veteran Ave.)*
Downtown 300 N. Los Angeles St., Los Angeles 90012 *(between E. Aliso St. and E. Temple St.)*

The Federal Building in Westwood, 2008.

The federal buildings in Westwood and downtown Los Angeles are key sites for protests and demonstrations aimed at the national government. For example, on the eve of Senator Joseph McCarthy's assault on civil rights, members of the Communist Party picketed in defense of workers. Likewise, during the 1980s, demonstrators expressed solidarity with the peoples of El Salvador and Nicaragua and supported amnesty for asylum seekers fleeing U.S.-financed paramilitary violence in both countries.

During the 1980s and 1990s, many protesters at the federal building demanded greater attention and responsiveness to the growing HIV/AIDS crisis. In 1987, the AIDS Coalition to Unleash Power (ACT UP) formed an L.A. chapter. Members were known for their stark visual and verbal confrontations designed to focus attention on federal neglect of the HIV/AIDS crisis. Their most

Maroug Sassounian leads an Armenian demonstration outside the Federal Building in Westwood, 1989.

recognized slogan was "Silence = Death," accompanied by the pink triangle that the Nazis had used to stigmatize lesbians and gay men. Another famous sign featured a photo of President Reagan over the slogan "He Kills Me." In 1990, more than 70 artists and supporters marched from the Los Angeles County Museum of Art on Wilshire Boulevard to the downtown federal building protesting federal censorship of AIDS issues in the arts and demanding federal funding to help fight AIDS. Twenty-seven people were arrested.

More recent protests have focused on the U.S. war in Iraq and Afghanistan, the federal response to Hurricane Katrina, U.S. support of Israel, and Immigration and Customs Enforcement raids, as well as on immigration policy in general.

NEARBY SITE OF INTEREST

Hammer Museum
10899 Wilshire Blvd., Los Angeles 90024
(310) 443-7000 (http://hammer.ucla.edu)

FAVORITE NEIGHBORHOOD RESTAURANT

Literati Café
12081 Wilshire Blvd., Los Angeles 90025
(310) 231-7484 (www.literaticafe.com)
Casual café fare includes homemade soups, fair-trade shade-grown coffee, and fresh mint lemonade.

5.5 Highways Performance Space

1651 18th St., Santa Monica 90404 *(nearest cross street: Olympic Blvd.)* (310) 315-1459 (www.highwaysperformance.org)

Highways Performance Space is an important site for art and activism in Los

Highways Performance Space, in the Eighteenth Street Arts Center complex, 2009.

Angeles and nationally. It was cofounded in 1989 by writer Linda Frye Burnham and performance artist Tim Miller. In the early 1990s, under Miller's guidance (Burnham stepped down as codirector in 1992), Highways mounted the world premiere of *AIDS! The Musical* as a benefit fund-raiser for AIDS Coalition to Unleash Power/LA (ACT UP/ LA). The play asserted that the medium of theater could serve as a venue for activist politics and "a site where the issues facing lesbians, gays, and/or AIDS activists could be voiced and heard," according to David Román in his book *Acts of Intervention*. Over the years, Highways' commitment to "socially involved artists and art forms" has led to collaborations with and performances by artists including Guillermo Gomez-Peña, Coco Fusco, Denise Uyehara, El Teatro Justo Rufino Garay de Nicaragua, Los Angeles Poverty Department, and Keith Antar Mason. The center's dedication to featuring

cutting-edge work by artists from groups that are marginalized by mainstream society has also led to controversy: in 1995, Highways made national headlines when, in response to complaints by Christian conservative Donald Wildmon, the National Endowment for the Arts revoked the center's funding because of the controversy over a flyer that depicted a naked African American man holding a Bible and wearing a cross.

Currently, Highways' mission is implemented via a performance lab, workshops, showings, discussions, and two galleries. The space also provides opportunities for emerging artists to develop exhibitions under a mentor. Highways' annual poetry festival brings together local and national poets, slam champions, actors, authors, teachers, and cultural workers from the literary, hip-hop, queer, Black, Asian, and Latina/o communities, while weekly "Queer Mondays" provide a consistent site for the development of new work.

NEARBY SITES OF INTEREST

Bergamot Station

2525 Michigan Ave., Santa Monica 90404

(310) 453-7535 (bergamotstation.com)

Art gallery and cultural center.

Co-opportunity

1525 Broadway St., Santa Monica 90404

(310) 451-8902 (www.coopportunity.com)

The only grocery cooperative in the L.A. area.

FAVORITE NEIGHBORHOOD RESTAURANTS

Teddy's Café

12043 W. Pico Blvd., Los Angeles 90064

(310) 444-9996

An old-school diner. Regulars recommend the breakfast deals.

Lares Restaurant

2909 Pico Blvd., Santa Monica 90405

(310) 829-4550 (www.lares-restaurant.com)

Mexican restaurant with a full bar and sometimes live music. Customer favorites include the fresh guacamole and arroz con pollo.

Nawab of India

1621 Wilshire Blvd., Santa Monica 90403

(310) 829-1106 (www.nawabindia.com)

A bit on the pricey side. Regulars enjoy the lunch buffet.

Café Bolívar

1741 Ocean Park Blvd., Santa Monica 90405

(310) 581-2344 (www.cafebolivar.com)

Pan–Latin American coffeehouse and art gallery with a café menu and high-quality coffee and tea drinks. Try the fresh *arepas* and café latte with *cajeta*.

TO LEARN MORE

David Román, *Acts of Intervention: Performance, Gay Culture, and AIDS* (Indiana University Press, 1998).

5.6 The Ink Well

Ocean Park Walk between Bay St. and Bicknell St., Santa Monica 90405

Pedestrians on the Santa Monica boardwalk in 2010 pass by a plaque placed there by the City of Santa Monica to commemorate the Ink Well as "a place of celebration and pain."

Los Angeles County's beaches have long been a major attraction for tourists and locals alike. Yet in the first part of the twentieth century, African Americans, Asian Americans, Latinas/os, and other people of color were excluded from virtually all of the area's public beaches, pools, and other recreational facilities. When parishioners of the Philips Chapel Christian Methodist Episcopal (CME) church, located at Bay and Fourth streets in Santa Monica, would head to the beach after services for picnics, games, and socializing, they would be harassed by police on behalf of white beachgoers, who protested the presence of Black people. Eventually, the Philips Chapel group located a place on the sand in a polluted, unwanted area and claimed it as their own. Known as "the Ink Well," this small beach area ran only the width of the street, about 200 square feet, but it was one of the few beaches in Los Angeles that was open to African Americans

Verna Williams and Arthur Lewis at the Ink Well, Santa Monica Beach's "Blacks only" section, 1924.

and other people of color, who flocked there from around the city. Even after racial restrictions on L.A.'s public beaches were lifted in 1927, African Americans continued to congregate here.

The Ink Well served a thriving African American community that was located nearby, clustered along Pico Boulevard between Fourteenth and Twenty-fourth streets in Santa Monica, as well as Black residents of nearby Oakwood. Oakwood was developed by Abbott Kinney in the early twentieth century to house the servants who worked in the homes of the Italian-inspired community of Venice. It was the only neighborhood within one mile of the coast where people of color could purchase homes. Before the civil rights era, segregated seaside resorts

and entertainment venues catered to the populations of these two neighborhoods. However, in the 1950s and 1960s, much of the Black community along Pico was demolished in preparation for the construction of the Santa Monica Civic Auditorium and the Santa Monica Freeway. Both developments stand on land once occupied by African American homeowners and businesses and then acquired via eminent domain. In February 2008, the City of Santa Monica dedicated a plaque commemorating the Ink Well and acknowledging L.A.'s history of segregated beaches.

NEARBY SITES AND EVENTS OF INTEREST

Palisades Park
Ocean Ave. north of the pier, Santa Monica 90403
(310) 458-8644
Park overlooking the beach, with beautiful views of the sunset.

Santa Monica Pier Twilight Dance Series
On Thursday evenings in the summer, the City of Santa Monica hosts a free music series on the pier. Highly rated and very popular (www.santamonicapier.org/twilight/). The pier itself offers an enjoyable walk at any time.

Third Street Promenade
Third St. between Broadway and Wilshire Blvd., Santa Monica 90401
Although this outdoor mall now consists primarily of upscale chains, it was one of L.A.'s first attempts at creating a pedestrian-friendly environment (see entry 5.9 Midnight Special and Sisterhood Bookstores).

Oakwood Recreation Center
767 California Ave., Venice 90291
(310) 452-7479 (www.laparks.org/dos/reccenter/facility/oakwoodRC.htm)

This community center features hand-painted tiles reflecting the Oakwood neighborhood's history.

Venice Boardwalk

Ocean Front Walk roughly between Rose Ave. and Washington Blvd., Venice 90291 (www.venicebeach.com)

The boardwalk at Venice Beach is famous for its street performers, restaurants, shops, and booths. Historically, it was important to the development of L.A.'s counterculture, and though it has recently experienced significant gentrification, it remains an excellent place to people-watch and enjoy the sun and sand.

FAVORITE NEIGHBORHOOD RESTAURANT

Fritto Misto

601 Colorado Ave., Santa Monica 90407
(310) 458-2829

Popular Italian restaurant offering a create-your-own-pasta option and a decadent flourless chocolate cake.

TO LEARN MORE

Alison Jefferson, "African American Leisure Space in Santa Monica: The Beach Sometimes Known as the 'Inkwell,' 1900s–1960s," *Southern California Quarterly* 91, no. 2 (2009): 155–189.

5.7 Los Angeles International Airport

1 World Wy., Los Angeles 90045
(310) 646-5252 (www.lawa.org/WelcomeLAX .aspx) WESTCHESTER

Los Angeles Municipal Airport (LAX) opened at Mines Field, formerly a 3,000-acre bean and barley field, in 1930. The airport's existence helped attract major aircraft manufacturers such as Northrop, Douglas, and North American Aviation to the region.

These firms worked with real estate developers to construct vast tracts of affordable homes for aircraft workers, leading to the creation of communities such as Westchester, El Segundo, Inglewood, and Lennox, most of which were occupied by working-class whites. The proximity of these residential communities to the airport would soon lead to major conflicts, as the health and quality of life of the workers were increasingly threatened by their very own employers—the aircraft manufacturers—and the airport itself.

During World War II, the federal government assumed operation of the airport to coordinate Pacific Rim defense activity and made many structural improvements that transformed LAX into the nation's first airport designed for the jet age. Building upon this competitive edge, civic leaders and business interests sought during the 1960s to expand and reconfigure LAX as an international airport. In order to add runways and terminals, however, they needed to re-establish in the surrounding communities a buffer zone for noise control. By the end of the decade, the L.A. Department of Airports had condemned and purchased more than 2,800 parcels of residential land and displaced many thousands of people.

The threat of displacement and the negative impacts of jet travel led the surrounding communities to organize. Grassroots groups such as the Inglewood Citizens Council, the Lennox Citizens Council, the Playa del Rey Civil Union, and the El Segundo Airport Noise Study Committee strongly opposed jet noise, which they claimed reduced residents' property values and damaged their health. They cited studies showing that noise pollution was linked to disrupted sleep, mental illness, heart disease, cardiovascular damage, high blood pressure, increased cholesterol, and shorter life spans. A 1972 study of schools under the flight path found noise levels so acute that researchers concluded the children were at risk of permanent hearing damage. Jet noise also prevented teachers and children from meeting their learning goals, as teachers frequently had to pause in their instruction while jets roared overhead—sometimes as often as every two minutes. Capturing this frustration, Sandrah Pohorlak, a teacher at Jefferson Elementary, wrote, "Tonight my nerves are shot! I struggled all day in a losing battle against those jets. The children couldn't hear me and I couldn't hear them, unless I stood 18 inches away from them." The neighborhood groups pursued various approaches, with occasional successes. In 1975, for example, a Superior Court judge ruled that LAX was indeed liable for damaging home values and awarded 520 homeowners a total of $740,000 in damages.

Such conflicts have grown particularly pronounced since the 1980s, as civic leaders' eagerness to make Los Angeles a hub of Pacific Rim trade, commerce, and tourism at virtually any cost has led to declining job quality and worsening quality of life for ordinary working people. By the mid-1990s, LAX was the fourth-busiest airport in the world, with the projected volume of passengers and air cargo expected to grow exponentially by 2015. Repeated iterations

of master planning have called for expansion of LAX's runways and terminals to accommodate ever-larger flows of people and goods. Meanwhile, the increased volume has had pernicious environmental effects. By the 1990s, LAX had become the third-largest source of smog in Southern California, and increases of local respiratory ailments (such as asthma) and cancer had been documented in surrounding neighborhoods. These effects are now concentrated among people of color and immigrants who, during the 1980s and 1990s, had moved into the aging tracts of small, single-family homes once occupied by white workers. In a sadly ironic twist, these residents suffer even worse environmental and quality-of-life issues than previous occupants, but are much less likely to enjoy the union wages and benefits of the earlier generation.

The organizing tradition continues. The LAX Coalition for Economic, Environmental, and Educational Justice formed in 2003 to ensure that LAX's most recent proposed modernization and expansion would benefit the communities most affected. The coalition was spearheaded by the Los Angeles Alliance for a New Economy (LAANE), which had helped to successfully negotiate the community benefits agreement (CBA) at the L.A. Live complex just a few years earlier (for more on the complex, see entry 1.19 L.A. Live). The coalition saw the potential to secure a similar or even stronger CBA as part of the airport's expansion. The coalition brought together community organizations, environmental groups, labor unions, and the Inglewood and Lennox school districts. In

2004, it negotiated the largest CBA to date with Los Angeles World Airports, LAX's governing body, which agreed to provide nearly $500 million to reduce noise pollution and mitigate negative environmental impacts such as smog and traffic congestion and to create job training and hiring mandates for local residents. The CBA also included specific provisions to address noise at schools in Lennox and Inglewood. Although airport expansion has recently been stalled, the CBA is legally binding and remains in effect even as smaller projects go forward. LAANE has also focused its organizing work on jobs in the hospitality, service, and tourism industries that cannot be exported (which creates some leverage for unions) and that are characterized by low wages, lack of health insurance, and poor working conditions. In 2009, LAANE worked with the Los Angeles City Council to successfully modify the city's existing Living Wage Ordinance, which had been created in 1997,

so that the wage paid by city contractors included an increased provision for health benefits. *(Quote is from W. C. Meecham, "Hazardous Jet Noise Radiation at Schools Near Los Angeles International Airport,"* Journal of the Acoustical Society of America *53 [1974]: 304.)*

TO LEARN MORE

Los Angeles Alliance for a New Economy, 464 Lucas Ave., Suite 202, Los Angeles 90017 (213) 977-9400 (www.laane.org).
Steven P. Erie, *Globalizing L.A.: Trade, Infrastructure, and Regional Development* (Stanford University Press, 2004).

5.8 Malibu Public Beaches

22126 Pacific Coast Hwy., Malibu 90265
(nearest cross street: Carbon Mesa Rd.)

The Malibu coastline, featured in countless films, television shows, and commercials, consists of 27 miles of beautiful public beaches. However, nearly 20 of those miles are lined with private development, creating

A cluster of signs along the Pacific Coast Highway illustrates competing public and private interests, 2009.

a wall of buildings (including the homes of many L.A. celebrities and other elites) that block both public access to the beaches and scenic views from the highway. In 1976, the California Coastal Act affirmed that private development must not inhibit public access to the seashore, and the California Coastal Commission has taken proactive steps toward this goal by, for example, creating legal standards for access and opening several access points. The beach access point at this address, known as the Geffen Accessway, was the result of more than 20 years of legal battles and is now maintained by the nonprofit group Access for All. Nonetheless, gaining access to Malibu's public beaches remains difficult. While the California Coastal Act requires approximately five access points per mile, there are currently only 18 accessways along the 20-mile stretch. Moreover, many of the existing points are sometimes illegally locked, and one has even been "closed for repairs" for more than six years! Wealthy homeowners use illegal tactics such as posting signs that claim the beaches are private or that parking is prohibited (both are usually false), hiring private security guards, and harassing beachgoers.

Sound intimidating? Don't let it be—you have the right to enjoy Malibu beaches! Here are some guidelines to keep in mind: The public always has the right to walk, sit, stand, sunbathe, and so on from the surf up to the mean high-tide line (the average high-tide line over the last 18 months). Since that line isn't visible, beachgoers are safe staying below the daily high-water line (where the sand was wet but has now dried). In addition, many (but not all) of the properties have public-private easements that allow visitors to occupy much of the dry sand. To find out where these public-private easements are, check out the California Coastal Commission web site (www.coastal.ca.gov)

PERSONAL REFLECTION BY THE LOS ANGELES URBAN RANGERS

From 2007 to 2010, the Los Angeles Urban Rangers ran our Public Access 101: Malibu Public Beaches project to show people how to find and use a public beach in Malibu—especially the 20 miles of the coast lined with private development. While beaches may be L.A.'s most cherished public spaces, using Malibu's glorious beaches safely and legally often requires advanced skills—whether you're visiting these public lands from the adjacent private houses or from farther away. Accordingly, we distributed a printed back-pocket guide, with an accessway map, safety tips, a taxonomy of common sign species, a beach etiquette checklist (don't use private furniture, and don't kick people off of public land), and all other necessary visitor information.

We also offered free, guided Malibu Public Beaches safaris—complete with skill-building activities that included trailblazing the public-private boundary, sign watching and species identification, a campfire song ("This Land Is Your Land"), a no-kill accessway hunt, and a public easement potluck. We're enormously pleased to report that a grand time was had by all—which is exactly as it should be when the public uses its beaches.

for a photographic map. These beaches are open 24 hours, although the access gates are locked on the street side at sunset (but not the beach side, so you can get out at any hour). Still confused? The Los Angeles Urban Rangers (www.laurbanrangers.org) offer a free downloadable map and guide of the Malibu public beaches, which clearly delineate access points and provide guidelines for using public beaches legally and safely. The guide also tells how to protect your rights in the event of resistance or harassment by private home-owners or guards.

NEARBY SITES OF INTEREST

Will Rogers State Historic Park

1501 Will Rogers Park Rd., Pacific Palisades 90272 (310) 454-8212 (www.parks.ca.gov/?page _id=626)

Museum and park dedicated to humorist and actor Will Rogers, who lived here from 1928 to 1935 and whose widow donated the land to the state of California in 1944. The park features equestrian facilities, horseback riding lessons, and hiking trails.

Santa Monica National Recreation Area

401 West Hillcrest Dr., Thousand Oaks 91360 (805) 370-2300

Topanga State Park

20829 Entrada Rd., Topanga 90290 (310) 455-2465

FAVORITE NEIGHBORHOOD RESTAURANTS

Reel Inn Fresh Fish Restaurant

18661 Pacific Coast Hwy., Malibu 90265 (310) 456-8221 (www.reelinnmalibu.com)

Casual place for fresh fish (grilled or fried) and a beer after a day at the beach.

Froggy's Topanga Fish Market

1105 N. Topanga Canyon Blvd., Topanga 90290 (310) 455-1728 (www.froggystopanga.com)

Cozy, rustic locals' spot in the heart of Topanga Canyon.

TO LEARN MORE

Los Angeles Urban Rangers, www .laurbanrangers.org.

5.9 Midnight Special and Sisterhood Bookstores

Midnight Special Bookstore   1318 3rd St., Santa Monica 90401 *(between Arizona Ave. and Santa Monica Blvd.)*

Sisterhood Bookstore   1351 Westwood Blvd., Los Angeles 90024 *(at Rochester Ave.)*

WESTWOOD

Midnight Special and Sisterhood were two beloved independent bookstores that have since gone the way of countless other indies, particularly in the face of megachains like Barnes and Noble and Borders. Midnight Special, located in Santa Monica, was a communal endeavor from its inception. Originally developed as a political project of radical political activists, the store was owned by Margie Ghiz and supported by her sister Geri Silva and a phenomenally committed staff. It first opened in Venice in 1970, then moved to Santa Monica's Third Street Promenade, where it became an "organic bulletin board" for the city—a community center as much as a bookstore. Midnight Special was able to locate on the promenade because it was subsidized by Wally Marks, who kept the rent below market value. The store offered an amazing collection of radical as

Staff at Midnight Special featured on the cover of the *L.A. Weekly* in 1996.

well as mainstream literature, in all genres and subjects. However, as higher-end corporate retailers such as the GAP, Starbucks, the Apple Store, and Barnes and Noble—who were willing to pay much higher rents—relocated to the area, Midnight Special was forced off the promenade in 2003 and reopened a block away for about nine months. Despite an outpouring of community support and donations, the lights went out for good in May 2004. The aisles that housed Gabriel Garcia Marquez, Octavia Butler, Noam Chomsky, and Howard Zinn were no match for the $50,000-per-month rent.

Sisterhood Bookstore was founded in 1972 by three women who were active in the L.A. women's movement: Adele Wallace, Simone Wallace, and Gahan Kelley. The women had previously worked together at

the L.A. Crenshaw Women's Center, which is where Sisterhood began to take shape. A room full of articles and books provided the original inventory. When the need outgrew the space, the three women opened a small storefront on Westwood Boulevard, and, within a matter of weeks, it seemed as if the L.A. women's movement had relocated there. Opening a mere two years after Midnight Special, Sisterhood Bookstore enriched the alternative bookseller landscape in Los Angeles by providing a place that not only showcased writing by women for women but also maintained the ethos and character of that small room at the Women's Center. Sisterhood became an important site of women's political activism and consciousness-raising where one could form relationships with like-minded people. Although the store was able to survive the onslaught of the superstore Crown Books throughout the 1980s, in 1992 its sales reached their peak and began to fall. In 1996, Borders moved in across the street and hastened the store's closure (ironically, at the time of this writing, Borders is in bankruptcy). Sisterhood celebrated twenty-five years of service to the Los Angeles community in November 1997, but the writing was on the wall. As the store struggled to compete with discounters like Borders, which offered a coffee bar and ample parking, Amazon entered the picture. In June 1999, Sisterhood Bookstore closed its doors for the last time. Interestingly, while Sisterhood closed because of direct competition with discount sales, Midnight Special's closure was mainly the result of rising rents; both are key factors in the diminishing num-

PERSONAL REFLECTION BY CRAIG GILMORE AND RUTHIE WILSON GILMORE, ACTIVISTS/ SCHOLARS AND FREQUENT PATRONS OF MIDNIGHT SPECIAL

Midnight Special helped you escape—not from life but into it. You could see a play written and performed by unemployed steelworkers, or run into Octavia Butler doing research in the science section. The man at the checkout admiring a Robbie Connel political portrait might be Eduardo Galeano. You could encounter Nelson Peery interviewed by Mike Davis, or hear Karen Tei Yamashita, Amiri Baraka, Luis Rodríguez, and hundreds more read their work. The bookstore hosted meetings and strategy sessions for countless justice struggles—concerning janitors, garment workers, antiapartheid, Central America, and prison abolition. Midnight Special was a place where curiosity and outrage were transformed into connection, activism, movement.

ber of independent bookstores across the United States. Yet these bookstores have not outlived their purpose. To the contrary, they are needed more than ever.

NEARBY SITE OF INTEREST

Social and Public Art Resource Center (SPARC)
685 Venice Blvd., Venice, 90291 (310) 822-9560
(www.sparcmurals.org)
A renowned public arts program; see entry 6.5
The Great Wall and Social and Public Art Resource Center (SPARC).

FAVORITE NEIGHBORHOOD RESTAURANTS

M Street Kitchen
2000 Main St., Unit D, Santa Monica 90405
(310) 396-9145 (www.mstreetkitchen.com)
Located near the former site of Midnight Special, this is a healthy café with seasonal offerings. Kids eat free 4–6 P.M. every day.

Real Food Daily
514 Santa Monica Blvd., Santa Monica 90401
(310) 451-7544 (www.realfood.com)
Also near Midnight Special, this organic, vegan restaurant serves delicious food. On the pricey side.

Attari Sandwich Shop
1388 Westwood Blvd., Los Angeles 90024
(310) 441-5488
At this Persian deli near Sisterhood Bookstore, customer favorites include the chicken *olivieh* sandwich, lentil soup, and kebab plates.

TO LEARN MORE

For information on independent bookstores and how to support them, check out the American Booksellers Association, www.bookweb.org.

5.10 West Hollywood City Hall

8300 Santa Monica Blvd., West Hollywood 90069 *(at N. Sweetzer Ave.)* (323) 848-6400 (www.weho.org)

Popularly known as the first "gay city" in the United States, West Hollywood was incorporated in November 1984. Before its incorporation, West Hollywood was part of unincorporated Los Angeles County and had long been known as a community tolerant of alternative lifestyles, where creative, nonconformist perspectives and identities could be expressed. During the 1920s, speakeasies, nightclubs, and casinos flourished along Sunset and Santa Monica Boulevards, West Hollywood's two main thoroughfares, because gambling was legal in the county, but not the city, of Los Angeles. In later years West Hollywood attracted many celebrities, actors, and tourists. By the 1960s its dense countercultural population made it a vibrant hub of the hippie movement. At that time, a club called Ciro's held the first gay dance nights on Sundays, which were known as "Tea Dances" (or "T-Dances"). At the time, it was illegal for two persons of the same gender to dance together in Los Angeles County, but in West Hollywood's loose political climate, such laws were not strictly enforced. Soon, many gay clubs and bars were established.

In 1970, inspired by the gay rights movement that was flourishing on the East Coast, activists formed the Gay Liberation Front of Los Angeles (see entry 1.14 Gay Liberation Front [1969–1972]/Former Home of Morris Kight). The GLF engaged in such activities as picketing Barney's Beanery, a West Hollywood restaurant that for many years posted a sign reading "Faggots Stay Out!," and coordinated Christopher Street West, the first Los Angeles Gay Pride Parade. The parade and its attendant festival moved to its current location in West Hollywood in 1978. By the mid-1980s, the gay population of West Hollywood was estimated at about 40 percent of the overall population, and the community was widely known as "Boys' Town" because of both the visibility of the gay male population and the growing number of businesses catering to gay-identified consumers.

West Hollywood City Hall, 2008.

These conditions made West Hollywood ripe for municipal incorporation. The campaign for cityhood began in 1983 in response to L.A. County's plans to dismantle rent control, which would have disproportionately affected West Hollywood's large renter population. A coalition of seniors, Jews, tenants, and gays led the successful movement to incorporate West Hollywood in 1984. The new city immediately adopted one of the strongest rent control laws in the country. Simultaneously, voters elected the nation's first gay-majority city council. Although incorporation brought together multiple constituencies, the campaign was widely perceived as a way to legitimize gay identity and to achieve local control over issues that affect gays. In 1985, West Hollywood became the first U.S. city to allow domestic partnership registration for its residents and to offer same-gender domestic partner benefits for its municipal employees.

More recently, West Hollywood's city hall has become a visible symbol of another important victory for LGBT rights activists. In May 2008, the California Supreme Court overturned a ban on same-sex marriage, stating that every Californian has a fundamental right to marry the person of his or her choice, and that the unequal statuses of marriage and domestic partnership violate the state constitution's guarantee of equal protection. The first couple to be married at West Hollywood City Hall was actor George Takei, also known as Mr. Sulu on *Star Trek,* and his partner, Brad Altman. In a Zap2it article, Takei linked the ban on same-sex marriage with the internment of Japanese Americans during World War II, stating, "With time, I know the opposition to same sex marriage, too, will be seen as an antique and discreditable part of our history." In November 2008, California voters passed Proposition 8, which amended the state constitution to recognize only marriages between a man and a woman. In August 2010, however, Justice Vaughn Walker of the Ninth Circuit Court ruled that Proposition 8 was unconstitutional, although as of this writing the case is still caught in legal appeals.

NEARBY SITES AND EVENTS OF INTEREST

Halloween Party
West Hollywood is famous for its annual Halloween Party, which takes place all along Santa Monica Blvd.

Center for the Study of Political Graphics
8124 W. 3rd St., Suite 211, Los Angeles 90048 (323) 653-4662 (www.politicalgraphics.org /home.html)
Has the largest collection of political posters in the United States and perhaps the world. An amazing resource for those interested in activism of all sorts. The center often takes volunteers and interns.

L.A. Free Press site (former)
8226 Sunset Blvd., Los Angeles 90046 (http:// losangelesfreepress.com)
The *L.A. Free Press* (1964–78), one of the country's most influential underground newspapers, operated out of the basement of the Fifth Estate Coffee House for its first two years. Currently, the site is occupied by the Den of Hollywood restaurant.

The Schindler House
835 N. Kings Rd., West Hollywood 90069 (323) 651-1510 (www.makcenter.org)
Considered the first house in Southern California to be designed using the principles of architectural modernism. Open to the public, but check its hours.

Silent Movie Theatre
611 N. Fairfax Ave., Los Angeles 90036 (323) 655-2510 (www.cinefamily.org)

FAVORITE NEIGHBORHOOD RESTAURANTS

Vegan Glory
8393 Beverly Blvd., Los Angeles 90048 (323) 653-4900 (www.veganglory.com)
Popular vegan Thai restaurant with an extensive menu.

Hugo's
8401 Santa Monica Blvd., West Hollywood 90069 (323) 654-3993 (www.hugosrestaurant.com)
Creative cuisine with many healthy options (vegan friendly). Not the cheapest, but worth the extra expense.

Barney's Beanery

8447 Santa Monica Blvd., West Hollywood
(323) 654-2287 (www.barneysbeanery.com)
Established in the 1920s as a stopover on Route 66. Extensive menu. Open 24/7.

Sahag's Basturma

5183 Sunset Blvd., Hollywood 90027
(323) 661-5311
Traditional Armenian sandwich shop.

5.11 Workmen's Circle/ Arbeter Ring

1525 S. Robertson Blvd., Los Angeles 90035
(at Horner St.) (310) 552-2007
(www.circlesocal.org)

PICO-ROBERTSON

The Workmen's Circle ("Arbeter Ring" in Yiddish) is a national organization with a progressive social vision, founded in 1900, that seeks to promote Jewish (particularly Yiddish) culture. The Los Angeles branch, known as the Karl Liebknecht Branch 248, was established in 1908 and has been in continuous operation since. In addition to providing camps for children and adults, the Workmen's Circle has been an active supporter of workers' and civil rights and features art exhibits at its Shenere Velt Gallery. The building also features a mural documenting the centuries-old Jewish struggle and its link to social justice. The Jewish population of the United States has been notable for its historic commitment to human and civil rights. Jewish Angelenos played an important role in the election of the city's first African American mayor, Tom Bradley, in 1973, and Jews are prominent members of the city's labor unions, nonprofits, and other progressive causes. Although anti-Semitism still exists in Los Angeles (in 2006, for example, 11 percent of all hate crimes in Los Angeles County were directed against Jewish people), it has decreased to an extent that many Jews have become fully integrated into mainstream society.

NEARBY SITES OF INTEREST

Museum of Tolerance

9786 W. Pico Blvd., Los Angeles 90035
(310) 553-8403 (www.museumoftolerance.com)
A unique and powerful museum that explores prejudice, discrimination, and the need for

A mural painted on the side of the Workmen's Circle building by Eliseo Art Silva (photographed in 2010) features civil rights leaders alongside traditional Jewish symbols, advocating "a more beautiful and better world."

respecting and accepting others. Its goal is to prevent genocide against any group, now and in the future.

Los Angeles Museum of the Holocaust

100 S. The Grove Dr., Los Angeles
(323) 651-3704 (www.lamoth.org)

Located in the Pan Pacific Park, this museum opened in 2010, across the street from The Grove shopping center's simulation of quaint Euro-urbanity.

FAVORITE NEIGHBORHOOD RESTAURANTS

Messob

1041 S. Fairfax Ave., Los Angeles 90019
(323) 938-8827 (www.messob.com)

Nyala

1076 S. Fairfax Ave., Los Angeles 90019
(323) 936-5918 (www.nyala-la.com)

Both Messob and Nyala are Ethiopian restaurants in the heart of Little Ethiopia. Los Angeles is home to one of the largest Ethiopian immigrant communities in the United States.

TO LEARN MORE

For more on Jewish history, visit the webpage of the Jewish Genealogical Society of Los Angeles, http://jgsla.org.

George Sanchez, "What's Good for Boyle Heights Is Good for the Jews: Creating Multiracialism during the 1950s," *American Quarterly* 56 (2004): 633–661.

6

The San Fernando Valley and North Los Angeles County

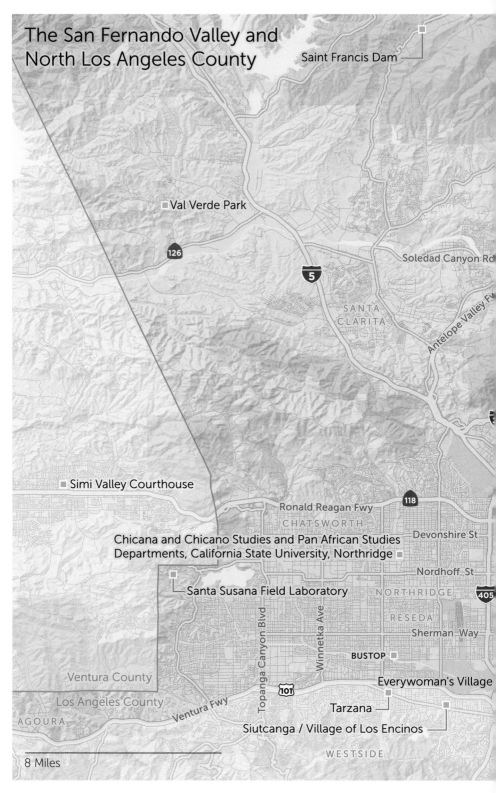

The San Fernando Valley and
North Los Angeles County

Saint Francis Dam

Val Verde Park

126

5

SANTA
CLARITA

Soledad Canyon Rd

Antelope Valley Fw

Simi Valley Courthouse

Ronald Reagan Fwy

118

CHATSWORTH

Devonshire St

Chicana and Chicano Studies and Pan African Studies
Departments, California State University, Northridge

Nordhoff St

NORTHRIDGE

405

Santa Susana Field Laboratory

RESEDA

Sherman Way

BUSTOP

Everywoman's Village

Ventura County

Los Angeles County

101

Tarzana

AGOURA

Ventura Fwy

Siutcanga / Village of Los Encinos

WESTSIDE

Winnetka Ave

Topanga Canyon Blvd

8 Miles

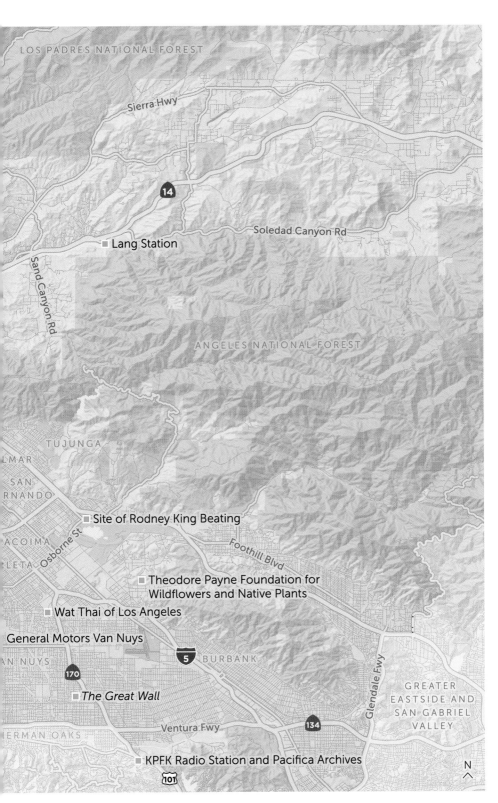

LOS PADRES NATIONAL FOREST

Sierra Hwy

14

Soledad Canyon Rd

Sand Canyon Rd

■ Lang Station

ANGELES NATIONAL FOREST

TUJUNGA

LMAR

SAN
RNANDO

ACOIMA

LETA

Osborne St

■ Site of Rodney King Beating

Foothill Blvd

■ Theodore Payne Foundation for
Wildflowers and Native Plants

■ Wat Thai of Los Angeles

General Motors Van Nuys

AN NUYS

170

5 BURBANK

■ *The Great Wall*

Glendale Fwy

GREATER
EASTSIDE AND
SAN GABRIEL
VALLEY

Ventura Fwy

134

ERMAN OAKS

■ KPFK Radio Station and Pacifica Archives

101

N

An Introduction to the San Fernando Valley and North Los Angeles County

The history and contemporary life of the San Fernando Valley is deeply informed by its unique geography. This area is bounded by mountain ranges, which create a natural bowl separating the northern and western parts of L.A. County from the vast central Los Angeles basin. "The Valley," as the San Fernando Valley is often called, is also the connector between L.A., the Central Coast, and California's Central Valley. Consequently, the San Fernando Valley is both a self-enclosed region and a gateway that connects L.A. to the rest of the state. Partly because of these geographic conditions, the San Fernando Valley and its edge communities are marked by a contradictory relationship with the rest of Los Angeles. On the one hand, many Valley residents conceive of themselves as socially, culturally, and geographically distinct from L.A. This sensibility has propelled recurrent attempts at secession (so far unsuccessful), as well as social movements, past and present, based on resistance to residential integration, school busing, and taxation that would create greater economic and political integration with the city of Los Angeles. On the other hand, residents of the San Fernando Valley are fundamentally dependent on the city of L.A. for employment, infrastructure, governance, and the cultural amenities of urban life. These tensions and contradictions are embedded in the area's landscapes and in the Valley's stories of power, resistance, and community.

The Valley and its environs are most commonly thought of as sprawling suburbs of Los Angeles formed by the historic process of white flight and populated primarily by middle-class white homeowners who periodically rebel and try to secede from the city. In popular culture, the Valley is frequently represented as an all-American suburb and parodied as the home of gum-cracking, ponytail-wearing, mall-hopping "Valley girls." Indeed, the fictional home of the Brady Bunch was located in the Valley (11222 Dilling Street, Los Angeles, for true fans). But while these images are true, they do not capture the whole story. Certainly, for much of its history, the Valley has been a place of exclusion and segregation, where middle-class white homeowners defined their suburban ideal through the exclusion of immigrants, people of color, and the poor, and by preventing unwanted land uses. Yet the Valley has also generated a complex history of grassroots resistance by students of color, workers, feminists, immigrants, and civil rights groups who have protested the efforts to exclude and dominate them, and who have struggled to claim the suburban vision as their own.

The Valley actually has a long history that precedes its incarnation as the postwar suburban ideal. Several flourishing indigenous settlements existed in the San Fernando Valley before the Spanish arrived;

these communities were ethnically and linguistically connected to the indigenous Tongva settlements located at Yang-Na and elsewhere in the central L.A. basin. During Spanish colonization, many of the Valley's Indian peoples were relocated to the Mission San Fernando Rey de España. During the Spanish colonial era (1769–1821) and the brief Mexican period of control (1821–48), the U.S. Southwest was divided into ranches through the land grant systems of the Spanish and Mexican governments. In the Valley, as in the rest of L.A., the Mexican government in particular allowed and encouraged wealthy white American and European male investors to apply for land grants. By the 1830s, much of the Valley's ranch land was already owned by white people. During the American era, beginning as early as the 1890s, agriculture drove the Valley's development, made possible by city-subsidized investments in irrigation and transportation infrastructure—including, most prominently, the completion of the Los Angeles Aqueduct, which diverted water from California's Owens Valley to Los Angeles and terminated in the San Fernando Valley. This monumental event, famously depicted in the film *Chinatown,* enabled the Valley and the larger city of Los Angeles to flourish as an agricultural empire in the prewar years.

During and after World War II, the Valley was transformed by the same process of suburbanization of people, housing, and industry that was occurring across the nation. This process was enabled by Federal Housing Administration and Veterans Administration home loans, decisions by

high-tech and defense firms to relocate at the suburban fringe, and the construction of federally subsidized interstate highways that connected expanding suburbs to the central city. This same process also produced the ranch homes, backyard swimming pools, strip malls, and often-gridlocked freeways that became emblematic of the San Fernando Valley's landscape. For the most part, as in the rest of the country, suburbanization of the Valley in the post–World War II years was indeed a racially exclusionary phenomenon that restricted new housing to white workers and their families. In the Valley, there were two exceptions to this phenomenon: the racially and economically integrated neighborhoods of San Fernando (which is an independent city) and Pacoima (a part of the City of Los Angeles), both in the northeast Valley. Before 1960, no other neighborhood in the Valley had a Black population that amounted to more than 1 percent of the whole. It was in Pacoima's and San Fernando's Black, Latina/o, Japanese American, and Jewish communities that most of the Valley's civil rights campaigns were launched. During the 1960s and 1970s, amid efforts to integrate neighborhoods, schools, and public facilities, many white homeowners in the Valley resisted fiercely, and often successfully. But there were gains, too, such as the ethnic studies programs established at California State University, Northridge; the plaque commemorating Chinese workers dedicated at Lang Station; and the largest Thai Buddhist temple in the nation, built in North Hollywood.

Beginning in the late 1970s, the same forces that led to the mass suburbanization of the Valley in the years after World War II propelled the "exurban"—or outer suburban—development of north L.A. County and the area west of the Ventura County line. In the years since, the suburban ideal continues to be redefined, and the people moving outward are much more diverse, both ethnically and economically. Nestled in the Valley and in the hills of north Los Angeles County are numerous master-planned and gated communities, created by real estate developers to satisfy the demands of upwardly mobile working-class and middle-class families, many of them Latina/o and Asian American, for affordable housing and a sanctuary from the perceived ills of urban life in L.A. In this respect, though they may be more racially and ethnically diverse, L.A.'s newest suburbanites are not all that different from their predecessors.

From its initial conception by Anglo-Americans as an agricultural investment, the Valley has boomed as a bedroom community. While traditional manufacturing (defense, auto production) did locate in the Valley, increasingly it is the home of television production (and of many celebrities) and pornography. Because of its proximity to Hollywood and "the industry," adult movie production has exploded in the Valley in the last few decades. According to one source, 90 percent of all legally distributed pornographic films are made in the San Fernando Valley, which nonetheless still clings to its image as a family-oriented collection of neighborhoods aspiring to the suburban ideal. Perhaps such seeming contradictions are inherent in contemporary suburbs. The struggle over who and what belongs in suburbia, and who and what does not, is vibrant and ongoing, though racial and economic concerns and a continued desire for prestige and exclusivity are often submerged in debates about the quality of schools, tax rates, and crime and safety. In this respect, suburban politics and the operation of hegemony and power—dynamics central to understanding the San Fernando Valley today—are becoming ever more complex and essential to study.

San Fernando Valley and North Los Angeles County Sites

6.1 BUSTOP

Reseda High School Auditorium

18230 Kittridge St., Reseda 91335 *(between Etiwanda Ave. and Lindley Ave.)*

Although school desegregation is often associated with the U.S. South, the issue also has a long and contentious history in Los Angeles. In 1978, following court decisions that required school boards to alleviate racial imbalances in schools regardless of the cause, the Los Angeles Board of Education implemented a desegregation plan via the mandatory busing of 40,000 students and the voluntary transfer of another 30,000. BUSTOP, a grassroots organization founded in 1976 by Bobbi Fiedler and Paul Clarke, both from the San Fernando Valley, brought suburban white parents together in opposition to the desegregation plan. Within just one year of its founding, BUSTOP had 50,000 members. BUSTOP hosted community forums and protests in local schools, such as an antibusing event at Reseda High School, pictured here. In addition to bringing several cases before local courts to halt implementation of the desegregation plan, BUSTOP mobilized state voters to approve Proposition 1, which released the school board from its obligation to actually implement busing and mandatory student reassignment unless *intent* of discrimination could be found—in other words, racially unequal *outcomes* were no longer sufficient cause for desegrega-

Reseda High School, 2008.

Rally at Reseda High School organized by BUSTOP to protest a school integration plan, May 20, 1980.

tion. In June 1982, the U.S. Supreme Court, in *Crawford v. Los Angeles Board of Education,* decided that Proposition 1 was constitutional and found no evidence of discriminatory intent behind its formulation. In its decision, the court argued that "the benefits of neighborhood schooling are racially neutral" and equally positive for both white and nonwhite students. The Board of Education eliminated the mandatory sections of the plan and reverted to voluntary desegregation only, with very poor outcomes. Many white families fled the city, and many of those who stayed enrolled their children in private schools. Within a few years, a two-tier system of education developed in Los Angeles—one private and white, the other public and nonwhite—which is still largely in place today. Bobbi Fiedler was elected to the Los Angeles Board of Education in 1977, and in 1980 she went on to the U.S. House of Representatives, representing Van Nuys in the twenty-first district. The history of struggles over educational integration in Los Angeles County, both in the courts and at the grassroots level, suggests that we need to rethink where and how white supremacy operates—that is, even in purportedly liberal California, through the allegedly race-neutral constructs of property rights, parental choice, and neighborhood schools.

FAVORITE NEIGHBORHOOD RESTAURANTS

Vinh Loi Tofu
18625 Sherman Wy., Reseda 91335
(818) 996-9779 (www.vinhloitofu.com)
Small Vietnamese vegan café and tofu factory in an unassuming strip mall.

Ramen Nippon
6900 Reseda Blvd., Reseda 91335
(818) 345-5946
One of the few ramen shops in the Valley. Regulars recommend spicy miso ramen, *gyoza,* and fried rice.

Fab Hot Dogs
19417 Victory Blvd., Reseda 91335
(818) 344-4336 (www.fabhotdogs.com)
Offers a wide variety of creative hot dog toppings.

TO LEARN MORE

Dan Martinez HoSang, "The Changing Valence of White Racial Innocence: The Los Angeles School Desegregation Struggles of the 1970s," in *Black and Brown Los Angeles,* ed. Josh Kun and Laura Pulido (University of California Press, forthcoming).

6.2 Chicana and Chicano Studies and Pan African Studies Departments, California State University, Northridge

Chicana and Chicano Studies

18111 Nordhoff St., 148 Jerome Richfield Hall, Northridge 91330 (818) 677-2734 (www.csun.edu/~hfchs006/)

Pan African Studies   18111 Nordhoff St., 221 Santa Susana Hall, Northridge 91330 (818) 677-3311 (www.csun.edu/csbs/departments/pan_african_studies)

In the late 1960s, CSU Northridge (then San Fernando Valley State College) was one of the most conservative public universities in the state. In part this was because of the low number of students of color compared to other public universities: in the fall of 1968, only 200 of the campus's 18,000 students were Black, and fewer than 100 were

Students promote a boycott of classes at San Fernando Valley State College (now CSU Northridge), demanding that the administration agree to add African American and Chicana and Chicano studies to the curriculum, 1969.

Chicana/o. After Martin Luther King Jr.'s assassination, Dean Edward Peckham claimed that he was unable to find a speaker from one of the local churches willing to pay tribute on campus.

In late 1968, racial tensions at Valley State boiled over. During a football game against Cal Poly San Luis Obispo, Black players were harassed by the other team, but unsupported by their white coach and teammates. After the game, fights broke out between Valley State's Black and white players in the locker room, and the Black Student Union demanded the coach's firing. Facing resistance from both the athletic director and the college president, Black students took over the administration building for four hours on November 4. University president Paul Blomgren agreed to a list of the Black Student Union's demands: the creation of a Black Studies department, recruitment of 500 new Black students a year, the firing of the football coach, an investigation of employment practices, and immunity from prosecution for the Black students involved.

The next day, he reneged on his promises, and police arrested 27 Black students on charges of kidnapping, false imprisonment, and conspiracy. Nineteen were convicted, with three student leaders receiving prison sentences of up to 14 years. In January 1969, a large multiracial rally was held in support of the arrested students. Among those attending was an active group of Chicana/o students involved in United Mexican American Students (which would later become part of MEChA [Movimiento Estudiantil Chicano de Aztlán]), who filled the void in student leadership on campus that had been created by the arrests. Almost 300 students and faculty, most of them white, were arrested at the rally. Community groups also got involved, demanding that the arrested students be released and that administrators meet the students' original demands.

CSU Northridge's Black Studies (now Pan African Studies) and Chicana and Chicano Studies departments were launched in 1969. Both were the first programs of their kind in the state. According to Rudy Acuña—who at that time was a newly hired professor, and who later became chair of the Chicana and Chicano Studies department—both departments were effectively under siege by local law enforcement during their first few years. The LAPD wiretapped a MEChA statewide conference held in the school cafeteria, and two undercover Mexican American police officers took Chicana/o Studies classes and reported back to the LAPD what was being taught and discussed. In spite of these challenges, both departments have gone on to achieve academic excellence and maintain a strong commitment to social justice. The Chicana and Chicano Studies department now has more than 20 full-time faculty and approximately 800 majors, and offers both a bachelor's and a master's degree. More recently, CSU Northridge has developed a Central American Studies program—one of the first in the country. The Pan African Studies department has ten full-time faculty and offers a bachelor's degree.

NEARBY SITES OF INTEREST

North Valley Jewish Community Center

16601 Rinaldi St., Granada Hills 91344
(818) 360-2211 (www.nvjcc.org)
Serves the needs of the Jewish community in the Valley, with a focus on programming for seniors and children. In August 1999, Buford Furrow Jr., a white supremacist, entered the center and shot and wounded three children and a receptionist. On his way there, he shot and killed Pilipino American postal worker Joseph Ileto because he was a person of color and a government employee.

Delmar T. Oviatt Library, CSU Northridge

(818) 677-2285 (http://library.csun.edu)

Houses the Special Collections department and Urban Archives Center (Tseng Wing, second floor west), which contains the papers of local labor unions and a range of political groups, and hosts the San Fernando Valley Digital History Collection, available online.

FAVORITE NEIGHBORHOOD RESTAURANT

Brent's Deli

19565 Parthenia St., Northridge 91324
(818) 886-5679 (www.brentsdeli.com)
The pastrami sandwiches are particularly popular.

TO LEARN MORE

Kevin Roderick, *The San Fernando Valley: America's Suburb* (Los Angeles Times Books, 2001), pp. 147–150.

6.3 Everywoman's Village

5650 Sepulveda Blvd., Van Nuys 91411
(between Hatteras St. and Burbank Blvd.)
Everywoman's Village was a nonprofit community adult school. It was founded in 1962 by Chris Edwards, Diane Rosner, and Lynn Selwyn, all former housewives who wanted to provide classes for women whose education or careers had been interrupted by marriage or motherhood. According to Selwyn, "One day we started talking about the problem women have finding creative outlets. Young girls live in a highly stimulated atmosphere during high school and college years, but often find themselves intellectually stagnant after a few years of marriage." At first, they had trouble finding qualified instructors because of the school's nontraditional approach, but the Village's reputation rapidly spread, and it attracted, on average, 1,000 students per year, nearly 25 percent of

The building at 5650 Sepulveda Blvd., Van Nuys, in 2008, currently a strip mall containing law offices, a Middle Eastern fast food restaurant, and a liquor store.

whom were men. Staff at the Village did not embrace an explicitly radical feminist philosophy. According to Thelma Solomon, the school's publicity director in the mid-1980s, they didn't have time to be radical because they were so busy. However, in addition to more strictly academic courses in engineering, psychology, and the arts, the Village offered workshops and lectures on sex and the law, adultery, and female masturbation; and it disseminated birth control information and sexual devices. The school also embraced an alternative educational approach by, for example, rejecting grades in favor of narrative evaluations. Everywoman's Village was an early model of innovative adult education, and of feminism, that addressed women's everyday lives, material needs, and psychological and sexual health. The school closed in 1999, after years of financial difficulties. (*Quote is from Ellen Shulte, "A Village Where Everyone Makes the Grade," Los Angeles Times, February 14, 1966, p. C1.*)

NEARBY SITES OF INTEREST

Sepulveda Basin Recreation Area
17017 Burbank Blvd., Encino 91316
(818) 756-8060 (www.laparks.org/dos/reccenter/facility/sepulvedaBasinRC.htm)

The Japanese Garden
6100 Woodley Ave., Van Nuys 91406
(818) 756-8166 (www.thejapanesegarden.com)
Located at the Tillman Water Reclamation Plant.

Encino Oak Tree Monument
Louise Ave., 210 feet south of Ventura Blvd, Encino 91316
A monument to the 1,000-year-old oak that survived the threat of developers, pollution, and various diseases but finally succumbed to a storm during the 1998 El Niño event.

FAVORITE NEIGHBORHOOD RESTAURANTS

Nat's Early Bite Coffee Shop
14115 Burbank Blvd., Van Nuys 91401
(818) 781-3040 (www.natsearlybite.com)
A favorite breakfast and lunch spot for more than three decades.

Salsa and Beer
6740 White Oak Ave., Van Nuys 91406
(818) 609-8877 (www.salsaandbeer.com)

Regulars rave about the carne asada combo and green enchiladas. Expect a wait during lunch hour and on weekends.

6.4 General Motors Van Nuys

7867–8010 Van Nuys Blvd., Panorama City 91402 *(between Lanark St. and Blythe St.)*

The General Motors (GM) plant formerly at this address was the last auto plant to close in Southern California during the region's painful process of deindustrialization. In the 1980s it was the site of a major struggle to keep the plant open, led by a multiracial group of United Auto Workers (UAW). GM's strategy included pitting its various factories against each other to see which would offer management the most desirable conditions. In this case, Van Nuys was in competition with a plant in Norwood, Ohio. UAW organizers struggled to get workers to see that they could wage a campaign against GM and had the right to insist that GM keep the plant open. According to a statement at that time by union activist Eric Mann, "The basic premise of the struggle—that we do not recognize GM's plant as 'private property' but see it as a 'joint venture' between capital, labor, and minority communities— flies in the face of GM's worldview and the dominant business ideology of the times." Activists stressed that corporations have a responsibility to their workers and to local communities, especially when the factories have been located in a community for many years. As part of their efforts to bring Latina/o, African American, and white workers together, as well as to build support in the larger community, UAW organizers connected with the

After the demolition of GM Van Nuys in 1998, the site was converted into a shopping center called "The Plant," 2008.

progressive political leadership of the time, including such figures as Jesse Jackson, Cesar Chavez, and Maxine Waters. By waging an extensive campaign, including a boycott, activists managed to get GM to stay ten years longer than anticipated. Although GM did eventually leave, the organizing work of the campaign led to the formation of the Labor/Community Strategy Center, which was later set up by the campaign's organizers and some of the workers. The center has developed such projects as the Bus Riders Union (see entry 1.3 Bus Riders Union and Labor/Community Strategy Center), which has organized for transit equity in Los Angeles since the early 1990s.

After the plant was closed, the lot sat barren for a few years until a redevelopment project was initiated. In a nod to the site's

United Auto Workers Local 645 President Pete Beltran, Cesar Chavez, and Maxine Waters (from left) march with a multiracial group of GM workers past the GM plant, 1983.

previous function, the new shopping center built there was called "The Plant." Although California was once the largest producer of autos and auto-related parts west of the Mississippi, at the time of this writing the state's last remaining auto plant (Toyota in Fremont) had just closed, leaving no auto plants in California. GM Van Nuys' transition from an auto plant to a shopping center signals the regional economy's shift away from durable manufactured goods to services and retail—a change that, for most workers, involves an equally important shift from high-quality, middle-class jobs with benefits to low-wage, insecure jobs with minimal benefits (like most of those in The Plant's retail stores). (*Quote is from Eric Mann, "Keeping GM Van Nuys Open," Labor Research Review 1, no. 9 [1986]: 36.*)

TO LEARN MORE

Eric Mann, *Taking on General Motors: A Case Study of the Campaign to Keep GM Van Nuys Open* (University of California, Los Angeles, Center for Labor Research and Education, 1987).

6.5 *The Great Wall* and Social and Public Art Resource Center (SPARC)

The Great Wall   Tujunga Flood Control Channel, North Hollywood 91606 (*along Coldwater Canyon Ave. between Oxnard St. and Burbank Blvd.*)

SPARC   685 Venice Blvd., Venice 90291 (*between Pisani Pl. and Shell Ave.; this site is located in the Westside*) (310) 822-9560 (www.sparcmurals.org)

The Great Wall is a mural painted by the Social and Public Art Resource Center. The mural tells the history of California from the perspectives of those excluded from dominant narratives: indigenous peoples, the poor, people of color, women, and gays and lesbians. The half-mile-long mural on the wall of the Tujunga Flood Control Channel was painted over multiple summers, beginning in 1976, when eighty young people, ten artists, and five historians completed the first 1,000 feet, which depicted the prehistoric era to 1910. Subsequent pieces of *The Great Wall* were painted over the summers of 1978, 1980, 1981, and 1983, and the mural was completed in 1984. *The Great Wall* draws on the aesthetic and political legacies of the great Mexican muralists as well as the public art of the Works Progress Administration. Most of the people who actually painted the mural were low-income and young people of color.

SPARC itself was founded in 1976 by muralist Judith Baca, painter Christina Schlesinger, and filmmaker Donna Deitch. Previously, Baca had been working for the City of Los Angeles' Department of Recreation and Parks as an art teacher in Boyle Heights. In that capacity she encouraged neighborhood youth to shift their focus from graffiti, which was often associated with gang-related disputes, to murals, which could express political themes while bringing art to the public. Baca initiated Los Angeles' first city-wide mural program, which culminated in more than 400 murals painted by teams of youth throughout the mid-1970s. However, censorship issues arose almost immediately,

Judith F. Baca, detail from the 1940s section of *The Great Wall of Los Angeles*. The mural, begun in 1976, is located in California's San Fernando Valley Tujunga Wash, a flood control channel built in the 1930s. Acrylic on cast concrete, 13' × 2,400', 1983.

and the use of public walls became more restricted, leading a group of artist-activists to create SPARC. SPARC is committed to the use of public art as an organizing tool, particularly in and for Los Angeles' disenfranchised and marginalized communities, and it embraces participatory art-making practices and processes.

The Great Wall inspired a larger Neighborhood Pride program that led to the painting of 105 murals, located in almost every ethnic community throughout Los Angeles. SPARC's murals are considered landmarks, and the organization's influence, as well as its emphasis on community-based art making, has spread globally. Restoration of The Great Wall began in 2009. There are also plans to add panels telling California's more recent history.

FAVORITE NEIGHBORHOOD RESTAURANTS

Porto's Bakery
3614 W. Magnolia Blvd., Burbank 91505
(818) 846-9100 (www.portosbakery.com)
Extremely popular Cuban bakery and sandwich shop. Among the numerous favorites are the guava cream cheese rolls, potato balls, crème brûlé, and mango mousse. Not in the immediate vicinity of The Great Wall, but an L.A. legend—and well worth the trip.

Jinya Ramen
11239 Ventura Blvd., Studio City 91604 (818) 980-3977 (www.jinya-la.com/ramen)
Small ramen shop serving up delicious savory pork broth, vegetable, and tomato-seafood ramens. Great gyoza as well.

6.6 KPFK Radio Station and Pacifica Archives

3729 Cahuenga Blvd., North Hollywood 91604 (nearest cross street: Lankershim Blvd.)
(818) 985-2711 (www.kpfk.org)

KPFK began transmitting in Los Angeles in 1959 as part of Pacifica Radio. Founded by a pacifist and former Washington, D.C., newsman, Lewis Hill, Pacifica is the oldest listener-sponsored independent radio station network in the United States. Since its founding, KPFK has served as an important alternative voice and progressive media outlet. This building on Cahuenga Boulevard houses the station's studios and contains a vast archive of public radio programming. The Pacifica Foundation recently began digitally restoring and preserving many of its unique programs, such as interviews with Alice Walker and Archbishop Oscar Romero and coverage of events like the Women for Peace rally in 1961 and the rally in support of Angela Y. Davis at UC Berkeley in 1968.

The radio station fell into disarray in the late 1990s, when programmers, staff, and audience members could not agree on how to respond to a declining audience, leading to infighting and a high turnover. Two events in recent years exemplify the turmoil at the station. In 2007, the elections for KPFK's board of directors were characterized by intense hostilities among competing factions after the station announced it would fire the general manager, who had been charged with sexual harassment and racism and had received a vote of no confidence. The camp defending the general manager argued that the claims were false and were actually part of an attempt to purge the station of Spanish programming and more radical content. These same programs also happened to be hosted in large part by people of color. Then, in the spring of 2009, the programming director took *La Causa,* a program about Chicana/o politics and issues, off the air. Conversation on the show often veered toward Palestine and Israel, Zionism and anti-Zionism, and the cohosts were accused of anti-Semitism and hate speech. The infighting and name-calling that characterized these two disputes are examples of the Left's tendency to self-destruct when it is unable to work across differences in class, race, ethnicity, and political ideology.

However, such tensions might also be read as examples of the crucial democratic debate necessary in any political community—in this case, a debate about the proper scope and focus of leftist media in the twenty-first century within a neoliberal regime. Despite the station's recent rocky history, KPFK remains one of the few alternative media institutions on the airwaves, which are otherwise dominated by a limited range of corporate and right-wing perspectives, and the station continues to be a vital resource for discussion of local issues. Favorite shows include *Uprising, Democracy Now,* and *Which Way, L.A.?*

NEARBY SITE OF INTEREST

Campo de Cahuenga

3919 Lankershim Blvd., North Hollywood 91604
(818) 762-3998, ext. 2 (www.campodecahuenga
.com)
Site of the signing of the Treaty of Cahuenga,

which ended the Mexican-American War in Alta California in 1847.

FAVORITE NEIGHBORHOOD RESTAURANTS

Daichan

11288 Ventura Blvd., Studio City 91604
(818) 980-8450
An eclectic selection of Japanese and Hawaiian-Japanese comfort foods.

Bollywood Cafe

11101 Ventura Blvd., Studio City 91604
(818) 508-8400 (www.bollywoodcafela.com)
Very popular Indian café. Try the chicken *tikka masala,* vegetable korma, and samosas.

Midori Sushi

11622 Ventura Blvd., Studio City 91604
(818) 623-7888 (www.midorisushi.net)
Not cheap, but it offers all-you-can-eat lunch and dinner specials with some of the freshest sushi and sashimi in the city.

TO LEARN MORE

KPFK regularly accepts volunteers and interns. Call the volunteer and outreach coordinator at (818) 985-2711 or visit www.kpfk.org/volunteer for more information.

Matthew Lasar, *Pacifica Radio: The Rise of an Alternative Network* (Temple University Press, 2000).

6.7 Lang Station

14212 Lang Station Rd., Canyon Country 91387 *(near Soledad Canyon Rd.)*

On September 5, 1876, the railroad line connecting San Francisco and Los Angeles was completed here at Lang Station. The railroad enabled California to develop as a single economic and political unit. Completing the connection required workers to bore numerous tunnels through the solid rock of the Tehachapi Mountains. Although many ethnic groups participated in this effort, Chinese workers were especially crucial. Despite their contributions to California's economy and infrastructure, however, Chinese laborers endured inhumane and discriminatory conditions, including segregated camps and inferior food, as they laid tracks and dynamited mountains. Death, paralysis, amputation, and injury were common. These workers were also much maligned and targeted by a fierce anti-Chinese movement (see entries 1.8 Chinatowns and 1.6 Calle de los Negros).

As the line neared completion, a contest was held to see if the workers from the north or from the south would be the first to complete the last 500 yards. The Los Angeles team won. Charles Crocker, president of the Southern Pacific Railroad, drove a gold spike into the track, surrounded by hundreds of prominent businessmen. While they celebrated the engineering prowess and massive public and private investment that made the railroad possible, the laborers were largely disregarded, except for a dehumanizing portrait by the *San Francisco Chronicle* that minimized the workers' contributions. The newspaper reported: "There were nearly 4,000 people on the ground, nearly 3,000 being Chinese employees of the railroad who with their picks, shovels and bamboo hats arranged on either side of

Lang Station, 2009.

Chinese workers and their boss near Lang Station, 1876.

the track looked on with wondering eyes and jabbering away like so many parrots. . . . After Crocker gave the signal and the locomotives whistled . . . the air was full of dust, steel rails and iron mauls hammering in the spikes. All the tracklayers were Caucasians and the Chinese simply looked on and cheered their favorite crew."

In 1976, the Chinese Historical Society of Southern California cosponsored Lang Station's centennial celebration, at which it installed a plaque that reads, in English and Chinese, "On this centennial we honor over three thousand Chinese who helped build the Southern Pacific Railroad and the San Fernando Tunnel. Their labor gave California the first north-south railway, changing the state's history." The original golden spike is housed at the California Historical Society in San Francisco.

NEARBY SITES OF INTEREST

Placerita Canyon Nature Center
19152 Placerita Canyon Rd., Newhall 91321 (661) 259-7721 (placerita.org)
The place where gold was first found in California.

Vasquez Rocks Natural Area and Nature Center
10700 W. Escondido Canyon Rd., Agua Dulce 91390 (661) 268-0840 (www.lamountains .com/parks.asp?parkid=657)
Former hideout of nineteenth-century California bandit Tiburcio Vasquez, and a nice place for hikes.

TO LEARN MORE

Alexander Saxton, *The Indispensable Enemy: Labor and the Anti-Chinese Movement in California* (University of California Press, 1995).

6.8 Saint Francis Dam

San Francisquito Canyon Rd., Santa Clarita 91390 *(GPS coordinates: 34.54704, -118.512504)*

Directions: From the intersection of San Francisquito Canyon Rd. and Copper Hill Rd., drive 7.5 miles. Take a sharp right on former San Francisquito Canyon Rd. and drive an additional 0.3 miles. The remains of the base of the dam will be to the left of the road. Note that the latter section of road is no longer in regular use and may be closed. For information and access, contact the U.S. Forest Service (Angeles National Forest) ahead of time at (626) 574-1613 or www.fs.fed.us /r5/angeles.

The Saint Francis Dam was constructed in 1925–26, after the completion of the Los Angeles Aqueduct, to provide sufficient water in case of an earthquake or sabotage by Owens Valley residents, who resented the Los Angeles Department of Water and Power (DWP) for diverting their water to L.A. When full, the dam held 28,000 acre-feet of water—one year's supply—weighing almost 52 million tons. The dam consistently suffered from small seeps and leaks, however, which Chief Engineer William Mulholland (who had also supervised construction of the aqueduct) insisted were normal. On March 12, 1928, Mulholland inspected the dam but reassured the dam keeper that it was fine and went home. However, just before midnight the dam broke and a wall of water 100 feet high plunged down the canyon. It hit the Santa Clara River at 18 miles per hour and then veered west, toward Ventura, until it spilled into the Pacific Ocean. The water traveled 54 miles in five and a

The remains of the Saint Francis Dam after its failure in 1928.

More than 80 years later, fragments of the Saint Francis Dam (foreground center; photographed in 2008) are still visible in the valley that it flooded.

half hours. Human survivors and livestock clung to trees or were snarled in fences. Ray Rising, a DWP employee, remembers: "I heard a roaring like a cyclone. . . . The water was so high we couldn't get out the front door. . . . In the darkness I became tangled in an oak tree, fought clear and swam to the surface . . . I grabbed the roof of another house, jumping off when it floated to the

hillside." The official death count was 450 people, but the actual number may have been closer to 700. Later reports concluded that the tragedy was not the result of design or engineering shortcomings; the dam was simply built in the wrong place—in a still moving landslide. The tragedy that occurred at Saint Francis Dam illustrates the risks inherent in city boosters' efforts to ensure that Los Angeles' growth and profit would not be impeded by its modest natural water supply. When you are willing to get water at any cost, such mishaps are inevitable. *(Quote is from "The Valley of Death," The Public "I," July 16, 2009, see http://thepublici.blogspot.com/2009/07/three-valley-of-death.html.)*

TO LEARN MORE

John Nichols, *St. Francis Dam Disaster* (Arcadia Publishing, 2002).

William Kahrl, *Water and Power: The Conflict over Los Angeles' Water Supply in the Owens Valley* (University of California Press, 1982).

Santa Clarita Valley Historical Society, 24101 Newhall Ave. (formerly San Fernando Rd.), Santa Clarita 91321 (661) 254-1275 (www.scvhs.org).

6.9 Santa Susana Field Laboratory

5800 Woolsey Canyon Rd., Canoga Park 91304

Directions: From the intersection of Woolsey Canyon Rd. and Valley Circle Blvd., drive approximately 2.5 miles on Woolsey Canyon Blvd., until the road ends at a T-shaped intersection. The entrance to the Boeing facility is on the left. Turn right and take the first left into the lower parking lot of Sage Ranch Park. A loop trail that begins at the southern edge of the parking lot affords views of the Boeing facility. The whole trail is 2.5 miles long, but you will see the Boeing parking lot and facilities almost immediately. Situated thirty miles from downtown Los Angeles on the top of the Simi Hills, Santa Susana is a 2,850-acre site that was devoted to military, aerospace, and energy testing and development. It represents well the in-

novations and achievements, as well as the risks and costs, of the high-tech industrial development that has been so important to Southern California's history and landscape. Because of its good year-round weather and culture of technological innovation, Southern California was key to early commercial aviation and World War II military production. In the 1940s, Boeing established the Santa Susana Field Laboratory as a test facility for nuclear weapons and rocket engines. Various U.S. agencies, including NASA, and corporations, such as Rocketdyne and the Marquardt Corporation, have used the facility over the years.

The Santa Susana Field Laboratory has produced two major environmental problems. First, it is the site of the first U.S. nuclear meltdown. In the 1950s, the facility operated the first commercial nuclear-power reactor in the country (which powered 1,100 homes in nearby Moorpark). Unfortunately, one of the reactors went awry on July 26, 1959. According to one account, this episode released more radiation than the meltdown at Three Mile Island. The second major environmental problem is vast soil and groundwater contamination. Both trichloroethylene (TCE) and perchloroethylene (PCE) have been found in the area. The full extent of the contamination is unknown, but it is estimated that there are more than 500,000 gallons of TCE beneath the site. An independent study published in 2006 concluded that the test site may be responsible for hundreds of cancers in the surrounding communities.

While efforts are now being made to ad-

The Boeing facility that houses the Santa Susana Field Laboratory, viewed from a loop trail in neighboring Sage Ranch Park, 2010.

Cartoon by Steve Greenberg for the *Ventura County Star*, 2003.

dress these problems, grassroots demands were ignored for years by the government. Under the George W. Bush administration, the Department of Energy (DOE)—without ever producing a full environmental impact report (EIR)—maintained that the site would pose no significant human health threat after it was cleaned, even declaring that it could be considered for a possible housing project. Then, in 2003, the DOE announced that it was changing its clean-up strategy and would leave 99 percent of the contaminated soil untouched. Fortunately, several organizations challenged these policies. In 2004 the Natural Resources Defense Council and the Committee to Bridge the Gap sued the DOE, charging that it had violated the National Environmental Policy Act, the Endangered Species Act, and the Comprehensive Environmental Response,

Compensation, and Liability Act (commonly known as the Superfund law). These groups have insisted that, at the very least, a comprehensive EIR must be produced. At present, the federal Environmental Protection Agency is the lead agency in an interagency agreement under which it must test for background radiation, produce an EIR, and develop a radiation cleanup plan. The California Department of Toxic Substances is charged with cleaning up the chemical contamination.

NEARBY SITE OF INTEREST

Sage Ranch Park

1 Black Canyon Rd., Simi Valley 93063
(818) 999-3753 (www.lamountains.com/parks
.asp?parkid=53)
A 625-acre park on the Los Angeles–Ventura county line. Hiking, picnicking, and camping.

TO LEARN MORE

Aerospace Contamination Museum of Education
(ACME), (310) 428-5085 (http://acmela.org).
The Los Angeles chapter of ACME promotes
awareness of and works to resolve the massive
environmental contamination associated with
the Santa Susana Field Laboratory.

Committee to Bridge the Gap, www.committee
tobridgethegap.org.

Natural Resources Defense Council, www.nrdc
.org.

Roger Lotchin, *Fortress California, 1910–1961: From
Warfare to Welfare* (University of Illinois Press,
2002).

6.10 Simi Valley Courthouse and Site of Rodney King Beating

Courthouse   3855-F Alamo St., Simi Valley 93063 *(at Valencia Ave.)*

Site of beating   11777 Foothill Blvd., Sylmar 91342 *(nearest cross street: Osborne St.)*

Simi Valley Courthouse, 2008.

On March 3, 1991, Rodney King, an African American motorist, was beaten with fifty-six baton blows and six kicks over a period of two minutes. While he was being beaten, seventeen police officers and four California Highway Patrol officers observed but failed to intervene. From a distance, local resident George Holliday videotaped the incident, producing a clip that would later be replayed across the world. In 1992, the case came to trial in Los Angeles. The district attorney charged four officers—Stacey Koon, Laurence Powell, Theodore Briseno, and Timothy Wind—with the use of excessive force. Because of the intense publicity and public outcry in Los Angeles, Judge Stanley Weisberg ordered a change of venue, and the case was moved to the Simi Valley Courthouse in neighboring Ventura County.

The demographics, culture, and politics of Ventura are radically different from those of Los Angeles—differences that favored the police officers. Both Simi Valley and Ventura County are whiter and more conservative than Los Angeles County. In 1990, Ventura County's population was 69 percent white (Simi Valley was 80 percent white) and just 2.2 percent Black, while Los Angeles was only 44 percent white and 10.5 percent Black. Simi Valley is home to many law enforcement professionals and is consistently ranked as one of the "safest cities in America." It is also home to the Ronald Reagan Presidential Library, and residents consistently elect conservative politicians such as U.S. Congressman Elton Gallegly, who has supported numerous anti-immigrant laws and English-only initiatives. All of these differences are highly significant because, according to legal scholar Patricia Williams, factors such as a community's racial composition and the percentage of the population associated with law enforcement are known to influence the outcome of a trial and are all taken into account when determining where a case will be moved to—suggesting that courts may rig the system to encourage particular outcomes. Not surprisingly, the jury in King's relocated trial was composed of ten white people, one Latino person, and one Asian person. According to one source, eight of the twelve jurors were either security guards, had served in the armed forces, or had spouses in the military.

On April 29, 1992, the jury acquitted the four defendants. Their decision led to the largest urban unrest in U.S. history: the L.A. uprising. After four days of upheaval, 53 people were dead, 2,383 were injured, and 12,545 were arrested. Seven hundred structures were destroyed, and damages totaled more than $1 billion. Partly because of public outrage over the acquittals, a subsequent federal civil rights trial was held. The jury found two of the defendants, Koon and Powell, guilty, while Wind and Briseno were acquitted. King also won a civil lawsuit in which he was awarded $3.8 million.

Although the Simi Valley Courthouse is not actually in Los Angeles, we thought it should be included in the *People's Guide*. Not only is it an important part of Los Angeles' history, but it also illustrates the importance of political borders—not just between nations, but also between cities and counties. While borders are entirely human creations, they have great power when consciously used by the state to determine political outcomes, as is so clearly illustrated by decisions to change a court venue.

NEARBY SITES OF INTEREST

Robert P. Strathearn Historical Park, Rancho Simi Recreation and Park District
137 Strathearn Pl., Simi Valley 93063
(805) 526-6453 (www.simihistory.com)
The former headquarters of a Spanish rancho and Chumash village.

Ronald Reagan Presidential Library
40 Presidential Dr., Simi Valley 93065
(800) 410-8354 or (805) 577-4000 (www.reagan library.com)

Want to find out what Reagan knew about U.S. military intervention in Central America? How about his attacks on affirmative action? His war on organized labor? Here is the place to start.

Mission San Fernando Rey de España

15151 San Fernando Mission Blvd., Los Angeles 91345 (818) 361-0186 (http://missiontour.org /sanfernando)
One of two Spanish missions in L.A. County. Also houses the archives for the Archdiocese of Los Angeles.

Tia Chucha's Centro Cultural and Bookstore

13197-A Gladstone Ave., Sylmar 91342 (818) 528-4511 (www.tiachucha.com)
A cultural space offering workshops, art exhibits, readings, family events, and performances.

TO LEARN MORE

Robert Gooding-Williams, ed., *Reading Rodney King/Reading Urban Uprising* (Routledge, 1993).

6.11 Siutcanga/Village of Los Encinos

Los Encinos State Historic Park, 16756 Moorpark St., Encino 91436 *(at La Maida St.)* (818) 784-4849 (www.parks.ca .gov/?page_id=619 or http://los-encinos.org)
The village of Los Encinos was the Tongva's largest settlement in the San Fernando Valley, with nearly 200 inhabitants (who are thought to have called the village Siutcanga) in the late 1700s. The Tongva people were drawn to this area because of its plentiful oak trees (acorns were an important food source) and warm springs.

When Spanish explorers, led by Gaspar de Portola and the Franciscan padre Juan Crespi, met the Tongva people here in 1769, they named the spot El Valle de Santa Cata-

lina de Bononia de los Encinos, or "Los Encinos" (The Oaks) for short. Later, the Tongva people from Los Encinos were forced into the region's two Spanish missions at San Fernando and San Gabriel, after Padre Fermín de Lasuén persuaded the owner of the land that would become the San Fernando Mission site, Francisco Reyes, to trade his land for a 4,460-acre ranch at Los Encinos village. The priest effectively traded indigenous land he did not own for a mission site on which to capture and convert the Tongva people. Reyes was later accused of mistreating the indigenous people who worked for him on his ranch, and in 1845 the Mexican governor Pio Pico regranted the land to three of the workers, recorded as Ramon, Francisco, and Roque, who raised cattle and corn there until their deaths a few years later. Vicente de la Osa acquired the Rancho Los Encinos from their widows in 1849. Though the U.S. Land Commission confirmed de la Osa's title in 1862 (a rarity in those days, when so many Mexicans were losing their land to American squatters and claimants), the ranch traded hands many times after the American conquest and eventually became the residential subdivisions of Encino and Sherman Oaks.

The State of California acquired five acres of the property in 1945 and created the Los Encinos State Historic Park, which features the original homes of two of the site's owners, as well as exhibits on the site's history. In 1984, construction workers excavating a foundation for a building complex on Ventura Boulevard, just across from the park, discovered an archaeological jackpot.

Native American workers Sanese and Napoleon (from left) at Rancho Los Encinos, 1906.

Los Encinos State Historic Park, 2008.

They found more than 2 million Indian artifacts, including arrowheads, beads, and various stone tools, and about 20 earthly remains that archaeologists dated at more than 3,000 years old.

San Vicente Mountain Park

17500 Mulholland Dr., Encino 90049
(www.lamountains.com/parks.asp?parkid=54)
Great views of L.A.

Versailles Cuban Restaurant

17410 Ventura Blvd., Encino 91316
(818) 906-0756 (www.versaillescuban.com)
A small, very popular local chain. The garlic
chicken is the house specialty.

6.12 Tarzana

18354 Ventura Blvd., Tarzana 91356
(between Ave. Hacienda and Ave. Oriente)

In 1910, General Harrison Gray Otis, owner
of the *Los Angeles Times,* bought the 550-acre
parcel of land that would become
the community of Tarzana. He
bought the parcel as his reward to
himself for investing in the Los Angeles Suburban Homes Company,
the syndicate that bought land in
the San Fernando Valley to take advantage of water from the new Los
Angeles Aqueduct. Otis named his
ranch Mil Flores, planted exotic trees
from Africa and Asia, and built both
a 20-room hacienda with a lookout
tower over the Valley and a log cabin
that he called Koonskin Kabin.

In 1919, Edgar Rice Burroughs,
author of *Tarzan: King of the Apes,*
purchased Otis's ranch, intending to
preserve it intact as his own personal
estate. As real estate values in the
Valley soared, however, Burroughs

subdivided the property and promoted
residential lots, using the language of colonization and exclusivity upon which his
Tarzan novel was based. In the novel, according to literary scholar Catherine Jurca,
the young Tarzan's home, replete with great
literary works left by his deceased British
parents, keeps him "civilized" despite being
surrounded by the "savagery" of African
tribes. Similarly, lots sold in Tarzana were
governed by racially restrictive covenants,
which mandated that "said premises or any
part thereof shall not be leased, sold, or
conveyed to or occupied by any person not
of the Caucasian race." According to Jurca,
"Tarzan justified the racial and class restrictions of burgeoning suburbs as a defense of
residential freedom on the part of besieged

Site of Edgar Rice Burroughs, Inc., 2008.

white inhabitants." The Tarzana subdivision helped to create an ideology of threatened white suburban homesteads and demonstrates the strange mix of colonial fantasy and racially exclusive land use policy that has characterized much of the San Fernando Valley's development.

This address on Ventura Boulevard represents just a small parcel of the original 550-acre ranch, but it is the site of Edgar Rice Burroughs, Inc., which manages a fan club, newsletter, magazine, all legal matters related to use of the Tarzan character, and Burroughs's personal archive. Burroughs himself was cremated, and his ashes were buried under the walnut tree outside the office.

NEARBY SITE OF INTEREST

Epicenter of 1994 Northridge Earthquake
Intersection of Wilbur Ave. and Saticoy St., Los Angeles 91335

TO LEARN MORE

Catherine Jurca, *White Diaspora: The Suburb and the Twentieth-Century American Novel* (Princeton University Press, 2001).

6.13 Theodore Payne Foundation for Wildflowers and Native Plants

10459 Tuxford St., Sun Valley 91352
(between Wheatland Ave. and Ledge Ave.)
(818) 768-1802 (www.theodorepayne.org)

The Theodore Payne Foundation is a non-profit nursery that promotes the cultivation of California native plants through retail sales and educational activities. Southern California has a Mediterranean climate, characterized by wet winters and dry summers, which is relatively rare around the world. Distinct plant communities such as chaparral and coastal sage have developed in the Mediterranean climate zones. California's native plants are ideally suited to their climate and need minimal irrigation and maintenance. Since the beginning of Spanish incursions in the 1500s, however, California's native species and plant communities have been under attack by invader species. Especially pernicious are the nonnative grasses (such as green lawns) and other plants with which Southern Californians seek to replicate eastern U.S. and European landscaping. The demise of California's native plants is a result of not only imperialist invasions but also the high regard in which we hold European tastes and fashion—despite the fact that they may be totally inappropriate for this particular environment. And, it is important to realize that our aesthetic tastes in plants and our incessant desire for land destroy habitats. Currently, one-third of California native plants (about 179 varieties) are considered rare, endangered, or threatened. Only 10 percent of the original coastal sage and less than 1 percent of California's native grasslands remain intact.

The Theodore Payne nursery is an important counter to these forces. The nursery occupies 22 acres and sells more than 300 native plant species. The foundation is named for Theodore Payne, who emigrated to Los Angeles from England. In 1903, Payne founded his own nursery to preserve native species that were being lost to agriculture

Native plants for sale by the Theodore Payne Foundation, 2008.

and housing. By the time he retired in 1958, Payne had made more than 400 species of native plants available to the public. Today, visitors can learn about growing and nurturing native plants by enrolling in the foundation's many classes or visiting its library and art gallery; the grounds are also a wonderful place to picnic, relax, or simply be inspired.

NEARBY SITE OF INTEREST

Hansen Dam Park

11770 Foothill Blvd., Lakeview Terrace 91342
(818) 899-6016 (www.laparks.org/dos/rec center/facility/hansendamRC.htm)
This 1,000-acre recreational facility includes an equestrian center, aquatic center (including a place to rent paddleboats), soccer fields, and more. Take a picnic and have lunch along one of the gently flowing streams. Since there are no trash cans along the dam, be sure to take a trash bag with you. And keep an eye out for snowy egrets, which are rare elsewhere in L.A. but common here.

FAVORITE NEIGHBORHOOD RESTAURANT

Rancheros Tacos

8447 Sunland Blvd., Sun Valley 91352
(818) 504-2789
Actually a great spot for Salvadoran *pupusas,* especially during the Wednesday specials.

TO LEARN MORE

Carol Bornstein, David Fross, and Bart O'Brien, *California Native Plants for the Garden* (Cachuma Press, 2005).

6.14 Val Verde Park

30300 W. Arlington St., Val Verde 91384
(nearest cross street: Euclid Ave.)
(661) 257-4014

A soccer game in Val Verde Park reflects the area's current demographics, 2008.

Val Verde was one of the few parks open to African Americans during the period of Jim Crow segregation. Beginning as early as the 1890s, African Americans were drawn to Los Angeles because of the opportunities available to Black people in the city and the relative freedoms they enjoyed here compared to cities in the Midwest and South. One reason for their relatively advantaged position was that other nonwhites, particularly Mexicans and Chinese, incurred the brunt of white racism in L.A.

However, as time went on and the Black population grew, discrimination against African Americans increased and they were barred from most public beaches, resorts, and parks. In the 1920s, a white Pasadena philanthropist donated land at Val Verde, which had originally been a mining town, to the county to be used as an outdoor area for African Americans. Val Verde soon became a prominent resort that featured such guests as Della Reese, Count Basie, and Duke Ellington. The park fell out of favor after the civil rights movement, when most segregationist barriers were dropped and African Americans were able to visit other recreational areas. Today Val Verde is a public park that serves the local population, which is now predominantly Latina/o.

Members of the White family at Val Verde Park in 1955.

Castaic Lake State Recreation Area
32132 Castaic Lake Dr., Castaic 91384
(661) 257-4050 (www.castaiclake.com)
Offers swimming, boating, canoeing, fishing, hiking, and more.

6.15 Wat Thai of Los Angeles

8225 Coldwater Canyon Ave.,
North Hollywood 91605 (at Cantara St.)
(818) 780-4200 (www.watthai.com)

Wat Thai (Thai Temple) of Los Angeles is the largest Thai Buddhist temple in the nation. It is also the religious, social, and cultural center of L.A.'s Thai community, which is the largest in the United States. Completed in 1979, the temple attracts thousands of visitors each year and has facilitated the development of a local Thai residential community in the surrounding neighborhoods. In addition to religious services, the temple provides a space in which to hold festivals that celebrate Thai holidays and, until recently, where Thais could operate food booths during weekends. These gatherings attracted diverse crowds, sometimes numbering in the thousands, leading to complaints from non-Thai residents of the surrounding communities. In the early 1980s, members of a neighborhood committee argued that events at the Wat Thai led to parking problems, litter, and noise; they invoked zoning laws in an attempt to prohibit the temple from sponsoring the festivals. After a series of investigations and meetings between temple officials and the neighborhood committee from 1982 to 1984, the city placed the Wat Thai on probation for violating zoning restrictions that had been established when it first opened. Despite the verdict, the Wat Thai continued to operate food booths on the weekends, but under conditions set by the neighbors and the city. Nearly 25 years later, in 2007, city officials

The Wat Thai of Los Angeles, visible from the surrounding residential streets, 2008.

PERSONAL REFLECTION BY TANACHAI MARK PADOONGPATT, ETHNIC STUDIES SCHOLAR

I remember the smell of incense and food wafting through the air. I remember discovering new places around the temple while playing hide-and-seek as a kid. My favorite hiding spot was behind the monks' quarters, next to a set of bathrooms that no one ever seemed to use. I remember being barefoot, a lot. I remember my grandfather's funeral in the recreation room on the bottom level of the school building. And I'll never forget watching my friend dangle from the ledge of the second-floor window of that very school building in an attempt to jump and join us below, so that we could all ditch Thai summer school.

called for a temporary moratorium on the sale of food at the Wat Thai. Responding to continuing complaints, city officials argued that the temple was essentially a food festival on weekends that generated problems for nearby residents. The moratorium became permanent, and as of this writing the Wat Thai is allowed to sell food only twice a year during major festivals; many of the vendors have since gone elsewhere to sell their food. For Thais as well as many other Asians, shutting down the food booths has meant they are without a central community space, vital for social interactions, cultural production, and economic opportunities. *(Courtesy of Tanachai Mark Padoongpatt)*

FAVORITE NEIGHBORHOOD RESTAURANT

Sri Siam Café
12843 Vanowen St., North Hollywood 91605
(818) 982-6161 or (818) 982-6262
(www.srisiamcafe1.com)
A favorite Thai spot. Try the crispy rice salad, spicy ribs, and mango and sticky rice dessert.

TO LEARN MORE

Tanachai Mark Padoongpatt, "Thais That Bind: U.S. Empire, Food, and Community in Los Angeles, 1945–2008" (PhD dissertation, University of Southern California, 2011).

7

Thematic
Tours

This chapter includes seven tours that will guide you to important places whose history and geography relate to a particular theme. All are full-day tours and will be most easily completed by car, for which we include point-to-point driving directions. Frequently, in addition to the main sites, we suggest nearby sites of interest to visit or organizations at which you may meet with staff members or arrange to volunteer. We also provide suggestions for good places to have a meal, although we invite you to choose any of the other restaurants listed in the "Favorite Neighborhood Restaurants" section of each site entry to accommodate your appetite and schedule.

First Peoples Tour

Contemporary Los Angeles has the largest urban concentration of American Indians in the United States. This tour visits important political, cultural, and spiritual sites of American Indians in Los Angeles County. You will travel through North L.A., the Greater Eastside and San Gabriel Valley, South L.A., and the Harbor and South Bay (specifically Long Beach).

Start at **YANG-NA** (200 N. Spring St., Los Angeles 90012), one of the largest villages of the Tongva people and a favorite trading spot for native peoples of the region before Spanish colonization. It is now the site of L.A. City Hall. The city of Los Angeles was founded on or near the site of Yang-Na in 1781, and the Tongva people were forced into the missions at San Gabriel and San Fernando. During the American period, they were auctioned off as slave laborers at the nearby **DOWNEY BLOCK** (312 N. Spring St., Los Angeles 90012), just around the corner from city hall. To get to the Downey Block from Yang-Na/city hall, walk north on Spring Street, make a right on Temple, and go to the corner of Temple and Main. Here, during the 1850s and 1860s, native peoples who had been imprisoned for crimes such as vagrancy or loitering were auctioned off, usually to Anglo and Mexican ranchers, for servitude.

The next stop is the **SAN GABRIEL MISSION** (428 S. Mission Dr., San Gabriel 91776). From the Downey Block, drive northeast on Main Street and take the first right, onto Aliso Street. Merge onto U.S.-101 south via the ramp on the left side. Take a slight left to get onto I-10 east heading toward San Bernardino, and travel for almost 7 miles. Exit at San Gabriel Boulevard and turn right at East Mission Road. The mission will be on the left side. Beginning in 1771, Tongva peoples were lured to this place with food, converted to Catholicism, and forced to perform agricultural and some manufacturing work. An estimated 6,000 indigenous people died here during Spanish rule. This mission was also the site of an unsuccessful uprising led by two young Indians, Toypurina and Nicolas José, in 1775. Call ahead if you wish to arrange a guided tour of the mission (although you may want to critique and challenge the official narrative), or explore the church, museum, gardens, and gift shop on your own. The mission is open seven days a week (except holidays) from 9:00 A.M. to 4:30 P.M. Admission is $5.00 for adults and $3.00 for children under 17.

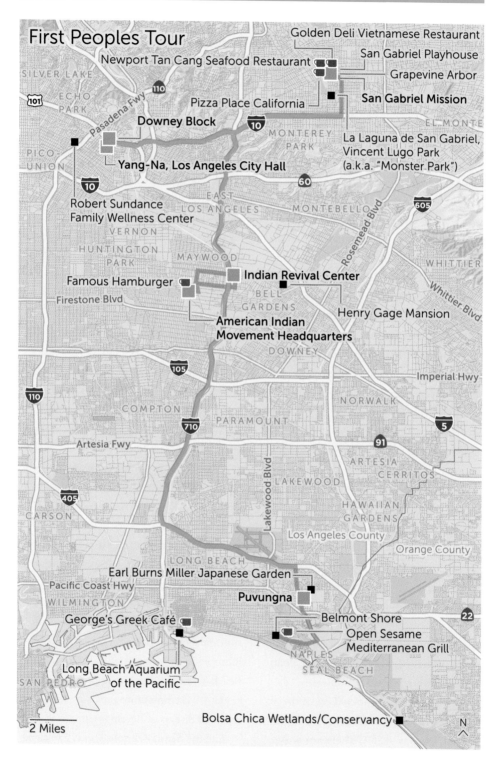

First Peoples Tour

Golden Deli Vietnamese Restaurant

Newport Tan Cang Seafood Restaurant

San Gabriel Playhouse

Grapevine Arbor

Pizza Place California

San Gabriel Mission

Downey Block

La Laguna de San Gabriel,
Vincent Lugo Park
(a.k.a. "Monster Park")

Yang-Na, Los Angeles City Hall

Robert Sundance
Family Wellness Center

Indian Revival Center

Famous Hamburger

Henry Gage Mansion

**American Indian
Movement Headquarters**

Earl Burns Miller Japanese Garden

Puvungna

Pacific Coast Hwy

George's Greek Café

Belmont Shore

Open Sesame
Mediterranean Grill

Long Beach Aquarium
of the Pacific

Bolsa Chica Wetlands/Conservancy

2 Miles

N

Stop for lunch in the neighborhood surrounding the mission. We recommend Pizza Place California (303 S. Mission Dr., San Gabriel 91776; 626-570-9622), which serves pizza and a variety of pan-Asian dishes; or Lunas Mexican Restaurant (343 S. Mission Dr., San Gabriel 91776; 626-576-7653), featuring fresh Mexican food. Both are located on Mission Drive very close to the mission.

After lunch, travel to southeast L.A.'s working-class suburbs, which now house some of the densest residential concentrations of American Indians, as well as some of the most historically important sites of American Indian activism in the county. First up is the **INDIAN REVIVAL CENTER** (5602 E. Gage Ave., Bell Gardens 90201), a church and hub of political activity that formed during the federal government's urbanization and relocation programs of the 1950s. To get to the Revival Center from the San Gabriel Mission, return to San Gabriel Boulevard and turn left so that you are traveling back toward I-10. Merge onto I-10 west heading toward Los Angeles. Take exit 21 heading toward I-710 South/Long Beach, merge onto Ramona Road, continue on to State University Drive, then get on I-710 south. Travel about 6.5 miles on the 710 freeway and exit at Florence Avenue. Turn left at Eastern Avenue, then turn left at Gage Avenue. The church will be on your left. It frequently hosts visiting indigenous speakers from across the nation, as well as cultural, political, and spiritual events.

Nearby are the historic offices of the **AMERICAN INDIAN MOVEMENT** (4304 Clara St. no. 1, Cudahy 90201), where AIM activists organized actions such as occupations of abandoned federal land, protests against governmental injustices, and resistance to state violence. To get there from the Indian Revival Center, head west on Gage Street toward Specht Avenue and travel 1.3 miles, turn left at Atlantic Avenue and drive for about 1 mile, and then turn right at Clara Street. The apartment complex that once housed the AIM offices will be on your left. Please respect the privacy of residents.

The last site on the tour is **PUVUNGNA** (1250 Bellflower Blvd., Long Beach 90840), in Long Beach, about 20 miles from the AIM offices but well worth the trip. To get there from the AIM offices, head east on Clara Street and turn left on Atlantic Avenue. Turn right on Florence Street and merge onto I-710 south heading toward Long Beach, then take I-405 south toward San Diego. Exit at Bellflower Boulevard and follow the signs for Bellflower Boulevard South. Turn left at Los Coyotes Diagonal and turn right at North Bellflower Boulevard. Make a right on East State University Drive and then turn left on Earl Warren Drive to enter the CSU Long Beach campus. Park in the first lot on the left. Walk north from the parking lot to arrive at Puvungna. This was once a Tongva village, and a very important one, for it was the birthplace of Chungichnish, their god and lawgiver, as well as a place of instruction and a burial ground. Given the site's location on the campus of Cal State Long Beach, it has also been an important site of student and community activism protesting repeated threats of development.

End the day at Belmont Shore, a relaxing

beach town within the city of Long Beach. Check out East Second Street between Pacific Coast Highway and Livingston Drive, where you'll find lots of charming little shops, eateries, and coffee shops. To get there from Puvungna, continue traveling south on Bellflower Boulevard and turn left at CA-1 (Pacific Coast Highway) south. Make a right on East Second Street, find a place to park, and walk around this enjoyable area.

Radical People-of-Color Movements of the 1960s and '70s Tour

This tour takes you to some of the places associated with the radical social movements among people of color in L.A. during the late 1960s and the 1970s, especially the Chicano Movement, Black Power Movement, and the American Indian Movement. You'll spend most of your time in the Eastside and South L.A., where most Black, brown, and red people lived at that time.

Start at **SELF-HELP GRAPHICS** (1300 E. First St., Los Angeles 90033), a community-based arts center that contributed to the Chicano Movement by supporting artists who created art reflecting the reality and perspectives of the Chicana/o and Latina/o communities. Self-Help Graphics is on the corner of Anderson and First Streets in a former warehouse with the lettering "Ocean Queen" still visible on its exterior. Its galleries are open Tuesday through Saturday, 10 A.M. to 4 P.M. Check their web site (www.selfhelpgraphics

.com) for workshops and special events.

Next, stop by **RUBEN SALAZAR PARK** (3864 Whittier Blvd., Los Angeles 90023), the site of the Chicano Moratorium in August 1970, which was the largest ethnic antiwar demonstration in U.S. history. Thirty thousand mostly Chicana/o demonstrators marched to Salazar Park (then named Laguna Park) from Belvedere to protest the fact that Chicanos were being disproportionately drafted and killed in the Vietnam War, even while they experienced discrimination and oppression at home. Upon their arrival, the demonstrators were met with intense police brutality; three people died and hundreds were injured or arrested. The park was renamed Salazar Park in honor of Mexican journalist Rubén Salazar, who was sympathetic to the Chicano Movement and who was killed while covering the event. To get to the park from Self-Help Graphics, travel east on First Street for one mile. Turn right on Soto Street, and left onto Whittier Boulevard. In 1.6 miles, you will see the entrance to the park on your right.

To see the actual place where Salazar was killed, travel to the former site of the **SILVER DOLLAR CAFÉ** (4945 Whittier Blvd., Los Angeles 90022). To get there from Salazar Park, head east on Whittier Boulevard for about 1.6 miles. The site will be on the left. Salazar had ducked into this store, which was then a bar, after reporting on the march, but he was hit in the head by a tear gas projectile fired by an L.A. County sheriff's deputy, who was never brought to justice. Before leaving East L.A., grab some lunch from El Mercado (3425 E. First St., Los Angeles 90063), an

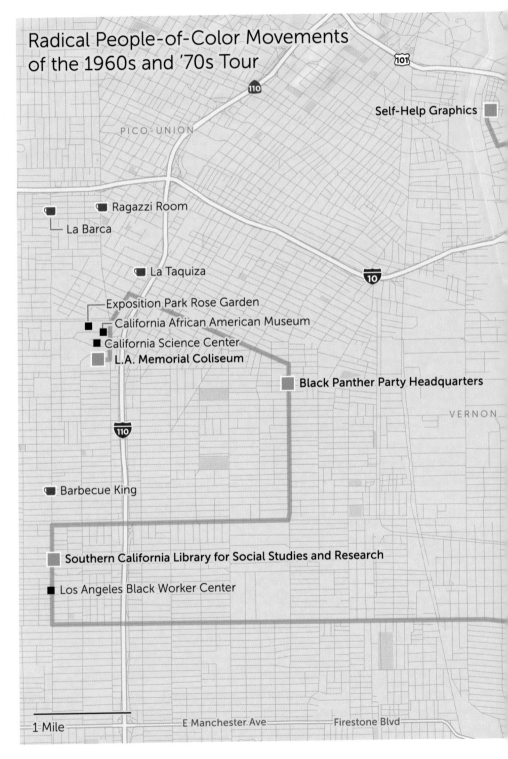

Radical People-of-Color Movements of the 1960s and '70s Tour

101

110

Self-Help Graphics

PICO-UNION

Ragazzi Room

La Barca

La Taquiza

10

Exposition Park Rose Garden

California African American Museum

California Science Center

L.A. Memorial Coliseum

Black Panther Party Headquarters

VERNON

110

Barbecue King

Southern California Library for Social Studies and Research

Los Angeles Black Worker Center

1 Mile

E Manchester Ave

Firestone Blvd

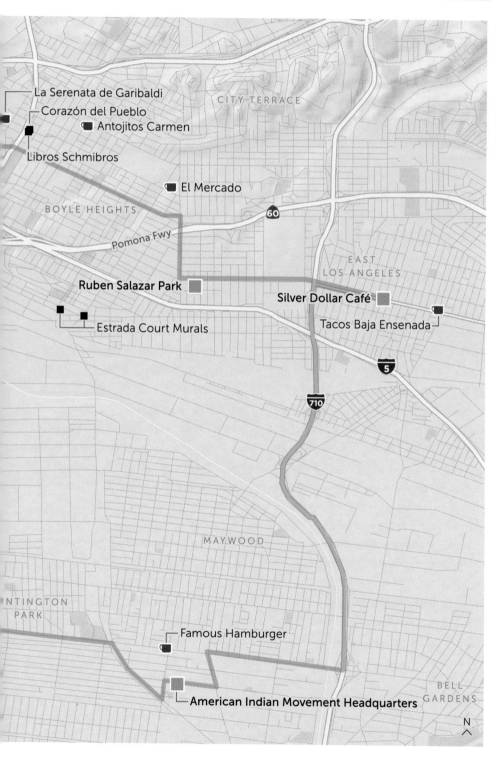

La Serenata de Garibaldi

Corazón del Pueblo

Antojitos Carmen

Libros Schmibros

El Mercado

CITY TERRACE

60

BOYLE HEIGHTS

Pomona Fwy

EAST
LOS ANGELES

Ruben Salazar Park

Silver Dollar Café

Estrada Court Murals

Tacos Baja Ensenada

5

710

MAYWOOD

NTINGTON
PARK

Famous Hamburger

BELL
GARDENS

American Indian Movement Headquarters

N

East L.A. institution and extensive market-place with numerous food options. For a closer option, try the Ensenada-style fish and shrimp tacos at Tacos Baja Ensenada (5385 Whittier Blvd., Los Angeles 90022). To get to Tacos Baja Ensenada from the Silver Dollar, travel half a mile east on Whittier Boulevard.

After lunch, travel about 8 miles to the former **AMERICAN INDIAN MOVEMENT HEAD-QUARTERS** (4304 Clara St. no. 1, Cudahy 90201), where AIM activists strategized and organized actions such as occupations of abandoned federal land, protests against continued governmental injustices, and resistance to state violence. From the Silver Dollar Café, go west on Whittier Boulevard for about three-quarters of a mile, then turn left on Eastern Avenue. After 0.2 miles, turn left to merge onto I-710 south toward Long Beach. Drive for about 3.6 miles on I-710 south, then exit on Florence Avenue toward Bell. Turn left at Atlantic Avenue, then take the third right, onto Clara Street. The apartment complex that once housed the offices of the L.A. branch of the American Indian Movement will be on your left.

Next up: **SOUTHERN CALIFORNIA LIBRARY FOR SOCIAL STUDIES AND RESEARCH** (6120 S. Vermont Ave., Los Angeles 90044; 323-759-6063; socallib.org), an invaluable archive of L.A.'s radical leftist organizations from the 1930s to the present, as well as a library and community center. From the AIM of-fice, head west on Clara Street toward Otis Avenue. Turn right at Salt Lake Avenue, then left on Florence Avenue. Turn right on Vermont Avenue to head north (total trip is

7 miles). The library will be on your right, about three-quarters of a mile up Vermont, near the corner of Sixty-first Street. If you intend to do extensive research or wish to take a more formal tour, contact the library staff ahead of time to make an appointment. Otherwise, enjoy browsing the library's extensive collection of radical books, posters, films, and ephemera.

Next, travel to the former **BLACK PANTHER PARTY HEADQUARTERS** (4115 S. Central Ave., Los Angeles 90011), where the LAPD initiated a four-hour raid and massacre in December 1969. The FBI had deemed the BPP the greatest threat to the internal security of the United States because of its revolutionary politics. To get there from the library, head north on Vermont Avenue, turn right on Slauson Avenue, then turn left on Central Avenue. The building that was at this address, and which was destroyed in the shoot-out, has been replaced by a paved lot. It will be on your right, between Forty-first and Forty-second streets. The shoot-out was a major factor leading to the eventual demise of the Southern California chapter of the BPP.

The last stop on the tour is the **L.A. MEMORIAL COLISEUM** (3939 S. Figueroa St., Los Angeles 90037; lacoliseumlive.com/joomla). In August 1972, the coliseum hosted the Wattstax concert, which was intended to help the community rebuild after the Watts uprising of 1965. It brought together more than 100,000 people and was the second-largest gathering of African Americans in U.S. history (after Dr. Martin Luther King's March on Washington). To get there from the BPP headquarters, travel north on Central Avenue, then turn left at Jefferson. Take a left onto Figueroa Street, then make a right at Exposition Park Drive, where you will enter the Exposition Park complex of museums and gardens. The coliseum is located in the middle of Exposition Park and is easily visible. After checking out the exterior of the coliseum, you can spend the afternoon strolling through the Rose Garden or visiting the California African American Museum (open Tues.–Sat. 10 A.M. to 5 P.M. and Sun. 11 A.M. to 5 P.M.; free admission), the Natural History Museum (open 9:30 A.M. to 5 P.M. daily; admission $9 adults, $6.50 children, students, and seniors), or the California Science Center (open 10 A.M. to 5 P.M. daily; free admission).

Have dinner in the Exposition Park–USC area. We recommend La Taquiza (3009 S. Figueroa St., Los Angeles 90007; 213-741-9795), which features a mammoth menu of Mexican foods, including their specialty, the *mulita;* or La Barca (2414 S. Vermont Ave., Los Angeles 90007; 323-735-6567), a family-style Mexican restaurant. Or stop for a coffee and pastry or a sandwich at the Ragazzi Room (2316 S. Union Ave., Los Angeles 90007; cross street is Hoover; 213-741-1723), a pleasant place to hang out and reflect upon your day. All three restaurants are north of the Exposition Park museums, which are bounded by Vermont and Figueroa.

Queer Politics and Culture Tour

This tour explores the historical development of queer social communities and political movements for LGBT rights in Los Angeles. It travels through the North L.A. and Westside regions of the *People's Guide,* focusing on those neighborhoods that have been and continue to be particularly important incubators of queer social critique and political mobilization.

Begin on Vermont Avenue between Eighth and Ninth streets, a block that once housed the **IF CAFÉ** (810 S. Vermont Ave., Los Angeles 90005) and **OPEN DOOR** (831 S. Vermont Ave.), two working-class, racially mixed lesbian bars that were crucial to the development of lesbian culture and community in L.A. from the 1940s to the 1960s—as well as frequent targets of police harassment and abuse.

Next, head to **PERSHING SQUARE** (532 S. Olive St., Los Angeles 90013), which was a popular cruising spot for gay men from diverse racial and economic backgrounds in the 1950s, as well as a common site for a broad array of protests. To get there from the If Café and Open Door, head north on Vermont and turn right on Seventh Street, then turn left at Olive Street. Pershing Square will be on your right. During the 1950s and 1960s, Pershing Square anchored a wide range of bars, apartments, and other centers of gay social life in the surrounding neighborhood, but like the two lesbian bars on Vermont, this area was subject to near-constant police sweeps and harassment.

Next stop: the former site of the L.A. branch of the **GAY LIBERATION FRONT,** which operated out of the home of gay rights activist Morris Kight (1822 W. 4th St., Los Angeles 90057). In addition to performing his work with the GLF, Kight was instrumental in founding both the gay rights parade now known as L.A. Pride and the organization now known as the L.A. Gay and Lesbian Center. To get to his former home from Pershing Square, head northeast on Olive Street toward Fifth Street, and turn left on Fifth. Stay left on Fifth as it goes under the freeway and

merges with Sixth Street. Turn right at Burlington Avenue, and take the third left, onto Fourth Street. Kight's former home, and the former offices of the GLF, will be on your right. As this is a private residence, please be respectful of the current occupants.

Now, you'll travel to the Silver Lake and Echo Park neighborhoods of L.A., which have long been queer-friendly places associated with a wide range of alternative communities and counterhegemonic social practices. First up: the historic site of the **BLACK CAT BAR,** now Le Barcito, in the Silver Lake neighborhood (3909 W. Sunset Blvd., Los Angeles 90029). In early 1967, this bar

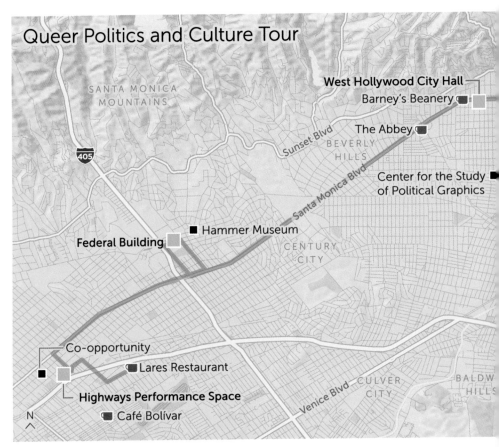

Queer Politics and Culture Tour

SANTA MONICA MOUNTAINS

West Hollywood City Hall
Barney's Beanery

The Abbey

Sunset Blvd
BEVERLY HILLS

Santa Monica Blvd

Center for the Study
of Political Graphics

Hammer Museum

Federal Building

CENTURY CITY

Co-opportunity

Lares Restaurant

Highways Performance Space

Café Bolívar

Venice Blvd   CULVER CITY

BALDW HILLS

N

was the site of L.A.'s first known protest for LGBT rights, sparked by an incident of police brutality the year before. The demonstration helped to mark Silver Lake as a gay neighborhood and to establish connections between the emerging gay liberation movement and the movements among other communities of color in L.A. and nationally.

While in the area, spend some time exploring Silver Lake's funky shops and street scene. There are also many wonderful spots here for lunch. Grab an espresso and pastry (the guava cheese pie is highly recommended) at Café Tropical (2900 W. Sunset Blvd., Los Angeles 90026; near the

intersection of Sunset and Parkman). For a heartier meal, try Bulan Thai Vegetarian Kitchen (4114 Santa Monica Blvd., Los Angeles 90029; one-quarter mile from Le Barcito; travel west on Sunset and go left at the split with Santa Monica Boulevard); or Downbeat (1202 N. Alvarado St., Los Angeles 90026), a jazz-themed coffee shop in Echo Park that serves up sandwiches and salads and is on the way to the next tour stop.

Staying in this general area, head to the **GAY WOMEN'S SERVICE CENTER** (1542 Glendale Blvd., Los Angeles 90026), founded in 1971, the first lesbian social services center in the United States. To get there from the

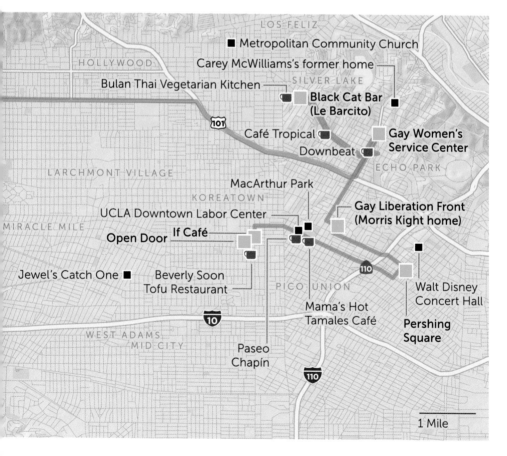

Black Cat area, continue east on Sunset Boulevard and turn left on Alvarado Street. Watch for the Downbeat, at 1202 North Alvarado, if that's where you wish to stop for lunch. The former site of the service center will be on your right, about a half mile up the street, at the corner of Alvarado Street and Glendale Boulevard.

The remaining stops on the tour take you to the Westside, to explore places that have been crucial to the more recent development of queer life, politics, and culture in L.A. Head to the **WEST HOLLYWOOD CITY HALL** (8300 Santa Monica Blvd., West Hollywood 90069) and the surrounding city of West Hollywood, which was incorporated in 1984 and is popularly known as the first "gay city" in the United States. From the Gay Women's Service Center, turn around on Alvarado to travel southeast, and turn right to merge onto US-101 north, traveling toward Sacramento. After 2.5 miles, exit on Santa Monica Ave/CA-2 toward Western Avenue. At the top of the off-ramp, turn left onto Santa Monica Boulevard and drive for 2.5 miles into West Hollywood. City Hall will be on your left. If you're so inclined, stop for a cocktail or other refreshment at The Abbey (692 N. Robertson Blvd.; at the corner of Santa Monica Blvd. and Robertson Blvd.), a beautiful bar and restaurant that has been at the center of WeHo nightlife for many years.

Next stop: the **FEDERAL BUILDING** (11000 Wilshire Blvd., Los Angeles 90024) in Westwood, which has been the site of numerous protests on behalf of gay rights and HIV/AIDS research, funding, and services. From WeHo City Hall, continue west on Santa Monica Boulevard for 5 miles and turn right on Sepulveda Boulevard. Take the third right, onto Wilshire Boulevard. The federal building will be on your right about a quarter mile up.

Finish the tour at **HIGHWAYS PERFORMANCE SPACE** (1651 18th St., Santa Monica 90404; 310-315-1459; www.highways performance.org). From the federal building, go northeast on Wilshire Boulevard toward Veteran Avenue and turn right on Veteran Avenue. Take the third right, onto Santa Monica Boulevard, then travel for almost 3 miles and turn left at Twentieth Street. Turn right onto Olympic Boulevard, then turn right onto Eighteenth Street. Highways will be on the right side of the street. Check the web site or call ahead to find out what performances, exhibits, or workshops will be available on the day of your visit.

Finish up the day with dinner at Lares Restaurant (2909 Pico Blvd., Santa Monica 90405; 310-829-4550), a Mexican restaurant with a full bar and occasional live music; to get there from Highways, head northeast on Olympic Boulevard, turn right on Cloverfield, and then make a left on Pico Boulevard. Or for delicious, if somewhat pricier, Indian food, try Nawab of India (1621 Wilshire Blvd., Santa Monica 90403; 310-829-1106); from Highways, head southwest on Olympic, turn right on Seventeenth Street, and turn left on Wilshire Boulevard.

Independent and Alternative Media Tour

This tour is for lovers of alternative and independent news media, libraries, and bookstores. The tour travels through several of the regions described in the *People's Guide,* so you'll get a good sense of the city's diverse neighborhoods, especially the places where working-class, immigrant, and Black communities have lived and developed their own interpretations—in newsprint, on the airwaves, and in fiction and film—of the conditions shaping their lives.

Start at the site of the old **L.A. TIMES BUILDING** (northeast corner of S. Broadway and W. 1st St., Los Angeles 90012), which represents the mainstream, corporate media perspective that independent news sources in L.A. have challenged for more than a century. In 1910, the McNamara brothers (James and John) planted a bomb in this building to protest the paper's staunch antiunion, antilabor politics and hostile coverage of local events. You can clearly see the footprint of the old building on this corner.

The next two sites feature the historic, now-demolished offices of two independent ethnic newspapers published during the 1910s and 1920s. First up, and very close to the L.A. Times building, is the site of the former offices of the **CABALLEROS DE DIMAS-ALANG** (126–128 Astronaut Onizuka St., Los Angeles 90012), a Pilipino fraternal organization that promoted liberation of the Philippines from U.S. colonialism, in part through

publication of its newspaper, the *Philippines Review,* at this address. From the L.A. Times building, walk southeast on First Street about a third of a mile, and turn right on Astronaut Onizuka Street. The former offices of the Caballeros will be on your left. Before this neighborhood became predominantly Japanese American, these buildings were at the heart of a thriving Pilipino community.

Next, walk or drive to one of the former offices of the **PARTIDO LIBERAL MEXICANO** (519 ½ E. 4th St., Los Angeles 90013), where the Mexican brothers Ricardo and Enrique Flores Magón published their newspaper, *Regeneración,* while in exile in L.A. during the Mexican Revolution. From the Caballeros offices, travel south on Astronaut Onizuka Street toward San Pedro Street and make a right at San Pedro Street. Turn left at Fourth Street. The former PLM offices will be on your left, approximately a half mile from the Caballeros offices. From this address, the Magón brothers promoted worker uprisings against the Porfirio Díaz dictatorship in Mexico, as well as advocated worker ownership and control of land and production.

While in the neighborhood, stop at the Studio for Southern California History (977 N. Hill St., Los Angeles 90012; www.socalstudio.org), a small gallery and museum dedicated to L.A.'s social history, located about 2 miles from the PLM offices (note that the Studio is currently open Friday through Sunday, 12 noon to 8 P.M., and by appointment, but check their web site to verify current hours). To get there from PLM, head southwest on Fourth Street toward Towne Avenue, then turn left on Towne and

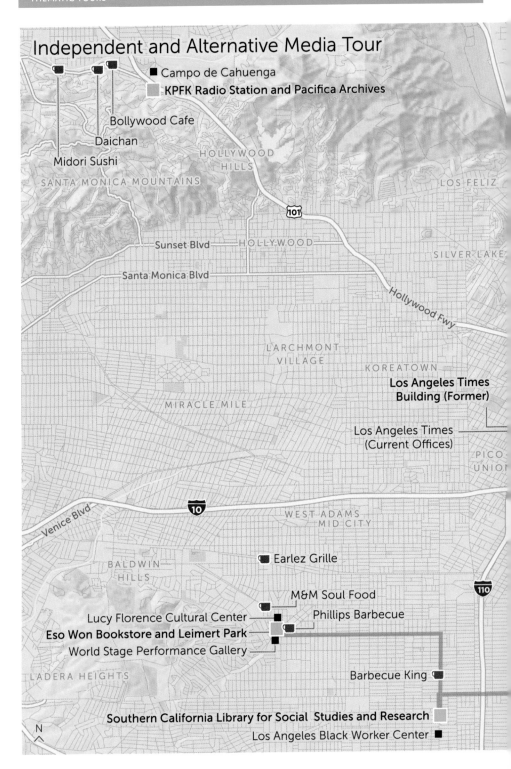

Independent and Alternative Media Tour

■ Campo de Cahuenga

■ KPFK Radio Station and Pacifica Archives

Bollywood Cafe

Daichan

Midori Sushi

HOLLYWOOD
HILLS

SANTA MONICA MOUNTAINS

LOS FELIZ

101

Sunset Blvd — HOLLYWOOD

SILVER LAKE

Santa Monica Blvd

Hollywood Fwy

LARCHMONT
VILLAGE

KOREATOWN

**Los Angeles Times
Building (Former)**

MIRACLE MILE

Los Angeles Times
(Current Offices)

PICO
UNION

10

WEST ADAMS
MID CITY

VENICE Blvd

BALDWIN
HILLS

110

■ Earlez Grille

M&M Soul Food

Lucy Florence Cultural Center — ■   Phillips Barbecue

Eso Won Bookstore and Leimert Park —

World Stage Performance Gallery —

LADERA HEIGHTS

Barbecue King

Southern California Library for Social Studies and Research

Los Angeles Black Worker Center ■

N

GLENDALE

134

EAGLE ROCK

San Fernando Rd

2

ATWATER
VILLAGE

GLASSELL
PARK

5

Glendale Fwy

CYPRESS
PARK

Old Partido Liberal
Mexicano office

Pasadena Fwy

HO PARK

Studio for Southern
California History

Hop Li Seafood
Restaurant

NOGA PARK
OUNTAINS

Philippe's
The Original

Daikokuya Ramen 10

Señor Fish

Partido Liberal Mexicano

Azusa Revival Commemorative Plaque

**Caballeros de Dimas-Alang
and *Philippines Review***

California Eagle

VERNON

HUNTINGTON PARK

1 Mile

make a slight left at Central Avenue. Turn left at East First Street and then make a right on Hill Street. The Studio will be about six blocks up the street on your right. Check out the web site ahead of time to see what exhibits and events are happening or to make an appointment with the director.

For lunch, stop at Philippe's the Original (1001 N. Alameda St., Los Angeles 90012; 213-628-3781; www.philippes.com), an L.A. institution specializing in French-dip sandwiches, near the PLM offices and the Studio for Southern California History. From the Studio, walk or drive south on Hill Street, make a left on College Street, then a right on Alameda. Philippe's is at the corner of Ord and Alameda streets, approximately one-half mile from the Studio. Or check out Hop Li (526 Alpine St., Los Angeles 90012; 213-680-3939; www.hoplirestaurant.com), an excellent Chinese restaurant located just around the corner from another address where the Partido Liberal Mexicano had its offices. To get to Hop Li from the Studio, walk or drive south on Hill Street, then turn right on Alpine Street (total trip is about one-third of a mile). The old PLM office at 809 Yale Street is just around the corner.

After lunch, head into South L.A. to check out some of the independent media sources, both historic and contemporary, that have germinated in this part of the city. First up are the former offices of the ***CALIFORNIA EAGLE*** (4071–4075 S. Central Ave., Los Angeles 90011), the longest running Black newspaper on the West Coast, published from 1879 to 1964. To get there from Philippe's, travel south on Alameda Street for 1.5 miles, turn right at Sixth Street, then make a quick left onto Central Avenue. The offices of the *Eagle* will be on your right side, near the intersection of Central and Forty-first Street. Here, under the leadership of Charlotta Bass (who later ran for vice president of the United States), the *Eagle* served as a leading defender of the rights and interests of people of color, and tackled racism in L.A. and the U.S. West, as well as elitism within the Black community.

A full run of the *California Eagle,* and an array of many other progressive and radical historical sources, is archived at the **SOUTHERN CALIFORNIA LIBRARY FOR SOCIAL STUDIES AND RESEARCH** (6120 S. Vermont Ave., Los Angeles 90044; 323-759-6063; socallib .org), the next stop on the tour. To get to the library from the *Eagle* offices, continue traveling south on Central Avenue, then make a right on Slauson Avenue, and then a left on Vermont Avenue. The library will be on your left, near the corner of Sixty-first Street. If you intend to do extensive research or wish a more formal tour, contact the library staff ahead of time to make an appointment. Otherwise, enjoy browsing the library's extensive collection of radical books, posters, films, and ephemera.

Last stop: **ESO WON BOOKS** (4331 Degnan Blvd., Los Angeles 90008; 323-290-1048; www.esowonbookstore.com), an independent Black-owned bookstore in Leimert Park, about 4 miles from the Southern California Library. From the library, head north on Vermont Avenue and make a left on Vernon Avenue. Travel 2.2 miles on Vernon and turn right on Eleventh, take a quick left on Forty-third Street, then take the second right, onto Degnan Boulevard. Eso Won Books will be on the left. Spend some time browsing this bookstore's thoughtfully curated selections.

Finish your day by grabbing a bite at M&M Soul Food (3552 W. Martin Luther King Jr. Blvd., Los Angeles 90008; 323-299-1302); Phillips Barbecue (4307 Leimert Blvd., Los Angeles 90008; 323-292-7613); or, for lots of vegetarian options, Earlez Grille (3630 Crenshaw Blvd., Los Angeles 90008; 323-299-2867). Head across the street from Eso Won to the World Stage Gallery (4344 Degnan Blvd., Los Angeles 90008; 323-293-2451; theworldstage.org), a renowned music and cultural center that sponsors workshops and cultural events most afternoons and evenings (check their calendar at their web site).

You can make your tour of L.A.'s independent media a two-day (or more!) affair by arranging to volunteer at **KPFK RADIO STATION AND PACIFICA ARCHIVES** (3729 Cahuenga Blvd., North Hollywood 91604; 818-985-2711; www.kpfk.org), particularly during their fund drives that occur throughout the year, or inquire about internships. Call the volunteer and outreach coordinator at 818-985-2711, or visit www.kpfk.org/volunteer, for more information.

Economic Restructuring and Globalization Tour

This tour illustrates the changing nature of the Los Angeles economy in the twentieth and twenty-first centuries, as the city has transformed from a vibrant hub of high-wage, often unionized manufacturing to a site of low-wage manufacturing, high-end and low-end service work, and global circuits of multinational finance, production, labor, and migration.

Begin in the morning at the **FIRESTONE TIRE AND RUBBER** plant (2323–2525 Firestone Blvd., South Gate 90280), a factory built in 1928 that once employed 2,500 well-paid, unionized workers. This plant represents the heyday of manufacturing in Los Angeles from the 1920s through the 1960s, when hundreds of factories dominated the landscape of this area and a strong working-class culture developed. The whole complex is still intact, and it now houses the South Gate Industrial Park and the South Gate Community Adult School, both of which represent Los Angeles' new manufacturing economy (which is predominantly low-wage, nonbenefited), as well as, in the case of the adult school, a collaboration between city governments and industry to prepare workers for such jobs.

From Firestone, walk or drive east on Firestone Boulevard for approximately one-half mile to the former site of the **TRIANON BALLROOM** (2800 Firestone Blvd., South Gate 90280), a dusty lot at the time of this writing, but once a thriving ballroom where working-class migrants from the Midwest (especially young single women) who worked at the area's manufacturing plants gathered for music, dancing, and socializing. Take the time to examine the contemporary industrial landscape along the way. Since the closure of Firestone and other branch plants in the 1970s and 1980s, most of the factories in this area now employ nonunionized workers, who are paid low wages to produce and assemble furniture, apparel, or electronics. The area's many warehouses coordinate shipping from the ports of Los Angeles and Long Beach to the Inland Empire and beyond.

Next, drive 4.6 miles to the **BICYCLE CLUB** (7301 Eastern Ave., Bell Gardens 90201), a casino built in 1984 that the city promised would revitalize southeast L.A.'s economy after the decline of manufacturing and the associated loss of corporate tax revenues. With its reliance on gambling as a strategy of economic development, the Bicycle Club represents the desperate measures taken by city governments in the aftermath of deindustrialization and Proposition 13. To get there from the Trianon Ballroom, head east on Firestone Boulevard toward Long Beach Boulevard and turn left at California Avenue. Then turn right at Florence Avenue, and make another right, onto Eastern Avenue. The casino will be on your right.

From the Bicycle Club, drive 7 miles to the former site of the **SOUTH CENTRAL FARM** (4100 Long Beach Ave., Los Angeles 90058). To get there, continue briefly south on Eastern Avenue, then make a U-turn to go north on Eastern, and turn left at Florence Avenue. Turn right at Alameda Street. The

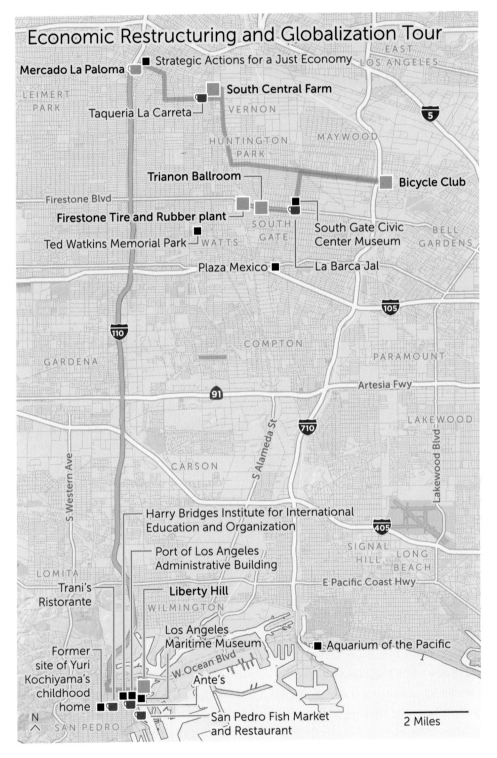

Economic Restructuring and Globalization Tour

EAST LOS ANGELES

Strategic Actions for a Just Economy

Mercado La Paloma

South Central Farm

Taqueria La Carreta

LEIMERT PARK

VERNON

HUNTINGTON PARK

MAYWOOD

5

Trianon Ballroom

Bicycle Club

Firestone Blvd

Firestone Tire and Rubber plant

SOUTH GATE

BELL GARDENS

Ted Watkins Memorial Park — WATTS

South Gate Civic Center Museum

Plaza Mexico

La Barca Jal

105

COMPTON

PARAMOUNT

GARDENA

Artesia Fwy

91

LAKEWOOD

710

CARSON

S Alameda St

Lakewood Blvd

S Western Ave

Harry Bridges Institute for International Education and Organization

405

SIGNAL HILL

LONG BEACH

Port of Los Angeles Administrative Building

LOMITA

E Pacific Coast Hwy

Trani's Ristorante

Liberty Hill

WILMINGTON

Los Angeles Maritime Museum

Aquarium of the Pacific

Former site of Yuri Kochiyama's childhood home

W Ocean Blvd

Ante's

N

SAN PEDRO

San Pedro Fish Market and Restaurant

2 Miles

former South Central Farm will be on your right. At the South Central Farm, immigrant workers—a great many of whom were and are employed in south and southeast L.A.'s contemporary manufacturing economy—created a community farm to grow food and medicinal plants that would supplement their low wages and lack of health insurance. The farmers situated their presence and occupation of public land within larger processes of labor migration compelled by free-trade policies such as NAFTA and the dislocation of poor people from the land in Mexico and Central America. The farmers were forcibly evicted in 2006 by L.A. County sheriff's deputies on behalf of a wealthy industrial property owner, whose ownership of the land was hotly disputed and perhaps illegal—and who has proposed to build yet another warehouse or truck-switching facility on the site.

For lunch, head to the Mercado La Paloma (3655 S. Grand Ave., Los Angeles 90007; 213-748-1963; www.mercadolapaloma .com), approximately 2.8 miles from the South Central Farm. Go south on Alameda toward Vernon Avenue, turn right on Vernon, then turn right on Avalon Boulevard. Make a left onto Jefferson Boulevard and another left onto Grand Avenue. The Mercado will be on your right. There is pay parking right in front of the Mercado, or free parking on the streets nearby or in the adjacent Department of Motor Vehicles parking lot. The Mercado is a small business incubator that seeks to address high rates of poverty by creating healthy economic development strategies, as opposed to gambling or other extractive and socially damaging industries. Restaurant options include several regional varieties of Mexican food (Oaxacan, Yucatecan), Thai, and North American foods, as well as an excellent *panadería;* several craft vendors also sell their goods here. You may also wish to stop by Strategic Actions for a Just Economy (152 W. 32nd St., Los Angeles 90007; 213-745-9961; www.saje.net), a community organization housed in a former garment sweatshop that is spearheading community-led economic justice initiatives. To get there, just continue north on Grand Avenue, pass Jefferson, and turn right on Thirty-second Street. Since this is a busy office and workspace, be sure to call ahead to find out if any events are happening, arrange to volunteer, or schedule a meeting with staff.

Spend the afternoon in the harbor area, about 20 miles south of central Los Angeles, where you can visit numerous places that bear witness to Los Angeles' immensely important role in the globalization of manufacturing and trade. Your first stop in the harbor area is **LIBERTY HILL** (100 W. 5th St., San Pedro 90731), the site of a critically important struggle in 1923 to protect freedoms of speech and assembly, and one that was key to the eventual birth of the International Longshore and Warehouse Union (ILWU). From Mercado La Paloma or SAJE, follow street signs to find your way to CA-110 south. The freeway will end. Then turn left on Gaffey, left at West First Street, and right at Harbor Boulevard. The site of the 1923 strike and struggle will be on your right. Within a very short walking distance are the

Port of Los Angeles Administrative Building (425 S. Palos Verdes St., San Pedro 90731) and Harry Bridges Institute (350 W. 5th St., San Pedro 90731; 310-831-2397; www.harry bridges.com). To get to both from Liberty Hill, walk west on Fifth Street toward Palos Verdes Street (one block); you'll see the administrative building on the corner to your left. Continue walking west on Fifth Street about one more block to the Bridges Institute, where you can check out its outstanding labor history library and video collection. Be sure to verify that the timing is right: the Bridges Institute is open Monday through Thursday 10 A.M. to 3 P.M.

While in the harbor area, you may wish to take a highly recommended urban ocean boat cruise (Saturdays and Sundays at 4 P.M. in the summer months; $29.95 adults, $10 children), offered by the Aquarium of the Pacific. The tour lasts 2½ hours and considers the interplay between trade and manufacturing and the ocean habitat in the port area. You can purchase tickets online or at the aquarium.

Complete your day with dinner in San Pedro. We recommend the San Pedro Fish Market and Restaurant (Ports O' Call Marketplace, Berth 78, 1190 Nagoya Way, San Pedro 90731; 310-832-4251; www.sanpedrofish market.com) or, for something more up-scale, Trani's Ristorante (584 W. 9th St., San Pedro 90731; 310-832-1220; www.jtrani.com), which specializes in Italian food, or Ante's (729 S. Ante Perkov Way, San Pedro 90731; 310-832-5375; www.antesrestaurant.com), for Croatian.

New Organizing Tour

Contemporary Los Angeles is the hub of some of the most dynamic and innovative labor organizing in the country. Since the 1980s, deindustrialization and the increasingly footloose nature of global capital have caused organized labor to reassess its traditional focus on factories and white male workers. Labor leaders have turned their attention instead to the service sector, especially restaurants, hospitality and tourism, and healthcare—all of which are major pillars of L.A.'s contemporary economy—and to the infrastructures and civic resources used by working-class people. Because L.A.'s service industry workforce has grown more diverse in the past half century and includes many Asian and Latina/o immigrants, organizers have also recognized the need to explicitly and actively work across racial, ethnic, gender, and cultural lines—which have historically hindered many unionization campaigns—to build strong alliances. This labor organizing is complemented by an array of social justice organizations centered on issues such as transportation, environmental justice, prison abolition, and youth empowerment. Frequently, organizers connect the struggles of immigrant workers and people of color in Los Angeles with those of people across the region and even around the globe. All of these dynamics are characteristic of the style of labor organizing called the "new organizing." This tour, centered primarily in the North Los Angeles region of the *People's Guide,* takes you to several key sites of the new organizing—some of the most important places where a new labor movement for the twenty-first century is being built.

Start in the San Fernando Valley at **GENERAL MOTORS VAN NUYS** (7867–8010 Van Nuys Blvd., Panorama City 91402). This place might be considered both the deathbed of the old organizing and the birthplace of the new organizing. This address is now a shopping center called The Plant, but in the 1980s it was the last auto plant in Southern California. A multiracial group of United Auto Workers, including African American, Latina/o, Asian American, and white workers succeeded in keeping the plant open for 10 years after GM first announced its plans to relocate to Canada. Even though the plant eventually did close, leaders went on to form the **LABOR/COMMUNITY STRATEGY CENTER** (LCSC) (3780 Wilshire Blvd., Suite 1200, Los Angeles 90010; 213-387-2800; www.thestrategycenter.org), the next stop on the tour, which has been at the forefront of the new organizing in L.A. ever since. One of the LCSC's most successful and innovative projects has been the Bus Riders Union, which successfully bridges Black, Latina/o, Korean, and white working-class transit users in demanding and creating a reliable, safe, and affordable mass transit system. To get to the Strategy Center from GM Van Nuys, head north on Van Nuys Boulevard

toward Lorne Street. Turn right on Roscoe Boulevard and merge onto CA-170 south, heading toward Los Angeles. Then merge onto US-101 south. Take the Western Avenue exit (which will actually deposit you on Lexington Avenue), then make a right to get on Western Avenue. The Labor/Community Strategy Center is at the corner of Wilshire Boulevard and Western Avenue, inside the beautiful Wiltern Theatre. Find a metered parking spot nearby and check out both the building and the Red Line stop on the opposite corner, which epitomizes the Bus Riders Union's fight for transit equity on behalf of working people. Then stop by the organization's offices on the twelfth floor; call ahead if you wish to schedule a meeting with staff or arrange to volunteer.

The remaining sites on this tour illustrate the range of outcomes associated with the new organizing in L.A. during the past 15 years: some were major successes, some less so. First up is the restaurant **CHOSUN GALBEE** (3330 W. Olympic Blvd., Los Angeles 90019; 323-734-3330; www.chosungalbee.com), in Koreatown. To get there from the Labor/Community Strategy Center, continue south on Western Avenue for 0.7 miles, and turn right on Olympic Boulevard. Travel about one block on Olympic, and you will see ChoSun Galbee on the south side of the street. In the late 1990s, the restaurant was the site of a successful organizing campaign among its Korean and Latina/o immigrant workers, who make up the bulk of the workforce in Koreatown's many restaurants. Led by the Koreatown Immigrant Workers Advocates (KIWA, which has since changed its name to

New Organizing Tour

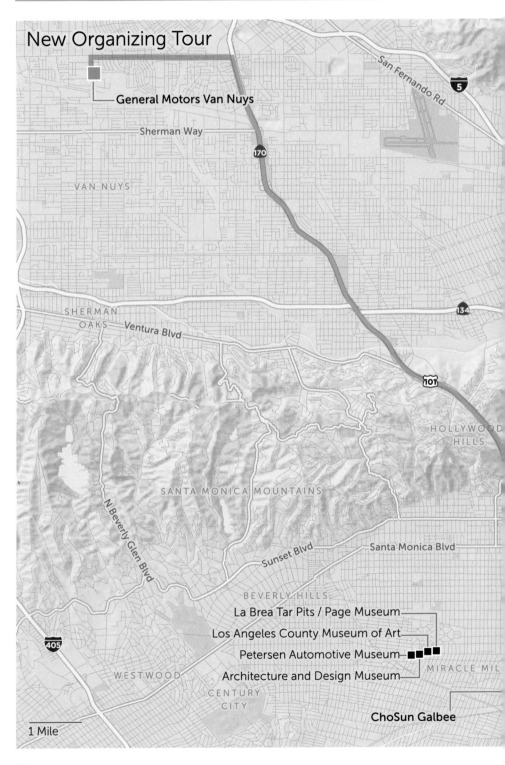

General Motors Van Nuys

Sherman Way

170

VAN NUYS

SHERMAN
OAKS — Ventura Blvd

San Fernando Rd

5

134

101

HOLLYWOOD
HILLS

SANTA MONICA MOUNTAINS

N Beverly Glen Blvd

Sunset Blvd

Santa Monica Blvd

BEVERLY HILLS

La Brea Tar Pits / Page Museum
Los Angeles County Museum of Art
Petersen Automotive Museum
Architecture and Design Museum

405

WESTWOOD

CENTURY
CITY

MIRACLE MIL

ChoSun Galbee

1 Mile

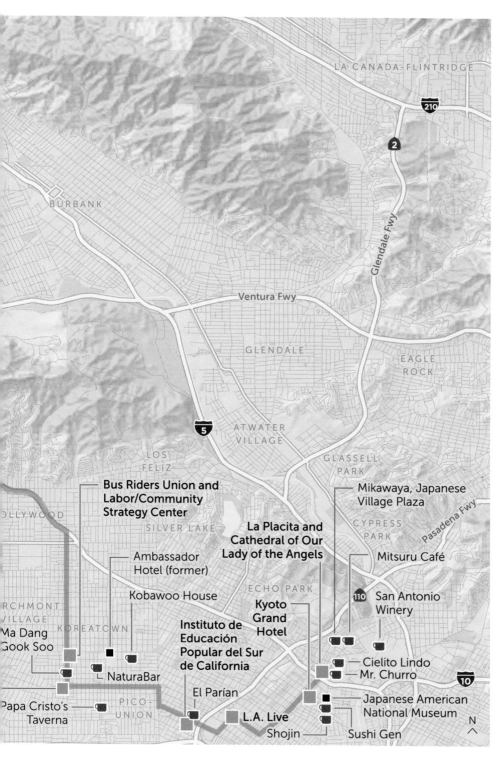

Bus Riders Union and Labor/Community Strategy Center

Mikawaya, Japanese Village Plaza

La Placita and Cathedral of Our Lady of the Angels

Mitsuru Café

Ambassador Hotel (former)

Kobawoo House

San Antonio Winery

Kyoto Grand Hotel

Instituto de Educación Popular del Sur de California

Ma Dang Gook Soo

NaturaBar

Cielito Lindo

Mr. Churro

El Parían

Papa Cristo's Taverna

Japanese American National Museum

L.A. Live

Shojin

Sushi Gen

BURBANK

LA CAÑADA-FLINTRIDGE

Glendale Fwy

Ventura Fwy

GLENDALE

EAGLE ROCK

ATWATER VILLAGE

LOS FELIZ

GLASSELL PARK

HOLLYWOOD

SILVER LAKE

CYPRESS PARK

Pasadena Fwy

ECHO PARK

RICHMONT VILLAGE

KOREATOWN

PICO-UNION

N

Koreatown Immigrant Workers Alliance), which embraced a multilingual and multi-ethnic approach, workers staged picket lines and demonstrations and were successful in winning back wages and fair working conditions. Today, ChoSun Galbee is one of the few restaurants in Koreatown where basic labor laws are obeyed.

The next stop is the **INSTITUTO DE EDUCACIÓN POPULAR DEL SUR DE CALIFORNIA** (Institute of Popular Education of Southern California), or **IDEPSCA** (1565 W. 14th Street, Los Angeles 90015; 213-252-2952; www.idepsca .org). IDEPSCA uses popular education methods to aid workers in identifying and theorizing the challenges they face, such as economic exploitation and anti-immigrant political sentiment. It also helps them to develop grassroots and cooperative solutions, including day-laborer centers and a housecleaning cooperative that uses environmentally friendly methods. To get to IDEPSCA from ChoSun Galbee, head east on Olympic Boulevard. Turn right on Hoover Street, make a left on Pico Boulevard, then a right at Union Avenue, and a left at West Fourteenth Street. This building, about halfway down the block, once housed refugee families from Guatemala and El Salvador and is now home to IDEPSCA's offices. If you call ahead to find out what is going on that day, you may be able to sit in on a meeting or training or arrange to volunteer.

For lunch, walk or drive to El Parían (1528 W. Pico Blvd., Los Angeles 90015; 213-386-7361), just around the corner from IDEPSCA, for excellent *birria,* burritos, or carne asada tacos with homemade tortillas and salsa. From the IDEPSCA offices, walk southeast on Fourteenth Street to Toberman, make a left on Toberman, and then take the second right, on Pico Boulevard. El Parían will be on your right.

Up next: **L.A. LIVE** (800 W. Olympic Blvd., Los Angeles 90015). From IDEPSCA or El Parían, head southeast on West Pico Boulevard, then make a left at Figueroa Street. You will almost immediately see the L.A. Live complex on your left, between Pico and Olympic boulevards. The total trip is 1 mile. L.A. Live, which includes the Staples Center, is home to the Lakers and a major concert venue, and is also the product of successful organizing to ensure that community economic redevelopment benefits the working class. In 2001, as part of L.A. Live's development process, the Figueroa Corridor Coalition for Economic Justice won an unprecedented community benefits agreement that secured permanent jobs and preferential parking for local residents, as well as money for parks. The agreement has since become a model for other economic justice groups around the country.

Now travel to the **KYOTO GRAND HOTEL,** formerly the New Otani Hotel (120 S. Los Angeles St., Los Angeles 90012; 213-629-1200; www.kyotograndhotel.com), where in the mid-1990s hospitality workers waged an unsuccessful unionization campaign that illustrates the tensions, difficulties, and possibilities of the new organizing. From L.A. Live, continue traveling north on Figueroa Street about one block, and turn right on Olympic Boulevard. Turn left at Main Street, and right at Second Street. The New Otani/ Kyoto Grand will be at the corner of Second and Los Angeles streets. The New Otani workers and organizers incorporated English-, Spanish-, Tagalog-, and Japanese-speaking peoples, as well as different generations of activists, in their campaigns. In addition, they explicitly connected their work with the global economy, specifically the hotel's ownership by a Japanese corporation and the city of L.A.'s recruitment of Japanese capital. While in Little Tokyo, stroll through the neighborhood to observe its many memorials and public art projects. You might also wish to drop by the Japanese American National Museum (369 E. First St., Los Angeles 90012; 213-625-0414; www.janm.org). To get there from the New Otani/Kyoto Grand, simply walk northeast on Los Angeles Street and turn right on First Street; the museum will be on your left. And be sure to stop for *mochi* ice cream at Mikawaya in the Japanese Village Plaza, across the street from the museum (118 Japanese Village Mall, Los Angeles 90012; 213-624-1681).

End the tour at **LA PLACITA** (535 N. Main St., Los Angeles 90012), the historic center of Los Angeles and the city's oldest church. Since the 1980s, the plaza has been the site of activism on behalf of immigrant rights, which is often associated with the New Sanctuary Movement. From the Kyoto Grand Hotel, continue traveling north on Los Angeles Street and turn left on First Street, then take the first right, onto Main Street. The plaza will be on your left, slightly less than a mile from Little Tokyo. Explore the shops, restaurants, public monuments and memorials, and activities at the plaza and nearby Olvera Street. If you're in the mood for a treat,

we recommend taquitos with guacamole at Cielito Lindo (23 Olvera St., Unit E) or decadent churros (plain or filled with chocolate, caramel, or strawberry jam) at Mr. Churro (12 E. Olvera St., near the public restrooms).

Environmental Justice Tour

Unlike the mainstream environmental movement, which tends to focus on species protection and the preservation of open spaces absent an analysis of unequal social structures, environmental justice integrates commitments to race, class, gender, and sexual equality with activism for ecological sustainability. This tour illustrates the dynamics of environmental injustice and environmental racism, as well as key places in the birth of L.A.'s environmental justice movement.

Start at the **LOS ANGELES RIVER CENTER AND GARDENS** (570 W. Ave 26, Los Angeles 90065; 323-221-8900). The River Center, which is open Monday through Friday, 9 A.M. to 5 P.M., features a free, self-guided exhibit on the history of the L.A. River (including historical efforts to cement the waterway), its current status (11 miles of natural river habitat have been restored), and a vision for the river's future. The River Garden Park, at the corner of San Fernando Road and West Avenue Twenty-Six, right at the entrance to the River Center and Gardens, is open daily from sunrise to sunset. It features a fountain, benches, and a lovely green space as well as a bicycle staging area, since numerous bike trails meet here. After checking out the

River Center's exhibits, you can walk along the river trail that begins at nearby Riverside Drive and check out a few of the "pocket parks" that are an important part of the greening effort in this high-density neighborhood close to several major freeways. To do so, from the River Center and Gardens continue down West Avenue Twenty-Six, make a right on Figueroa Street, cross over the 5 freeway, then make a right on Riverside Drive and look for the trailhead. Small pocket parks in the vicinity include Egret Park, which features native plantings and interpretive displays of river wildlife, and Steelhead Park, which has a small outdoor amphitheater. Walk as far as you like along the pedestrian/bike trail.

Next, you'll travel to the heavily industrial suburbs of south and southeast Los Angeles County, which are primarily home to Latinas/os, African Americans, and native peoples. The next three locations to visit are the sites (both existing and proposed) of major producers of industrial, chemical, and toxic waste pollution, but they also bear witness to histories of resistance to environmental toxicity among working-class people, people of color, and immigrants of many different national origins. Though their exteriors are benign and unassuming, the impacts of the activities that take place in these landscapes (or would have taken place, if not for concerted grassroots resistance) are profoundly unjust. First up is **AMVAC CHEMICAL CORPORATION** (2110 Davie Ave., Commerce 90040), a manufacturing plant that produces pesticides that have been banned in the United States; it distributes them for use in

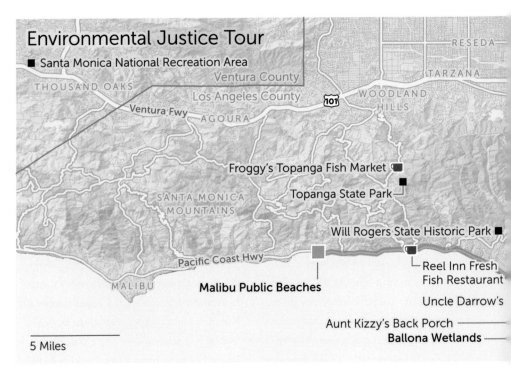

Environmental Justice Tour

■ Santa Monica National Recreation Area

THOUSAND OAKS
Ventura County
Los Angeles County
RESEDA
TARZANA
WOODLAND HILLS
Ventura Fwy
AGOURA

SANTA MONICA MOUNTAINS

Froggy's Topanga Fish Market ■
Topanga State Park ■

Will Rogers State Historic Park ■

Pacific Coast Hwy
Reel Inn Fresh Fish Restaurant
MALIBU
Malibu Public Beaches
Uncle Darrow's
Aunt Kizzy's Back Porch
Ballona Wetlands

5 Miles

less-industrialized countries. To get there from the L.A. River Center, head southeast on West Avenue Twenty-Six toward Jeffries Avenue, then turn right and merge onto I-5 south. Exit at Washington Boulevard toward Commerce and turn left at the bottom of the off-ramp onto Washington; then turn left at Gayhart Street. Take the first right, onto Davie Avenue. AMVAC's production facility will be on your right.

Next, travel to the proposed site of the **VERNON INCINERATOR** (3961 Bandini Blvd., Vernon 90058), about 4 miles away from AM-VAC, in the industrial city of Vernon. To get there from AMVAC, head southwest on Davie Avenue toward Corvette Street, and turn left at Gayhart. Turn right on Washington Boulevard and drive approximately 2 miles, then turn left at Atlantic Boulevard. Take the

ramp to Bandini Boulevard and turn right at Bandini. The proposed site of the Vernon incinerator will be on your right. Here, the City of Vernon had agreed to allow California Thermal Treatment Service to build a hazardous waste incinerator that would release many tons of hazardous waste each year into the surrounding communities, without requiring a full environmental impact report. The Mothers of East L.A. (MELA) saw this proposition as a blatant act of environmental racism, since Latina/o and Black communities are already disproportionately burdened with such facilities, and mobilized to successfully defeat the project. While this site sits empty now, imagine what could have been there—yet another toxic polluting facility in a predominantly Latina/o, low-income neighborhood.

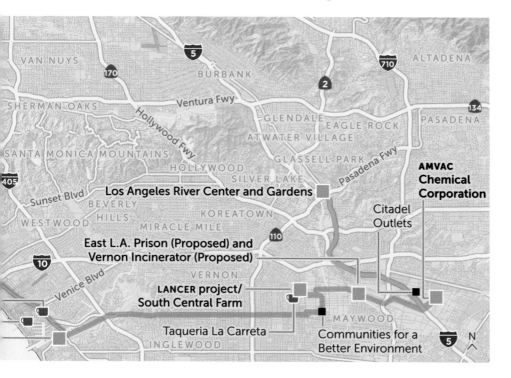

Next up: the former site of the **LANCER PROJECT** and, more recently, the **SOUTH CENTRAL FARM** (4100 Long Beach Ave., Los Angeles 90058). In the mid-1980s, a group of mostly African American women formed Concerned Citizens of South Central Los Angeles and successfully defeated the city's plan to locate a waste-to-energy incinerator, called the LANCER project, at this address. Then, after the urban uprising in 1992, a group of mostly Latina/o immigrants created a community farm on this site that was meant to address and partly ameliorate the negative environmental impacts of facilities such as AMVAC and the Vernon incinerator on poor and working-class communities of color. Although the farm was destroyed by L.A. sheriff's deputies on behalf of a wealthy property owner in 2006, you can still get a sense of what the farm—which was the largest urban garden in the United States—was like before its destruction. To get there from the Vernon incinerator, head northwest on Bandini Boulevard toward Downey Road; travel on Bandini for 1.4 miles and continue on as Bandini becomes Thirty-seventh Street. Turn left at Santa Fe Avenue, take the second right, onto Vernon Avenue, and turn right at Long Beach Avenue. The former farm site will be on your right.

Stop for lunch at **TAQUERIA LA CARRETA** (1471 E. Vernon Ave., Los Angeles 90011; 323-232-7133), a popular neighborhood Mexican restaurant known for its quesadillas made with homemade tortillas. From the South Central Farm, make a U-turn so you are heading south on Long Beach Avenue, back to Vernon Avenue. Turn right on Vernon Avenue. The taqueria will be on your right, at the corner of Vernon and Compton avenues.

While you're in the area, you may wish to drop by Communities for a Better Environment (5610 Pacific Blvd., Huntington Park 90255; 323-826-9771; cbecal.org), an environmental justice organization that advocates toxin-free communities in Los Angeles and California. CBE also offers a "Toxic Tour" that goes into greater depth about toxicity, health risks, and environmental justice activism in this part of the city. To get there from the LANCER/South Central Farm site, drive south on Long Beach Avenue, then turn left at Vernon Avenue; curve right to follow Vernon Avenue as it turns into Pacific Boulevard, heading south. Or, from Taqueria La Carreta, head west on Vernon Avenue (back toward the former South Central Farm), and follow it as it turns into Pacific Boulevard. The organization's offices will be on your left. Call ahead if you wish to arrange to volunteer, schedule a meeting with staff, or find out when a Toxic Tour will be offered.

To visit the remaining sites on the tour, head out to the Westside, where you can examine the flip side of environmental justice: overdevelopment and privatization of public environmental spaces within more privileged communities. The first Westside location is the **BALLONA WETLANDS,** one of two remaining wetlands in L.A. County. To get there from the South Central Farm, go south on Alameda Boulevard (you'll need to make a quick right on Vernon, then a left to stay on Alameda) and then turn right at Slauson Avenue. Turn left at Jefferson Boulevard and pass Lincoln Boulevard. Make a U-turn and park alongside the marsh on the south (eastbound) side of Jefferson Boulevard. Originally occupying more than 2,000 acres, most of Ballona was destroyed in the 1950s and 1960s by oil development and residential and commercial construction, such as the nearby upscale Playa del Rey project. Since 1978, environmental activists have been working to restore the wetlands. To date, they have succeeded in recovering hundreds of acres. The freshwater marsh has an excellent public trail, with interpretive signs, along the perimeter. Friends of Ballona Wetlands also offers occasional community programs and can arrange guided tours; call (310) 306-5994 to make arrangements.

Spend the rest of the afternoon, and perhaps catch the sunset, at the beach: specifically, **MALIBU PUBLIC BEACHES** (using the Geffen Accessway at 22126 Pacific Coast Hwy., Malibu 90265). There, you can examine the attempted privatization of some of L.A. County's most beautiful public spaces by wealthy homeowners who block access

by the public, especially the poor and working-class people you saw, and perhaps met, earlier in the tour. To get there from the Ballona Wetlands, take the beautiful Pacific Coast Highway, which winds along California's magnificent coastline; compare this landscape with the industrial suburbs where you spent your time earlier today. Begin by heading northeast on Jefferson Boulevard, and turn left at Lincoln; then travel for 3.6 miles and make another left at Ocean Park Boulevard. Turn right at Neilson Way, and continue on as Neilson Way becomes Ocean Avenue. Turn left at California Incline (signs will direct you toward the Pacific Coast Highway), and make a slight right onto the Pacific Coast Highway; follow it for about 9 miles. The Geffen Accessway and the beaches beyond will be on your left.

Finish the day with dinner at the Reel Inn Fresh Fish Restaurant (18661 Pacific Coast Hwy., Malibu 90265; 310-456-8221; www.reel innmalibu.com), a favorite among Malibu locals; just turn around and head east on the Pacific Coast Highway, back toward Santa Monica, for 4.5 miles. The restaurant will be on your left.

Recommended Reading

Landscape Studies

Baker, Alan R. H., and Gideon Biger, eds. *Ideology and Landscape in Historical Perspective: Essays on the Meanings of Some Places in the Past.* New York: Cambridge University Press, 1992.

Cosgrove, Denis E. *Social Formation and Symbolic Landscape.* Madison: University of Wisconsin Press, 1984.

Duncan, James S., and Nancy G. Duncan. *Landscapes of Privilege: Aesthetics and Affluence in an American Suburb.* New York: Routledge, 2004.

Hayden, Dolores. *The Power of Place: Urban Landscapes as Public History.* Cambridge, MA: MIT Press, 1995.

Lippard, Lucy R. *The Lure of the Local: Senses of Place in a Multicentered Society.* New York: New Press, 1998.

Meinig, Donald W., ed. *The Interpretation of Ordinary Landscapes: Geographical Essays.* New York: Oxford University Press, 1979.

Mitchell, Don. *Cultural Geography: A Critical Introduction.* Malden, MA: Blackwell, 2000.

———. *The Lie of the Land: Migrant Workers and the California Landscape.* Minneapolis: University of Minnesota Press, 1996.

Schein, Richard H., ed. *Landscape and Race in the United States.* New York: Routledge, 2006.

Critical Cartographies

Blaut, J. M. *The Colonizer's Model of the World.* New York: Guilford Press, 1993.

Center for Land Use Interpretation, http://clui.org.

Counter-Cartographies Collective, www.countercartographies.org.

Harley, Brian. "Deconstructing the Map." *Cartographica* 26 (1989): 1–20.

Lewis, Martin W., and Kären E. Wigen. *The Myth of Continents: A Critique of Metageography.* Berkeley and Los Angeles: University of California Press, 1997.

Los Angeles Urban Rangers, http://laurbanrangers.org.

Mogel, Lize, and Alexis Bhagat, eds. *An Atlas of Radical Cartography.* Los Angeles: Journal of Aesthetics and Protest Press, 2008.

Monmonier, Mark. *How to Lie with Maps.* 2nd ed. Chicago: University of Chicago Press, 1996.

———. *No Dig, No Fly, No Go: How Maps Restrict and Control.* Chicago: University of Chicago Press, 2010.

Paglen, Trevor. *Blank Spots on the Map: The Dark Geography of the Pentagon's Secret World.* New York: Dutton, 2009.

Smith, Neil. "Contours of a Spatialized Politics:

Homeless Vehicles and the Production of Geographical Scale." *Social Text* 33 (1992): 55–81.

Solnit, Rebecca. *Infinite City: A San Francisco Atlas.* Berkeley and Los Angeles: University of California Press, 2010.

Stringfellow, Kim. *Greetings from the Salton Sea: Folly and Intervention in the Southern California Landscape, 1905–2005.* 2nd ed. Chicago: Center for American Places at Columbia College Chicago, 2011.

Thompson, Nato, and Independent Curators International. *Experimental Geography: Radical Approaches to Landscape, Cartography, and Urbanism.* New York: Melville House, 2009.

Wood, Denis. *The Power of Maps.* New York: Guilford Press, 1992.

Los Angeles and Southern California Studies

Acuña, Rodolfo. *Anything but Mexican.* New York: Verso, 1995.

Almaguer, Tomás. *Racial Fault Lines: The Historical Origins of White Supremacy in California.* Berkeley and Los Angeles: University of California Press, 1994.

Avila, Eric. *Popular Culture in the Age of White Flight: Fear and Fantasy in Suburban Los Angeles.* Berkeley and Los Angeles: University of California Press, 2004.

Banham, Reyner. *Los Angeles: The Architecture of Four Ecologies.* New York: Harper and Row, 1971.

Barraclough, Laura. *Making the San Fernando Valley: Rural Landscapes, Urban Development, and White Privilege.* Athens: University of Georgia Press, 2011.

Benavides, Jose Luis. "'Californios! Whom Do You Support?' *El Clamor Público*'s Contradictory Role in the Racial Formation Process in Early California." *California History* 84, no. 2 (2006): 54–73.

Bernstein, Shana. *Bridges of Reform: Interracial Civil Rights Activism in Twentieth-Century Los Angeles.* New York: Oxford University Press, 2011.

Bobo, Lawrence D., Melvin Oliver, James H. Johnson Jr., and Abel Valenzuela Jr., eds. *Prismatic Metropolis: Inequality in Los Angeles.* New York: Russell Sage Foundation, 2000.

Bonacich, Edna, and Richard P. Appelbaum. *Behind the Label: Inequality in the Los Angeles Apparel Industry.* Berkeley and Los Angeles: University of California Press, 2000.

Bornstein, Carol, David Fross, and Bart O'Brien. *California Native Plants for the Garden.* Los Olivos, CA: Cachuma Press, 2005.

Camarillo, Albert. *Chicanos in a Changing Society: From Mexican Pueblos to American Barrios in Santa Barbara and Southern California, 1848–1930.* Cambridge, MA: Harvard University Press, 1979.

Carpio, Genevieve, Clara Irazábal, and Laura Pulido. "The Right to the Suburb: Rethinking Lefebvre and Immigrant Activism." *Journal of Urban Affairs* 33, no. 2 (2011): 185–208.

Center on Urban and Metropolitan Policy. *Los Angeles in Focus: A Profile from Census 2000.* Washington, DC: Brookings Institution, 2003.

Charles, Camille Zubrinsky. *Won't You Be My Neighbor? Race, Class, and Residence in Los Angeles.* New York: Russell Sage Foundation, 2009.

Cheng, Wendy Hsin. "Episodes in the Life of a Place: Regional Racial Formation in Los Angeles's San Gabriel Valley." PhD diss., University of Southern California, 2009.

Creason, Glen. *Los Angeles in Maps.* New York: Rizzoli International Publications, 2010.

Cuff, Dana. *The Provisional City: Los Angeles Stories of Architecture and Urbanism.* Cambridge, MA: MIT Press, 2000.

Culver, Lawrence. *The Frontier of Leisure: Southern California and the Shaping of Modern America.* New York: Oxford University Press, 2010.

Davis, Mike. *City of Quartz: Excavating the Future in Los Angeles.* New York: Vintage Books, 1990.

Dear, Michael J., ed. *From Chicago to L.A.: Mak-*

ing Sense of Urban Theory. Thousand Oaks, CA: Sage Publications, 2001.

Dear, Michael J., Eric Schockman, and Greg Hise. Rethinking Los Angeles. Thousand Oaks, CA: Sage Publications, 1996.

De Graaf, Lawrence B. "The City of Black Angels: Emergence of the Los Angeles Ghetto, 1890–1930." Pacific Historical Review 39, no. 3 (August 1970): 323–352.

DeLyser, Dydia. Ramona Memories: Tourism and the Shaping of Southern California. Minneapolis: University of Minnesota Press, 2005.

Deverell, William Francis. Whitewashed Adobe: The Rise of Los Angeles and the Remaking of Its Mexican Past. Berkeley and Los Angeles: University of California Press, 2004.

Erie, Steven P. Globalizing L.A.: Trade, Infrastructure, and Regional Development. Stanford, CA: Stanford University Press, 2004.

Escobar, Edward J. Race, Police, and the Making of a Political Identity: Mexican Americans and the Los Angeles Police Department, 1900–1945. Berkeley and Los Angeles: University of California Press, 1999.

Ethington, Philip J. "Los Angeles and the Problem of Urban Historical Knowledge." American Historical Review 105, no. 5 (December 2000), www.historycooperative.org.

Ethington, Philip J., William H. Frey, and Dowell Myers. "The Racial Resegregation of Los Angeles County, 1940–2000." 2001, www-bcf.usc .edu/~philipje/Segregation/CensusSegregation.html.

Faderman, Lillian, and Stuart Timmons. Gay L.A.: A History of Sexual Outlaws, Power Politics, and Lipstick Lesbians. New York: Basic Books, 2006.

Flamming, Douglas. Bound for Freedom: Black Los Angeles in Jim Crow America. Berkeley and Los Angeles: University of California Press, 2006.

Fogelson, Robert M. The Fragmented Metropolis: Los Angeles, 1850–1930. Berkeley and Los Angeles: University of California Press, 1967.

Fong, Timothy P. The First Suburban Chinatown: The Remaking of Monterey Park, California. Philadelphia: Temple University Press, 1994.

Fulton, William B. The Reluctant Metropolis: The Politics of Urban Growth in Los Angeles. Baltimore: Johns Hopkins University Press, 2001.

García, Mario T. Memories of Chicano History: The Life and Narrative of Bert Corona. Berkeley and Los Angeles: University of California Press, 1994.

———. Mexican Americans: Leadership, Ideology, and Identity, 1930–1960. New Haven, CT: Yale University Press, 1989.

Garcia, Matt. A World of Its Own: Race, Labor, and Citrus in the Making of Greater Los Angeles, 1900–1970. Chapel Hill: University of North Carolina Press, 2001.

Gilmore, Ruth Wilson. Golden Gulag: Prisons, Surplus, Crisis, and Opposition in Globalizing California. Berkeley and Los Angeles: University of California Press, 2007.

Gooding-Williams, Robert, ed. Reading Rodney King/Reading Urban Uprising. London and New York: Routledge, 1993.

Gottlieb, Robert, Regina Freer, Mark Vallianatos, and Peter Dreier. The Next Los Angeles: The Struggle for a Livable City. Berkeley and Los Angeles: University of California Press, 2005.

Gottlieb, Robert, and Irene Wolt. Thinking Big: The Story of the Los Angeles Times, Its Publishers, and Their Influence on Southern California. New York: Putnam, 1977.

Griswold del Castillo, Richard. The Los Angeles Barrio, 1850–1890. Berkeley and Los Angeles: University of California Press, 1982.

Hamilton, Nora, and Norma Chinchilla. Seeking Community in a Global City: Guatemalans and Salvadorans in Los Angeles. Philadelphia: Temple University Press, 2001.

Harwood Phillips, George. "Indians in Los Angeles, 1781–1875." In The American Indian Past and Present, edited by Roger Nichols. New York: Alfred Knopf, 1986.

Healey, Dorothy Ray, and Maurice Isserman. *California Red: A Life in the Communist Party*. Urbana: University of Illinois Press, 1993.

Heizer, Robert. *The Destruction of the California Indians*. Lincoln, NE: Bison Books, 1993.

Herbert, Steve. *Policing Space: Territoriality and the Los Angeles Police Department*. Minneapolis: University of Minnesota Press, 1997.

Hise, Greg. *Magnetic Los Angeles: Planning the Twentieth Century Metropolis*. Baltimore: Johns Hopkins University Press, 1997.

Hondagneu-Sotelo, Pierrette. *Doméstica: Immigrant Workers Cleaning and Caring in the Shadows of Affluence*. Berkeley and Los Angeles: University of California Press, 2001.

Horne, Gerald. *Fire This Time: The Watts Uprising and the 1960s*. Charlottesville: University Press of Virginia, 1995.

HoSang, Daniel Martinez. *Racial Propositions: Ballot Initiatives and the Making of Postwar California*. Berkeley and Los Angeles: University of California Press, 2010.

Hunt, Darnell, and Ana-Christina Ramón. *Black Los Angeles: American Dreams and Racial Realties*. New York: New York University Press, 2010.

Hurtado, Albert. *Indian Survival on the California Frontier*. New Haven, CT: Yale University Press, 1990.

———. *Intimate Frontiers: Sex, Gender, and Culture in Old California*. Albuquerque: University of New Mexico Press, 1999.

Kahrl, William. *Water and Power: The Conflict over Los Angeles' Water Supply in the Owens Valley*. Berkeley and Los Angeles: University of California Press, 1983.

Kenney, Moira. *Mapping Gay L.A.: The Intersection of Place and Politics*. Philadelphia: Temple University Press, 2001.

Klein, Norman. *The History of Forgetting: Los Angeles and the Erasure of Memory*. New York: Verso, 1997.

Kropp, Phoebe S. *California Vieja: Culture and Memory in a Modern American Place*. Berkeley and Los Angeles: University of California Press, 2006.

Kun, Josh. "What Is an MC If He Can't Rap to Banda? Making Music in Nuevo L.A." *American Quarterly* 56, no. 3 (September 2004): 741–758.

Kurashige, Lon. *Japanese American Celebration and Conflict: A History of Ethnic Identity and Festival, 1934–1990*. Berkeley and Los Angeles: University of California Press, 2002.

Kurashige, Scott. *The Shifting Grounds of Race: Black and Japanese Americans in the Making of Multiethnic Los Angeles*. Princeton, NJ: Princeton University Press, 2007.

La Chapelle, Peter. *Proud to Be an Okie: Cultural Politics, Country Music, and Migration to Southern California*. Berkeley and Los Angeles: University of California Press, 2007.

Li, Wei. "Building Ethnoburbia: The Emergence and Manifestation of the Chinese Ethnoburb in Los Angeles' San Gabriel Valley." *Journal of Asian American Studies* 2 (February 1999): 1–28.

Lopez, Ian Haney. *Racism on Trial: The Chicano Fight for Justice*. Cambridge, MA: Harvard University Press, 2004.

Los Angeles Alliance for a New Economy. *The Other Los Angeles: Executive Summary*. Los Angeles: Los Angeles Alliance for a New Economy, 2000.

Lotchin, Roger. *Fortress California, 1910–1961: From Warfare to Welfare*. Urbana: University of Illinois Press, 2002.

Macias, Anthony. *Mexican American Mojo: Popular Music, Dance, and Urban Culture in Los Angeles, 1935–1968*. Durham, NC: Duke University Press, 2008.

Mann, Eric. *L.A.'s Lethal Air*. Los Angeles: Labor/Community Strategy Center, 1991.

McWilliams, Carey. *Southern California: An Island on the Land*. 2nd ed. Salt Lake City: Peregrine Smith Books, 1973.

Merrifield, Andy. "The Urbanization of Labor:

Living-Wage Activism in the American City." *Social Text* 62 (Spring 2000): 31–54.

Milkman, Ruth. *L.A. Story: Immigrant Workers and the Future of the U.S. Labor Movement.* New York: Russell Sage Foundation, 2006.

Molina, Natalia. *Fit to Be Citizens? Public Health and Race in Los Angeles, 1879–1939.* Berkeley and Los Angeles: University of California Press, 2006.

Monroy, Douglas. *Rebirth: Mexican Los Angeles from the Great Migration to the Great Depression.* Berkeley and Los Angeles: University of California Press, 1999.

———. *Thrown Together: The Making of Mexican Culture in Frontier California.* Berkeley and Los Angeles: University of California Press, 1990.

Nicolaides, Becky. *My Blue Heaven: Life and Politics in the Working-Class Suburbs of Los Angeles, 1920–1965.* Chicago: University of Chicago Press, 2002.

Ochoa, Gilda. *Becoming Neighbors in a Mexican American Community.* Austin: University of Texas Press, 2004.

Oropeza, Lorena. *¡Raza Si! ¡Guerra No! Chicano Protest and Patriotism during the Viet Nam War Era.* Berkeley and Los Angeles: University of California Press, 2005.

Pagán, Eduardo Obregón. *Murder at the Sleepy Lagoon: Zoot Suits, Race, and Riots in Wartime L.A.* Chapel Hill: University of North Carolina Press, 2003.

Pardo, Mary. *Mexican American Women Activists: Identity and Resistance in Two Los Angeles Communities.* Philadelphia: Temple University Press, 1998.

Parson, Don. *Making a Better World: Public Housing, the Red Scare, and the Direction of Modern Los Angeles.* Minneapolis: University of Minnesota Press, 2005.

Pastor, Manuel, Jr. "Common Ground at *Ground* Zero? The New Economy and the New Organizing in Los Angeles." *Antipode* 33 (2001): 260–289.

Pastor, Manuel, Jr., James L. Sadd, and Rachel

Morello-Frosch. "Environmental Inequity in Metropolitan Los Angeles." In *The Quest for Environmental Justice: Human Rights and the Politics of Pollution,* edited by Robert Bullard. San Francisco: Sierra Club Books, 2005.

Pitt, Leonard. *The Decline of the Californios: A Social History of the Spanish-Speaking Californians, 1846–1890.* Berkeley and Los Angeles: University of California Press, 1999.

Price, John. "The Migration and Adaptation of American Indians to Los Angeles County." *Human Organization* 27 (1968): 168–175.

Pulido, Laura. *Black, Brown, Yellow, and Left: Radical Activism in Los Angeles.* Berkeley and Los Angeles: University of California Press, 2006.

———. "Rethinking Environmental Racism: White Privilege and Urban Development in Southern California." *Annals of the Association of American Geographers* 90 (2000): 12–40.

Roderick, Kevin. *The San Fernando Valley: America's Suburb.* Los Angeles: Los Angeles Times Books, 2001.

Romo, Ricardo. *East Los Angeles: History of a Barrio.* Austin: University of Texas Press, 1983.

Rosenthal, Nicolas. "Re-imagining Indian Country: American Indians and the Los Angeles Metropolitan Area." PhD diss., University of California, Los Angeles, 2005.

Sackman, Douglas Cazaux. *Orange Empire: California and the Fruits of Eden.* Berkeley and Los Angeles: University of California Press, 2005.

Saito, Leland. *Race and Politics: Asian Americans, Latinos, and Whites in a Los Angeles Suburb.* Urbana: University of Illinois Press, 1998.

Sánchez, George J. *Becoming Mexican American: Ethnicity, Culture, and Identity in Chicano Los Angeles, 1900–1945.* New York: Oxford University Press, 1993.

———. "What's Good for Boyle Heights Is Good for the Jews": Creating Multiculturalism on the Eastside during the 1950s." *American Quarterly* 56, no. 3 (September 2004): 633–661.

Saxton, Alexander. *The Indispensable Enemy: Labor and the Anti-Chinese Movement in California.* Berkeley and Los Angeles: University of California Press, 1975.

Schrank, Sarah. *Art and the City: Civic Imagination and Cultural Authority in Los Angeles.* Philadelphia: University of Pennsylvania Press, 2008.

Scott, Allen J. *Technopolis: High-Technology Industry and Regional Development in Southern California.* Berkeley and Los Angeles: University of California Press, 1993.

Sides, Josh. *L.A. City Limits: African American Los Angeles from the Great Depression to the Present.* Berkeley and Los Angeles: University of California Press, 2003.

Smith, R. J. *The Great Black Way: L.A. in the 1940s and the Lost African-American Renaissance.* New York: PublicAffairs, 2006.

Soja, Edward W. *Postmodern Geographies: The Reassertion of Space in Critical Social Theory.* New York: Verso, 1989.

———. *Seeking Spatial Justice.* Minneapolis: University of Minnesota Press, 2010.

Soja, Edward W., and Allen J. Scott, eds. *The City: Los Angeles and Urban Theory at the End of the Twentieth Century.* Berkeley and Los Angeles: University of California Press, 1998.

Sonenshein, Raphael J. *The City at Stake: Secession, Reform, and the Battle for Los Angeles.* Princeton, NJ: Princeton University Press, 2004.

———. *Politics in Black and White: Race and Power in Los Angeles.* Princeton, NJ: Princeton University Press, 1993.

Stevens, Errol Wayne. *Radical L.A.: From Coxey's Army to the Watts Riots, 1894–1965.* Norman: University of Oklahoma Press, 2009.

Studio for Southern California History, http://www.socalstudio.org.

Valle, Victor M., and Rodolfo D. Torres. *Latino Metropolis.* Minneapolis: University of Minnesota Press, 2000.

Villa, Raúl. *Barrio-Logos: Space and Place in Urban Chicano Literature and Culture.* Austin: University of Texas Press, 2000.

Waldie, D. J. *Holy Land: A Suburban Memoir.* New York: W. W. Norton, 1996.

Waldinger, Roger, and Mehdi Bozorgmehr, eds. *Ethnic Los Angeles.* New York: Russell Sage Foundation, 1996.

Widener, Daniel. *Black Arts West: Culture and Struggle in Postwar Los Angeles.* Durham, NC: Duke University Press, 2010.

———. "'Perhaps the Japanese Are to Be Thanked?' Asia, Asian Americans, and the Construction of Black California." *Positions: East Asia Cultures Critique* 11, no. 1 (2003): 135–181.

Wild, Mark. *Street Meeting: Multiethnic Neighborhoods in Early Twentieth-Century Los Angeles.* Berkeley and Los Angeles: University of California Press, 2005.

Wolch, Jennifer, Manuel Pastor Jr., and Peter Dreier, eds. *Up against the Sprawl: Public Policy and the Making of Southern California.* Minneapolis: University of Minnesota Press, 2004.

Acknowledgments

It takes a village. This book has been a major undertaking, evolving slowly over almost 15 years. Many, many people have helped throughout the years, in ways both small and large, and perhaps in ways they did not even know. It would be impossible to list all the folks who lent a hand, but we will attempt it nonetheless.

First and foremost we thank Tony Osumi, who first thought of creating the *People's Guide* and gave it its name. Tony is a longtime L.A. activist and teacher who is constantly coming up with new and innovative political ideas. While Laura P. worked alone for a number of years collecting sites and writing about them, she knew that this project had the potential to be much bigger, but she didn't quite know how to get it there. Many different people spurred the project along through its various incarnations. Sharon Sekhon played a transformative role in the development of the *People's Guide*. She took it from pieces of paper to a poster (an idea first suggested by Alexis Moreno) and then a web site. Sharon had the technical expertise, vision, and passion to make the *People's Guide* real while she worked for USC's Institute of Multimedia Literacy (IML) and continued to contribute to the project in her role

as executive director of the Studio for Southern California History. We are deeply grateful for all of Sharon's efforts, not only on behalf of this project but also toward building a more inclusive social history of Los Angeles generally. We are also thankful to Priscilla Ovalle, who helped with web site design; Alex Tarr of the Institute for Multimedia Literacy, who designed the map for the original poster version for the *People's Guide;* and Robert Drwila, who took photos. Daniel Martinez HoSang played a key role in helping to conceptualize this early phase of the project and researched and wrote several entries. Others became involved later as the poster evolved into a book. Mizue Aizeki designed a beautiful prototype, and David Deis made the initial maps. Craig Gilmore offered continuous advice on publishers, Ben Ehrenreich and Jen Lin-Liu offered publishing contacts, Justin Kestler assisted with negotiating contracts, and Chuck Morse of AK Press provided much-needed encouragement and advice. Trevor Paglen, Nicholas Brown, and Lize Mogel assisted with cartography contacts. John Emerson was our official cartographer and produced the beautiful maps that grace this book.

Conducting the research for the *People's Guide*

and taking the early photographs was a monumental task that involved the work of many people. While we did the vast majority ourselves, many students, faculty, acquaintances, friends, and relatives throughout the Los Angeles area assisted along the way: Art Almeida, Deborah Al-Najjar, Christine Bacareza Balance, Shamell Bell, Brittany Berryman, Adam Bush, Umayyah Cable, Genevieve Carpio, Glen Creason, Ofelia Cuevas, Tyler Daly, Thang Dao, Noah Dauber, Michelle Franco, Laura Fugikawa, Diane Fujino, Jerry Gonzalez, Kai Green, Sarah Gualtieri, Christina Heatherton, Jesús Hernández, Emily Hobson, Pierrette Hondagneu-Sotelo, Roark Honeycutt, Daniel Martinez HoSang, Jessica Kim, Jenni Kuida, Josh Kun, Viet Le, Ron Lopez, Roberto Morales, Kyle Morgan of ONE National Gay and Lesbian Archives, Lorena Muñoz, Shigeko and Don Murashige, Steven Murashige, Lata Murti, Phuong Nguyen, Viet Thanh Nguyen, Chris Nyerges, Tanachai Mark Padoongpatt, Eduardo Obregón Pagán, Marlom Portillo and IDEPSCA, Suyapa Portillo, Bertha Pulido, Craig Pulido, Louis Pulido, Richard Pulido, Ron Pulido, Geoff and Kikanza Ramsey-Ray, Sonia Rodriguez, Denise Sandoval, Damien Schnyder, Orlando Serrano, Geri Silva, Karen Tongson, Chiquita Tuttle, Paul Von Blum, Michaela Wagner, and Clyde Woods. Meghan McDowell, Sarah Guzy, and Toni Skalican fact-checked the final manuscript. Emily Hobson deserves a special mention as she essentially "curated" the LGBT sites in the People's Guide. She identified, researched, and wrote them and often secured photos. Mike Murashige, in addition to providing continuous information and feedback, was also an explorer extraordinaire who helped to find the exact site of Chavez Ravine; Ruthie Wilson Gilmore and Craig Gilmore accompanied us on various People's Guide journeys and explorations. Jake Peters served as a patient conavigator, driver, and traffic spotter for numerous photography expeditions. Gwen Gary

was our official "foodie," trying many of the restaurants listed in the People's Guide and writing descriptions of them. Emerson Marroquin was enthusiastic about the project's philosophical and political convictions and deeply supportive of the research and writing process. Juan De Lara provided support, insight, and Eastside expertise in the final stretch.

One of the greatest joys of writing this book was the opportunity to listen to the stories of people who had been personally involved in the struggles we document here. These stories, in their tellers' own words, are highlighted in the "personal reflections" sprinkled throughout the text. For their contributions in this regard, we thank Craig Gilmore and Ruth Wilson Gilmore, Gilda Haas, Dolores Hayden, Christina Heatherton, Tony Osumi, Tanachai Mark Padoongpatt, Gary Phillips, the Los Angeles Urban Rangers, Louis Pulido, Margarita Ramirez, Leland Saito, and Grace Summers.

Acquiring the archival images included in the People's Guide involved the cooperation and enthusiastic support of many people and institutions. We are thankful to Michelle Zack and the Altadena Historical Society; Erica Varela and Ralph Drew at the Los Angeles Times' Department of Rights and Permissions; Sarah Allison at University of California, Riverside, Special Collections; Judy Baca and Pilar Castillo of SPARC; Rachelle Balinas Smith at USC Special Collections; Lynn Beahm at Arcadia Publishing; Simon Elliott and Carol Nishijima at UCLA Special Collections; Renee James at California State University, Los Angeles, Special Collections; Elisa Marquez at Associated Press Images; Jane Nakasako at the Japanese American National Museum's Hirasaki National Resource Center; Christina Rice at the Los Angeles Public Library (special shout-out to the LAPL for its tremendous generosity); David Sigler at California State University, Northridge, Special Collections; Ali

Trachta at the *L.A. Weekly;* Robin Walker at the ILWU Library; Loni Shibuyama of ONE National Gay and Lesbian Archives; Rebekah Kim of the GLBT Historical Society; and Fern Tiger of Fern Tiger Associates. Several individuals allowed us to use photographs from their personal or family collections, for which we are extremely grateful: Arvis Ford, Ignacio Gomez, Steve Greenberg, Gloria Ruelas, Frank Villalobos, and Mark Weber. Finally, Eliseo Medina gave us permission to print a photograph of a mural he painted, and Ruth Judkowitz of Workmen's Circle helped us get in touch with him.

We have been fortunate to work with dedicated, visionary representatives of the University of California Press. Kim Robinson has been a helpful, responsible editor who saw the possibility of the *People's Guide* from the beginning and helped the project live up to its potential. Thanks also to Kalicia Pivirotto and Stacy Eisenstark, who assisted with many technical questions and procedural issues. Jacqueline Volin capably guided the project through production, and Bonita Hurd was an excellent copy editor. We are deeply indebted to our two not-so-anonymous reviewers, Scott Kurashige and Gilda Haas. They did a wonderful job of engaging the text and were full of great suggestions and corrections. Special thanks to Gilda for following up with us and lending her expertise. Thanks also to Mike Davis, who reviewed the manuscript and offered an additional set of sites.

Special thanks to the wonderful staff of the Department of American Studies and Ethnicity at USC: Sandra Hopwood, Kitty Lai, Jujuana Preston, and Sonia Rodriguez. They have contributed to this project in more ways than they can imagine. The good people at the College's Business Office also did a superb job of processing countless photo permission invoices: Fabian Ledesma, Flo Ner, Lois Nishimoto, and Allison Welsh.

We have tried to thank as many people as possible, but we also know that we have left out some names, and for this we apologize. Fifteen years is a long time, and we collected a lot of debts. We received a lot of wonderful help and encouragement along the way, and there are, no doubt, omissions and mistakes, and these remain our responsibility.

Credits

Page 24: © 2004. Fern Tiger Associates. All rights reserved.

Page 30 (top): Courtesy of Los Angeles Public Library.

Page 32 (center left and right): Courtesy of Los Angeles Times Photographic Archive, Department of Special Collections, Charles E. Young Research Library, UCLA.

Page 34: Photo by Harry Quillen. Courtesy of Los Angeles Public Library.

Page 37: Courtesy of Los Angeles Public Library.

Page 38 (bottom): Courtesy of International Longshore and Warehouse Union Library and Archives.

Page 40: Courtesy of Los Angeles Public Library.

Page 45 (top): Photo by Walter Blumoff, courtesy of the Gay, Lesbian, Bisexual, Transgender Historical Society.

Page 47 (bottom): Photo courtesy of Los Angeles Public Library.

Page 49 (top): Photographer unknown.

Page 49 (bottom): Associated Press / Koji Sasahara.

Page 54: Gift of the Family of Kenzo and Ikuko Nakawatase, Japanese American National Museum (2007.37.8).

Page 56: Photo by Gary Leonard. Courtesy of Los Angeles Public Library.

Page 58: Courtesy of Los Angeles Public Library.

Page 59 (bottom): Courtesy of Los Angeles Public Library.

Page 61: Photo by Mark Weber. Courtesy of Mark Weber.

Page 62 (top): Courtesy of Herald Examiner Collection / Los Angeles Public Library.

Page 64: Artist unknown. Courtesy of Wikimedia Commons.

Page 66 (bottom): Photo by Roy Hankey. Courtesy of Los Angeles Public Library.

Page 70: Courtesy of Laura Barraclough.

Page 71 (right): Courtesy of University of Southern California, on behalf of the USC Libraries Special Collections.

Page 79: Courtesy of the Altadena Historical Society.

Page 85 (right): Ignacio Gomez, artist and designer, www.ignaciogomez.com.

Page 87: Photographer unknown.

Page 88 (bottom): Photo by Bob Cary. Copyright © 1995, Los Angeles Times. Reprinted with permission.

Page 95 (bottom): Used by permission of Special Collections and Archives, University of California, Riverside Libraries, University of California, Riverside, CA.

Page 103 (top): Courtesy of Los Angeles Public Library.

Page 105 (top): Photo by Sal Castro. Courtesy of Los Angeles Public Library.

Page 105 (bottom): Photo by Frank Q. Brown. Courtesy of Los Angeles Times Photographic Archive, Department of Special Collections, Charles E. Young Research Library, UCLA.

Page 109: Courtesy of Los Angeles Public Library.

Page 112: Courtesy of Southern California Library for Social Studies and Research.

Page 114: Photographer unknown. Courtesy of Los Angeles Public Library.

Page 124 (bottom): Photo by Jonathan McIntosh.

Page 127: Courtesy of Herald Examiner Collection/Los Angeles Public Library.

Page 131 (top): Courtesy of Los Angeles Public Library.

Page 131 (bottom): Photo by Jack Carrick. Courtesy of Los Angeles Times Photographic Archive, Department of Special Collections, Charles E. Young Research Library, UCLA.

Page 132 (bottom): Courtesy of Los Angeles Public Library.

Page 135: Photography by Willie Ford, courtesy of California State University, Los Angeles, John F. Kennedy Memorial Library, Special Collections, Compton Communicative Arts Academy Collection.

Page 136 (bottom): Courtesy of Herald Examiner Collection/Los Angeles Public Library.

Page 138: Courtesy of the Ruelas family.

Page 141: Photo by Dean Musgrove. Courtesy of Herald Examiner Collection/Los Angeles Public Library.

Page 143 (top): Courtesy of Los Angeles Public Library.

Page 144 (bottom): Photograph by Toyo Miyatake Studio. Gift of the Alan Miyatake Family, Japanese American National Museum (96.267.780).

Page 145: Courtesy of Herald Examiner Collection/Los Angeles Public Library.

Page 149: Courtesy of Herald Examiner Collection/Los Angeles Public Library.

Page 152: Photographer unknown.

Page 155 (bottom): Photo by William Reagh. Courtesy of Los Angeles Public Library.

Page 169 (bottom): Courtesy of Los Angeles Public Library.

Page 172: Courtesy of Los Angeles Public Library.

Page 174 (bottom): Reprinted with permission from *Cambodians in Long Beach,* by Susan Needham and Karen Quintiliani. Available from the publisher online at www.arcadiapublishing.com or by calling 888-313-2665.

Page 179: Illustration by Nick Podue. Special thanks to Art Almeida.

Page 183 (top): Photographer unknown. Courtesy of Los Angeles Public Library.

Page 199: Courtesy of Los Angeles Times Photographic Archive, Department of Special Collections, Charles E. Young Research Library, UCLA.

Page 201: Courtesy of Herald Examiner Collection/Los Angeles Public Library.

Page 203: Courtesy of Herald Examiner Collection/Los Angeles Public Library.

Page 206: Courtesy of Shades of L.A. Collection/Los Angeles Public Library.

Page 212: Courtesy of *L.A. Weekly.*

Page 225 (bottom): Robert Franklin Collection. Urban Archives Center. Oviatt Library. California State University, Northridge.

Page 227: University Archives. Urban Archives Center. Oviatt Library. California State University, Northridge.

Page 231: Photo by Mike Sergieff. Courtesy of Herald Examiner Collection/Los Angeles Public Library.

Page 232: ©SPARC www.sparcmurals.org.

Page 235 (bottom): Photographer unknown. Courtesy of Los Angeles Public Library.

Page 237 (bottom): Photographer unknown. Courtesy of Los Angeles Public Library.

Page 239 (bottom): Cartoon by Steve Greenberg for the *Ventura County Star,* 2003.

Page 243 (top): Photographer unknown. Courtesy of Los Angeles Public Library.

Page 247 (bottom): Photographer unknown. Courtesy of Shades of L.A. Collection/Los Angeles Public Library.

Index

DESIGNER AND COMPOSITOR NICOLE HAYWARD

TEXT 10/14.5 DANTE

DISPLAY MUSEO SANS AND MUSEO SLAB

PREPRESS EMBASSY GRAPHICS

INDEXER KEVIN MILLHAM

CARTOGRAPHER JOHN EMERSON, BACKSPACE.COM

PRINTER AND BINDER SHERIDAN BOOKS, INC.